D1739905

Freedom of Speech in Russia

This book traces the life of free speech in Russia from the final years of the Soviet Union to the present. It shows how long-cherished hopes for an open society in which people would speak freely and tell truth to power fared under Gorbachev's *glasnost*; how free speech was a real, if fractured, achievement of Yeltsin's years in power; and how easy it was for Putin to reverse these newly won freedoms, imposing a 'patrimonial' media that sits comfortably with old autocratic and feudal traditions. The book explores why this turn seemed so inexorable and now seems so entrenched. It examines the historical legacy, and Russia's culturally ambivalent perception of freedom, which Dostoyevsky called that 'terrible gift'. It evaluates the allure of western consumerism and Soviet-era illusions that stunted the initial promise of freedom and democracy. The behaviour of journalists and their apparent complicity in the distortion of their profession come under scrutiny. This ambitious study covering more than 30 years of radical change looks at responses 'from above' and 'from below', and asks whether the players truly understood what was involved in the practice of free speech.

Daphne Skillen has degrees from London, Sydney and Colorado universities. Her doctorate is from University College London. She has lived and worked in Moscow for many years as a journalist and as a consultant for international development agencies and donors. She has also worked in countries of the former Soviet Union besides Russia and in South-East Asia.

BASEES/Routledge Series on Russian and East European Studies

Series editor: Richard Sakwa, Department of Politics and International Relations, University of Kent

Editorial Committee: Roy Allison, St Antony's College, Oxford, Birgit Beumers, Department of Theatre, Film and Television Studies, University of Aberystwyth, Richard Connolly, Centre for Russian and East European Studies, University of Birmingham, Terry Cox, Department of Central and East European Studies, University of Glasgow, Peter Duncan, School of Slavonic and East European Studies, University College London, Zoe Knox, School of History, University of Leicester, Rosalind Marsh, Department of European Studies and Modern Languages, University of Bath, David Moon, Department of History, University of York, Hilary Pilkington, Department of Sociology, University of Manchester, Graham Timmins, Department of Politics, University of Birmingham, Stephen White, Department of Politics, University of Glasgow

Founding Editorial Committee Member:
George Blazyca, Centre for Contemporary European Studies, University of Paisley

This series is published on behalf of BASEES (the British Association for Slavonic and East European Studies). The series comprises original, high-quality, research-level work by both new and established scholars on all aspects of Russian, Soviet, post-Soviet and East European Studies in humanities and social science subjects.

Freedom of Speech in Russia

Politics and media from Gorbachev to Putin

Daphne Skillen

LONDON AND NEW YORK

First published 2017
by Routledge
2 Park Square, Milton Park, Abingdon, Oxon OX14 4RN

and by Routledge
711 Third Avenue, New York, NY 10017

Routledge is an imprint of the Taylor & Francis Group, an informa business

© 2017 Daphne Skillen

The right of Daphne Skillen to be identified as author of this work has been
asserted by her in accordance with sections 77 and 78 of the Copyright,
Designs and Patents Act 1988.

All rights reserved. No part of this book may be reprinted or reproduced or
utilised in any form or by any electronic, mechanical, or other means, now
known or hereafter invented, including photocopying and recording, or in
any information storage or retrieval system, without permission in writing
from the publishers.

Trademark notice: Product or corporate names may be trademarks or
registered trademarks, and are used only for identification and explanation
without intent to infringe.

British Library Cataloguing in Publication Data
A catalogue record for this book is available from the British Library

Library of Congress Cataloging in Publication Data
Names: Skillen, Daphne, author.
Title: Freedom of speech in Russia : politics and media from Gorbachev to
Putin / Daphne Skillen.
Description: Abingdon, Oxon ; New York, NY : Routledge, [2017] | Series:
Routledge series on Russian and East European studies ; 108
Identifiers: LCCN 2016022535| ISBN 9781138787667 (hbk) | ISBN
9781315766256 (ebk)
Subjects: LCSH: Mass media–Political aspects–Soviet Union. | Mass media–
Political aspects–Russia (Federation) | Freedom of speech–Soviet Union. |
Freedom of speech–Russia (Federation) | Mass media policy–Soviet Union. |
Mass media policy–Russia (Federation) | Soviet Union–Politics and
government–1945-1991. | Russia (Federation)–Politics and government–
1991-
Classification: LCC P95.82.S65 S55 2017 | DDC 302.230947084–dc23
LC record available at https://lccn.loc.gov/2016022535

ISBN: 978-1-138-78766-7 (hbk)
ISBN: 978-1-315-76625-6 (ebk)

Typeset in Times New Roman
by Taylor & Francis Books

MIX
Paper from
responsible sources
FSC
www.fsc.org   FSC® C013604

Printed and bound by CPI Group (UK) Ltd, Croydon, CR0 4YY

To Tanya, Jack, Louis and Marcel

Contents

Introduction

The breakup of the Soviet Union offered Russia an unprecedented opportunity to become an open society in which people could speak freely without fear of the consequences for almost the first time in its history. The freedom to speak, express opinions, publish – this it would seem was the dream not of decades but of centuries. The censor, that 'soured eunuch prowling amongst the muses', was Pushkin's description in 1822 of the enemy of free speech, who made writers' lives a misery. When the barriers did finally come down in 1991, free speech was the first and most intoxicating part of the freedoms let loose in the rough and tumble of Yeltsin's years in power. It seemed that the commitment to speak freely had finally taken hold of a once politically oppressed society. Yet Russia entered the twenty-first century with a different president and a different agenda that saw the gradual but relentless erosion of the freedoms that had been accumulated.

Since 2000, under the Putin regime, the majority of mainstream media have reverted to their usual role as Kremlin mouthpieces, and nationwide television channels have been reinvented as instruments of war and hate, introducing a new and dangerous form of 'soft power' that has baffled and challenged the West. Putin's popularity has soared to 80–90 per cent. But Yeltsin had also once inspired the largest demonstrations in the country calling for democracy. The question is: why and how did the dream of democracy and free speech go so wrong, and what can be learned from it?

There had always been a degree of scepticism that free speech in Russia could work. In the early days of *glasnost*, commentators often saw a fable of their times in the tale of Moses, who took forty years to lead his people to the promised land. But that was the wrong way of looking at it: it was precisely not about being 'led', but about what people could do themselves. Others quoted Chekhov's words that you had to 'squeeze the slave out drip by drip' first. It might take some time before ruler and ruled were able to appreciate and make good use of free speech and perhaps, some thought, it would only be those born after the demise of the Soviet state who would be able to make a success of it. Today that person would be 25 years old and is further than ever from that goal. It was startling with what ease the genie of free speech, as Russians called it, was shoved back into its bottle. Despite all the handicaps – the turmoil of the 1990s, the absence of traditions of free speech and democracy, the violations of media impartiality – the urge to speak freely in the media and on the streets played such a central role in changing society and bringing about radical reform that it seemed incredible it could have been hijacked so quickly. Freedom of speech was the main catalyst for reform that helped bring down the Soviet state and start the transition to western-style democracy. It was considered one of the few indisputable achievements of *glasnost* and the post-Soviet regime.

An early example of its transformative role can be seen in1989. In that most euphoric year of populist political engagement that emerged out of Gorbachev's *perestroika*, the historian Yury Afanasyev shocked communist apparatchiks at the USSR Congress of People's Deputies by his straight talking, addressing them as 'esteemed aggressively obedient majority', supporters of the 'Stalin–Brezhnevite' system to block reforms: 'while you, Mikhail Sergeyevich', he added, turning to Gorbachev, 'are either listening attentively to this majority or else cleverly influencing it'.[1] Never in Soviet political life had such outspoken criticism been heard in public. As permission had been granted to broadcast the congress proceedings live on nationwide television, it could have been heard potentially by the then 250 million viewers of the Soviet Union. In fact, so many people were watching the coverage of the ten-day congress that, according to the USSR Supreme Soviet, it resulted in a 20 per cent drop in industrial output. Viewers heard for the first time the outpourings of delegates from the vast Soviet empire and its ethnically diverse people: from Moscow's and Leningrad's intellectuals to opposition activists in the rebellious republics to the feisty woman delegate from the Nenets ethnic minority of the Chukcha autonomous republic.

The public demonstration of a pluralism of views revealed the country's vast wealth of talent and human resources, a matter of surprise in a state that had allowed no alternative to Kremlin positions. The excitement of new ideas showed up the old guard in the Politburo and the dullness of the entrenched bureaucracy. The hostility between the sides was visceral. When Andrei Sakharov spoke to boos and slow-clapping from party stalwarts and Gorbachev, in the chair, turned off Sakharov's microphone for overstepping the time limit it was, for the reformers, proof of Gorbachev's flawed grasp of events. Gorbachev may have freed Sakharov from political exile and house arrest in one of the first acts of *perestroika*, but the fact that he was now silencing a man accorded almost saintly reverence for his courageous struggle on human rights, was unforgivable. The contrast between the *ancien régime* and the liberal reformers was stark.

It was a historic moment for the power of free speech, a symbolic throwing off of chains that corresponded to the enlightening functions of free speech as understood by John Stuart Mill and other classical libertarians. The act of free speech, through the free flow of knowledge and the competitive 'marketplace of ideas', would project the most rational solutions for the improvement of societal ills and the most suitable leaders to implement them. It was the first time the public was able to see a contest between incumbents and aspiring political leaders, many of whom later became leading politicians and public figures; to listen to previously censored information vital to their lives about economic shortages, corruption, the centralisation of power, the KGB and much else; and to realise that a plethora of political and economic solutions existed to vie with the old ones.

A number of newspapers characterised this moment as one when Soviet people could rightly say they were living in 'another country', one where public discussion was normal. These words reappeared once again in the press to capture another dramatic historic moment in 1991 when Gorbachev returned to Moscow from Foros after the coup: he had returned to 'another country' full of promise of a new democratic era with Yeltsin at its head. When opposition leader Aleksei Navalny was detained in prison for more than two weeks for taking part in the first large-scale anti-Putin protests in 2011 he emerged proclaiming that he had spent '15 days in one country and come out into another'. The reference to living in another country seems to hold a certain resonance for Russians, as if one could finally do away with that tiresome long-suffering Mother Russia, so obdurate in her ways, and begin to lead normal civilised lives, as people apparently did in the developed world. The point was to avoid a legacy which, as Yeltsin's prime minister, Chernomyrdin had comically put it: 'we wanted it better, but it turned out as always'. The 'as always' factor can be seen today in the dysfunctional nationalist state which the Kremlin calls its version of democracy. It can be seen in the reappearance of an 'aggressively obedient majority' prepared to toe the Putin line. It can be seen in a largely muzzled media and a state monopoly of mainstream television that has almost entirely eliminated alternative views leaving behind, as always, a spark of determination and dissent but another failed experiment in liberation.

This book traces the development of free speech in the Soviet Union and Russia over thirty-one years, from the beginning of *perestroika* in 1985 to the present day. To understand some of the background to free speech I dip occasionally into the country's past history. My main focus is the nationwide media: the press and electronic media with a substantial national reach. The regional media, a vast topic in itself, is beyond the scope of this work. From the 2000s in Russia, with the expansion of digital technology, the book also looks at the internet and social media. I examine how the media have exercised free speech in which, by rights of their profession, they should have a vested interest. These 'interests' have not always been straightforward. However, no other institution over this period has tested the limits of free speech in the same way. For free speech to be a reality in modern society it has to be exercised by the mass media and conveyed to the mass of the public. As free speech declined from the 2000s, protest spread in the arts, which have always played an oppositionist role in Russian and Soviet society. The banning of the arts on grounds of politics or of blasphemy and obscenity tells us a great deal about Russia's return to its oppressive roots.

I use the term 'free speech' generically to encompass all forms of expression. The term 'free press' is used to specify the media industry. The term 'freedom of expression' is more extensive than 'speech' and better expresses artistic protest (music, the arts, images). Nevertheless, the term 'free speech' adequately embraces all these activities and fits my wider concerns. When J. S. Mill speaks of 'freedom of thought and discussion' and Herzen discusses the 'freedom to hear' (*svoboda slukha*), they are elaborating on the concept of free speech. The same is true for the 'freedom to remain silent', an important act under the Soviet totalitarian system when proactive expressions of party loyalty were required.

What is essential to the concept of free speech is the expression of opposing views. A free press is not a forum to lavish praise or obloquy on a political leader. It is by its nature politically critical and, in repressive societies, usually subversive. Thus, in the historical context, in pushing for the right to speak freely, the Russian media were taking part in a struggle for a different society with open institutions, public debate and the right to scrutinise and criticise the Kremlin and other institutions of power.

For this to succeed the media needed to exercise their role as the fourth estate, a term the first post-Soviet press minister, Mikhail Poltoranin, claims to have let loose on Russia. I shall focus on political journalism, as seen in news and current affairs, opinion and commentary. One criterion is the extent to which pluralism and diversity in the media provided the public with views corresponding to reality. 'Soviet reality', so oddly called, had been a concoction of distortions and lies: more wishful thinking than fact. 'Virtual reality' as fabricated by media gurus to conceal Putin's kleptocratic goals is another form of blocking the truth. From Macaulay's famous observation in 1828, when the ban on reporting the proceedings of parliament was lifted, that 'in the Reporters' Gallery yonder, there sits a fourth estate more important than them all' – than all the other institutions of power, the lofty notion arose of the media's role in holding politicians and governments accountable and acting as the 'watchdog' of the public interest. The idea of the fourth estate asserts the media's right of access to information and the public's right to know. In taking its commitment to free speech seriously, the liberal democratic movement in Russia based its precepts on the Anglo-American model and the belief that a free and independent media were fundamental to eradicating the endemic secrecy of their country's government and preventing the abuse of state power.

Russia's politically repressive past should not in itself have precluded its chances of success as a democracy, even though inevitably its route would not be easy. If we take the former Soviet republics, it was always expected that the Baltics would be successful, but Georgia and Ukraine have also persevered in their long struggle to exercise free speech and maintain their independence even against Russian military aggression. By contrast, Russia had only its internal battles to fight, and it had enjoyed almost a decade of free speech and democracy under Yeltsin, yet the media succumbed easily to Putin's control. He did not need to use physical force, just a few well-placed punitive examples were sufficient to start the downward decline. Although today campaigning journalists are targets for assassination, in 2000 when Putin first became president there was every chance of confronting the authorities in defence of free speech and democracy without fear of dire reprisals.

This raises a number of questions. How did journalists change so rapidly from being almost preternaturally sensitive to any encroachment upon their freedom during the Gorbachev and Yeltsin years to exercising so little concern when Putin took office? Was it a loss of faith in democracy? Did the media ever fully comprehend what was involved in the practice of free speech? Were journalists complicit in the destruction of their own profession? Was it a cynical trade-off of freedom in exchange for material benefits and the good life? Was the allure of imperial pride and superpower status more important than freedom? Did free speech ever have a chance?

The book is divided into two parts, four chapters in each part and a conclusion. Part one examines issues thematically; Part two is arranged chronologically. In reporting events chronologically, the devil is in the detail and in the alternative choices that were available. For the media to exercise free speech, the interests of four institutions are of concern – the Kremlin, media oligarchs, media professionals and the public. Examining their roles indicates whether power is being implemented 'from above' or 'from below'; whether it is a 'gift' from those in power for their purposes or whether it is sought by the media and the public for the betterment of society.

I am indebted to Martin Dewhirst, Roger Hewitt, David McLellan, Alex Pravda, Anthony Skillen and Yevgenij Yanushevich for reading the draft of this work and sharing their exceptional knowledge and insights with me. Sincere thanks to Andrei Richter not only for reading the draft and providing helpful comments, but for sharing and discussing experiences of many of the events in Russia recounted in this book. Thanks as well to Pete Duncan for his helpful comments on Chapter 8. Any flaws are obviously mine. Having lived and worked for many years in Russia, and studied it for longer, I am grateful to many people for their thoughts and ideas for more than the 31 years covered in this book: in particular, I want to mention Mikhail Fedotov and Anna Kachkaeva; and to remember the late Svetlana Kolesnik and the late Sergei Muratov. My warm gratitude to Yelena Kovalenko for looking after me so often in Moscow. My appreciation to Richard Sakwa and Peter Sowden at Routledge for supporting me all along the way.

In transliterating Russian names and words, I have used familiar and easily understood renderings into English, or people's own rendering of their names in English. In the notes, I follow the British Standard system with some modifications.

Note

1 *Pravda*, 27 May 1989.

Part 1

1   Liberties and rights

Starting from unlimited freedom, I arrived at unlimited despotism.
(Dostoyevsky, *The Devils*, 1871–2)

I Liberty or licence?

The discussion of freedom, its intrinsic appeal and 'what is to be done' to attain and sustain it has a long-established history in Russian political thought and literature. Reflections on the meaning of freedom of speech, however, have been surprisingly rare. Perhaps the very magnitude of censorship under tsarism and the totality of its grip in the Soviet era made a discussion of the subject vague and irrelevant, other than in poetic lament. If the concept of free speech was considered at all, it tended to be seen as the flip side of state censorship. Once censorship was removed, free speech would naturally follow. When the Soviet Union collapsed, Russian commentators and international observers alike assumed that as the barbed wire had been torn down free institutions and values would flourish. Of all the pillars of democracy – good governance, free and fair elections, the rule of law, civil society – it was thought that free speech would be the simplest and fastest to implement. It turned out not to be so.

In signing up to the model of western democracy, the Russian media could turn for examples to the Anglo-American tradition with its belief in the pre-eminence of free speech. Illustrious moments in the development of free speech run like a golden thread from Milton to Mill, from the First Amendment to Franklin D. Roosevelt's 'Four Freedoms' that lie at the heart of the Universal Declaration of Human Rights. They could have turned to Voltaire and the French Enlightenment. Russians also have their own illustrious figure in Aleksandr Radishchev who, in denouncing serfdom in the eighteenth century found time in his *Journey from St Petersburg to Moscow* to elaborate, in Voltairean tones, on the value of free speech. Radishchev might well have been a role model, much as the English might turn to Milton for a rousing defence of free speech, but as the father of radical thought with its thread running all the way to communism, Radishchev was not an acceptable icon in post-communist Russia.

Yet Radishchev had a great deal to say that was in fact relevant to Russia's launch into democracy. Having emerged out of the freer climate for the press instituted by Catherine the Great, who had embraced the values of the Enlightenment, he became a victim of that dilemma common to the Russian scene between declarative liberalism and political ruthlessness. Self-printing his *Journey* in 1790 after the French Revolution, not the best of times, Radishchev incensed Catherine by his critique of her corrupt court and the brutal conditions of serfdom. He was sentenced to death, to be beheaded. His book was banned, seized and burned, but copies were in great demand and were circulated and read secretly (the ban was lifted only in 1868). Although the day after his arrest he had pleaded for mercy and apologised for his 'insane' book, it was some time before Catherine commuted his sentence to ten years' exile in Ilimsk in central Siberia. Radishchev was clear about why autocratic governments prohibited freedom of the press:

> The free thinker … will stretch forth his … fearless arm against the idol of power, will tear off its mask and veil, and lay bare its true character. Everyone will see its feet of clay.[1]

Like J. S. Mill, he believed in the power of truth and the destructiveness of censorship where even 'a single stupid official' in the police can hold back the advance of knowledge and progress. He saw no reason for censoring religion and in a very modern tone, pornography. Censorship made a mockery of human dignity, a value he saw everywhere desecrated. It demeaned and infantilised its subjects, like a 'nurse' who has outstayed her welcome:

> censorship has become the nursemaid of reason, wit, imagination, of everything great and enlightened. But where there are nurses, there are babies and leading strings, which often lead to crooked legs; where there are guardians, there are minors and immature minds unable to take care of themselves. If there are always to be nurses and guardians, then the child will walk with leading strings for a long time and will grow up to be a cripple.[2]

Radishchev's disinterested passion for truth could have inspired the democracy movement when the assaults on free speech began, but if anyone had called Putin a 'nanny' (*nyanka*), as a nod to history, instead of acquiescing to his macho image, the cultural reference would have been lost. Radishchev also produced Russia's first essay on the history of world censorship, entitled 'A Brief Account of the Origins of Censorship' in which he, like Milton before him, attributed censorship to the Inquisition. The ancient Greeks and Romans may have put truth to the sword, Radishchev argued, but censorship *qua* prior restraint was the invention and exclusive prerogative of the Roman Catholic clergy. Once the darkness had spread, he said, the fetters of 'clerical superstition' were replicated in 'political superstition'. In all cases the rule of censorship is 'to strike out, blot out, prohibit, tear, burn everything that is opposed to natural religion and Revelation, everything in opposition to the government, every personal reflection, everything contrary to public morality, order and peace'.[3]

Free speech 'above all other liberties'

Although centuries of political struggle had gone into the development of free speech in the West, Russia, like other unexpectedly liberated societies, would have to do it in one leap. As Russians say, you can't take two leaps to jump over the abyss. Yet everything was being done on the hoof, with little time for reflection or study of the experiences of other countries. What did a free press mean and how was one to deal with the obstacles to its exercise: intolerance, prejudice, conformity, ignorance, vested interests? The playwright Aleksandr Gelman pondered how much time had been spent in cursing the Soviet Union, all those free radios beaming from the West and spies everywhere, yet no preparation for the day when Russia would be free: not one scenario, no programmes – 'what a strange country, wouldn't you say, such intellectual nonchalance?'.[4]

With hindsight, leading politician Boris Nemtsov admitted the reformers' naivety: 'I was sure that to cancel communism meant a great life in a few months ... Not only me, but Yeltsin and all of our team ... But unfortunately reality looks much more serious and much more complicated than we believed at the time'.[5] The Soviet experience had given reformers scant understanding of time or scale. The belief in Yavlinsky's 500 Day Plan to deal with the huge problems of the economy was another delusion. When Karl Popper, whose book *The Open Society* had some circulation in the country, was asked if the plan stood any chance of success, he answered that it might – in 500 years rather than days.[6] Yeltsin's generals were also confident it would take a few weeks to suppress Chechen rebellion, but its issues are still not resolved even if the general fighting has ended. Neither were the issues of free speech as simple as journalists thought.

They could have started by looking at the first modern defence of free speech and the rights of journalism: Milton's *Areopagitica: For the Liberty of Unlicensed Printing* (1644). The censorship structure that Milton confronted was not dissimilar to the Soviet Union's Glavlit. Milton, writing as a Puritan at the time of the English civil wars, was outraged by the onslaught on the publication of pamphlets, books and news sheets produced by religious dissenters. In *Areopagitica*, he attacked the state-controlled machinery of censorship that had been instituted in 1643, preventing publication without prior permission. All materials needed to be licensed and registered by the Stationers' Company, which was also responsible for the seizure and destruction of offensive literature and the arrest and imprisonment of offending writers, printers and publishers. In the same way, Glavlit was a state-controlled machine, where censorship took place at the point of publication and nothing could pass without the censor's stamp. Although Milton demonstrated his courage in refusing to license or register *Areopagitica*, he was not, as was Radishchev, punished.

What Milton and free thinkers despised about censorship was the implication of the government's 'infallibility and uncorrupted-ness'. Milton mocked those who feared that free expression would lead to anarchy, the ploy of most repressive governments and one overused by Putin. 'Whoever knew truth put to the worse, in a free and open encounter?' he asks.[7] For Milton free speech was God-given and it was his duty to God to defend it, introducing for the first time the role of conscience over the will of monarch and state, with these famous words – 'Give me the liberty to know, to utter, and to argue freely according to conscience, above all other liberties'.[8] For Russians free speech came 'from above', but as a gift from the tsar: to act according to conscience was rebellion. Milton, however, lacked Mill's belief in pluralism and tolerance. He feared that if the Roman Catholic Church was given the rights accorded to other religions, it would bring the Inquisition and the banning of books to England. He had seen the effect on Galileo in Florence, grown old as a prisoner for voicing heretical views on astronomy. Thus Milton failed the test of tolerance – 'not tolerated popery, and open superstition, which as it extirpates all religions and civil supremacies, so itself should be extirpate'.[9]

If Milton's nightmare was Roman Catholicism, democratic Russia's was the Communist Party. The argument is a familiar one – those who advocate intolerance lose the right to be tolerated. Philosophically, however, there is no logical validity to be illiberal to illiberals, as Anthony Skillen points out in his article on free speech: 'Intolerance, injustice or cruelty do not justify, *a priori*, retributive intolerance, injustice or cruelty. The vision of a society in which only liberals have the right to liberty is conceptually as well as actually comic'.[10] Free speech is not innocuous, but whether it is so injurious and dangerous as to warrant censorship, whether the danger can be diluted by increasing the plurality of voices rather than eliminating incendiary ones, whether it is ever justified to stop the flow of the creative imagination and discussion – these are the issues that revolve around the debate on free speech. For the democrats in new Russia tolerance was a frightening proposition: to give an equal voice to opponents or subscribe to honest elections ran the risk of the communists returning to power. Arguably, Putin's repressive regime stems from the way these issues were resolved by the media industry in the 1990s.

Free speech as an end in itself

A different approach to censorship would have come from readers convinced by John Stuart Mill's *On Liberty* (1859), the classic liberal thesis in defence of freedom of speech. Although in many Russian universities this text was on the list of courses of foreign journalism, few students appear to have read it from what I have been told by different generations of graduates. Mill's view that

censorship was 'evil' because it robbed people of truth and justice was especially relevant to Russia. Mill had a special word to say about Russia's 'mel-
ancholy condition'. He considered the problem lay in Russia's permanent
bureaucracy, which was so strong that even the tsar could not dislodge it. As
a result, it would crush individualism and 'not all the freedom of the press
and popular constitution of the legislature would make this ... country free
otherwise than in name'.[11] Mill's analysis of mid-nineteenth-century Russia
has an authentic ring for today's Russia, free in name but not in fact, and
burdened by a bureaucracy considerably larger than the one that had served
tsarism and the whole of the Soviet Union.

The supremacy of the individual was central to Mill's thesis, so that every
opinion was valuable. Mill argued that all human beings should be free to
form and express opinions without interference from governments or other
individuals provided the voicing of these opinions did not directly harm or
threaten anyone, as would be the case if a person incited an angry mob to
lynch a suspect. In the creativity of discussion, people would be able to seek
the truth because: 'if the opinion is right, they are deprived of the opportunity
of exchanging error for truth; if wrong, they lose, what is almost as great a
benefit, the clearer perception and livelier impression of truth, produced by its
collision with error'.[12] As people are not perfect and may not be able to
recognise all sides of the truth, a reconciling and combining of opposites is
required so that conflicting doctrines 'instead of being one true and the other
false, share the truth between them'.[13] He went further, saying that if either of
two opinions had a better claim than the other, it was the minority, because
that view represented neglected interests.[14]

Mill believed the benefits of free speech to humanity were manifold: the
development of individuality would lead to more responsible and rational
citizens; a free and tolerant society would contribute to greater happiness; and
the ever increasing number of uncontested truths, having survived the cut and
thrust of rational argument, would assist in a genuine consolidation of opinion. Mill did not only see free speech as a means to the betterment of
society, he saw it as good in itself. Because freedom was intrinsic to a highly
civilised society and to mature human beings, the exercise of judgement and
individual spontaneity was not simply a means to happiness but the very
essence of happiness.

These views were startlingly alien to Russian culture. Mill's horror of the
unanimity of views, where even the silencing of one opposing voice would
diminish the pursuit of truth, was obviously hard to accommodate to an
autocratic society with rigidly enforced political values brokering no opposition. The Leninist dictum of 'those who are not with us are against us'
showed political loyalties overrode issues of truth. Tolerance of minority
views was never a part either of the tsarist or Soviet empires. The Marxist
class-based ideology focusing on the primacy of workers gave official justification in the Soviet Union for the persecution of whole classes and groups –
the bourgeoisie, kulaks, 'enemies of the people', ethnic and cultural

minorities. We can see a return today to the scapegoating of minorities in Putin's Russia. The idea that free speech is good in itself has not found currency in Russian practice where media have been and continue to be used principally as a means to an end: either a tool of the state or of opposition to the state.

Nor does the role of reason hold the same Enlightenment aura in Russia as it does in the West. Apart from some of its intellectuals, Russia did not experience the Reformation or the Enlightenment, and many concepts borrowed from there remain alien. Mill's belief in individuality was not easy to superimpose on a society that has had a feudal–communal and collective political heritage. Herzen, who was grateful to England for giving him political refuge and allowing him the freedom to produce his Free Russian Press in London from 1853, never saw liberalism as a political solution for Russia, looking instead to what he considered Russia's unique rural communal traditions. At its freest, the communal ideal was envisaged as a cooperative anarchist utopia (Kropotkin, Tolstoy); at its worst, a cog-in-the-machine nightmare in the name of communism. Of course, since the fall of the Soviet Union many of these values have taken contradictory and often surprising forms. In Russia today one is more likely to witness rampant individualism, bordering on social Darwinism, in a society that is not collective or communal but atomised, grouped around family and friends, in response to a hostile mafia state. These adaptations are responses to old perceptions and fears and Russia, historically, tends to keep turning to its past.

Mill and Dostoyevsky

A comparison between Russian attitudes to freedom and those of the West become clearer if we look at two classic statements from Mill and Dostoyevsky, each quotation famous in its own right:

> If all mankind minus one, were of one opinion, and only one person were of the contrary opinion, mankind would be no more justified in silencing that one person, than he, if he had the power, would be justified in silencing mankind.
>
> (Mill, *On Liberty*, p. 20)

> I renounce higher harmony altogether. It is not worth one little tear of that tortured little girl who beat herself on the breast and prayed to her 'dear, kind Lord' in the stinking privy with her unexpiated tears.
>
> (Dostoyevsky, *The Brothers Karamazov*, p. 286)

Each statement presents what is considered to be the highest ethical valuation. One silenced opinion against one anguished tear: the balance of values lying between freedom and justice. It is within this dichotomy that much of Russia's political thinking has been conducted. Can freedom be the ultimate dream of a society whose history has been one of misery, bondage and suffering, or is it justice and the fair distribution of power, wealth and respect? Neither freedom nor justice has any meaning without equality, and it was the emancipatory philosophies – socialism, communism, anarchism – and movements towards distributive justice that provided the main alternative to autocracy in Russia. The unspoken social contract between individual and state has moved between these priorities: freedom, public order (security/stability) and prosperity (social and material justice). The attitude to freedom – and concomitantly to free speech – plays out within these tensions.

For both Mill and Dostoyevsky freedom was the highest value, but within wildly divergent cultural narratives. Mill prioritises free speech as part of a secular, progressive moral world view. The quotation from Dostoyevsky prioritises justice; but it is not Dostoyevsky's view, it is part of a debate he conducts with his anti-hero Ivan Karamazov, who believes that man can control evil and build a just society based on reason and science. Dostoyevsky, who finds Ivan's views simplistic, propagates the value of freedom and individualism but within a conservative religious framework quite remote from Mill's, yet expressed with such paradox and perversity that he exemplifies Mill's belief in opposite ideas 'sharing' truths. For Dostoyevsky freedom is one's only salvation, but it is such a 'terrible gift'[15] that people are happy to rid themselves of it. Dostoyevsky throws the question of freedom or justice into a kind of Millian debating ring in which Ivan's socialist secular views are tested against Dostoyevsky's religious conservative ones and, so typical of Dostoyevsky, gives his opponent's side greater coherence and dramatic form than his own. Even at the end of his life Dostoyevsky was still attracted by the socialism and atheism of his youth which he later derided.

Ivan has renounced God for not preventing the torments of the world, such as the suffering inflicted on innocent children. He has also rebelled against God for rejecting the only banner that human society can understand – the banner of earthly bread – replacing it with nothing better than:

> some promise of freedom, which men in their simplicity and their innate lawlessness cannot even comprehend, which they fear and dread – for nothing has ever been more unendurable to man and to human society than freedom![16]

The just society Ivan has in mind is embodied in the Legend of the Grand Inquisitor, who offers a trade-off: he revokes man's freedom in return for material wealth and security. Knowing that people are weak and easily seduced by material goods, the Grand Inquisitor uses the manipulative spin of *'miracle, mystery, and authority'* to control society and persuade it that he knows what is in its best interests.[17] But, for Dostoyevsky, there can be no morality or justice without God. If the Grand Inquisitor thinks self-interest can keep society under control, he has ignored the subconscious or people's 'underground', that which is not subject to reason and can erupt unexpectedly in acts of violence, irrationality and caprice. Thus, simply to spite himself, Dostoyevsky's earlier Underground Man denies his own self-interest as the most 'advantageous advantage'.

This parable enabled Dostoyevsky to sound off against most of the progressive schools of thought after the 1860s that attempted to lay down theories for an equal and just society based on Enlightenment principles. Most of all he was annoyed by socialism and the naive views of thinkers such as Chernyshevsky, who saw man as a calculating machine devoid of mystery. He disliked utilitarianism for considering the greatest happiness of the greatest number as a proper ethical goal for humanity (while Mill seeks to justify individual liberty on utilitarian terms); and lambasted Roman Catholicism (but not Russian Orthodoxy) for its intolerance, authoritarianism and claims to infallibility.

The grand dilemma Dostoyevsky raises is between freedom and justice. Ivan's first premise was justice. Yet Ivan's view of reality based exclusively on reason moves him to accept an unjust society under the paternalistic tyranny of the Grand Inquisitor. Ivan's mistake, and that of the socialists, is to identify human happiness with socio-economic interests, reducing desires and conflicts to simple practical issues. For Dostoyevsky, the deeper problem was the existential one of freedom and the way people cope with this 'terrible gift'. It is terrible because they are responsible for their own salvation and must exercise their own judgement to choose between good and evil, truth and falsehood. Mill also emphasised the importance of choice, but he based it on reason and not faith:

he who does anything because it is the custom, makes no choice.[18]

One can understand why Russians see Dostoyevsky's works as prophetic of the Soviet state, the Grand Inquisitor pointing the way to the later crushing of individuality and freedom and the consequent bloodbath in the name of a communist earthly paradise. Ivan's 'not one tear' stands in grim contrast to the flood of tears suffered by Soviet society. Dostoyevsky's parable is an indictment of a censored, infantilised, apathetic world, which he calls elsewhere an ant heap, the unthinking collective which Russians tend to identify with the horrors of the 1930s. In twentieth-century literature the Grand Inquisitor became a potent symbol of totalitarianism, metamorphosed into the Benefactor in Zamyatin's 1922 mockery of Bolshevism in the dystopian novel *We*; and later still into Orwell's Big Brother.

But Dostoyevsky's view of freedom as more important than social justice did not offer any hope of social liberation, only an ahistorical quietism of higher moral awareness that we, like the Karamazov brothers, are all guilty and all responsible each for the other. This is a bleak alternative to the socialist vision of people creating their own destiny. Moreover, like much else in Dostoyevsky's thinking, freedom is two-sided: freedom is necessary to attain goodness, truth and beauty, but it is also wild, volatile and unpredictable. Man's 'underground' is a dark place threatening anarchy and chaos. Images of freedom have always contained this anarchic quality in Russian public consciousness, symbolised as a whirling snowstorm, a cleansing force of nature, the wild Scythian galloping across the endless steppes. These are evocative literary images, but much of Russia's philosophy came out of its novelists. Freedom is responsible for 'rebellion' (*bunt*), the mindlessness of failed peasant revolts led by charismatic heroes such as Pugachov or Makhno or Antonov, which worried Lenin so much that freedom played little part in his organised and elitist revolution.

So much, then, we might say, for Dostoyevsky's spectacular denunciation of the Inquisitor's despotism if it failed to change his attitude of subservience to the oppression of tsar and church. It was a position which 'lesser minds have reached with smaller effort', said Freud, for whom *The Brothers Karamazov* was the most magnificent novel ever written. 'Dostoyevsky threw away the chance of becoming a teacher and liberator of humanity and made himself one with their gaolers'. The compromise with morality, said Freud, was a typical Russian trait.[19] Dostoyevsky had suffered under the tsarist system, subjected to a mock execution and Siberian exile for no more than taking part in the Petrashevsky circle's progressive literary salon in St Petersburg, and it left him with a complicated attitude to authority. His double-sidedness leaves an ambiguous legacy in perceptions of freedom. Much as he disliked materialism he saw this to be the strongest urge in an impoverished and wretched society. One can wonder, with Ivan Karamazov, if it makes sense to talk of freedom in such conditions. Mill assumed a certain standard of living for his views of free speech to prevail.

Svoboda *and* volya

The attitude to freedom is made more confusing by the two words that express it in the Russian language: *svoboda* and *volya*. Both are fuzzy at the edges. The two words are sometimes interchangeable, but they denote different states of mind. Although *svoboda* is a Russian word (from *sloboda*, a settlement of free men), its meaning and usage are western. It is the word used to denote ideas originating in the Enlightenment, such as freedom of speech, conscience and religion. *Svoboda* means you can do what you want but responsibly and according to the law. *Volya* is the older Russian word. It means you can do what you want without restraint – 'freedom for me but not for you', in effect. Linguist Tatyana Surikova of Moscow State University's faculty of journalism says that when Russians use the word *svoboda*, they may also have *volya* in mind:

> Why? Because Rus' was a vast space only partially settled and you could feel free without restrictions. This is a feeling, almost a national trait.

> Behind the word 'volya' lies our history, geography, ethnography, a vast array of factors that lead us to understand 'svoboda' as 'volya', because we don't want to accept that there are restrictions. We feel we should accept these restrictions, but we can't. Deep down, most people, even the most enlightened of us, mean 'volya' when we say 'svoboda'. I think the western meaning of 'svoboda' will need much more time to take root.[20]

Many of Russia's contradictions come from such not fully absorbed foreign concepts. *Svoboda* is the word that is used today to express freedom, but the anarchic *volya* lurks behind the word. If, off the cuff, you put a question to an ordinary person in the form of: 'Do you want Russia to be free?', the answer would probably be 'No way!', because it would be taken as freedom running amok. Tolstoy, who struggled all his life with the conflict between morality and the will to freedom, articulated this distinction in his play *The Living Corpse* when one of the characters, exhilarated by the music of an old gypsy song exclaims, 'This is the steppe. This is the tenth century. This isn't *svoboda*, it's *volya*' – when tribes still roamed freely over the vast flatlands of Kievan Rus'.[21] In the same way the philosopher, Pitirim Sorokin, observing the 1917 February revolution is quoted as saying: 'So we have freedom, so everything is permitted' – reiterating Dostoyevsky's formula 'if God does not exist, everything is permitted'. The general implication is that earthly freedom, as distinct from spiritual and heavenly freedom, is a curse entailing egoism, narcissism and random acts of violence, not at all a sunny and healthy liberation.

A symbiosis of these two perceptions of freedom can be observed in public opinion polls. When respondents are asked to explain their view of freedom, they more often than not see it in terms of Dostoyevsky's dark 'underground', related to excess and linked to violence, pornography, obscenity and nihilism. In the 2000s Romir surveys showed that more than 70 per cent of the population supported censorship, because they understood it to mean showing sex and violence on television. The Levada Centre, Russia's internationally respected sociological and polling research institute, whom I tend to refer to where possible, has made some interesting findings on this topic. It appears that censorship does not necessarily have negative connotations for Russians; nor do respondents make distinctions about what should be available to adults and children. In the Centre's 2012 survey of online censorship, more than two-thirds agreed with the proposition that 'because there are many dangerous sites and materials on the internet it is necessary to impose censorship' – 63 per cent referred to adults, 65 per cent – to children. The urge to control free speech predominates because people are scared, says the Centre's Aleksei Grazhdankin: 'not only of the internet, they are scared of freedom and the free dissemination of information': their ideal model is the traditional one 'in which the state protects people and takes responsibility for everything in their lives'.[22]

The distrust of other people possessing freedom does not relate to having freedom oneself, to do what one wants, turning J. S. Mill's social precept on its head. The Russian approach to grab what freedom one can willy-nilly without worrying about the effects on others shows a legacy where taking responsibility for society was not the prerogative of the individual and discouraged or criminalised by the autocratic state. Only in emergency situations, in periods of war and crisis when leaders have abandoned society or shown huge incompetence do we see citizen responsibility on a large scale coming to the fore, such as in the paradoxical freedom Leningraders experienced in dealing with the terrible Nazi blockade of their city. Levada Centre's surveys regularly find these nuances entangled in the concept of 'freedom' (*svoboda*):

> It is obvious that in the concept of 'freedom' (svoboda) the view that clearly dominates is not one that is valuable to civil society, such as individual freedom and responsibility, but freedom seen as arbitrary rule or anarchy. For oneself, this freedom is valued because it removes restrictions and liberates one from control and supervision; for others, it is perceived more negatively, as something from which only a 'strong hand' can save you.[23]

Wrapped in such ambiguity, freedom is easily misunderstood and misinterpreted, a creature of mistaken identity or a conversation at cross purposes. An interesting analogy, culturally puzzling to Europeans, is the way many Americans identify freedom with the right to bear arms. If the Second Amendment to the US Constitution enshrined in 1791 to protect the individual in wild hostile lands may no longer serve its purpose, it is still part of folk memory. By contrast, Russia has only recently retreated from a long and repressive history, and its current state is hardly stable, so that the word freedom is still something that provokes caution.

Svoboda and *volya* can also be differentiated by external and internal attributes. *Svoboda* is a condition contrary to that of being enslaved or imprisoned; *volya* is closer to ideas of personal liberation and willpower. Each conveys different sets of meaning and experience. As such they reflect contrasting ways of interpreting freedom, which Isaiah Berlin famously identified in his essay *Two Concepts of Liberty*.

Berlin draws a distinction between negative and positive freedom. He applied negative freedom to liberals such as Mill and Locke who perceived freedom as the absence of external restraint: the idea that an individual should be left alone to do what he wants, provided his actions do not interfere with the freedom of others. In this respect negative freedom characterises the Yeltsin era when censorship was abolished and external restraints were genuinely as well as legally removed, allowing citizens to pursue their own good to the best of their abilities. Such freedom is supposed to be limited by law and regulation, although historically this is problematic in Russia. It may also be limited by the fact that there are other goals in society that compete with freedom and may be seen as carrying a higher value, such as justice, or happiness, or security or prosperity. Berlin's point is that in sacrificing freedom to gain security or justice or any other value we should not be fooled into thinking that freedom has not been decreased.

The idea of positive freedom requires more than just the right to say or do what you want. At its crux is the realisation of one's 'true' purpose or one's 'real' self. This is the meaning it holds in Marxism, socialism and messianic beliefs. To fulfil this potential, it may be necessary to involve the state in ways that would be impermissible to liberals. In Marxism positive freedom attaches not simply to the individual but to the collective, to human beings' 'species essence'. According to Marx's theory of alienation, workers in selling their labour power under capitalism become so alienated from their productive activity and their fellow workers that they fail to recognise their objective class interests. In such cases people may think it is justifiable to force others to be free in a higher cause, because they may be too ignorant or oppressed to know it themselves. The basis of this idea, Berlin explains, lies in the Enlightenment notion of the divided self; that a person is torn between one's 'higher' nature, based on reason, and one's 'lower' nature, consistent with irrational impulses. From this position it is easy to descend into tyranny by replacing the actual wishes of citizens or societies with their 'true' wishes. In the words of one of Dostoyevsky's revolutionaries, 'starting from unlimited freedom, I arrived at unlimited despotism'[24] – and no more than a stone's throw away from the Grand Inquisitor, the Soviet 'dictatorship' of the proletariat or Stalin's engineering of the soul. It is also implied in Putin's 'managed' democracy, that paternalistic guidance is necessary to fulfil 'real' needs.

Berlin suggests that, despite the human diversity of choice and preference, ideologues illegitimately deem only certain choices to be valid in terms of our 'real' human nature. This might be, for example, choices that are seen to be morally good for us, as ensuring we only watch serious documentaries instead of tabloid trash. The point is that such attitudes are tendentious and rhetorical and should be seen for what they are. When political-technologist Gleb Pavlovsky manipulates television screens to show there is 'no alternative' to Putin, the multiplicity of choice has been eliminated, just as it was on Soviet screens.

'Bourgeois' freedom

In Marxist-Leninist theory concepts such as free speech, independent media, human rights and parliamentarianism are institutions of liberal 'bourgeois' democracy and consequently downgraded in value. They are seen as perpetrating double standards by facilitating economic exploitation and promoting the interests of the bourgeoisie while passing off as neutral institutions. The media's 'superstructural' status, dependent on the economic base in society, makes them instruments and expressions of the ruling class. Thus, for Lenin, the free speech that was proclaimed after the February revolution was illusory. The bourgeois liberal concept of freedom of the press, to abolish censorship and give all parties and organisations the right to publish, was too narrow and did not take into account the powerful role played by finance and advertising. It meant freedom was for the rich and not for the oppressed, as Lenin was never tired of repeating:

> the publication of newspapers is a profitable and major capitalist enterprise into which the rich invest millions and millions of roubles. 'Freedom of the press' in bourgeois society consists of the freedom of the rich systematically, unwaveringly, on a daily basis, in millions of copies to dupe, corrupt and fool the exploited and oppressed mass of the people and the poor.[25]

Such incisive awareness! One is baffled as to why Russian journalists, so many of whom had been well-meaning Leninists, were not more sceptical in their initial embrace of the oligarchs. But pro-Putin statist-neoliberals reverted seamlessly to Marxist arguments to disparage free speech as an expression of western double standards and no more than a covert ploy to import regime change to Russia.

II Human rights or human obligations?

Part of the notion of free speech in western society is the belief that men and women have a 'right' to express themselves. If that right is denied, they may claim they are justified in revolting against the political system restricting them. This sense of entitlement did not develop in Russia's extreme form of autocracy and constantly confronts the liberal's urge for freedom. The monarch's subjects had duties, not rights.

The Universal Declaration of Human Rights of 1948, which endorsed the inalienable rights of all people regardless of race, religion or creed, was never signed by the USSR.[26] Partly this reflected cold war animosities, partly different value systems. The main conflict in the drafting of the Declaration was the relationship of the individual to the state. Western human rights theory asserts that the individual is the bearer of human rights, whose protection requires limiting the powers of the state. In Soviet thinking freedoms were contingent on the collective, and society as a whole was the bearer of human rights. The state was seen not as a potential violator of freedoms, but as their guarantor. What the Soviet Union claimed to be human rights can be seen in early amendments to the Declaration that were not included in the final document: to define the duties of citizens to their state; to guarantee national sovereignty; to ensure the rights of certain groups rather than the rights of individuals; and the right of people to self-determination (this last proposition was pointedly directed at western powers, whose empires were at stake after the war). Eleanor Roosevelt, chairperson of the drafting commission, was exasperated by the Soviet delegation:

> Long ago in London during a discussion with Mr. Vyshinsky,[27] he told me there was no such thing as freedom for the individual in the world.

All freedom of the individual was conditioned by the rights of other individuals. That of course, I granted. I said: 'We approach the question from a different point of view, we here in the United Nations are trying to develop ideals which will be broader in outlook, which will consider first the rights of man, which will consider what makes man more free; not governments, but man'. The totalitarian state typically places the will of the people second to decrees promulgated by a few men at the top.[28]

The Universal Declaration of Human Rights is undoubtedly a western creation, but concessions were made to the communist bloc. In his 'Four Freedoms' speech,[29] Franklin D. Roosevelt set out the basic rights to be incorporated in the Declaration. Two of the freedoms – freedom of speech and freedom of religion – were classical Enlightenment principles based on 'natural rights', that man is born free and each individual is unique. The other two freedoms did not fit the traditional reading of human rights in western thought – freedom from want and freedom from fear. The latter referred to an internationalist approach in settling questions of war and peace. The former – freedom from want – was the main concession to the Soviet Union, which gave socio-economic rights parity with civil and political rights. The UN booklet on the Four Freedoms describes these freedoms as separate, but not independent: 'Denied education, denied information, suppressed or enslaved, people grow sluggish; their opinions are hardly worth the high privilege of release. Similarly, those who live in terror or in destitution, even though no specific control is placed upon their speech, are as good as gagged'.[30]

Although many western thinkers view socio-economic rights more often as government services than as rights, that which is attained through political struggle rather than birth, they are not questioned today in international relations. The Declaration's two-pronged attempt to straddle the ideological differences of countries making up the UN produced constant disagreement in draft amendments about how to define the right of free speech, as the UN summary records show:

> [The Soviet representative] considered that the article dealing with the freedom to disseminate ideas did not solve the problem of freedom of expression, as the diffusion of dangerous ideas, such as war-mongering and fascist ideas, should be prevented. That same article, he submitted, made no provision for the free dissemination of just and lofty ideas. If freedom of expression was to be effective, the workers, he argued, must have the means of voicing their opinions, and for that they must have at their disposal printing presses and newspapers.[31]

Socio-economic rights, as embodied in Soviet constitutions, include the right to work, healthcare, education, housing, rest and security – rights provided by the state. Writing in a preamble to a booklet on human rights published in

1981, Konstantin Chernenko, later penultimate General Secretary of the CPSU, asserted: 'Communists are convinced that there is no such thing as "pure democracy" or political rights and freedoms in general. Our political system is a complex of state and public organisations'.[32]

Opinion polls show that socio-economic concerns dominate. Conducting a survey covering the period from 1994 to 2010, the Levada Centre asked respondents to name which human rights they considered most important. They found that free education and medical provision for the elderly rated the highest – 64 per cent (1994), 74 per cent (2004) 69 per cent (2010); followed by the right to life, housing and employment. By contrast, freedom of speech for these same years was rated 18 per cent, 24 per cent, 34 per cent. The right of access to information received 8 per cent, 17 per cent, 22 per cent.[33] The gap between socio-economic and political rights is evidenced in most polls. The Centre's Boris Dubin explains that freedom is seen not as what a person himself does, but what the state does to protect his social well-being. In effect, the fewer choices a Russian has to make, the freer he or she feels.[34] Dubin cites figures that indicate that 70 per cent of Russians considered themselves free in 2010 after a decade of suppression of freedom but the raising of living standards; while only 40 per cent considered themselves free in 1990 as the country opened up to new freedoms but in a situation of economic instability.

If Soviet leaders gave low priority to political rights, their record of implementing socio-economic rights was a devastating failure, unable as they were to provide basic consumer goods and material comforts. Instead, through the servile media, they insisted that problems of food and consumer production and distribution were not the fault of the system but of individual instances of corruption and incompetence. There was a special TV programme for this in the early 1980s called *More and Better Goods*, where various factory bosses were roundly scolded for not implementing their set tasks and blamed for the endless queues. The gap between truth and reality was one of the absurdities of the system that enabled it to implode so easily. The cover-ups in most sectors of society were easy to see through. Formally, for example, unemployment did not exist in the USSR because it had been officially eliminated in 1930, the day that unemployment benefits were stopped. It existed as unemployment between jobs, employment below skill levels and overmanning.[35] The tacit social contract of those years was 'we pretend to work, they pretend to pay us'. Moreover, if you had, by virtue of being employed, the freedom to realise yourself through work, you did not have the freedom to choose to be unemployed, because that was illegal. If you did not work, you were legally a 'parasite', even though you did not receive social security benefits. One of the most absurd cases of the absence of free choice was when the brilliant poet Iosif Brodsky was imprisoned for choosing not to do more than the odd job and write poetry. The judge asked Brodsky: 'Who has recognized you as a poet? Who has enrolled you in the ranks of poets?' 'No one', replied Brodsky. 'Who enrolled me in the ranks of the human race?'[36]

The struggle for civil and political rights, which had been downgraded by Soviet ideologists, became the focus of the human rights movement in the 1960s and 1970s. The dissidents called for the freedom to write and publish, to assemble and protest. Once the Soviet Union had signed the Helsinki Accords in 1975, human rights activists were able to use one of its guiding principles of 'respect for human rights and fundamental freedoms, including the freedom of thought, conscience, religion or belief' to legitimise their protests. Their defence against persecution was to refer to this international agreement.

Are human rights 'Russian'?

In Yeltsin's new Russia all the basic provisions of the Universal Declaration of Human Rights became part and parcel of the Russian legal system. Article 17 of the new Constitution states: 'The basic rights and freedoms of the human being shall be inalienable and belong to everyone from birth'. Looking back at the Constitution in 2008, its co-author Sergei Shakhrai saw at least the beginnings of a change in the perception of his countrymen:

> For the first time in Russian history the Constitution said that rights and liberties are given to us at birth, not by gift of the lawmaker. From this follows the conclusion that human rights have priority over state interests. This goal has not been achieved at this point, but in 15 years significant progress toward it has been made.[37]

This is no longer the case. The 'Russianness' of human rights has come into question again in Putin's policy of a resurgent Russia. New policy initiatives began to take effect after Putin's second term in office, one of which was the attempt to design a church–state ideology, an alliance which was officially unconstitutional. Prior to becoming Patriarch in 2009, Metropolitan Kirill revived the issue of whether citizens had rights or duties. At the Tenth World Russian People's Convocation in 2006 he rejected the 'universality' of the Universal Declaration of Human Rights, because it had originated in the West; and he denied the individual's 'moral autonomy' inherent in the idea of 'inalienable' rights.[38] Instead, the convocation brought out its own declaration *On the Rights and Dignity of Man*, asserting that 'values exist that are not inferior to human rights. They include faith, morality, the sanctity of sacred objects, and the Fatherland'.[39] The declaration repeated the suspicion held by nationalists that the West's adherence to human rights was based on principle: 'We reject the politics of double standards in the sphere of human rights, as well as attempts to exploit these rights in order to promote political, ideological, military, and economic interests, or to impose a particular governmental or social order'.

Following two years of discussion, the church's official position challenging freedom and human rights was proclaimed in a document called *Basic*

Teachings of the Russian Orthodox Church on Dignity, Freedom, and Human Rights, adopted in 2008. According to it, freedom is 'one of the manifestations of God in human nature', but at the same time 'freedom of choice is not an absolute or ultimate value', because human nature is 'darkened by sin'. If people are left to their own devices to make choices, they may choose evil; so it is the church in its pastoral role that provides people with spiritual guidance:

> The weakness of the human rights institution lies in the fact that while defending freedom of choice, it tends to increasingly ignore the moral dimension of life and freedom from sin. The social system should be guided by both freedoms … Free adherence to goodness and truth is impossible without freedom of choice, just as free choice loses its value and meaning if it is made in favour of evil.[40]

In the West human rights belong to all people at all times; they are not denied to 'sinners'. Responsibilities accompany rights in most treatises on freedom (such as in Mill or in Article 29 of the Universal Declaration of Human Rights), without reference to the church. As stated in the Basic Teachings, however, the church is justified in intervening to prevent such 'inhumane actions towards human beings as abortion, euthanasia, use of human embryos in medicine, experiments changing a person's nature and the like'. Human rights should not contradict love for the 'fatherland', it says, and freedom of expression can never justify the 'public defilement of objects, symbols or notions cherished by believers'. The outrage at 'defilement' can be seen in the Pussy Riot case and the introduction of a law on blasphemy, the first since tsarist times (see discussion in section III).

One of the thinkers involved in *Basic Teachings* was Aleksandr Dugin, at the time head of the Eurasia movement, whose ultranationalist views, sometimes mixed with Nazi sentiment, mysticism and imperialism, have had a significant impact on Putin's search for an ideology, and whose vision it is said was behind the annexation of Crimea. In 2006, Dugin expressed his views as 'ecumenical democracy', saying the only reason 'liberal' democracy had been accepted under Yeltsin was because nobody had understood these subtle distinctions. Instead: 'we should "subordinate" democracy to sovereignty; refuse to blindly copy western examples; bring back moral and family values; stop the propaganda of sin and vice in the media'.[41] In 2015 these have become the dominant views behind the setting up of religious channels such as Tsargrad TV and, noticeably, despite anti-western feeling, the channel has found affinity with the right-wing Tea Party values of Fox News, one of whose executives has been working in Russia to help disseminate shared traditional values.

In Russia religious conservatism is rooted in the nineteenth-century Slavophile tradition. The courageous Solzhenitsyn, very much the fearsome prophet of yore, shocked the secular West with these views after he had been forced into exile in 1974. Westerners, knowing him to be the grand dissident against the Soviet regime's forced labour camps, were bewildered by his non-liberationist philosophy. As a conservative nationalist, Solzhenitsyn believed human obligations to be superior to human rights, and equated freedom with excess: 'Destructive and irresponsible freedom has been granted boundless space. Society appears to have little defence against the abyss of human decadence, such as, for example, misuse of liberty for moral violence against young people, motion pictures full of pornography, crime and horror', he said in a speech to a stunned audience at Harvard University in 1978.[42]

Sausages or freedom?

In the 2000s commentators tried to explain the political apathy under Putin's first two terms in office as an agreeable trade-off, whereby free speech and free assembly were exchanged for economic prosperity and security. Relinquishing political and civil rights was known crudely as exchanging freedom for sausages. The freedoms that kept most people satisfied were the opportunity to buy food and clothes, acquire private property and land, build one's own country 'dacha', travel abroad, enjoy access to the world's films, books and music, practise religion (at least Russian Orthodoxy) and not feel ostracised from the global community. In developed societies these are the normal accoutrements of life, and Russians were making up for long periods of deprivation and isolation: but had the Grand Inquisitor's miracle and mystery duped them into a deal at the expense of political and civic freedoms?

Political analyst Stanislav Belkovsky doubted in 2010 that ordinary citizens had reaped any real benefit from the supposed trade-off, quoting Putin's own statistics from one of his TV studio discussions, that teachers were earning the equivalent of £147 per month and midwives £105. After a decade of alleged and shameful obloquy, Belkovsky argued, neither statists, communists, nor liberals ('who saw Putin as Pinochet-lite') got much out of it except a kind of 'monstrous freedom':

> Sex, drugs, and rock 'n' roll … help yourself! The only question is – what will you give in exchange … No, not your soul; in the zero years, no one needs a soul, you can stick it up your a___. Just one thing – give up the right to elect and to be elected. If only because the people never choose correctly, and the chosen one is always doomed.[43]

Belkovsky's 'monstrous freedom' is more appropriate to the early period of Putin's regime when the main taboo was politics, but as the church's role in society increased, so did religious moralism in the arts and society. In the Yeltsin period there had been only one scandal connected with religious censorship, when NTV advertised that it would broadcast Martin Scorsese's film *The Last Temptation of Christ*. It caused some protest and NTV bowed to the church and viewers' pressure at the time, but showed the film a year later to hardly any reaction. Now, major art exhibitions were being banned at the church's insistence. The controversial art on display broached religious and political themes, juxtaposed with images of consumerism, in a medley of Jesus, Lenin, Coca-Cola and Mickey Mouse. Prominent art curator, Marat Gelman was charged in 2005 for inciting religious hatred and political extremism in his exhibition, 'Russia2', which set out to explore the 'other' Russia 'beyond the scope of the para-governmental, officious culture'.[44] He was cleared, probably because of his earlier work for the Kremlin as a PR guru. This was not the case with the Andrei Sakharov Museum and its director, Yury Samodurov, who had two exhibitions banned for confronting religious censorship – 'Beware, Religion!' and 'Forbidden Art-2006'. Samodurov was charged with 'inciting religious hatred', fined heavily on both occasions and lost his job. The six members of the congregation of St Nicholas of Pyzhi, who wrecked the first exhibition, and the outraged altar boys who vandalised the second, all got off scot-free. These first cases of censorship in the arts were a forewarning of things to come. There was a sense of déjà vu in the air, recalling the infamous 1962 exhibition of avant-garde art which had signalled the end of Khrushchev's 'thaw', when he harangued the artists as 'pederasts' and some of their work as 'dog shit'.

The bleakness of an unreformed church and a repressive state engendered protest art designed to shock and shake up an apathetic society, witnessed in Pussy Riot's joyous iconoclasm, on the one hand, and the masochistic asceticism of Pyotr Pavlensky, on the other. To support Pussy Riot's right to free expression, St Petersburg's performance artist Pavlensky sewed up his lips: he has also wrapped his naked emaciated body in barbed wire, nailed his scrotum to the ground in Red Square and more recently set the main door of the Lyubyanka, the HQ of the secret police, alight. His stated aim is to free himself from the 'phobia of pain and fear': after all, the state cannot harm him more than he has done to himself. His 'art' has received some acclaim, but it seems to me more akin to the martyrdom of the religious dissenter-sectarians and the self-destructiveness of old sects like the Flagellants, Self-Immolators and Self-Castrators (Khlysty, Samosozhentsy, Skoptsy). Marat Gelman sees Pavlensky's acts as gestures of hopelessness: 'People have been forced into a corner – the choice is between leaving, going to prison, or joining up with those in power'.[45] Both Gelman and Samodurov have emigrated.

III The trial of Pussy Riot

The trial of Pussy Riot became an international *cause célèbre* when several young women from a feminist punk group tested the boundaries of freedom of expression and freedom of religion (or non-religion) and exposed, like no other protest action had done, the medieval trappings of the Orthodox Church, aided and abetted by Putin's state. It was a moment when the modern, western, secular mindset clashed with religious obscurantism. The crushing of this most flamboyant example of the anti-Putin protest movement of 2012 ushered in a whiff of the Inquisition. Radishchev would have bewailed these fetters of 'clerical superstition' when Patriarch Kirill said of Pussy Riot: 'the devil has laughed at us'.[46]

What was distinctive about Pussy Riot's protest was its provocative nature, calculated to cause offence to many people in order to prove a wider principle. Opposition leader Aleksei Navalny thought their act was idiotic, but he was in the front row of the public gallery to support their right to do it. It was all about the Voltairean principle, the *sine qua non* of free speech: 'I disapprove of what you say, but I will defend to the death your right to say it'. On Putin's side, the goal of the authorities was to disguise the fact that political free speech was being suppressed, preferring to turn the case into one of blasphemy. For veteran human rights activist Lev Ponomaryov, the Pussy Riot case showed the church and state inexorably drifting towards the most conservative and uneducated sectors of the population. 'The educated part of Russian society, which condemns this trial outright, is up against a brainwashed majority. All this may lead to Russia turning into an Orthodox Christian version of Iran'.[47]

The issue revolved around a 30-second anti-Putin punk-prayer. On 21 February 2012 five women entered Moscow's Cathedral of Christ the Saviour wearing balaclavas pulled over their faces and dressed in a jumble of brightly-coloured clothes to confront the 'traditional' values Putin and the church had begun to enforce. In front of the golden iconostasis, they belted out their protest hymn: 'Mother of God, Virgin, drive Putin away ... Gay parade despatched to Siberia in irons ... Holy shit, shit, shit ... Mother of God, Virgin, become a feminist ... black limousines form the Procession of the Cross ...'.[48] Combining music from the Church's litany with abrasive punk, they stomped and shouted, genuflected and made signs of the cross, threw themselves on the ground in prostration. It was a funny cartoonish performance, intentionally tasteless and done in high spirits. A nun tried to interfere, while several elderly people watched in shock. Cathedral guards ejected the group and that might have been the end of it, except that the video the group's friends had filmed appeared on YouTube and went viral. It was at this point that the alliance between church and state, which the group had so wickedly satirised, showed its full force.

Two of the women, Nadezhda Tolokonnikova (22) and Maria Alekhina (24)[49] were accused of 'hooliganism motivated by religious hatred', a charge carrying a maximum sentence of seven years. They were refused bail, detained for five months, and were not allowed to see husbands, children, friends. They were sentenced to serve two years in a penal colony (general regime) because they had 'undermined social order'. The judge refused to accept the defence's argument that the performance was a political protest against Putin, ruling that the act was motivated by hatred of the Orthodox Church. The judge claimed that Putin's name had not been heard by the witnesses in the cathedral and that the words had been added to the video of the performance later, after it had been edited. The women were therefore branded not as political critics but as 'blasphemers', although at the time there was no law on blasphemy in Russia. TV presenter Arkady Mamontov found it a convenient word to repeat many times on state television to demonise the women in the eyes of Russia's massive television audience. An opinion poll showed that 43 per cent of the population felt the sentence was too lenient.[50]

To prove the charge of blasphemy the prosecution went to risible lengths. Part of the expert evidence against the women came from ancient canon law decreed by the Church Fathers. They had violated the laws of the Council in Trullo (seventh century), which had banned the use of 'comic' or 'satyric' dress and public dancing in church (canon 62), as well as 'undisciplined vociferation' and shouting (canon 75). To boot, canon 15 of the Council of Laodicea (fourth century) allowed only canonical singers into the ambo.[51] The case was riddled with procedural and legal violations which mobilised Russia's usually apathetic professional classes. About a hundred psychologists and linguists signed an open letter protesting against the prosecution expert's misuse of psycho-linguistic methodology, allowing Alyokhina to be evaluated as 'suffering from mixed personality disorder displayed by an active position in life'. The Lawyers' Association wrote an open letter pointing out there was no such crime in the Criminal Code of the Russian Federation as 'offending the feelings of believers'.

Pussy Riot was part of a radical performance art group. Some of them had belonged to the anarchist art collective Voina ('War'), which had already organised a number of sensational happenings as part of the protest movement.[52] Tolokonnikova and her husband Pyotr Verzilov took part in one of them, an orgy staged in a museum on the eve of Medvedev's election in 2008 to mock Medvedev's national project to increase the birth rate. It was called 'Fuck for the Baby Bear Successor' (the word *medved'* meaning 'bear').[53] Pussy Riot's acts of *épater les bourgeois* had everything to do with politics. In particular, they objected to statements by Patriarch Kirill that Orthodox believers should not go on protest demonstrations and that Putin's reign had been 'a miracle of God'. They were appalled that he had interfered in the elections, urging believers to vote for Putin and the United Russia party. They had carefully chosen the Cathedral of Christ the Saviour, the official seat of the church, for their performance to highlight the corruption and vast wealth the church had accrued by its alliance with the state. According to them, the cathedral was a money-making enterprise where halls could be rented out for $10,000 an event. Patriarch Kirill already had a reputation for making money. Before he had become patriarch, newspapers had named him 'Tobacco Metropolitan' for allegedly profiteering from the duty-free import of foreign cigarettes, which Yeltsin had granted the church to allow it to re-establish itself.

It was only to be expected that many people would be shocked and offended by Pussy Riot's performance at the altar, but the contrary was also true, that Pussy Riot had every right to be offended by the Patriarch's political interference in a secular state. People pointed out that if the song had said

'Mother of God, keep Putin safe', there would have been no court case. In normal circumstances the charge would have been hooliganism with fifteen days' detention. Pussy Riot had knowingly thrown a stone in the water, but the ripples caught more shades of Russian historical dissent than they might have envisaged. Their protest resounded with literary nuances, from Maya-kovsky's 'A Slap in the Face of Public Taste', to Yesenin with the Imaginist wild bunch daubing the walls of the Passion monastery in Moscow with his verse: 'Here the nuns at night/Remove Christ's trousers', to the absurdists that Tolokonnikova loves, to Dostoyevsky's famous device of 'skandal'. But it was their bravery and humour that caught the western world's imagination and support.

Putin was in London during the trial, and confronted by the media frenzy he called for leniency but: 'I think if the girls were, let's say, in Israel, and insulted something in Israel … it wouldn't be so easy for them to leave or if they desecrated some Muslim holy site, we wouldn't even have had time to detain them'.[54] It is this kind of moral relativism (a common Soviet-era defence known as 'whataboutism') that Tolokonnikova mocked when she quipped: 'A Putin maxim could be "Jail is better than stoning"'. The women were sent to penal colonies and released only a few months before the end of their sentences. They continue to be politically active and have funded an NGO in support of female prisoners (http://zona.media).

Notes

1 *A Journey from St Petersburg to Moscow*, ed. Roderick Page Thaler, trans. Leo Wiener, Cambridge, MA: Harvard University Press, 1958, p. 169.
2 Ibid., p. 165.
3 Ibid., p. 167.
4 'Nogi bez dorogi', *Literaturnaya gazeta*, 21 October 1998.
5 Interview with Boris Nemtsov, August 1991 Putsch, RFE/RL, 19 August 2011, JRL 2011, 152, no. 15.
6 *Guardian*, leader, 22 March 1993.
7 *Milton and the Modern Media: A Defence of a Free Press*, introduction by Granville Williams, London: B&D, 2005, pp. 80, 102.
8 Ibid., p. 101.
9 Ibid., p. 103.
10 'Freedom of Speech', *Contemporary Political Philosophy*, ed. Keith Graham, Cambridge: Cambridge University Press, 1982, p. 141.
11 J. S. Mill, *On Liberty and Other Writings*, ed. Stefan Collini, Cambridge: Cambridge University Press, 2000, p. 110.
12 Ibid., p. 20.
13 Ibid., p. 47.
14 Ibid., p. 49.
15 *The Brothers Karamazov*, trans. David Magarshack, vol. 1, London: Penguin, 1969, p. 301.
16 Ibid., p. 296; italics in original.
17 Ibid., p. 301.
18 Mill, *On Liberty and Other Writings*, p. 59.

19 'Dostoevsky and Parricide' (1928),*The Standard Edition of the Complete Psychological Works of Sigmund Freud*, James Strachey (ed.), London: Hogarth Press, 1961, vol. 21, p. 177.
20 Author's interview, 3 June 2011.
21 *Zhivoi trup*, Sobranie Sochinenii v 14 tomakh, tom 11, Gosudarstvennoe izdatel'stvo khudozhestvennoi literatury, Moskva 1952, p. 221.
22 Levada Centre, 10 October 2012. www.levada.ru/2012/10/10/tsenzure-v-internete-o bespechena-obshhestvennaya-podderzhka-63-grazhdan-vystupayut-za-ogranicheni ya-v-seti/ (accessed 18 July 2016).
23 L.D. Gudkov, B.V. Dubin, N.,A., Zorkaya, *Postsovetskii chelovek i grazhdanskoe obshchestvo*, Moskovskaya shkola politicheskikh issledovanii, 2008, pp. 35–6.
24 *The Devils*, trans. David Magarshack, London: Penguin, 1960, Pt II, Ch. 7, p. 404.
25 'Kak obespechit' uspekh uchreditelnogo sobraniya (o svobode pechati)', *Rabochii put'*, September 15 (28), 1917 in *V.I. Lenin o Pechati*, A.P. Okorokov (ed.), Politizdat, 1982, p. 362.
26 However, in the early 1970s the USSR ratified all the documents adopted to develop the Declaration, including the Pact on Economic, Social and Cultural Rights, the Pact on Civil and Political Rights and attached documents.
27 Ironically, Andrei Vyshinsky, who headed the Soviet delegation in discussing human rights was the notorious state prosecutor who had presided over the Stalin show trials in the 1930s, on one occasion calling for the accused, previously top Bolshevik leaders, to be 'shot like rabid curs'.
28 'The Struggle for Human Rights', delivered 28 September 1948, Paris. The Eleanor Roosevelt Papers Project. https://www.gwu.edu/~erpapers/documents/speeches/doc026617.cfm (accessed 23 November 2015).
29 Address to Congress, 6 January1941. www.wwnorton.com/college/history/ralph/workbook/ralprs36b.htm (accessed 23 November 2015).
30 *The United Nations Fight for the Four Freedoms*, a booklet originally published by the Office of War Information, Washington, DC, 1942. https://archive.org/details/TheUnitedNationsFightForTheFourFreedoms (accessed 23 November 2015).
31 *Yearbook of the United Nations 1948–9*, Ch. V., Social, Humanitarian and Cultural Questions; Section A., Human Rights, (2) Discussion by the General Assembly Plenary meeting, (a) Views expressed by Representatives, p. 532. www2.ohchr.org/english/issues/education/training/docs/UNYearbook.pdf (accessed 24 November 2015).
32 *The CPSU Society: Human Rights*, Moscow: Novosti Press Agency Publishing House, 1981, p. 13.
33 Levada-Tsentr *Obshchestvennoe mnenie: ezhegodnik* 2010, Moskva 2010, p. 172.
34 Peter Fedynsky, 'Insider's view of Russian public opinion polls', *Voice of America*, 8 June 2010.
35 Aaron Trehub, 'Social and Economic Rights in the Soviet Union: Work, Health Care, Social Security, and Housing', *Radio Liberty Research Bulletin*, RL Supplement 3/86, 29 December, 1986, p. 3.
36 Efim Etkind, *Protsess Iosifa Brodskogo*, London: Overseas Publication Interchange Limited, 1988, p. 61.
37 'The point of no return has not been passed yet', *Nezavisimaya Gazeta 2008*; in JRL 2008, 226, no. 10.
38 Victor Yassmann, 'Russia: The Orthodox Church and the Kremlin's new mission', RFE/RL, 10 April, 2006. www.rferl.org/content/article/1067551.html (accessed 23 November 2015).
39 Deklaratsiya o pravakh i dostoinstve cheloveka X Vsemirnogo Russkogo Narodnogo Sobora.
40 Osnovy ucheniya Russkoi Pravoslavnoi Tserkvi o dostoinstve, svobode pravakh cheloveka, 26 June 2008. Russkaya Pravoslavnaya Tserkov'. http://www.patriarchia.ru/db/text/428616.html (accessed 23 November 2015).

41 *Argumenty i Fakty*, 19 April 2006.
42 BBC News. http://news.bbc.co.uk/go/pr/fr/-/2/hi/europe/7540077.stm (accessed 23 November 2015).
43 'Rossiya chudovishchno svobodna', *Moskovskii Komsomolets*, 23 December, 2010.
44 SRAS. www.sras.org/news2.php?m=445&popup=1#Russia2 (accessed 23 November 2015).
45 Shaun Walker, 'Petr Pavlensky: why I nailed my scrotum to Red Square', *Guardian*, 5 February 2014. www.theguardian.com/artanddesign/2014/feb/05/petr-pavlensky-nailed-scrotum-red-square (accessed 23 November 2015).
46 Patriarch Kirill, 'U nas net budushchego, esli my nachinaem glumit'sya pered velikimi svyatunyami', 24 March 2012. *Pravoslavie.ru*. http://www.pravoslavie.ru/news/52433.htm (accessed 23 November 2015).
47 *Kommersant*, 17 August 2012; in JRL 148/6.
48 'Bogoroditsa, Devo, Putina progoni … Gei-praid otpravlen v Sibir' v kandalakh … Sran', sran', sran' Gospodnya … Bogoroditsa, Devo, stan' feministkoi … Krestnyi khod iz chernykh limuzinov …'. In court Tolokonnikova said they had translated into Russian the equivalent of the English word 'holy shit' to convey the sense of something unpleasant. http://webkind.ru/text/56256202_62007434p906071039_text_pesni_pank-moleben-bogorodica-putina-progoni-pussy-riot.html (accessed 23 November 2015).
49 The third woman who was accused, Yekaterina Samutsevich, was later freed on appeal after her lawyer argued she had been ejected from the church before the performance.
50 2 October 2012, Interfax; in JRL173/9.
51 Mark Feygin, 'Imenem Trul'skogo i Laodikiiskogo soborov …', *NoNaMe*. http://nnm.ru/blogs/assa82/imenem-trulskogo-i-laodikiyskogo-soborov/#comment_18484848 (accessed 24 November 2015).
52 One of *Voina*'s happenings was painting a massive phallus on half of the Liteiny bridge in Petersburg, so that when the bridge opened at night the drawing faced FSB headquarters. It was called 'Dick captured by FSB' (*Khui v plenu u FSB*). The British graffiti artist Banksky sent £80,000 to support two members of Voina , who had been arrested.
53 '*Yebis' za naslednika Medvezhonka!*'
54 'Pussy riot trial: Vladimir Putin calls for leniency', *Guardian*, 3 August 2012. www.guardian.co.uk/world/2012/aug/03/pussy-riot-trial-vladimir-putin (accessed 23 November 2015).

2 Dimensions of free speech

If freedom of the press were accorded to Russia for twenty-four hours, what you would see would make you recoil with horror. Silence is indispensable to oppression.

(Marquis de Custine, 1839)

I What size free space?

How much free speech is enough? In Russia, where there was hardly any experience of uncensored speech, freedom paradoxically meant something that was boundless and wild. As we saw in the last chapter, the idea of unlimited freedom (*volya*), the urge to break boundaries in an autocratic society, has struggled with the concept of freedom with responsibilities (*svoboda*). It has created confusion in what is already a difficult terrain about where to plot ethical boundaries between liberty and licence, freedom and order, regulation and censorship. Playwright Aleksandr Gelman acknowledged the problem towards the end of the 'free' Yeltsin years: 'When we had no freedom we dreamed of it as something that was not and should not be subjected to regulation. The very expression "regulating freedom" seemed blasphemous to us. It's only now that we're beginning to realise that the most important thing is to regulate freedom. You must regulate freedom to strengthen, consolidate and make it irreversible'.[1]

This confusion has produced oddities. Some hare-brained experiments took place in the early years of free speech, such as the short-lived news programme, *The Naked Truth*, read by a topless female presenter. Complaints that there was 'too much' freedom in the 1990s usually meant two things: either an obsessional fear of chaos, repeated almost as a mantra by pro-Putin supporters today, or the perfectly rational demand for more regulation. In the Putin years when silencing political opposition was officially encouraged, examples of bizarre zealotry became common. Moscow city council's decision to limit free speech to two people per square metre at political rallies in a law that was passed in 2007 was mocked by the newspaper *Kommersant* ('Businessman') as 'Opposition Demonstrators Invited to March on the Spot'.

Various ploys by the Putin regime are used to pretend restrictions on free speech do not exist. During the Sochi Winter Olympics in 2014, a zone for demonstrations was set up in a park 7 miles out of town. The Deputy Prime Minister Dmitry Kozak explained that in this way people were able to 'freely express their opinion without breaching the rights of other citizens'[2] – of course, if a protester wanted to speak to an empty field. Another 'free' option has come from Russia's idea of Speakers' Corner in Hyde Park, London, despite its reputation in England today as a venue for cranks. Such corners have been set up in two of Moscow's large parks, including Gorky Park. Even then, if more than one person wishes to speak, it is necessary to notify the authorities. Prior permission is required to hold a meeting in any other location.

In the Anglo-American tradition, limits to free speech are usually set by laws and regulations that attempt to safeguard social harmony. The notion of absolute free speech was classically rebutted by the American judge Oliver Wendell Holmes who laid down in law that the right of free speech did not permit a man falsely to shout 'fire' in a crowded theatre and cause panic. As we do not live in a vacuum, there is no absolute free speech, though critics who cry out 'chaos and anarchy' tend to latch onto this fear. Liberal philosophers such as Mill and Locke have argued that a certain area of personal freedom must be safeguarded to enable individuals to benefit from the virtues of free speech. According to Isaiah Berlin, the area is determined by 'haggling'.[3] The crisis of global terrorism today is a case in point of haggling between advocates of individual freedom and those seeking to extend the powers of security and law enforcement. But a wider space need not make free speech more effective. The United States' First Amendment gives the media about as close to absolute freedom as any country is likely to be, yet in important political matters the American media can be inordinately feeble. The country's top newspapers, the *New York Times* and the *Washington Post* felt honour-bound to make a public apology in their newspapers for failing to investigate properly the government's claims that Iraq possessed weapons of mass destruction, thus colluding in the country going to war. They had let their readers down. Much the same was implied by Russia's former Human Rights Ombudsman, Sergei Kovalyov, when he said in the Yeltsin years that 'our press is free but not independent'. Even if the institutions of freedom are in place, they may not guarantee that free speech will prevail in the face of informal and overwhelming constraints of deference or greed.

Although free speech and democracy largely go together, J. S. Mill points out that liberty is not incompatible with some kinds of autocracy. Just as democracies may deprive the individual of a great many liberties, so the despot may leave his subjects a wide area of freedom while clamping down on other values.[4] Under tsarist autocracy and Soviet totalitarianism, the freedom that writers or journalists enjoyed depended on how willing the monarch or leader was to permit independent thought. Catherine the Great opened up freedoms that allowed writers and publishers such as Radishchev and Novikov to flourish, but as soon as rebellion erupted in the hinterlands she stamped down on free thinking with brutal force. The fragile freedom that exists under repressive systems leads to a sense of unpredictability and a fear of the 'arbitrariness' of power. The Russian's longing for order may well lie not so much in a fascination with the 'iron fist' as in the desire for predictability.

Free speech at any one stage is difficult to measure with certainty and is best plotted on a continuum of more or less freedom. Historically there has been no gradual progression of free speech in Russia as there has been in many countries in Western Europe and the Americas. In Russia it has been a series of ups and downs, steps forward and back. After the gains of the 1905 reforms a steady increase of free speech might have been anticipated except for the Bolshevik coup that took Russia in another trajectory. When the Utilitarian Jeremy Bentham attempted to measure happiness by determining the index of pleasure and pain according to his felicific calculus, it became clear that weighing the balance between duration and intensity was fairly arbitrary. This is well known on television where 10 seconds can make or break your career. An overview of the existence of free speech in Russia shows it to be more a matter of intensity than duration, but whether the intensity can survive long fallow years without distortion is arguable. How far can Yeltsin's eight years of relative freedom be sustained by 16 years (so far) of Putin's stamping on it?

There are only two periods in Russia's history of the last 300 years when it can be said to have enjoyed relatively full free speech. If we evaluate the level of free speech in society according to legal, political and economic conditions conducive to the manifestation of free speech, then it is only the 1917 February Revolution and Yeltsin's years as president that comply with the criteria. Other liberalising periods have propelled the development and experience of free speech and kept the flame of liberties alight, but journalists and writers did not have any guarantee that they would be protected from arbitrary and indiscriminate punishment. With a history like that of Russia or the Soviet Union where you could be put to death, sent into exile or suffer imprisonment in a labour camp, jail or psychiatric hospital for writing, or for that matter reading, such guarantees are not without significance.

Most liberal reforms in Russia were begun and carried out 'from above' – Alexander II, Khrushchev and Gorbachev. None of these freedoms which were granted as a 'gift', usually for political reasons and not for freedom *per se*, survived to develop normally with their leaders. Although the February Revolution was a popular, spontaneous uprising, it did not last long. We are left with the Yeltsin era, the only example of freedom being won by forces 'from below' that succeeded in bringing a leader of their choice to power and surviving for a decent period of time. This then was potentially the best chance of success Russia has had to create a liberal society.

Three centuries of censorship

Russia's press started its life more than 300 years ago when Peter the Great founded the newspaper *Vedomosti* ('Gazette') in 1702. Like so much else in

Russia, the idea came from what Peter had observed on his travels in Europe, but what in Europe was a grass-roots, evolutionary process set up by publicists and private printers, in Russia became an institution imposed 'from above' by the tsar on a perhaps not unwilling but neither clamouring populace. The newspaper was to serve his ambitions to modernise Russia, to inform the public of his domestic and foreign policies and publicise the military exploits of his Swedish campaign. Peter was involved in every aspect of running the paper: he wrote for it, controlled its editorial policy, and censored articles he disapproved of – in one case, banning the whole of issue 24 of the paper. Peter can thus be called Russia's first journalist, first oligarch and first censor. A pattern was established from the very beginning.

The reform movements of the eighteenth and nineteenth centuries, which inaugurated the grand literary and publicist movement, took place under severe pre-publication censorship laws. A softer regime under Alexander II lasted ten years when prior censorship was replaced by a punitive system based on legal responsibility. The works of Pushkin, Belinsky, Herzen, Dostoyevsky, Tolstoy and so many others showed that censorship was not sufficient to silence the great free thinkers, although their struggles with the censors of the day or the tsar's diktat traumatised their lives. The censor A. V. Nikitenko noted with painful honesty in his diary that none of these writers had criminal intentions, yet they found themselves 'every day and every hour in danger of perishing for nothing, because of some secret denunciation or slander or misunderstanding or out of haste or because of someone's bad mood or false interpretation'.[5] Censorship bred an ambivalence towards authority in writers, who were dependent on officialdom for their survival. Pushkin had to endure the literary advice of the despotic Nicholas I, who decided to be his personal censor, as well as that of the tsar's dreaded Chief of the Gendarmerie, Count Benckendorff, and the regular censors. It is understandable that Pushkin might at one moment pay tribute to the tsar, 'No, I'm no flatterer when I freely Praise the tsar', and at another time disclaim 'Autocrat and Evildoer! I hate you and your throne, your violence is the death of children' – a verse not published in his lifetime.[6]

It was not until the 1905 Revolution that serious cracks began to appear in autocracy. The October Manifesto of 1905 granted a parliament (the Duma), and promised civil liberties based on 'principles of genuine inviolability of the person, freedom of conscience, speech, assembly and association'. This brought about an upsurge of press activity as all political parties were granted the right to own their own newspapers. The expansion of the opposition press of liberals and socialists – Kadets, Socialist Revolutionaries, Mensheviks, Bolsheviks – and their newspapers – for workers, peasants, soldiers, youth, trade unions and soviets – thrived and provided a plurality of political views on the turbulent events. With troops still loyal to the tsar, however, Nicholas II was able to renege on many of these concessions and the persecution of opponents continued. There was frenetic media activity, but journalists were still jailed and newspapers were closed and sometimes heavily fined.

Nevertheless, reforms had changed political consciousness and unless a complete overhaul of the political system occurred the monarchy was doomed.

The grass-roots revolution that spread through Russia in February 1917 provided a free press for all persuasions. The provisional government abolished censorship for the first time, newspapers multiplied and opposition views and revolutionary politics proliferated. But the government was at war, and by the July days military censorship was imposed and Bolshevik newspapers were banned as subversive for calling for an end to war with Germany. This first flowering of officially endorsed free speech was intense, but lasted only five months. The Bolsheviks' first act on coming to power was to close down the bourgeois and non-Bolshevik socialist press. Having seized power, Lenin considered it suicidal to give his political opponents a say through their newspapers, even if they were socialists. As early as two days after the Bolshevik coup, the Decree on the Press was passed closing down newspapers as a 'temporary measure', but one which was never rescinded in the Soviet Union's almost 74-year-old history.

In the Soviet period, liberalisation and greater media freedoms were a result of decisions made by the party Central Committee to implement policy changes. As private initiative on a large scale was not possible, change could only come top-down. Khrushchev's 'thaw' in the late 1950s and early 1960s, after a long period of terror and war, was directed at reforming the party and, in the process, justifying his own succession to the Politburo after Stalin's death. The policy of *destalinisation* was an attempt to bring the party closer to what were seen as more humane Leninist principles. Khrushchev's secret speech at the 20th Party Congress in 1956 against Stalin's 'cult of personality' electrified and traumatised a nation that had not only believed in the lies of the Communist Party but idolised Stalin. For such a campaign to succeed, Khrushchev had to give editors and journalists enough space to use their own initiative. The media were meant to serve the state, only this time the propaganda was directed at a campaign of reform which progressive journalists could throw themselves into with enthusiasm as their minds cleared of the fog of Stalinism. Together with poets, writers and the public, the media were invigorated by this period of partial freedom, but Khrushchev's goals for reform were limited. A beginning was made, political and economic reforms were started and, as abruptly, taken away. This devastated a young generation that had hoped to build a new and better communist future, a generation known as the *shestidesyatniki* (people of the sixties), those who were activated by Khrushchev's reforms and experienced the disillusionment of their short duration. Starting as an *Izvestiya* journalist, the famous Aleksandr Bovin, later to become Brezhnev's speech writer and still later a diplomat in the Yeltsin era, expressed the frustration of his generation:

> For young party functionaries of that time (I was 25 then and worked as head of the propaganda department of a party district committee) the 20th Congress was a purifying storm which made it possible to look to

the future with hope. We began to learn to think, to act, to speak our mind. And it was with bewilderment, pain and a terrible sense of my own helplessness that I and my generation saw the ideas of one of the truly historic congresses of our party sink into the quicksands of bureaucracy.[7]

Despite state brutality to keep the lid down, free speech erupted in another domain – the dissident movement. Dissident Soviet writers who could not get past the censor would bring their works out in *samizdat* (self-publishing), which were copied by hand or typed and circulated in carbon copies. This was a dangerous occupation, even for those taking part in the most menial tasks, let alone helping to distribute such subversive works as Solzhenitsyn's *Gulag Archipelago*. Sometimes these works circulated in copies published abroad (*tamizdat*). In this underground world that broke the silence of a totalitarian system, the dissidents felt they were 'internal émigrés' in their own country. Dissident information bulletins monitored and recorded violations of human rights and the fate of writers and dissidents. The *Chronicle of Current Events* (*Khronika tekushchikh sobytiy*) was the longest running *samizdat* journal, lasting from 1968 to 1983, producing a total of 63 bulletins with regular sections entitled 'Arrests, Searches, Interrogations', 'In Prisons and Camps', 'Persecution of Religion', 'Persecution of Crimean Tatars' and so on. Its style was factual and non-judgemental. In the 18 years of Brezhnev's regime this was the main form of protest and government accountability.

After the 'thaw', the media reverted to their normal role as servants of the state, and careers were made and broken on that basis. Journalists of progressive views did not on the whole take the extra step into the dissident movement that would have ostracised them from society; but neither were they able to overcome their discontent and frustration. Their malaise was a suffocating sense of moral and political entrapment. They worked within the system, but baulked at it, sabotaged it in many small ways, wrote in Aesopian language that the public was skilled at reading, criticised the system deftly and deviously when possible. Some lost their jobs, others moved around in different positions, yet others were sent abroad by sympathetic editors to get them out of harm's way. It was this generation that came into its own when Gorbachev took office and proclaimed the need for *glasnost*.

The 'people of the sixties' were made of tougher stuff than the younger generation that had grown up under the Brezhnev years of cynicism and conformism. They were offered a second chance and weren't about to be duped by party machinations. Most of the early editors-in-chief who took up Gorbachev's call for reform came from this generation and their agenda was wider than the one Gorbachev conceived for them: people such as Yegor Yakovlev (*Moskovskiye novosti*/'Moscow News'), Igor Golembiovsky (*Izvestiya*/ 'News'), Vitaly Korotich (*Ogonyok*/'Little Flame'), and many other journalists, academics and intellectuals, who envisaged how the media would spearhead a new society with *glasnost* at its crux. In many ways they were the lucky generation: they had been through the demystification process which cured them of political gullibility and uncritical party allegiance, while still retaining a sense of purpose and the belief that they could improve society. They could still turn to an ideology which gave shape to their ideas of building socialism with a human face. In practical terms, they were alert to the forces opposing *glasnost* and quicker off the mark at struggling against the conservative backlash when the time came.

Like Khrushchev's 'thaw', Gorbachev's *glasnost* started as a top-down reform. From the very beginning it was intended as a measure to assist his policy of *perestroika* (restructuring), the plan to reform and revitalise the Soviet system and halt its economic decline. The media, as the right arm of party and state, would mobilise support and win the hearts and minds of the people for his programme. Gorbachev never intended *glasnost* to open up a Pandora's box revealing the whole range of crimes committed by the party during the years of Soviet power. *Glasnost* was not meant to be an invitation to free speech. But he miscalculated the limits he could place on *glasnost* and the control he could exert on the media in their effort to push forward the frontiers.

In his first speech on 11 March 1985 as General-Secretary of the Communist Party, Gorbachev inadvertently exposed the dilemma at the heart of his policy. 'We are obliged to extend *glasnost* further', he said. 'The more that people are informed, the more actively they will support the Party, its plans and its programme aims'.[8] In fact, precisely the opposite was true. The more people learned about how their lives had been cruelly mismanaged by the party, the less likely they were to support it. Gorbachev's goal of reforming the party and making it more open, humane and effective was welcomed with great enthusiasm in the first years of his rule. The freedoms he allowed were almost unimaginable to people at the time, each day widening the chinks in their knowledge of the past and the suffering people had been through. *Glasnost* was Gorbachev's most successful policy, but it was the one that largely contributed to bringing him and the Soviet Union down.

How the media responded to the freedoms that *glasnost* allowed changed as expectations grew. If at first *glasnost* was gratefully accepted as making life freer, a few years later the media were complaining that it did no more than let off steam. They labelled the policy '*glasnost* in doses'. By 1989 journalists were demanding guarantees in law of their right to speak freely, reasoning they had no certainty that the freedoms that had been so tortuously acquired over the past years might not be removed overnight, as they had been after the 'thaw'.

The broadcaster Eduard Sagalayev, famous for the earliest excursions of *glasnost* on television, expressed how he felt in 1990 at the peak of discontent with Gorbachev's unwillingness to take reforms further:

> I constantly feel that *glasnost* is free speech in the dose prescribed and determined for us by the leadership ... everything we write and say, we say not because we are free, but because we are allowed to. And all the laws

that have been passed and will be passed in the near future about the press, about freedom of conscience, about the right to travel in and out of the country – all this, I feel, makes democracy a house of cards and the rule of law a house of cards that can be swept away in an instant with a single puff.[9]

It was not long before the Soviet Union itself fell, like a house of cards. Hardly anyone forecast it. The leap from Soviet society to western-style democracy and free market capitalism was unchartered territory and anything was possible. Yeltsin's popularity at this initial stage was so great that he effectively had a mandate to push forward any radical reform he wished in order to modernise the country and dismantle its totalitarian past.

Expanding free speech: Yeltsin

Yeltsin's era is distinguished by the first real attempt to provide the conditions and infrastructure for freedom of speech to exist and flourish. This period lasted from December 1991 to December 1999. Yeltsin took it upon himself to be the guarantor of free speech. He was indebted to the progressive media for keeping his name alive after he had been ostracised by Gorbachev, and for supporting him throughout his rebellion against the party. The media had helped to bring him to power and he realised the tactical advantage it gave him. When push came to shove, as in the 1996 re-election campaign, he was proved right. Although journalists were extremely tough on him as president, he allowed them to criticise and lampoon him – something no leader had allowed during the Soviet period or, so far, after it.

A new chapter was opened in political satire on the commercial channel NTV's show *Kukly* ('Puppets'), with its sharp wit and fiendish life-size dolls modelled on the UK's *Spitting Image* and France's *Guignol-Info*. A buffoonish bear-like Yeltsin, mumbling inconsequentialities in a slurred voice, would appear regularly on screens with his villainous team of ministers. One show on 8 July 1995 based on Gorky's play *The Lower Depths* with Yeltsin and his officials portrayed as tramps living in filthy dosshouses, claiming the state minimum wage, incensed the Prosecutor General's office so much that it sued the programme on Yeltsin's behalf. The hardline paper *Sovetskaya Rossiya* ('Soviet Russia') recommended 'corrective labour' with a maximum of two years for the offenders. When Yeltsin found out, he fired the Prosecutor General. When Putin came to power it did not take him long to indicate his displeasure. Neither had Gorbachev allowed such familiarity. As USSR president a law was passed to protect his honour and dignity, according to which publicly insulting the president could be punishable by three years' imprisonment. In terms of the mystique Russian leaders have created around themselves, Yeltsin's acceptance of the liberties that are taken when free speech is exercised was a serious standard-setter of democratic change.

For all the criticism Yeltsin endured, he was touchy and easily offended. His press secretary from 1992 to 1995, Vyacheslav Kostikov, was never certain how much information Yeltsin was receiving from his entourage if the messages were unpleasant. He himself was anxious about showing Yeltsin newspaper reports of his performance in Germany in 1994 when after a champagne lunch he had seized the bandmaster's baton and drunkenly conducted the orchestra. With footage travelling the globe treating him like a figure of fun, Kostikov felt it was his duty to show him the coverage. The next day, for the first time, Yeltsin did not shake his hand and ignored him entirely, but 'fortunately the president turned out to be forgiving and the thickening clouds began to disperse the following day'.[10] There was always a kind of blustering integrity to Yeltsin that endeared him to the public. It was a period that had as much to do with unlearning old habits as picking up new ones. The 1990s breathed a different atmosphere, with shifting and flexible attitudes and an informality that came with a freer way of life that seemed unthreatened.

II Laws and rules of the game

The Yeltsin era was conceived as a transition to democracy. In this period the institutions of free speech, some of which were introduced during Gorbachev's reforms, were confirmed and expanded. Censorship was abolished and free speech enshrined in the new Constitution of the Russian Federation, approved in 1993, which states under article 29:

> 29.1 Each person is guaranteed freedom of thought and speech.
>
> 29.2 Propaganda or agitation arousing social, racist, nationalist or religious hatred or enmity is not permitted. It is prohibited to promote propaganda of social, racist, nationalist, religious or language supremacy.
>
> 29.3 No one can be forced to express their opinions and beliefs or to reject them.
>
> 29.4 Each person has the right freely to seek, get, transfer, produce and disseminate information by any lawful means. The list of information constituting a state secret is determined by federal law. Freedom of the mass media is guaranteed. Censorship is prohibited.[11]

The reason for the double emphasis, that censorship is prohibited and free speech guaranteed, was to overcome the suspicion in Russian minds that any legislation permitting freedom was probably a sham. If you were naive enough to be taken in, you'd probably be punished in due course. Thus the legal term 'everything that is not prohibited is allowed' made little sense to Russians, who were used to a system where 'rules of the game' were paramount. The informal way of doing things – with a nod and a wink – was what counted. The dark humour of Soviet anecdotes usually spelled out the true nature of things. Three lawyers meet. The English lawyer says: 'everything that is permitted is permitted; everything that is prohibited is prohibited'. The French lawyer says: 'everything is permitted even if it is prohibited'. The Soviet lawyer says: 'in the Soviet Union everything is prohibited, what is permitted is obligatory'.

It is not laws alone that encourage free speech, but the political climate that is shaped by those in power. Most of the laws safeguarding free speech that were approved during the Yeltsin period exist today under Putin, but the majority of the media is not free or independent and although anti-censorship laws have not been repealed, self-censorship is rampant. 'No one tells me what you can and can't do. It's in the air. If you know what is permitted and what is not, you're in the right place. If you don't, you're not', says broadcaster Nikolai Svanidze.[12] That does not mean that laws have no real effect, only that citizens need to sniff out which way the wind is blowing, and leave room for contingencies. Draconian laws introduced from 2000 by Putin, as well as the long list of new laws that came into effect after military intervention in Ukraine in 2014 have had a catastrophic effect on traditional media and the internet. On the other hand, the Constitution's Article 29.2 (cited above) had no effect in preventing a year of the worst hate speech against Ukrainians that Russian television has ever broadcast.

Law of the mass media

Censorship was first officially abolished by the USSR Law on the Press and Other Mass Media on 12 June 1990 in the year before Gorbachev resigned. This law was superseded by the Russian Federation's Law of the Mass Media signed by Yeltsin 18 months later on 27 December 1991, coming into force on 14 February 1992.[13] These two laws freed the media, helped in the transformation from *glasnost* to free speech and provided the stimulus for Russia's aspirations to become a democracy. The 1991 law is the closest Russia has to a Millian document in defence of free speech. Both laws were authored by the country's eminent reformist lawyers, Yury Baturin, Mikhail Fedotov and Vladimir Entin. Baturin and Fedotov, with a string of academic publications on constitutional law and, in the case of Fedotov, intellectual property, have participated imaginatively in political and intellectual life (Entin remained in the academy). Baturin became Yeltsin's legal and security adviser and secretary of the Security Council from 1996 to 1997, and later trained as a cosmonaut, flying on two space missions. Fedotov was Yeltsin's Press Minister, UNESCO's Russian Representative in Paris, Secretary to the Union of Journalists, becoming head of the Human Rights Council and its adviser to the president, when it was founded by President Medvedev – and today still one of a handful of organisations that speaks out in defence of liberties.

The media law's existence started almost as comic relief, in one of those magical moments when things in Russia happen in impossible conditions. Fedotov had written a dissertation on the need for a press law in 1976 when no one thought he had picked a sensible project – but he was the offspring of three generations of jurists. Ten years later Gorbachev announced the need for a press law and gave the official task to a conservative member of the party Central Committee, Vadim Medvedev. Although Medvedev's draft law was meant to be widely publicised and discussed within the terms of *glasnost*, the date kept being put off. There were a few insider draft laws competing with Medvedev's, but unsolicited drafts were unwanted and such brazenness could even be dangerous. But it seemed like a good idea to Fedotov and Baturin as they were chopping wood and cooking shashliks at a country dacha. They were pretty certain Medvedev's party document would be inadequate, so they wrote their own, under the aegis of the Union of Journalists, which gave them some protection. As Medvedev was opposed to their version, no editor would publish it. As luck would have it, when Fedotov and his family were on holiday in Estonia, their Estonian journalist friends managed to get the draft published in a supplement, inserted into an Estonian-language youth sports newspaper – but the ice was broken. If an article had been published on the territory of the Soviet Union, it did not have to pass the Russian censor. After that, the draft law was published in Russian newspapers and began to be circulated.

The next step was to publish 5,000 copies to hand out to delegates coming to the First Congress of People's Deputies in 1989. As that required money they did not have, Fedotov used his car as a taxi until he had earned enough. There were lots of volunteers happy to distribute the slim paperback, but people were not permitted to bring literature or briefcases into the Kremlin, where the congress was held. Fedotov's wife, Maria, sewed booklet-sized pockets inside the volunteers' jackets and in this way, moving in and out of the Kremlin to re-stock, they managed to distribute all the copies. Promoted by pro-democracy reformers and at least ten deputies who represented the Union of Journalists, the alternative draft law was discussed in the most important lobby, the corridors and halls at the congress, where the real politics was taking place. A volunteer went up to Yeltsin to give him a copy, but Yeltsin said he already had one, and intended to push through the draft law. Gorbachev neither promoted nor rejected the alternative law.

As soon as the Soviet Press Law had come into force in the summer of 1990, censors from Glavlit began to leave newspaper offices, where they had worked. The second law, which was more liberal and western in scope, helped newspapers and journals to escape the party stranglehold. Although some media outlets began to set themselves up as independent almost immediately the Communist Party's 'guiding role' was revoked in March 1990, basing their action on the policy of *glasnost*, the law provided solid foundations. In the Soviet system no concept of 'owner' existed. *Pravda* ('Truth'), for example, was an 'organ' of the Central Committee of the Communist Party of the Soviet Union, with its badge stamped on the front of the paper. The Media Law introduced the entity 'founder' (*uchreditel'*), which helped break the tie between newspapers and their previous owners. A court case in which Fedotov defended the right of the literary journal *Znamya* ('Standard') to dissociate itself as an 'organ' of the USSR Union of Writers, set a precedent. 'What rights did a founder have?', Fedotov explained to me:

> It had to have founded a newspaper. But *Znamya* was founded in 1931 and the Union of Writers was set up in 1934, so it's doubtful that the son was born before the father. Going back into the archives, we found out that the decision to make *Znamya* an 'organ' of the Union of Writers came from the Central Committee of the All-Union Communist Party (Bolsheviks), which had no connection at all to the Union of Writers. After that, there was not a single court case where owners managed to get back their previous newspapers and journals.

Such acrobatics were necessary to extricate journalists from the intricate tangle the party had created to cover up its political supremacy. Media lawyer Andrei Richter, who set up Russia's first media law and policy centre in Moscow in 1996, explains:

> It happened not exactly according to the rule of law, in my opinion, but in a bizarre way, like stealing newspapers from their owners, except that they were not really owners, because newspapers had been established by party decisions and not solid law. In this way the law allowed editors and journalists to leave their official owners but keep their titles. This involved hundreds of Party, Soviet and Komsomol newspapers and journals. It was not according to the law, but it was legal.[14]

The other way the media law extended the exercise of free speech was by spelling out media rights in detail. This was the necessary formality for Russian laws to be effective. 'The fact that a journalist has rights does not mean he can use them, but at least we've written in that he has these rights; otherwise journalists would have had nothing to go on', Fedotov says. Among the list of rights, the law guarantees journalists access to information and editorial independence. The journalist has the right to remove his signature from reports which contradict his convictions or that have been distorted in the process of editorial preparation, which meant a journalist's freedom was also protected from editorial pressure (although no journalist has ever tested this article). The law safeguards the confidentiality of sources. It asserts media responsibilities as well as rights. If the media publish or broadcast information that is inaccurate or false, the law requires that an apology is printed in the same place or broadcast at the same time as the original information. The activity of a media outlet may only be suspended or ended by a decision of a court of law or by its founders. It can be closed down only after it has received two warnings in a year.

The media law's principles began to be distorted when Putin came to power. As a result, Andrei Richter believes, the law can now obstruct free speech. The share of journalists' responsibilities and rights, delicately balanced in the law, have been skewered to focus mainly on journalists' obligations. The requirement of state registration of media outlets, which helped editorial offices gain independence from the party, is now used punitively to remove a recalcitrant media outlet. 'Twenty-five years ago you couldn't start a media outlet because there was no procedure to avoid the state's ban on independent media. Today, when a media outlet needs to register, it again needs to get permission from the state. The European Court of Human Rights made this point in the case of Dzhavadov *versus* Russia, that this permission has been abused', says Richter. To add to this, he says, the media law has been amended so that if extremist speech is found in the media, the law can punish not just the individual who disseminated supposedly extremist speech but the whole media organisation.

In the Yeltsin years about 30 federal statues regulating the media were adopted between 1991 and 1999. Richter believes that overall they created a sound and operational base for the mass media:

> Most editors and journalists take it for granted that there is an absence of state censorship, easy procedures to start a newspaper, inadmissibility to arbitrarily shut down a news outlet, certain availability of information resources, access to sources, possibility to investigate and attack the government – all unheard of under the Soviet regime, and all guaranteed by the new press freedoms.[15]

Today these laws can still work to curb excesses. Because of the Putin regime's pretence that Russia is a democracy, pliant legislators need to juggle with these liberal laws if they want to issue punitive sentences or draft new amendments. 'I can't imagine how we'd be able to live today if some traces at least of the 1990s hadn't remained', former TV owner Irena Lesnevskaya said in 2014. 'Censorship didn't exist in the nineties, although everyone knocks and criticises [it now]. I don't agree with that for a second'.[16] It was the combination of a permissive climate and the introduction of liberal laws that made the Yeltsin era free.

Law against extremism

While the media law encouraged a free and open society, Putin's 2002 law 'On Counteracting Extremist Activity' has substantially narrowed the domain of free expression, with amendments in 2006 and 2014 making it ever more threatening to speak freely in the traditional media and online. The impact on free speech has been toxic. The term 'extremist' is so vaguely defined that it can apply to almost anyone who displeases the authorities. It allows journalists to be branded as extremists if they criticise public officials, they can be sentenced to jail for up to five years and, if they are charged, their media outlet can be closed down or suspended after two warnings. The list of extremist activities includes, for example, 'public slander directed toward figures fulfilling the state duties of the Russian Federation or the state duties of subjects of the Russian Federation' and 'hindering the legal duties of organs of state authorities'.[17]

Almost any derogatory remark in the media can be interpreted as extremist if the author cannot prove his statement to be true in a court of law. 'I have always understood extremism to be connected with violence: if there is no violence, there is no extremism', countered Fedotov. As the media's traditional justification of being the fourth estate in liberal democracies is to hold officials to account, this law prevents their basic functions. A perfectly adequate law existed before, covering terrorism and hate speech in Article 282 of the Criminal Code. But the Criminal Code, says Andrei Richter, could not be used to close a media outlet, 'so they changed a small article in the Criminal Code, which was not often used, into a tool to bring liability to a huge number of people'.

The idea that public officials should benefit from increased protection under defamation law contravenes internationally established standards based on the European Court of Human Rights that says that public officials should tolerate a *higher degree* of criticism than ordinary citizens. This was not the way Aleksandr Kotenkov, the president's representative to the Federation Council, perceived the role of public officials in Russia: 'There cannot be any assumptions in the media about state officials ... [they] enjoy the presumption of innocence, like any other citizen. But accusing a state official of engaging in extremist activity doesn't only insult the person in question, it also undermines trust in the state. That is extremism. And so, my dear journalists, you'll now have to think before you speak'.[18]

Self-regulation

In the Yeltsin years, efforts were made to encourage self-regulation, giving journalists the right to supervise their own profession and protect it from government interference. Given that the media tended to see freedom as boundless, these efforts were often ignored, although a start was made. Surpassing all expectations was the ad hoc arbitration court that was set up in 1993 to resolve media disputes on the spot during the first democratic elections. The court could pass on recommendations to the government, but it had no real power to impose fines or other sanctions. It was thought that without an 'arbitration prison', no one would take the institution seriously. Yet its respected media experts and chairman, law professor Anatoly Vengerov, made it a surprise success. It later became the media's permanent co-regulatory body on ethics and professional standards, known as the Judicial Chamber of Information Disputes attached to the President's Office, the direct connection with Yeltsin as 'guarantor' of liberties gaining the chamber protection from outside pressure. This quasi-independent regulator, which was evolving into a powerful moral corrective to media violations within the profession, was disbanded by Putin in 2000 in one of his first acts against media independence.

There have been other attempts at self-regulation, with a variety of groups and media outlets drafting their own ethical codes and charters. The Union of Journalists had a minor success with its self-regulating body, the Grand Jury, that heard disputes and made moral assessments on some of the worst media complaints; and today a Public Collegium is trying to do the same thing, but has had little success with state media. In the year Putin came to power a media union was set up 'from above' to incorporate top managers and compete with the Union of Journalists, but it also had limited success.

With the tightening up of freedoms, power over the media remains with the law and formal regulation. In 2008 two institutions on culture and media were joined under the Ministry of Communications to form a federal executive body, Roskomnadzor, which supervises electronic media, the internet and mass communications.[19] On one occasion only, an attempt was made by senior broadcasting executives to introduce self-regulation with regard to media coverage of terrorist acts after the Moscow hostage crises of *Nord-Ost* and Beslan. The aim was to prevent harsh legislation that would have banned reports containing remarks intended to obstruct counter-terrorist operations or encourage or justify opposition to it. Receiving the go-ahead from Putin, journalists agreed to abide by guidelines they defined in a 2003 Counter-terrorism Convention. The Convention took into account aspects of reporting that had most incensed the Kremlin, such as live interviews with terrorists and journalists assuming the role of mediator; but it also dealt with matters of taste and decency, such as avoiding gruesome images and showing tact for the feelings of family and relatives of victims. No sooner had the Convention been adopted, says Andrei Richter, than it was forgotten both by the media and the authorities, which could be witnessed in the coverage of later terrorist acts that took place in the centre of Moscow.[20] Self-regulation has not had great success, because it requires agreement between the profession, owners and the state of the value of free and independent media.

Restricting free speech: Putin

Whereas Yeltsin came to power on a wave of liberation after the coup, Putin's popularity was based on fighting the second Chechen war. As the saying goes, truth is the first casualty of war, and anti-terrorism and anti-extremism legislation has been a useful way of silencing journalists and citizens. Deep suspicion about the reasons behind the Chechen war and whether it had been instigated to boost Putin's popularity and bring him to power have never been disabused. A repeat 'war' scenario 14 years later in Crimea and Ukraine after massive 'Russia without Putin' protests gives further substance to these early suspicions and raises new ones about the level of FSB operations behind the scenes to protect Putin and his entourage.

Putin's attitude to free speech demonstrated from the very start what Yeltsin called 'that severe nervous reaction at the sight of a newspaper', which he said was characteristic of the security services.[21] The public example of this pathological approach came in the media policy document, Doctrine of Information Security, which Putin approved in 2000, as early as six months into his presidency. Drafted by the Security Council, many of whose members were former KGB generals, it exudes a chilling effect for the future of free speech. All the seeds of war paranoia and resentment directed at Ukraine and the West in 2014 are embedded in this document that sets out so early the preconditions for turning the media into a Kremlin-approved propaganda machine. Putin's spin doctor Gleb Pavlovsky confirmed that, although Putin's manipulation of the Ukraine crisis was an improvisation, 'the logistics and plans existed a long time ago'.[22]

Nominally supporting the right of free speech, the greater part of the Doctrine of Information Security consists of a list of threats that news and information pose to the country's national interests. The main villains in the document are privately owned domestic media and foreign media. The word 'terrorist' is mentioned only once, but the whole spirit of the document is permeated with a sense of menace and the need to provide:

> trustworthy (*dostovernyy*) information to the Russian and international public about the Russian Federation's state policy and its official position on socially significant events in Russian and international life.[23]

The document also emphasises the state's duty to protect society from foreign influences and the dissemination of spiritual and moral values that 'violate norms accepted by Russian society'. The aim is to stop 'manipulated information (disinformation, concealed and distorted information)'. For this reason, it is necessary 'to bolster the state media, expanding their capabilities to promptly convey trustworthy information to Russian and foreign citizens'. With a straight face, the doctrine assumes the state possesses no interests of its own that will affect 'trustworthiness'.

In these statements we have the thinking behind the later expansion of state-owned and state-affiliated media and the emasculation of the independent sector. Although the threat from private and foreign media allegedly came in the 'monopolisation of individual or all sectors of the Russian information market' and their 'blocking of activities of state media', there was no basis to this premise. In Russia the most powerful mainstream television channels have always been state-owned and the state has always had a near monopoly on licensing and registration. According to the Union of Journalists in 2000, at the time of this document, 80 per cent of the print and broadcast news media was controlled directly or indirectly by the federal government or the 89 regional governments or local authorities.[24] The then general secretary of the Russian Union of Journalists, Igor Yakovenko, noted quizzically: 'the state is the sole monopolist of information resources, while no private company is a monopoly. This concept does not seem to be aimed against state monopoly. Rather it makes a bogeyman of private media'.[25]

The bogeyman at the time the doctrine emerged was NTV, the largest and most successful private channel owned by Vladimir Gusinsky. NTV had not supported Putin in the 1999/2000 elections. But the problem lay not so much in this fact as in the matter of power: rival oligarch Boris Berezovsky, who was the main engineer behind the television campaign to elect Putin, was also under attack. The doctrine's goal was to enable the state to regain control over private media oligarchs, who had emerged in the competitive market of the Yeltsin years. If the Kremlin did not engineer Soviet-style control, it would not be able to plant 'trustworthy' messages without interference from independent or foreign sources or from such loose cannons as Berezovsky.

The doctrine encapsulated some of the main ideas of Putin's regime: suspicion of foreign intrusion on its sovereignty, ideas of Russian Renewal after years of kow-towing to the West and the IMF, the rollback of democratic freedoms and the promotion of Russia's traditional values as a defence against the West. Crucially, it needed to block accurate media coverage of the Chechen war that could destabilise the government. The tragedy of 9/11, coming exactly a year to the day after the doctrine came into effect, helped the process of labelling Chechen rebels as terrorists. Putin was the first leader to ring the American president after 9/11 to offer his commiserations. It was his way of putting what many saw as a separatist war in Chechnya on the same footing as Islamic world terrorism. As a war against world terrorism, it was easier to curb the right to free speech that had come to be accepted in the Yeltsin period.

The public liked Putin because he was young, healthy and 'normal', a trait much prized by Russians used to a dysfunctional society. But there was nothing 'normal' about a former KGB lieutenant colonel becoming president of a country that had relinquished its totalitarian past. Not only was Putin KGB, but he was proud of it. The fact that his mentor was Anatoly Sobchak granted him some liberal credentials, but his KGB qualifications and his previous posting as head of the KGB's successor organisation, the FSB, were particularly relevant to dealing with a merciless round of terrorist acts connected with Chechnya. His decisive response and the 'strong man' image he conveyed in launching the second war in Chechnya, only a few weeks after being appointed prime minister, added enormously to his popularity at a time when Yeltsin seemed to have completely vanished from the scene. So convenient were these events in building up Putin's popularity that suspicion has remained ever since that those promoting Putin were responsible for provoking the war.

The stuff of conspiracy theories, largely because it is hard to imagine that such ruthlessness could be perpetrated against one's own people, although it happened often enough under Stalinism, the second invasion of Chechnya has been attributed to the so-called apartment bombings: a series of explosions that blasted four apartment blocks in Volgodonsk, Buynaksk and two in Moscow, all in September 1999, killing 293 people and injuring over 600. At about the same time there were other explosions in Moscow and Dagestan. Suspicion was aroused when a bomb was found in Ryazan, also in September, and defused by local authorities whose evidence was later denied by the FSB. The bags that were alleged to contain hexagon tied to a detonator were apparently, the FSB announced, bags of sugar used in a military training exercise. Suspicion has intensified as three people not content with this official version of events, all well-known figures, have died in strange circumstances. There was the shocking death of former KGB operative Aleksandr Litvinenko, who was poisoned by a lethal radioactive substance polonium-210 in London in 2006. The public inquiry held in London ten years later concluded that Putin had 'probably' sanctioned his assassination. Before that, investigative journalist Yury Shchekochikhin from *Novaya gazeta* ('New Newspaper') had died in Moscow in 2003 of symptoms similar to Litvinenko's, and opposition parliamentarian Sergei Yushenkov, the deputy chairman of the independent investigative committee into the bombings, was shot dead in the same year. There is no direct evidence of a conspiracy, but the fact remains that the apartment bombings catapulted a virtually unknown KGB officer to become president a few months later. His tough talk helped, as did the first public expression of his gangster-like slang, when he vowed he would get the Chechens wherever they were – 'we'll wipe 'em out, even in the outhouses'.

The tandem

Policy on the media did not change substantially under the Putin–Medvedev tandem, but the political climate was softer and Medvedev presented himself as a more moderate figure. After the 2008 elections, with Medvedev replacing Putin as president and Putin becoming prime minister, a switching of posts that no one seriously believed would affect Putin's predominance, the vital question was the extent to which Medvedev would be independent of his mentor.

Throughout his period in office, analysts wondered if he would bring back some of the freedoms that had been lost under Putin's hardline politics. Medvedev's rhetoric raised hopes of liberalisation with remarks such as 'freedom is better than non-freedom'.[26] There was some cause for optimism as Medvedev had never served in the security services and his background as a lawyer seemed to make his promises more credible, to install the rule of law, stop the 'legal nihilism' in society and fight corruption. Cultivating the image of a man younger and more responsive to the demands of modern society than Putin, Medvedev was internet savvy, had his own blog and Twitter account and liked rock music.

He showed greater respect for media freedoms than Putin ever had. This he showed in his state-of-the nation address, but he spoke in a curiously timorous way:

> Freedom of speech should be strengthened by technological innovations. Experience shows that trying to persuade officials to leave the media alone is useless. Instead of trying to persuade them we should more

actively expand the free space of the internet and digital television. No official is able to obstruct discussion on the internet or censor a thousand channels at one and the same time.[27]

One wonders why he did not simply instruct his officials to stop obstructing journalists. Such signs of weakness in a president became irritating and were described as 'pathetic' by journalists and bloggers. There were incidents of Medvedev making promises to the public which were simply ignored by his bureaucracy. One of these, to hold an inquiry into compensation for families of victims of the 2008 war in Georgia was never carried out. With hindsight, we can see he was more junior in the tandem than people assumed at the time. Nevertheless, protocol was maintained on television: Medvedev – first, Putin – second, corresponding to their formal status. If one appeared in the news, the other tended to as well. According to some journalists, two-thirds of news items on national state channels were inserted not because of their newsworthiness but to maintain this balance.

As head of state, Medvedev was committed to developing technology and modernisation. He attempted to expand the domain of the Russian internet in political life, posting his manifesto and articles online, urging politicians to start their own blogs, and suggesting that laws and issues of importance should be posted on the web for public discussion. His own LiveJournal video blog was launched in October 2008 and his Twitter account in June 2010. Unlike Putin, Medvedev understood the inevitability of the internet to modernisation, even as many began to use the freedom of the web to change the political stupor that had characterised the first eight Putin years.

There was a lack of clarity to Medvedev's overtures to the opposition press. During its darker hours he visited the offices of *Novaya gazeta* to express his condolences after the assassination in 2009 of the newspaper's young reporter Anastasiya Baburova and the prominent human rights lawyer associated with the paper, Stanislav Markelov. The newspaper had already seen four of its investigative journalists murdered in recent years. This visit was in stark contrast to Putin's indifference to earlier assassinations. Yet Medvedev's ambivalence was not lost on many of Moscow's more critical journalists, who asked why it took him ten days before approaching the editor of *Novaya gazeta*, during which time there had been total silence from the Kremlin. Why, they also asked, were the press and TV cameras banned from the meeting? Medvedev's reply that 'as a lawyer' he did not want to put pressure on the prosecution's investigation was mocked, especially by prominent journalist Aleksandr Minkin, who represented the anger felt by his colleagues that the perpetrators of only one of the many contract killings of journalists had been solved at that time. Minkin wrote in his series, 'Letters to the President' in *Moskovsky komsomolets* ('Moscow Komsomol Member'):

Don't be angry, but do you run a legal advice bureau in the Kremlin? You are not working there as a lawyer but as President ... Your words

will always be the words of the *President* (as long as you remain President) ... and no one sees you either as a lawyer or as an 'ordinary
person' ... Why precisely in this instance did you want to speak without
the press? ... Why not let ... society know that you condemn this murder
and see it as your duty to ensure that with all the means at your disposal
the killers will be apprehended and brought to trial?[28]

The lingering question was whether Medvedev lacked the power to introduce
liberal reforms or didn't wish to. As Putin's handpicked successor, he never
openly confronted Putin, yet he did not appear content to play second fiddle,
calling for the modernisation of society to deal with the consequences of
Putin's policies which, as he spelled them out in his manifesto, *Forward, Russia*,
were quite onerous – 'an inefficient economy, a semi-Soviet social sphere, an
unformed democracy, negative demographic tendencies and instability in the
Caucasus'.[29] It was such examples that kept the hope alive that he was a
liberal at heart.

Did Medvedev have any discernible impact on increasing free speech? The
fact of a tandem meant some restrained competition was taking place within
the power structures. It gave more room to breathe and people took advantage of the situation. There was an increase in street action and protest, despite
constant police interventions. Without this breathing space, the massive anti-
Putin protests when he returned to power would probably not have occurred.
Journals and websites started to cater for a new young and wealthy middle
class, who were close to Medvedev's professional values. In the last year of his
term in office, Medvedev ventured to support more liberal causes, perhaps
staking his political future on the urban liberal elite. He attended the anniversary celebrations of the founding of the new sophisticated online TV news
channel Dozhd' ('Rain'), he set up the Presidential Council for developing
Human Rights and Civil Society, and started a public service channel which,
good as it sounded, received minimal financing after his departure. He was
moving in a more moderate direction, which may have threatened the interests of the pro-Putin clans. With the switch back to Putin as president and
Medvedev as prime minister in 2012, he has not stood out as an independent
political figure.

Measuring free speech

When journalists are asked what period they consider the freest of the past 30
years, they usually point to 1989–91 as the golden years when censorship had
virtually disappeared but the communist party was still bankrolling their
media outlets, salaries and privileges that went with subjection to the Soviet
system. It was an illusionary moment that could not last, even if the market
had been introduced in a less radical way.

In 1999, a map of free speech in Russia's 89 republics (except Chechnya)
was drawn to determine how much free speech had spread during Yeltsin's

eight years in office. The 'Public Expertise' project, conducted by media and human rights organisations, set out to examine which regions promoted a climate favourable to free and pluralistic media. The results were ranked in three sections: freedom to access information, freedom to produce information and freedom to distribute information. The results surprised researchers, because none of the regions reached a favourable rating. The rankings out of 100 points ranged from a low of 10 in Bashkortostan to a high of 63 in Moscow. Most of European Russia fell into a mixed category of over 45 points. The study concluded:

> We in Russia have entirely respectable legislation, proclaiming basic human rights on the federal level, and entirely cannibalistic conditions on the local level. Real life does not take place on the basis of federal laws but on the basis of local conditions. And the difference between conditions in various regions within Russia are greater than the difference between conditions in, for example, the US and Poland.[30]

There were a few surprises about Moscow as well, which received unfavourable results on access to information. Moscow's public officials failed to respond to journalists' questions adequately, breaking the media law's article 38 ('the right to receive information'), article 39 ('request for information') and article 40 ('denial or delay in providing information'). The study also found that to open a news stand in Moscow required permission from 29 different authorities.

The enormous distance Russia still had to travel to overcome its entrenched bureaucracy and traditional disregard for the law needed time and favourable circumstances, which it did not have. The rapidity with which Putin reverted to repressive measures gave little breathing space. The annual monitoring by Freedom House of world press (media) freedom reflected the rapid deterioration, although its comparisons between Russia and other countries do not always make sense. Based on its monitoring of conditions in 2002–3, Freedom House downgraded Russia's press freedom level from 'partly free' to 'not free', mainly as a result of the closure of the last independent national broadcaster (TV6).[31] The narrowing of free space has continued. In 2004, Russia was ranked as 148th out of 193 countries; ten years later, in 2014, it was 176th out of 197 countries, on a par with Sudan and Ethiopia. The internet, according to Freedom House, fell to 'not free' in 2015 as a result of the Ukraine crisis, which began the campaign against independent websites and blogs.[32]

The Yeltsin years offered the greatest promise of establishing the institutions of free speech, despite political conflicts and economic crises. Under *glasnost*, the 'generation of the sixties' knew they had to strike while the iron was hot, but the struggle became less fraught once Yeltsin came to power. Yet there were many instances that showed reforms were not irreversible, and Yeltsin was under attack from nationalists and conservatives during most of his period in office. The question to ask, then, is why did journalists fail to make the most of their opportunities when they were available to safeguard the newly found freedoms that they had fought for?

Notes

1　*Dos'e na tsenzuru*, 1/1997 p. 26.
2　Nuck Zaccardi, 'Sochi protest zone will be 7 miles away from Olympics', NBC Sports, 10 January 2014. http://olympictalk.nbcsports.com/2014/01/10/sochi-olymp ic-protest-zones/ (accessed 11 November 2015).
3　'Two Concepts of Liberty', *Political Philosophy*, ed. Anthony Quinton, Oxford: Oxford University Press, 1967, p. 143.
4　Ibid., pp. 147–8.
5　Yury Baturin, 'Tsenzura protiv glasnosti: ot Ivana Groznogo do 1917g', *Dos'e na tsenzuru*, I/1997. p. 69.
6　'Net, ya ne l'stets, kogda tsaryu Khvalu svobodnuyu slagayu', *Druz'yam* 1828; and 'Samovlastitel'nyi Zlodei! Tebya, tvoi tron ya nenavizhu', *Vol'nost'. oda* , 1817.
7　*New Times* (no. 5) 9 February 1987, SWB (SU/8495/B/1, 18 February 1987.
8　*Pravda*, 12 March 1985.
9　'Ya rasstalsya s illyuziyami', *Zhurnalist*, 9 September 1990, p. 8.
10　*Roman s prezidentom*, Moksva, Vagrius, 1997, p. 321.
11　http://constitution.ru/10003000/10003000-3.htm (accessed 11 November 2015).
12　Gary Neill, 'The hand that feeds them', *The Economist*, 7 August 2008. www.econom ist.com/world/europe/displaystory.cfm?story_id=11880594 (accessed 11 November 2015).
13　Zakon Rossiiskoi Federatsii 'O sredstvakh massovoi informatsii', 27 December 1991, Garant. http://base.garant.ru/10164247/1/#block_100 (accessed 11 November 2015).
14　Author's interview, 4 June 2011.
15　'Media Regulation: Foundation Laid for Free Speech', *Russian Media Challenge*, ed. Kaarle Nordenstreng, Elena Vartanova, Yassen Zassoursky, Helsinki: Kikimora Publications, 2002, p. 121.
16　*Hard Day's Night*, Dozhd' TV, 5 February 2014.
17　Federal'nyi Zakon 'O protivodeistvii ekstremistskoi deyatel'nosti' (s izmeneniyami i dopolneniyami'), 25 July 2002, *Garant*. http://base.garant.ru/12127578/ (accessed 11 November 2015).
18　*Kommersant-Vlast'*, 29, 24 July 2006.
19　The Federal Service for Supervision of Telecommunications, Information Tech-nologies and Mass Communications (Federal'naya sluzhba po nadzoru v sfere svyazi, informatsionnykh tekhnologii i massovykh kommunikatsii).
20　See Andrei Richter, *Post-Soviet Perspective on Censorship and Freedom of the Media*, Moscow: UNESCO, 2007, pp. 291–2.
21　*Midnight Diaries*, London: Phoenix, 2000, p. 200.
22　David Remnick, 'After the crash', *New Yorker*, 17 July 2014. www.newyorker.com/ news/daily-comment/after-the-crash (accessed 11 November 2015).
23　Doktrina informatsionnoi bezopasnosti Rossiiskoi Federatsii, 9 September 2000. http://www.femida.info/14/19002.htm (accessed 1 December 2015).
24　Statement of the Russian Press Freedom Support Group, House of Journalists, Moscow 13 July 2000.
25　Interfax, 15 September 2000.
26　'Svoboda luchshche, chem ne svoboda', *Rossiiskaya gazeta*, 21 February 2008. http:// www.rg.ru/2008/02/21/svoboda.html (accessed 12 November 2015).

27 Poslanie federalnomu sobraniyu RF, *Kremlin.ru*, 5 November, 2008. http://kremlin. ru/events/president/transcripts/1968 (accessed 31 November 2015).

28 *MK, RU*, 29 January 2009. www.mk.ru/politics/article/2010/07/22/518425-otdohni te-ot-.html?action=comments&#comments (accessed 11 November 2015).

29 'Dmitry Medvedev, Rossiya, vpered!', *Gazeta.ru*, 10 September 2009. www.gazeta. ru/comments/2009/09/10_a_3258568.shtml (accessed 11 November 2015).

30 *Obshchestvennaya ekspertiza, Anatomiya svobody slova*, Moskva: Nauka, 1999, p. 3.

31 *Freedom House*, http://freedomhouse.org/report/freedom-press/2003/russia#.VET-b_ nF8uc (accessed 11 November 2015).

32 'Freedom on the Net 2015', *Freedom House*. https://freedomhouse.org/sites/default/ files/FOTN%202015%20Full%20Report.pdf (accessed 12 November 2015).

3 What price free speech?

Yesterday they gave me freedom
What am I to do with it?

(Vladimir Vysotsky, a ballad, 1965)

I A lucrative profession

The media was a powerful force in Russia by the time Yeltsin came to power.
Journalists had fought for their right to free speech by rejecting the limits that
Gorbachev had imposed on *glasnost*, and they had helped repulse anti-
democracy forces in the 1991 coup. Their freedom had not been bequeathed
'from above', as was usual in the case of reform. They were indebted to
Yeltsin for their victory only in the same measure as he was indebted to them.
To that extent free speech was not intended as a 'means' to anything other
than the normal everyday workings required of a democracy.

This was the moment of truth for media professionals. Editors and journalists had an opportunity to practise their profession in a normal and civilised way and build on the role of the media as the fourth estate. Yet this is
not what happened. Instead, much of the blame for the demise of free speech
must be laid at the feet of media professionals. If it was not only possible but
relatively easy for Putin to clamp down on free speech almost immediately
Yeltsin resigned, then journalists had done little to consolidate their status. It
meant that the unprecedented chance to create institutions to safeguard journalists' rights had been squandered. It showed the journalist community to be
atomised and competitive, when it had been feasible to band together in
solidarity against state and corporate interests. Although journalists the world
over are a fractious tribe, Russia had been lamenting its absence of free
speech for centuries.

As there was no Kremlin diktat to tell the media what to do, it was possible
to set up normal relations with two other institutions connected to the media
industry: private investors and the public. Under *glasnost* the media had
worked to champion the interests of the public, but under the stringent conditions of the market the scales tipped towards owners and finance. As soon

as the bulk of journalists began to identify their self-interest with oligarchic or state interests, rather than serving the public, the media reverted to their traditional role in Russia, as an organ for somebody or something other than truth-telling. *Novaya gazeta*'s Sergei Sokolov was in no doubt that journalists were to blame:

> It all started in the 1990s when they sold out to the oligarchs for gigantic amounts of money and they themselves began to lie and in fact made lies their business and their way of earning money. Strictly speaking, journalists themselves sold out their profession and their free speech. Now the government has changed and there are no more oligarchs; instead, the security services use them, and it's too late to jump back. They started it themselves; this must be remembered.[1]

There is a world of difference, however, between attitudes in the Yeltsin and Putin years. The Yeltsin years were charged with creative energy and aspired to great heights. If the long-awaited freedoms were misused and misunderstood, it was done without the overt cynicism of the Putin regime. Pro-Putin media executives have been indiscriminate in propagating the wishes of the regime. If they share Putin's politics of nationalism, they serve it uncritically, with little self-respect or professional standards. By comparison with the Yeltsin austerity years, the 2000s was a period heading towards an oil boom; and part of their rationale for protecting the wealth of the oligarchic clans cohering around Putin was to jump on the same lawless bandwagon.

There were many factors that contributed to the demise of free speech in the mainstream media. The allure of money was a primary cause. The need to work and feed one's family is always a reason for caution, but no stick was being brandished in the Yeltsin years; and it is normal for a person committed to an idea to be prepared to take some risks for it. If greed was a substantial factor, it was not the only one. A serious handicap was the legacy inherited from the Soviet past: its illusions, isolationism and deformed thinking, together with the delusions of grandeur of a former superpower. Media professionals were creatures of the Soviet Union, they had grown up and been educated in the Soviet system and were members of what was called Homo Sovieticus, which they themselves saw as a strange and absurdist breed that had mutated after years of fear and lies. They could not be expected so quickly, as TV presenter Vladimir Pozner said of the ruling elite, 'to chop off their tails'. Moreover, the media had dubious partners to keep them on the straight and narrow and provide financial and moral support. On the one side, a predatory oligarchy concerned with its own interests and, on the other, a passive public which could no longer even afford to subscribe to newspapers.

It would be glib to think it was easy. Dostoyevsky called freedom a 'terrible gift' because it forced individuals to make difficult choices. For journalists, as for most citizens, it meant making moral, political and economic choices in a society undergoing profound change. It forced them to navigate between idealism, survival, enrichment, careerism and cynicism. Moreover, it was not hard to take bribes when the country was almost bankrupt and wages were hardly paid. While other previously respected professions – scientists, engineers, teachers – were forced to bargain and barter, and sell goods in the market to feed their families, journalists' skills were in high demand in a capitalist economy. The starting up of business and competition turned advertising and information into a valuable commodity. Using their position irresponsibly, making money on the side through bribery and corruption, the media became embroiled in politics and crime.

It began with *dzhinsa* or concealed advertising. For cash, a journalist would pass off an advertisement as an item of news. The term came from 'jeans', that fashionable item to kill for in the dark old days. It was coined when *perestroika*'s most popular TV programme, *Vzglyad*, agreed to interview the Levi Strauss company if they were paid not in cash but in Levi jeans. The other name for this sort of bribery is *zakazukha* – from the verb 'to put in an order'. Taking a hundred dollars here and there seemed an innocent enough way of making a quick buck. For many press journalists, who were often not getting a salary, it helped them and their media outlet to keep going. But the system escalated rapidly. When top western corporations began to seek advertising to attract the vast Russian market for their consumer goods, unimaginable luxuries beckoned. This bonanza created massive wealth for those individuals and television production companies who exploited these opportunities for their own gain, without sharing it with the television channel. In 1995, if a businessman wanted to win a lucrative licence for an oil contract and *dzhinsa* on the main news would provide him with good publicity, he would think nothing of dolling out $20,000–$100,000 to media professionals in an envelope or, if the money did not fit into the envelope, a sports bag.[2] During the election period, by producing commissioned material for candidates and parties you could earn enough money to buy a car or a flat. It put media professionals into a different social class, a part of the *nomenklatura*, and further distanced them from ordinary people. It meant not only hobnobbing with the rich and powerful, but having the instruments of power in their own hands.

The system of paying salaries to media professionals had its tricks, which came in two parts. One was the official salary, which made up about 10 per cent of the real wage. The other was 'grey' money in envelopes, which made up 90 per cent of wages, tax-free. In the early years, *dzhinsa* was a matter of private initiative, but editors were not happy to be left out of this profitable business and *dzhinsa* became part of a pool shared out among the staff by the editor of a newspaper or TV programme. This put journalists into a situation of dependency, because if the editor did not like them, he could withhold their 'bonus', and there were no documents to prove otherwise.

Dzhinsa continued, even when economic conditions improved. A Moscow public relations company, Promaco, carried out a sting operation in 2001 to see which newspapers would accept money to print a story they did not know was faked. The company sent out press releases for the opening of a fictitious electronics store to 21 publications. Out of that number, 13 printed the press release after accepting money for it. The commissions ranged from \$90–\$1,200.[3] As the oil boom brought wealth to the country, the practice of *dzhinsa* not only did not peter out but became institutionalised as part of endemic corruption. In the 1990s the practice had been based on informal agreements, but under the Putin regime it became formalised as a contract for 'information services'. This system today is seen as absolutely normal: almost everyone does it, both in Moscow and in the regions. It means you can never be sure if a news item is an advertisement. This is known as 'black PR'. There have also been instances where media outlets have forced contracts on companies through extortion, pumping out negative coverage until the firm signs up. Money coloured everything, and first and foremost the quality of news gathering, as Anna Politkovskaya deplored:

> The purpose of self-censorship is to keep your hands on a large, very large, salary. The choice is not between a job or being unemployed, but between earning a fortune or a pittance.[4]

The most difficult task for media professionals was to build the foundations of a democratic media for the first time in their country's history. There were no blueprints that had been drafted and circulated for discussion during the years in opposition for when the day came, because hardly anyone thought it ever would. Only the media law, which had been fomenting for years in the thoughts of its co-authors, was ready to greet the new world. There had always been a tradition of struggle in Russia, with its revolutions and rebellions, but there was no tradition of construction. Leaders had not been in the habit of entrusting the rank and file to shape their own lives and that of their workplace without tough 'guidance' from above. While people had always shown enormous resilience and ingenuity in the face of war and deprivation, these were heroic exploits in the struggle against a common enemy or a repressive leader. Journalists had always played a fundamental role in these struggles, as did the great journalists-cum-opposition leaders, Lenin and Trotsky, supreme masters of prose and campaigning journalism, but greater in struggle than in fulfilling their ideals. Legendary ruses had been created to keep opposition papers afloat in the history of journalism. The redoubtable *Pravda*, after it was established in 1912, was closed down nine times by the authorities in two years and reopened eight times under new names, its unflappable staff appointing a nominal editor, whose main task was to sit in jail on occasion, so that the real editors could get on with the job.[5]

In 1992, one year into the new democracy, Vladislav Flyarkovsky, from Russia TV's news programme *Vesti* ('News') could see that things were going wrong. As long as there had been collisions, there were sparks: Gorbachev vs

Yeltsin, right vs left, the Soviet Union vs Russia, but after the August coup the flame went out:

> damn us, it was simpler to work when there was nothing but enthusiasm to keep us going, than to work in normal conditions. It was easier for us to fight than to build – that's the case not only with the government and the president. And if, as on Russian television, you don't have enthusiasm or normal conditions, then things are really bad.[6]

Flyarkovsky had tried unsuccessfully to whip up interest among the famous rebels on *Vesti* to form a joint stock company independent of state television. Many of the efforts to start more modest enterprises around programmes or production companies were unsuccessful although, with hindsight, the ones that managed to pull it off maintained their independence far longer. REN TV's independence lasted way into the Putin regime, and radio Ekho Moskvy ('Moscow Echo') is still a beacon of hope today. A greater number of smaller entities would have distributed the takings from advertising and created a more pluralistic environment. It was also a more democratic project to start from the media grass roots and build up.

Instead, many of *Vesti*'s team moved over to oligarch Vladimir Gusinsky, to start a big commercial station, NTV, in 1993. This was an exciting project, but also the more conventional top-down model familiar to media professionals. It was glamorous, it had money and status – but it survived intact as a full-time channel determining its own politics for only five years. The lure of money and wealth, getting rich quick by using media for power games, lost sight of the democratic process.

The glamour of imperialism

The former Soviet Union and Eastern Europe, after decades of post-war deprivation and shortages, were beguiled by the consumerism offered by the West. Russia seemed more than normally hypnotised by wealth and status. It was a hunger for material goods that was understandable, if not for the primacy it held in many people's lives. But Russia as an empire has always been obsessed with façade and grandeur: the awesome Byzantine trappings of power have accompanied its leaders throughout the history of tsarism, changing the form if not the essence of grandeur in Bolshevik internationalism, a kind of megalomania that attempted to liberate the world from its chains, while crushing its citizens under poverty and terror. Big was always good. Nothing provokes Putin's resentment more than a perceived disrespect from the West of Russia's imperial grandeur based on its size, power and history. Power says might is right, it does not quibble about ethics. That is why the word 'power' (*vlast'*) in Russian can stand on its own: it is not some government in power, it is raw power. The over 80 per cent popularity Putin gained through showing his iron fist to Georgia and Ukraine shows this belief to be shared. People will say – don't forget, Napoleon looked tough until he came to Russia. Yeltsin's policy of self-determination for the USSR's republics and greater freedom for Russia's regions was seen, even by woolly liberals, not as a vital federalisation of the country's politics if it ever wished to abandon authoritarian rule, but as a risk to its imperial future. Grandeur was meant to shock and awe, a method of control and a companion of fear.

It was also, says Nina L. Khrushcheva, great-granddaughter of the former Soviet leader, 'the gulag that imprisons the Russian mind'. The sense of destiny and mission, of fifteenth-century Moscow as the Third Rome, saviour of Christianity after the fall of the Byzantine Empire, encourages illusions of grandeur and exceptionalism. Status comes with pomposity. Editors in disgrace have known what it feels like to sit in their office with 11 telephones on their desk, plus the 'vertushka' connected to the Kremlin, and endure deathly silence until relieved of their duties. When Yeltsin fell from grace, he would have become a nobody if the media had not kept his name in the public eye. 'I was only nominally alive. Politically I didn't exist; politically I was a corpse. And then another thing that made me vaguely depressed was the absence of telephone calls from people who had once been constantly phoning me', he wrote.[7]

The price of superpower status has caused great suffering as well. When people learned in the early 1990s that the Kremlin had been funding communist parties all over the world while they had stood in endless queues, it was barely news in the West, but came as a shock to the nation. Superpower status at the expense of ordinary people has exacerbated feelings of victimisation, a profound belief that Russians have suffered more than anyone else, an inverted form of grandstanding. No one can deny Russia's long-suffering history, but the tendency has been to look for blame not to its leaders or the nation but to scapegoats – the West or the Jews or the enemy within – the latter particularly resonant in a multi-ethnic state (of, precisely, 185 large and small ethnic groups), which holds its 'colonies' within its borders. For a population that has never been allowed to solve its own problems, it has produced a culture of complaint and a demand that the world owes it a debt. Would the allies have won the war if not for Russia? It never matters in these endless conversations to point out that if Stalin had not murdered thousands of military personnel and their top command a few years before the war began things might have been less horrific.

Cultural imperialism says a great deal about the way television broadcasters perceived their role in a democracy. They could have concerned themselves less with property and state-of-the-art technology and more with balanced and truthful news coverage. The addiction to drama and intrigue in the corridors of power outweighed stories to assist people in understanding the bewildering world of western capitalism that was turning their lives upside down. Three large TV channels replaced Gosteleradio's one main national channel that had served the whole Soviet Union. In terms of pluralism, three is better than one, but they could have all been smaller, especially when the country was bankrupt and journalists in the regions were living on miserly wages. Official salaries ranged from $20 to $7,000 per month in 1995.[8] Although the three big nationwide TV channels used their money to make serious programmes and high-quality entertainment as well, they were built big to be organs of power and ensure survival. The aim was imperial and elitist, not democratic.

The imperialist mentality also affected the way journalists related to the West, as competitors in the superpower stakes. The force of Putin's views a decade later of 'getting off one's knees' expressed this sense of resentment at having to 'succumb' to the more sophisticated developed world. It made it hard for Russian journalists in the early days to acknowledge they had something to learn from the West, even at the height of friendship, even about democracy when most of them had been isolated from western ideas all their lives and were attempting to duplicate them for their own country. That would have been to lose face. Instead of catching up and devouring the fruits of world knowledge from which they had been isolated, the response was often denial. On one occasion, I was surprised by the reaction of prize-winning regional journalists, who had taken part in a Soros Foundation contest and been awarded $1,000 each, a considerable amount of money at the time. The rewards were for writing the best election articles in the run-up to the first Russian democratic elections in 1993. There was little expectation of good journalism: after all, reporters had no practice in writing about free elections. The articles by the prize-winners (with a few exceptions) were mediocre, mainly paraphrasing candidates, but part of the idea had been to provide financial support to tide them over difficult economic conditions. When the winners were receiving their cash (no cheques existed at the time), I talked to some of them. A number replied that they weren't pleased with the prize, that they had expected to receive more money for their efforts, and that their work merited it.

Dissident writer Andrei Sinyavsky saw censorship as the cause of such high self-esteem. Sinyavsky's 'fantastic' stories which circulated in *samizdat* in the 1960s explained some of the grand delusions of Soviet consciousness. In his satire on the disease of 'graphomania', he examined compulsive behaviour and plagiarism as a way of identifying the true artist from the hack, referring to a genre called 'writing for the desk drawer' (*pisat' v stol*), because it would never pass the censor. Political repression and the lack of open discussion allowed self-deception and illusions to flourish:

> We live in a remarkable country. Everybody writes, even schoolgirls and pensioners ... Do you know what we owe it to? To Censorship! It's simpler and harsher abroad ... Some lord publishes a little book of vers libre and everyone can see it's crap. Nobody reads it, nobody buys it, and the lord takes up some useful work like energetics or stomatology ... But we live our whole lives in pleasant ignorance, flattering ourselves with hopes ... Damn it, the state itself gives you the right – the priceless right! – to think of yourself as an unrecognised genius.[9]

The mentality inherited from the Soviet system was not conducive to building democratic institutions. Values that over centuries of struggle and institution-building in the West had enabled and strengthened the exercise of free speech emerged in travestied forms when refracted through the distorting mirror of Soviet reality. Ideas of equality, social justice, solidarity, consensus were theoretically all part of the humanity of the Soviet system, promising a glorious future for all humankind, so who would deny them, except for the gap between words and deeds, ideology and reality. Debased by the lies and deceit of the system, they lost their currency to inspire. Ideology was equated with political pressure and lies, education with didacticism, campaigning with indoctrination. It affected open-mindedness, the search for knowledge and experience, the ability to trust and compromise. In 2010 Mikhail Fedotov complained that journalists had not heeded his warning to study and broaden their horizons, which would have prevented the 'terrible thing that has happened':

> I warned about this in 1991 … when I said 'the media law is only the first step. We have to learn what a free press is. We have to learn to work in conditions of freedom – we have to study'. Unfortunately, after that, Maksim Sokolov's comment in Kommersant was: 'What if found out by God/That Fedotov is a pedagogue?' But it turned out I was right that this education never took place. A culture of freedom has never developed. For some, free media was the chance to earn money by concealing advertising as news – but that is not journalism.[10]

Significantly, the kind of solidarity that was needed to build strong professional institutions had been thoroughly discredited. Through the prism of Soviet ideology, solidarity was a way of herding members into creative or trade unions so they could be controlled by the party. Such unions had never defended their members. An interesting book published in 1995, initiated by media-support advocates, very gingerly raised the possibility of journalists getting together to exhibit 'team spirit'.[11] So worried were the editors not to put journalists off, that the book avoided the word 'union' for a newly coined business term from the 1990s, *korporatsiya*, meaning much the same thing but with an emphasis on team work or collegiality. The aim was to see if journalists could come together and agree on 'rules of the game': to draft a code of conduct, organise a self-regulatory mechanism to resolve ethical conflicts, and find out whether journalists had a 'mission'; if they did, was it to be that of messenger or fourth estate?

The majority of editors and journalists who contributed to the book saw no prospect of journalist solidarity. How could there be, wrote state TV's future executive Oleg Dobrodeyev, when journalists had been brought up on the notion of political expediency? Newspaper editor Vitaly Tretyakov asserted that 'we have no common values, and neither does society', seeing a merciless Darwinian world of rivalry and survival. An article by Anna Politkovskaya, who was assassinated in 2006, is poignant to read today because of her lack of faith in any organised unity among journalists, one of the reasons why she was almost alone in exposing the brutality of the war in Chechnya:

> A group's ethical norms, like the group itself, must be born of ITSELF, by itself, without any outside help – no forceps or midwives ... There's no sincerity in the trade, no trust in each other. Only someone's shocking death will bring us together ... and even that is semi-artificial and semi-hysterical. It is more likely that most people's pain is not for the profession but for something else ... Alas, the regular death of journalists in Chechnya is not as great a concern as the two that took place in Moscow. The capital has its smart set. And those who hang out there take a break from ethics, at least those who cry out only when one of theirs has died.[12]

Politkovskaya felt people had to discover their own individuality before they could join a group, or they would be subsumed by it. Boris Dubin from the Levada Centre explained to me how alarming the idea of solidarity was to people who had experienced Soviet collectives: 'no one dared to stand out because the loner always destroys the collective; therefore, solidarity acted as a restraining force, an act of anonymous collective repression, that you must not break ranks or, why, do you think you're something special?'.[13]

Misconceptions of free speech

The concept of free speech carries with it a number of principles without which it cannot properly exist: pluralism, diversity, tolerance, dialogue, openness, transparency. Because free speech in Russia has so often been taken to mean 'freedom for me but not for you', the importance of pluralism as the right for others to speak freely has often been ignored. 'All journalists are sympathetic to free speech, but not so much to pluralism', says media pundit Aleksei Simonov, 'because it doesn't enter their heads that free speech and pluralism are practically synonymous. Our socialisation of consciousness is still developing. Bolshevisation gave us two points of view: mine and the wrong one, and tolerance doesn't come into it'.[14]

A central argument for the value of pluralism is that truth and justice are given a chance to emerge through the clash of opposing views. When Putin asked *Kommersant*'s then editor Andrei Vasilyev why he thought television was better in the 1990s when channels belonged to the oligarchs, Vasilyev replied, 'but they belonged to different oligarchs, that means there's already a choice' – something Putin did not seem to understand.[15] Surely, media analyst Aleksei Pankin asked rhetorically, 'one big lie is better than a pluralism of lies?'[16] But if there is only one big lie, it could be mistaken for the sole truth. Historically, Russia has already had the 'one big lie scenario' under the party's Central Committee, and for many it was more comfortable than a mass of conflicting views and opinions, crying out to be heard.

The practice of critical inquiry in the democratic spirit of give and take was alien to the Soviet experience. When censorship was lifted, criticism often felt like freedom to harm. At times it sounded like denunciation, a hangover from Communist Party meetings where criticism of troublemakers was accompanied by penalties and mini purges, zealotry and moralism. The term 'constructive criticism' had been accepted by Soviet ideologues, although what it really meant was that it was okay to criticise lowly officials but not the 'gensec'. Criticism had more often been used not for constructive but destructive purposes, to punish or 'rehabilitate'. In the relative safety of the kitchen, language was no less harsh and aggressive because frustrations were being vented that could not be expressed in public. It made the language of criticism trenchant even when civilised debate became possible.

It showed the country was not ready to take on the virtues and nuances of a seasoned liberal culture. A mature sense of proportion would have prevented ideas careering between pragmatism and idealism, eulogy and damnation. Compromise and consensus were often seen simply as 'selling out'. A more tolerant approach might have seen merit in being cautious or non-opinionated or collectively inclusive. It might have prevented the sectarianism of journalists, political leaders and public figures. It might also have softened the invective that was heaped on Yeltsin and the government, not only by his opponents but by his supporters. Conservative TV presenter, Andrei Pushkov, once Gorbachev's speechwriter and today Putin's ideological ally, could not understand why Yeltsin's supporters spent so much time slagging him off. It would be their fault, he said, if Yeltsin lost the elections: 'when 80 per cent of your information is criticism of the authorities, who happen to be liberal, then you play into the hands of the communists'.[17] Putin's spin doctor Gleb Pavlovsky also feared the chattering dissidents because he saw the chatter as endless and uncompromising. His way of getting around the dissident mentality was not to confront but manipulate it, the core of his PR strategy.

Under *perestroika*, Aleksandr Yakovlev as ideology chief always worried about the nation's capacity to tolerate political, cultural and ethnic diversity. 'It is necessary to learn to respect the opponent, not to regard him as necessarily a malicious plotter trying to loosen the screws that hold socialism together', he warned. The bitterness and envy people felt towards each other stoked by repression, deportations, denunciations and *anonimki* – the practice of sending anonymous information to party committees usually for malicious purposes, which was stopped by law only in 1988 – were matters that needed to be treated with kid gloves. He feared compromise and tolerance would be stifled by the maximalist approach common to Russian and Soviet history:

> Why does it have to be 'either–or'? Either the Plan or the market. Either internationalism or patriotism. Either rock music or folk poetry. Either democracy or discipline ... We cannot live at the extremes, dashing from one impasse to another.[18]

The bigotry Yakovlev feared resurfaced with venom under Putin's state-sanctioned policy of Russian resurgence, which saw a marked increase in xenophobia, football racism, anti-immigrant hostility and race-related murders. It was not helped by remarks from Putin, attacking 'tolerance of the genderless and infertile'.[19] The Levada Centre calculated that 46 per cent of people rejected other ethnic groups in 2011.[20] The *anonimki* culture has not faded away either – 84 per cent of people say colleagues snitch on each other at the office.[21] Moreover, reported Roman Super, with the hysteria over Ukraine in 2014, the atmosphere in television newsrooms became poisonous, with journalists fearing denunciations for being 'disloyal'.[22]

II 'A journalist in Russia is more than a journalist'

Another reason the media failed in their role as advocates of free speech was the exceptionally heavy burden they were expected to carry. The Russian-Soviet journalist has always had more functions to perform than report a story. The saying – 'a poet in Russia is more than a poet' – from Yevgeny Yevtushenko's 1965 poem, applies to the journalist as well, because he or she is pushed into becoming the 'conscience' of society in a country where the institutions of checks and balances against absolute power tend not to work. What the poet could get past the censor with imagery, the journalist could do with Aesopian refinement.

Journalism as a profession has always been respected in Russia precisely because of these additional roles, despite the plethora of hacks and liars on the landscape. The multitasking was also evident in Lenin's definition of a journalist as a 'collective agitator, propagandist and organiser', whose functions were like a 'scaffold' that would rebuild society. In the pre-*perestroika* period, although political propagandists were largely understood to be Kremlin cyphers, journalists writing on social matters gained the public's trust by giving much needed practical information and advice on topics ranging from the cradle to the grave at a time when there were no private customer services or civil society organisations to turn to. And then there were the letters, millions of them that the public wrote to the press and television to complain and seek advice – the main reflection of public opinion that existed under the Soviet system.

When the Soviet Union fell, it was the media people turned to. Journalists became catalysts of reform, ready to solve political problems. They were seen to be more prepared for democracy, because they had access to information unavailable to most citizens and they were familiar with western ideas. Their popularity got some of them elected to be people's deputies at the first semi-democratic People's Congress in 1989. They were 'more than' journalists because they were political activists, visionaries, economic advisers and agony aunts. They took on all the roles that Soviet media had undertaken, as well as engaging in new institutions that had not existed in the Soviet system, such as genuine political parties and civil society, which were in the process of being formed. Gorbachev had asked the media to be a 'loyal' opposition, but the media were soon contesting for power. Media under the oligarchs unabashedly took political sides, so that TV channels were sometimes called Gusinsky's or Berezovsky's political parties. In 2002 when Putin's TV executive, Oleg Dobrodeyev, declared that television and radio are 'more than just mass media, they play a very special role',[23] he had the Leninist tradition of journalist in mind.

The loftiness of the term 'more than a journalist' has its ironic side, referring to people who bang on about things they know nothing about. Journalists can be 'less than' journalists when they are propagandists and hacks. Those who refuse to toe the line in a despotic society are thrown back on their conscience. The arguments about whether Anna Politkovskaya was a human rights worker or a journalist are pointless because in being 'more than a journalist' she was both. People came to solicit her advice from all over the country and not only the North Caucasus, because no one else would help them. She did not simply write stories about them, but helped them find 'disappeared' sons and daughters, fill in forms, petition bureaucrats and negotiate to free hostages. She did the investigative work of law enforcement agencies, seeking out bits of evidence they had missed which could prove useful in a court case. Almost 40 criminal investigations were opened up on the basis of her work.

A distinct division between groups of journalists began to emerge in the second Chechen war between the outsider and the Kremlin insider. Politkovskaya demonstrated just how different the aims and resources of these two groups were in a 2001 report, when she accused Russian paratroopers of holding local Chechens in pits in the ground, where they were beaten and tortured until a ransom was paid. To check out the story that villagers had told her, she travelled in a private car to the remote village of Khatuni in the mountains. She saw no one in the pits when she visited, but small details and ropes on the site were exactly what people had told her about. After leaving the paratrooper unit, she was detained and held for two days by the military, and her newspaper *Novaya gazeta* found out her location only from unofficial sources. With the help of separatist Chechen leaders, she was smuggled out in the middle of the night back to Moscow. Politkovskaya's treatment caused a scandal, and the Kremlin sent ultra-nationalist Mikhail Leontyev to test her report. He had earlier advocated bombing Chechnya to the ground. Leontyev arrived in a military helicopter embedded with the paratrooper's commander. He reported that Politkovskaya's story was nothing more than 'delirious fantasy' and that she was obviously 'crazy'.[24]

Politkovskaya's colleague Sergei Sokolov dismisses those critics who have complained that her evidence is not always foolproof:

> How can you prove a crime has been committed by soldiers when even prosecutors aren't allowed into army regiments? ... if a percentage of the evidence was enough to open a criminal case, then I consider that is what

the 'fourth estate' is all about ... because to get information on such sensitive matters, to put it mildly, can be done only at great risk – which is, in fact, what Anya did.[25]

Out of Ostankino TV's overcoat

Many of the national TV presenters who became the brightest stars of *perestroika* and the Yeltsin years came from privileged backgrounds. They studied at top institutions, such as Moscow State University's Faculty of Journalism or MGIMO, Moscow's State Institute of International Relations under the Ministry of Foreign Affairs, out of which many diplomats emerge. They spoke foreign languages and some of them had worked abroad. Many began their careers at Gosteleradio's overseas broadcasting department, Moscow Radio. The three *Vzglyad* presenters all worked for the overseas radio service. Yevgeny Kiselyov worked in the Farsi section of Moscow Radio and taught for four years at the KGB Higher School, something he had to live down. Many were children of the *nomenklatura*. *Vzglyad*'s Aleksandr Lyubimov was the son of a charming spy at the London Embassy. As a child he had lived abroad with his family, he studied at MGIMO and worked at Moscow Radio's Scandinavian Service. Most of these young television journalists who took over in the 1990s were in their twenties and thirties.

Moscow Radio was probably one of the freest places in the country. There were fewer censors in the studios because the programmes were not for domestic consumption, and journalists could even edit Brezhnev's speeches for overseas listeners, quite unthinkable in domestic broadcasting. 'Those were fantastic times', remembers Lyubimov. 'There was freedom of expression and artistic freedom, and they paid you for it. We had every chance to read the western press, listen to western radio and compare conflicting viewpoints'.[26]

The real awakening came with *perestroika* when many of them moved over to Ostankino TV's Youth Department, run by pioneering broadcasters Eduard Sagalayev and Anatoly Lysenko. This became the hotbed of *glasnost*, the creative centre for freeing television from its old bonds. It was said these young journalists had come out of the Youth Department's 'overcoat', so vital and inspiring was the experience that it was compared with Gogol's seminal short story *The Overcoat*, out of which emerged the grand writers of the nineteenth century. They were the bright young things who would change new Russia.

On the surface, people working in the media were definitely more prepared to welcome democracy, but whether they were democrats is another matter. It was the simplest terminology to use at the time. It was unlikely they themselves knew who they were. Primarily they wanted reform and change: to obliterate the stifling and punitive atmosphere of oppression that dogged their every step; and to become part of the western community. 'I don't know what democracy is', said *perestroika*'s most famous editor, Yegor Yakovlev, who was actually a Leninist. 'I don't consider myself to be a democrat'.[27] He noted that in 1992 anyone connected with the party apparatus was rejected as backward, while lots of opportunists were pretending to be democrats to get a piece of the pie. Being a democrat was rather vague: it could mean no more than liking the Beatles. If journalists knew more than the rest of society, they still knew relatively little about democracy and suffered the same disenchantment as anyone else at the way the country was suffering in the name of democracy.

This goes some way to explain the startling metamorphosis of many previously feted journalist-democrats who now hold the frontline in Putin's reactionary regime. From pro-western reformers to strident nationalist conservatives and revanchist statists, the Jekyll-and-Hyde transformations have shown how undigested the reforms were and how volatile and extreme Russian society is.

Metamorphoses

Some of these contradictions are startling. Today's top TV executive, Oleg Dobrodeyev, wrote eloquently in 1995 about the sad state of affairs in the Soviet past when journalists were no more than 'transmission belts of the ideological system'. He lamented how those who did not follow the party line would pitifully end their careers on radio, broadcasting to the pavilions of the Soviet Exhibition of National Economic Achievements.[28] Today, as head of the most powerful state television machine, VGTRK, which manages national and regional television and radio output, Dobrodeyev is no longer the man who lets journalists say what they think. This is the station that has broadcast the most strident disinformation programmes on Ukraine and has been used to tarnish and scapegoat opponents.

Many of today's most voluble anti-American propagandists were trained at US Congress-financed Radio Liberty in Moscow, one of the most popular and informed news venues in the 1990s. NTV's pugnaciously pro-Putin general director, Vladimir Kulistikov, was a liberal at the Moscow Bureau of Radio Liberty where he worked from 1993 to 1996. Many journalists from Gusinsky's 'independent' channel NTV, who were trained by Dobrodeyev, then its head, are unashamed bigots today, notably Arkady Mamontov, who has fronted some of the most odious programmes on TV, doing hatchet jobs on Pussy Riot and gays, whom he refers to as 'perverts' and 'sodomites'. Mikhail Leontyev was once a Soviet dissident and a liberal on Gusinsky's newspaper *Segodnya* ('Today'), but became a patriot over the Chechen war. Leontyev is now top PR man at the largest state oil company, Rosneft, and a friend and personal adviser to the powerful Igor Sechin. Gruff and hard-hitting, he has presented the TV mini slot *Odnako* ('However') since 1999, which broadcasts straight after the first Channel's *Vremya* news and is therefore watched by most of the country. The title reminds me of Aleksandr Bovin's warning to beware of the word *odnako*, because it is always followed by a stream of propaganda. Dubbed by his opponents as ten minutes of hate, *Odnako*'s paranoid, eccentric views are mainstream in Putin's post-Crimea world.

The most infamous turncoat is Dmitry Kiselyov, who was rewarded for his hate speeches arousing enemy mania during the Ukraine crisis in 2014 by being appointed head of the new state media conglomerate, *Rossiya Segodnya* ('Russia Today'), that replaced the more even-handed RIA Novosti. As the regular presenter of state TV's Sunday current affairs programme *Vesti nedeli* ('Weekly News'), Kiselyov received international condemnation as an anti-gay basher with his vampire-like images:

> I think that just imposing fines on gays for homosexual propaganda among teenagers is not enough. They should be banned from donating blood and sperm and their hearts, in case of an automobile accident, should be buried in the ground or burned as unsuitable for the continuation of life.[29]

That one of the highest media posts went to a caricature figure with cranky views, not dissimilar to the so-called 'crazies' of the American Tea Party, shows how low television has sunk. As a Scandinavian expert, Kiselyov was also offended by a Swedish TV programme for children about potty-training, implying that Ukraine would fall into the depravity of early sex and child abortions if it joined the European Union. The reason Sweden supported Euromaidan was to avenge centuries-old battles fought against Russia, he claimed.[30] When Kiselyov was put on the West's blacklist of sanctions, he cried foul that slapping sanctions on journalists was a blatant attack on freedom of speech, while his pro-Kremlin colleagues signed a letter to protest what they said was a ban on the profession. One-time editor, Sergei Parkhomenko wrote in his blog: 'but who said they were journalists?'.

Dmitry Kiselyov, as a baby-faced reporter in 1991, made his name as a rebel who refused to broadcast false information on killings at the Vilnius TV station. Since then, some interesting relics of Kiselyov's past have turned up on YouTube. I was surprised to find that I was indirectly involved in one incident, when I worked for the UK's Department for International Development and commissioned the NGO, Internews, to do a seven-part training video on how to make television. In 1999 Kiselyov was invited on episode six to discuss ethics. He says:

> For me, a journalist shows the world in its true proportions, he gives the whole picture of the world. People sitting in front of the screen have to know if they are watching a journalist or an agitator; after all, we are talking of professional journalism. If we talk crap, there will be a constant decline in standards – more vulgarity, more nudity and sensational reporting. Any lowering of standards, any lowering of morals and rules, and we will be left with a load of crap. Then one sunny day we'll find ourselves swimming in the dirt like pigs and we'll have a society where we all talk crap, smeared in dirt, and we won't be able to fall any lower.[31]

Unfortunately, there was more room to fall. Bloggers have posted a diploma Kiselyov received for participating in a US State Department Visitor Leadership Programme on International Security as late as July 2012. In 2014 it did not stop his anti-American rants during the Ukrainian crisis and his threat that Russia could reduce the United States to 'radioactive ash' – which he displayed on animated maps of nuclear missiles.[32] His anti-America tirades continue in different locations. In 2015 during the Syrian campaign, he implied that America had done a deal with Islamic State because, unlike Russia's tragic civilian air crash, America had suffered no crashes for two years.[33]

The Vilnius event was one of the most significant moments in the unravelling of the Soviet Union. No doubt this has irked Kiselyov and his even more famous rebel partner at the time, Tatyana Mitkova, in their current quest to push Russia along the path of imperial revival. Mitkova sent back the medal she had won from the Lithuanians after receiving a prize from Putin for coverage of the annexation of Crimea.

The irony is that anti-westernism does not mean Russians do not want to live in the West: this kind of double thinking is not unusual. Putin's powerful media enforcer Mikhail Lesin, mastermind behind the satellite channel RT and its propaganda against western decadence, was happy to acquire $28 million worth of prime Los Angeles-area real estate, where members of his family live. Although he was being investigated in America for money laundering, he was planning to move there with a new family after retiring in 2015, but died suddenly at the age of 57 in Washington, DC, in allegedly suspicious circumstances. The novelist Viktor Yerefeyev sees this divided consciousness everywhere; in the masses, among young people, on the internet:

> They do not like America, and are convinced that America wants to take away Russia's sovereignty. At the same time, they are prepared to emigrate to America on a moment's notice. They are convinced that Navalny is a secret agent of the Kremlin, but if told that in this case they are also agents of the Kremlin, they get angry. Europe for them is rotten and decadent, but they yearn to get a residence at least in Bulgaria. In the morning they dislike the authorities; at noon they dislike the opposition, and then it all gets mixed up. Their brains are like a wrecking ball.[34]

Can the media be trusted? (Surveys)

The majority of today's journalists have pruned their functions to comply with the state capitalist marketplace. They see themselves as professionals, a notion which they link to the writer's craft and to self-expression but, oddly, not to truth or morality. According to Svetlana Pasti, who has conducted a series of valuable in-depth interviews on journalist attitudes, 'journalism is no longer a mission of humanism *en route* to a radiant future, but a means to earn money and forge a career. There are no values: only the interests of the political and economic groups striving for power'.[35] She found that almost all post-Soviet journalists justified bribery in their profession as a necessary evil. As one respondent put it: 'journalists are not from another planet, but take bribes just as doctors and teachers do'.[36] But linking professionalism with corrupt practices is exclusive to the later Putin period. One respondent explained his understanding of his job:

> Professionalism is when you are bought by money ... They want to use your professionalism for their own aims. They do not turn to just anybody but to the professional, who competently organises the black PR campaign, who is competently able to raze a character and his business to the ground.[37]

Our crass interviewee sees his profession as fulfilling a task, which is good writing to purpose (a hitman could say the same); but ethics is not his responsibility. Such sentiments are not unusual in the Putin camp to justify self-interest. In Pasti's studies, only 14 per cent of journalists said ethics played a part in their work.[38]

Comparing two generations of journalists, those working in 1992 and in 2008, Pasti wanted to find out how often journalists were able to put their ideas into practice. In 1992, 61 per cent claimed they were always successful in getting their material into print; in 2008 only 20 per cent were successful.[39] But the greater restrictions on freedom in the Putin years did not lessen job satisfaction. If in 1992, 62 per cent of journalists said they were happy in their work; in 2008 this number increased to 72 per cent.[40] The reasons they gave were independence in the newsroom, career prospects and privileges that came with the job. One can conclude that these journalists either shared the views of their media organisation or uncritically accepted self-censorship as part of the 'rules of the game'. Pasti says: 'Journalists keep close to the government and business, being the main sponsors of their existence, but maintain distance from their audience, who are not seen as important or influential'.[41] In one of her studies, to the question 'Do you disclose the name of rape victims before the court's decision?', one respondent answered: 'It depends who has suffered. If s(he) is some official, so naturally not'.[42]

How does the public respond to the media and the loss of free speech? In the 16 years since Putin came to office respondents show they are aware that free speech has declined. If in 2000 58 per cent said the authorities were not threatening free speech and 18 per cent were uncertain, by 2016 it was only 35 per cent who believed the Kremlin was not attacking free speech, with 44 per cent uncertain.[43] But there is often little apparent logic to responses. In Levada Centre's ongoing survey of the percentage of trust accorded to TV, radio and print we find that in 1989, the year of the flowering of *glasnost*, only 38 per cent trusted the media absolutely, despite the fact that the popularity of newspapers was huge and people were fixed to their TV sets. In 1996 when free speech was considered normal, only 24 per cent fully trusted the media. In 2001 as NTV was being crushed under government pressure, trust in the media rose to 30 per cent.[44] In 2014 when Russian channels were spewing hate against Ukraine, full trust in the media was 50 per cent. State TV was watched without regard to whether respondents trusted it or not: 92 per cent of those who trusted it, 88 per cent of those who did not.[45]

Whether or not people trust television, they still watch it. They watch it out of habit, it is what they do when they get home after work, it is a family ritual, and it requires no extra effort. Thus, against all expectations, the limited number of independent traditional media outlets does not spur people to turn to the internet for their news. In the 2014 study only 5 per cent received news solely from the internet, while 20 per cent turned to both the internet and television for news. In Moscow the figure was higher: 33 per cent regularly and 37 per cent occasionally watched the news on the internet. But those who refer to the internet do not necessarily watch non-state independent sources, whose ratings generally do not exceed 17 per cent. Television continues to be the dominant venue, watched by more than 90 per cent of the population. To further narrow the type of news that the public receives, the European Audiovisual Observatory points out that 77 per cent of content broadcast by Russian TV channels are of Russian origin, with only 6 per cent coming from Europe.[46]

The Kremlin's monopoly of mainstream television explains the relative ease with which the regime has been able to manipulate hysteria over Ukraine, but we cannot assume that people subscribe to this narrative because they are ill informed. What appears to be a lack of logic in surveys may be ingrained fear or caution about telling the truth or a scrambled consciousness from too much propaganda or imperialist swagger and 'wannabee' aspirations. People may accept what they see on television without actually believing it, a question which is raised in Chapter 4 on the normalisation of lying. The accuracy of news reports do not appear of paramount importance when we learn from the Levada Centre's 2014 survey that 25 per cent of Russians are content to depend on friends, relatives and neighbours to get their news, a habit of acquiring information from the Soviet grapevine and partially responsible for reinforcing dubious stories and conspiracy theories. The fact that television is watched by 90 per cent, whether or not people believe it makes it today's opium of the people. Like journalists, the public appears to be satisfied by what requires the least effort and provides the most comfort. The majority of journalists appear to share with the public the same political apathy, conformism and subservience to the ruling class.

Is this a journalist I can shake hands with?

If a journalist behaves shamefully, he is not someone you 'shake hands with' (*nerukopozhatnyy*). That is how Russians refer to those who have overstepped the mark of morality and decency. Over the years it is surprising how rarely journalists will ostracise their disreputable colleagues. In the Soviet Union almost everyone contributed in some way, however minor, to the repressive nature of the state, because the state's hold was total. It was part of forced collective responsibility, to which the party Politburo was also subject. It meant that if everyone was responsible, no one was to blame. It has had a strange impact on morality.

Today, as in the past, journalists are likely to shake their colleagues' hands, whatever they do. Moscow is a village, as they say: everyone in the media knows one other and when they get together at their smart trendy gatherings (*tusovki*) these quarrels can be put aside. In the 1990s, Sergei Dorenko's behaviour as Berezovsky's well-paid attack dog did not ostracise him from the community. Whether the failure to name and shame in Russia, given its history, is magnanimous or foolish is a moot point. I asked academic and radio journalist Anna Kachkaeva, one of the country's top media experts who knows almost everyone in the media world, how she felt about her colleagues' personality shifts:

> We've all been too closely connected with each other over these 20 years. We've all failed to do something we should have done or agreed to do something we shouldn't ... Some people have retained their principles, others have betrayed them consciously or cynically, some think they were wrong then and right now ... Who are we to judge? It's not my right to call someone a scumbag or a bastard, although you might want to with some people, not because of what they've done to their colleagues but because of what they've done to their viewers and listeners – that's the crime, they're engaged in fooling them, and then to say it's the same in every country is truly monstrous. But I prefer to discuss this publicly than to have personal duels.[47]

The question of whose hand not to shake erupted in a scandal after an editor's birthday party when 'selfies' appeared on Instagram of pro-Putin and opposition journalists pulling funny faces.[48] How was that possible in 2014, people asked on social media, after the horrors of war in Eastern Ukraine? The 'victims' – *Ekho Moskvy*'s editor, Aleksei Venediktov, who had been hauled over the coals that week and nearly lost charge of the only independent national radio left, Marianna Maksimovskaya, a courageous journalist who had recently been sacked from REN TV, and rock star Andrei Makarevich, who had been hounded as a traitor for defying the authorities and performing for refugees in a part of the Donbas controlled by the Ukrainian army – were socialising with, of all people, Mikhail Leontyev and Putin's press secretary, Dmitry Peskov. The same Peskov who was known to have said of the Bolotnaya demonstrators, who were sitting in jail for what was seen as grossly trumped up charges, that 'their livers should be splattered on the asphalt'.

TV Dozhd' ran a discussion, asking what it meant to say 'it's nothing personal'? Predictably, journalists defending the happy snaps feared falling into what they understood as Soviet-style moralism ('do we want to be like the Communist Party's comradely courts to decide what's right and wrong for everyone?'; 'we're all tarred with the same brush'; 'half of TV centre is responsible for propaganda and sending people to fight and die in Ukraine, so why pick on any one person?'), etc. Others took a clear moral position. Socialite blogger Bozhena Rynska said the Putinites had crossed a line and 'you don't French-kiss criminals'. Academic Sergei Medvedev argued that media professionals 'with blood on their hands' was a new factor and we, who have survived totalitarian and criminal systems, know there is always a way out in the 'ethics of non-participation'.[49] Blogger Arseny Bobrovsky expressed suspicion of journalists' motives: 'all these "political differences" are rightly seen by the mass of the population as squabbles about whose status will increase by the next trendy gathering, and the majority rightly refuse to be cannon fodder in this battle'.[50]

Venediktov himself was unrepentant when questioned. 'But they are trying to close down *Ekho Moskvy*', exclaimed the surprised interviewer. 'Not Peskov, nor Leontyev, personally', Venediktov replied. It is partly his friends in high places who have enabled Venediktov to keep his independent station and website going, and it cannot be said that he is indiscriminate. When he had the dubious honour of being invited by Putin to be his proxy in the 2012 elections, he refused – not an easy thing to do.

'Do you embrace your persecutor?' is a Dostoyevskian question. In Russia nothing gets done without friends and contacts, because institutions do not work and there is no other way to deal with the system. But the system is made by people, so when does the vicious circle end? Journalists, like everyone else, need to work. But the lessons of history also warn of the dangers of going along with the system. Communist Party officials in the 1930s all knew each other very well, both the victims and the persecutors, and they nearly all eventually went through the 'meat grinder', as Solzhenitsyn called the machine of death. Alfred Kokh, blogging from his refuge in Germany, gives the example of the writer Isaak Babel, who became pals with the NKVD and even observed them shooting innocent people, none of which spared him when his time came.

If you fell off the radar in the Soviet Union, you might become a janitor on the sly, as dissidents did. In the 1990s journalists saw themselves as independent for the first time, even when they were tied to an oligarch, precisely because they could leave him if they wanted and find another job. Various groups of discontented journalists left their newspapers to start their own in those days. If a troublemaker in Putin's regime is pushed out for not abiding by the rules of state media, he would have to either change professions or emigrate. Other outlets will not take troublemakers for fear of reprisals, while there are too few 'free' outlets left to accommodate those who disagree with the Putin line. There are rows of houses in Latvia bought up by Russian media professionals, says reporter Roman Super, in case they lose their jobs and need to make a get-away.

What happens when a journalist can take no more of the system? In 2010 the man who introduced stylish cultural programming to Russian television, Leonid Parfyonov, caused a sensation when collecting the prestigious Vladislav Listyev prize he had been awarded. He had come straight from the hospital after visiting Oleg Kashin, a sharp young blogger who had been brutally beaten with steel pipes and had almost died. Addressing the high-powered officials and guests, many among whom were those who had first opened up television in the early days and whom he regarded as his mentors, he said nervously – 'I have no right to blame any of my colleagues: not being a fighter myself, I don't expect heroic deeds from others' – something he had to say, because he had been compromised by not leaving NTV with some of his colleagues after Putin had Gusinsky pushed out. As it was, he was derided online with sneers of 'look who's talking!'. Parfyonov spoke of the brilliant breakthroughs on early television, while now news was just Kremlin PR. 'The top officials behind a correspondent on a federal channel are not newsmakers but his boss's bosses. Institutionally the correspondent can no longer be called a journalist, but a bureaucrat following the logic of service and subordination'.[51] The *crème de la crème* in the audience looked on po-faced, applauding politely. Parfyonov's speech was not broadcast on TV (only two tiny bits and not the harsher parts). The newspapers speculated: was it an act of rebellion or approved by the Kremlin?

The talented Parfyonov no longer works regularly on television. Basically that had ended a long time before, when he took an interview with a Chechen rebel leader's widow. His absence from television shows the return of Soviet priorities where ideology and not talent counts. Advertising per minute for his programme was the highest on the channel. When such celebrities are forced to move off-centre they don't necessarily vanish into obscurity: Parfyonov makes documentaries, writes books and runs a restaurant with his chef wife.

'We will do it our way'

If you're a democrat one moment and a statist the next, sincerely or cynically, who are you, anyway? The question of identity in Russia is a traumatic one, turned over and dissected incessantly by Russians and the world, an endless masochistic exploration of the 'elusive' Russian soul or what is now called 'mentality'. China seems not to have this problem. Kissinger recalled that when he told Chinese Premier Zhou Enlai in 1972 that China seemed mysterious, Zhou pointed out that China was not at all mysterious to 900 million of his compatriots. But as satirist Mikhail Zadornov says about his compatriots: 'Russians think one thing, say another, do a third, and don't themselves know what they feel'.[52]

The duality that runs through the heart of Russian culture, its European and Asian heritage, keeps it divided within itself. On the one hand, the highest European learning and culture, which looks to reason and the rule of law; on the other, the Tatar-Mongol yoke and the rule of an implacable and arbitrary autocracy. If it is possible to understand the political apathy of the masses and their acceptance of the cruelties of absolute power, the ostentatious syco-phancy on the part of some of the educated classes comes as a shock (Minister Volodin gushing at Valdai in 2014 that 'without Putin there is no Russia' or election chief Churov's remark that 'Putin is always right'). It can be seen in the fawning reception to Putin's presence in a studio audience, or when top bureaucrats accept the humiliation of being publicly scolded on television.

Writer Mikhail Shishkin sees the imperial symbol of the two-headed eagle as explaining Russia's fate: 'we are a nation of Siamese twins – one body, but the heads don't understand each other'.[53] This metaphor has many variations (Herzen's was: 'the heads look in different directions, the heartbeat is one'), indicating the absence of any resolution. Shishkin explains today's world: 'This head doesn't want to live in a patriarchal dictatorship, it demands free-dom, rights and human dignity. The other head has its own medieval way of life: sacred Russia – an island encircled by an ocean of enemies and only the Father in the Kremlin can save the country. That's We and Them'. Satirist Zadornov says calling 'us' Eurasians is a bit highfalutin. 'We're not Eurasia, we are – Asiopa', he exclaims, eyebrows raised, rhyming it with the word 'arse' (*zhopa*). This is the side Lenin called 'Asiatic barbarism' and equated with tyranny. The balance tips between the two sides. Under Yeltsin it tipped towards Europe, under Putin it has tipped towards Asia. Trying to combine the two can produce schizoid-like responses, which liberals experience in Putin's society as it increasingly takes on medieval and traditional trappings. Putin cheerleaders have a word for liberals – *liberasty*, to rhyme with *pederasty* (pederasts), as state-induced hatred is whipped up between liberals and tradi-tionalists. The problem of reconciling a divided society and, sometimes, a divided self, can be sensed in the nervous energy and agitation of Russian life, always on the edge of hysteria.

Historically, the dichotomies collided most painfully in 1917 between Wes-terners and Slavophiles, city and country, proletariat and peasant, atheist and believer. Poets, writers and artists tried to find synthesis (Yesenin, Leonov, Zamyatin, Tatlin) in symbols of fluidity and dissolution in literature and art, which caused so much pain in real life. So did the proletarian poets by reconciling industry with nature (the 'iron rose').[54] The anarchist writer Boris Pilnyak described the adjustments that were necessary when a western Marxist ideology was imposed on eastward-facing peasants, rooted in age-old traditions, prepared to adapt to the Bolsheviks because it is a Russian word, and even to Lenin after they had transformed him into a water sprite from folklore, but rejecting the foreign word 'communist' and the German Marx and his western ideas. Peasant Nikon drawls:

'Kammun-ests!' – and with an energetic gesture (eyes glinting in the torch light): 'We're for the Bolsheviks! for the Soviets! We'll do it our way, Roossian style. We've been under the masters – enough of that! The Roossian way, our way! By ourselves!'[55]

What exactly does it mean to do it 'our way', which is heard so frequently these days in the media? What does it mean in a divided society and in a situation where public opinion fluctuates so wildly between extremes? When Gorbachev's press secretary, Gennady Gerasimov, was questioned about the nature of reform he was the first to quip 'we'll do it our way', the witty reference to Frank Sinatra's song much appreciated in the West, although no doubt there was steel behind Gerasimov's smile. Putin's Defence Minister Sergei Ivanov was not smiling when he told journalists scathingly in 2006 that democracy was not a potato 'that grows where you plant it'.[56] Doing democracy Russian style, however, must at least retain what is distinctive about democracy. When Putin felt it expedient to be seen as a democrat, his PR team made every attempt to reconcile the irreconcilable by inventing such artificial constructs as 'managed' democracy and government-financed non-governmental organisations. The result was imitation democracy or 'virtual' reality, a duality that was no more reconciled than Peter the Great's boyars, having been forced to shave their beards and dance the minuet, became Europeans.

The Soviet system has left behind unexpected adaptations. Much of politics to be found in the Russian media today veers towards the far right, defined in terms of attitudes to the state, usually taken to their extremes: on the one hand, the communist–nationalist–imperialist tendency; on the other, neo-liberal ultra-conservative views. Social democratic or moderate positions are often out on a limb. The irony was lost on no one to hear America's senior conservative Pat Buchanan ask: 'is Putin a paleo-conservative? ... is he one of us?'. On the whole, pro-Putin media professionals exult in imperial or super-power greatness and believe serving the state to be more significant than the concerns of individuals. Against the statists, the liberal democratic opposition veers towards libertarianism, bordering on social Darwinism. There are constant surprises to be had among liberal anti-Putin journalists. Popular investigative journalist Yuliya Latynina, whose fierce criticism of crime and corruption has helped to keep public accountability of the Putin regime on the radar, sings the praises of dictator Pinochet as 'creating the most blooming economy in South America ... He killed opponents by the thousands – but he never took a bribe'.[57] Andrei Illarionov, Putin's one-time economics adviser and now powerful critic, resigned in 2005, denouncing the lack of freedom in all areas of life. Illarionov shares an admiration with other neo-liberals (such as Alan Greenspan) for Ayn Rand, the Russian-born economist and novelist who moved to America in the 1920s and became one of the most fanatical exponents of laissez-faire capitalism and supreme Nietzschean individualism over the grey masses. In these extremist positions, both sides often share role models. Pinochet is a hero to Mikhail Leontyev and attracted many advocates in the 1990s. The cult of Lee Kuan Yew attracts Putin and his arch opponent, Aleksei Navalny. Both sides are attracted to imperialism, the aristocracy, elitism. The liberal editor of the magazine *Snob* interprets the English word positively to mean a person who has achieved success in life. On both sides xenophobia and racism are never far from the surface. Both sides feel close to the American ultra-right and the European anti-immigrant parties. When five prominent human rights advocates petitioned the intelligentsia to counter 'anti-immigrant hysteria' in 2013 after 20 race-related deaths, hardly anyone responded.[58]

These attitudes do not harmonise with the traditional role of the intelligentsia. In the nineteenth century the intelligentsia identified itself with the 'progressive' part of society, which meant those who cared for justice and truth, and protected the 'little man'. It meant 'going to the people' and not standing aloof from them, but such views carry the taint of communism. As a result, humanism, which was part of Soviet ideology (if not Soviet practice) has been dismissed in a way that has thrown the baby out with the bathwater. According to human rights lawyer Tatyana Volkova, many Russian intellectuals no longer understand the issues that concern western intellectuals. 'Americans and Europeans look at us and are baffled', she says, 'we seem educated and cultured, but we have such primitive reactionary views that even a brutal, savage redneck seems decent by comparison'. The old intelligentsia has died, she says, but a new progressive social class has not emerged. It means that 'there is no one to tell the families of Manning and Snowden such simple words of support as "for your and our freedom!"'[59]

A research programme at Moscow's Higher School of Economics compared Russian values with those of 31 European countries. Researchers Magun and Rudnev showed the average Russian to be committed to 'values of wealth and power, as well as to personal success and social recognition'. But these values were not linked to a readiness to take risks or actions 'beyond the scope of performing routine duties'. The researchers stressed the extent to which Russians appreciate security and protection from a strong state, and their lack of interest in the values of 'novelty, creativity, freedom, and independence':

> Compared to those surveyed in other countries, this strong focus on self-interest leaves less room in the minds of Russians for concerns about equality and justice in their own country and in the world, about tolerance, nature and the environment, and even about people they are very close to.[60]

The researchers show that the rejection of communist ideology and the formation of market institutions changed moral priorities. Self-interest and competitiveness, previously denounced, moved into the category of approved behaviour, while concern for the welfare of others lost its positive moral evaluation:

> These results demonstrate that there is no adherence whatsoever to collectivist values, which are considered essential for the 'Russian soul' by

traditionally minded ideologists. Just the opposite, public concern about the low level of altruistic, solidarity values and the exaggerated importance of self-interest orientations in Russian society is well founded.[61]

Apart from this 'average', Magun and Rudnev point to a sizeable 'value minority', whose members share values not typical of most Russians, which embraces 19 per cent of the population – about 26 million people. The figure of 15–20 per cent is also given by several Levada Centre polls from different years. This minority is committed to 'openness and self-transcendence' typical of European countries with more prosperous populations. Magun and Rudnev hypothesise that this is the 'resource group for the country's advancement'. This 19 per cent refers mainly to the liberal democratic section of urban educated Russia, that sympathises with the West and wants to be part of it – a 'value minority' that constantly chafes against backwardness and reaction. It is mainly journalists and activists within this minority that continue to struggle for free speech and the basic principles of democracy.

III The ultimate price

In a country like Russia, to fight the state when it has shown its iron fist takes courage. The fact that many journalists have been willing to seek the truth and act as the fourth estate at any price testifies to the fact that free speech continues to play a powerful role in Russia, as it always has. It is a minority voice today, but a defiant one that keeps the Putin regime unsettled.

Russia is one of the most dangerous countries in the world for critical journalists. Any investigation into the abuse of power embroils a journalist in toxic interconnections between politics, business and organised crime that make up the 'mafia' state. This means it is often impossible to establish the motive behind a killing. *Novaya gazeta*'s legal reporter, Leonid Nikitinsky, quipped: 'Unless you are killed in a very interesting way, don't come and see me'.[62] So many journalists have been killed, he said, and no matter what he and his colleagues write or what corruption they expose 'nothing ever happens'. A new Investigative Committee was set up in 2007 to improve the situation, headed by Aleksandr Bastrykin, but he himself was caught intimidating the deputy editor of *Novaya gazeta* in June 2012. Sergei Sokolov reported that Bastrykin had taken him to a forest and threatened to decapitate him. Bastrykin denied this at first but later acknowledged he had 'had a chat' and apologised. Bastrykin was not reprimanded or removed from his post.

Putin's obsession with seizing control of the media and imposing censorship in everything but name makes his public indifference to the murders no surprise. If he has not been personally involved, he is responsible for having created an environment where it is possible to kill journalists with impunity. His unresponsive behaviour is a signal to his chain of command that there is no urgency in solving these murders or punishing those involved. The whole legal process – investigative, prosecutorial and judicial – is tainted by politics. Although a greater number of investigations have recently led to prosecutions of those who have actually perpetrated killings, the masterminds – those who have ordered hits for their own personal vendettas, often with the money to procure murder – have managed to escape arrest. The astonishing fact is that only one mastermind has been convicted – and he got away with it because of the statute of limitations (the case relating to Igor Domnikov – see below).

The total figure of deaths of media professionals stands at 359, killed between 1993 and 2015, about 100 of them in Chechnya.[63] These figures are based on Russian media monitoring results, which differ from that of the New York-based Committee for the Protection of Journalists (CPJ), which records journalists killed worldwide. The CPJ lists 56 work-related deaths in Russia between 1992 and 2016, of which 36 were directly targeted murders, 23 of them since Putin came to power.[64] The enormous discrepancy between results lies in the fact that in every case a decision has to be made as to whether the journalist died in the performance of professional duties (as a result of investigations, publications or broadcasts, accidents, war or conflict) or because of involvement in private business and criminal activities. The chance of making 'black cash' deals on the side is not uncommon. Aleksei Simonov, head of the Glasnost Defence Foundation (GDF), told me that the American mentality in monitoring these deaths differs from the Russian: 'for CPJ a killing is based on professional duties if it is confirmed by law enforcement agents, while I say it's always based on professional duties unless law enforcement agents prove otherwise'. The cases are rarely clear-cut, although CPJ's figures are on the conservative side. A case in point was the death of Artyom Borovik, prominent editor of the newspaper *Sovershenno Sekretno* ('Top Secret'), who was killed after his small charter plane crashed in suspicious circumstances in March 2000. Many people attributed the crash to Borovik's investigations into the infamous apartment bombings. Borovik was a man with friends in high places and his tabloid, full of conspiracy theories and murky secrets, might well have had new information. Because the real cause of death is uncertain, he is not on CPJ's list.

As well as the risk or threat of death, a range of violations from state and criminal structures can make it extremely difficult for critical journalists to work and for their outlets to survive. They face harassment, intimidation, beatings, arrests, detention, legal claims, threats to family and children. Pressure can be technical through eviction from premises, electricity blackouts, water and gas turned off, repeated fire inspections, tax penalties, and damage to equipment and property. There have been many instances of masked riot police swooping on offices, removing computers and documents because of an alleged crime. Denial to access information, censorship and cyberattacks are numerous. To take one year, 2008, as an example, GDF counted 1,450 conflict situations.[65]

Society's attitude to the death of journalists changed radically between the early 1990s and 2000s. In pre-*perestroika* days, dissidents were thrown into prison by the state, they were not killed by gangsters in the streets, but after the collapse of the Soviet Union the criminal world invaded many aspects of life. There were guns for hire to kill troublemakers. Why so much fuss about journalists, when citizens also get killed? – can be heard on the streets. Because journalists are supposed to work in the public interest and without them it is unlikely we would ever know about the killings of citizens or much else. Leonid Parfyonov expressed it this way: 'A journalist does not get beaten up because of what he has written, said or filmed. He gets beaten up because it has been read, heard or seen'.[66]

A few cases are included here briefly to show the price some journalists have paid to keep free speech alive.

The first high-profile targeted assassination occurred in 1994 and caused shock and disbelief. Dmitry Kholodov, a 27-year-old war correspondent on the wide-circulation daily *Moskovsky komsomolets*, picked up a briefcase at the Kazansky railway station in Moscow, believing it contained top-secret information from a source in counter-intelligence, and brought it back to the office. The briefcase was booby-trapped and when he opened it, it exploded, killing him and injuring three others. Kholodov had been writing a series of articles on corruption in the western group of the armed forces which had been withdrawn from East Germany and was known to be heavily involved in trafficking arms. Kholodov had alleged the connivance of Defence Minister Pavel Grachev and top officials in the corruption. At the time of his death he was investigating the 'uranium mafia'. As the first snow fell on 19 October, the day of Kholodov's funeral, 10,000 people gathered in a demonstration in support of free speech before marching to the cemetery. A minute's silence was observed on television and Yeltsin expressed his commiserations, but more was expected from Yeltsin and he was criticised for not attending the funeral in person.

Kholodov's colleagues refused to be silenced and *Moskovsky komsolomolets* launched an attack on Grachev, calling him a murderer. An article by Vadim Poegli printed three days after the murder entitled 'Pasha-Mercedes', with a subheading: 'A thief should sit in jail and not be minister of defence', revealed that two Mercedes-600s had been purchased for Grachev at a price equivalent to 'two buildings with 16 apartments for 32 officers and their families', as it was later revealed in the slander trial Grachev brought against the paper and won. But this sort of money was nothing compared to the sums changing hands in the army scandals. The other question to ask, as always, was: in whose interest was it to create an outcry against the Ministry of Defence? Kholodov had written many damning articles without any reaction from the army, and the ministry would not have sought a spotlight on its activities. An outcry against Grachev, who had supported Yeltsin in the coup, could serve the political ends of those who wished to discredit Yeltsin, a version Yeltsin agreed with. The motive was never uncovered and the political mastermind never exposed. Days after the murder, the Moscow city police already knew that the 45th regiment was behind the crime, but the serving officers on trial were acquitted for insufficient evidence. Various appeals for a retrial right up to 2005 have failed.

In 1995 the biggest shock came at the audacity of the murder of the country's most famous TV personality, Vladislav Listyev (39), whose death put an end to the only chance of turning state television into a public service broadcaster. Television went off the air for a whole day as thousands grieved over their favourite TV star, and Yeltsin denounced this 'evil and cowardly act' (see Chapter 7). Another shock came in 1998 with the killing of Larisa Yudina (53), editor of the newspaper *Sovetskaya Kalmykia Segodnya* ('Soviet Kalmykia Today'), almost the sole critical voice against the president, Kirsan Ilyumzhinov (who hosts world chess championships in the capital, Elista, of this small autonomous republic). Yudina was violently assaulted and killed in what many alleged was a political murder. Such remote areas are considered to be fiefdoms of their presidents, but as the outcry against Yudina's death was so strong, both in Kalmykia and in Moscow, the case was taken over by Moscow prosecutors. Several men were sentenced, one a former aide of Ilyumzhinov, but no one was implicated in ordering the killing.

Yudina's murder, as in other 1990s cases, gathered enormous support from colleagues and showed the capacity for solidarity in moments of urgency. Moscow and regional papers rallied to support the running of Yudina's paper, taking turns every week to write for it and get it published. In the Kholodov case a joint venture *Obshchaya gazeta* ('Everyone's Newspaper') consisting of contributions from many of Moscow's newspapers brought out a memorial issue. Vitaly Yaroshevsky, then working for the regular *Obshchaya gazeta*, described how quickly the media responded in those days to support their colleagues. When war reporter Nadezhda Chaykova was brutally murdered in Chechnya, Yaroshevsky flew to collect her body, promising an article to *Izvestiya* on his return, as his paper was a weekly. It took a week to find Chaykova's body, then bring it to Grozny and back to Moscow. The plane arrived later than expected, but the editor, Igor Golembiovsky, held up the paper's schedule so that Chaykova's story could be printed on the front page. 'That's an enormous paper, they had to pay serious fines to hold up the press, delay trains and distribution', Yaroshevsky explains. NTV's Dobrodeyev also sent out a film crew to meet them at the airport, so that it would be the first item on the news – 'not a story about Yeltsin or a government session, mind you. I couldn't imagine it today', Yaroshevsky adds. 'We were different people, we seemed to have different heads and hearts. Then everything changed when we were told to serve the state and not the truth'.[67]

In the 2000s, the number of targeted journalists increased. The killing of prominent American-Russian editor of *Forbes Russia*, Paul Klebnikov (41), an expert on the country's gangster capitalism, happened in 2004 in Moscow with nine shots from a passing car. Many people suspected that Klebnikov's publication of the 100 wealthiest people in Russia had been responsible for his murder, but media rights monitor Oleg Panfilov denied this would worry anyone: 'Rich people don't hide that they are rich, they don't ride bicycles like in Sweden or go to McDonald's like Americans. They show off their $150,000 Rolex watches, ride around in Mercedes, and live in huge houses'.[68] With some prompting from the US State Department, two Chechens were charged but later acquitted; another Chechen was suspected for a while. Klebnikov's family and friends continue to search for his contract killer and for those who commissioned the murder.

The newspaper that has suffered the most is *Novaya gazeta*, which has seen six of its colleagues murdered.[69] A consistently independent paper from 1994, it has been the choice of workplace for equally determined independent journalists. An early case in the Putin period was that of Igor Domnikov (42), the first in the list of journalists from *Novaya gazeta* to be killed. He was bludgeoned to death with a hammer by members of a criminal gang after he had written a series of critical articles on the Lipetsk regional administration. The murderers were found because the police were already hunting them for another 23 killings. Although *Novaya gazeta* was certain who the mastermind was, it was only in 2014 that enough evidence was gathered by investigators to sentence a former Lipetsk vice-governor to seven years in prison. A month later the case against him was dropped due to the statute of limitations.

The newspaper's internationally famous colleague was Anna Politkovskaya. Her desk remains in the office as it was – no one sits there – when she was gunned down at the age of 48 by an assassin in the entrance to her apartment building in Moscow on 7 October 2006, Putin's birthday. For three days Putin said nothing, but he was caught off guard at a press conference with Angela Merkel in Germany. He replied cynically that it was her death that had caused more harm to public officials than her reporting, whose impact was 'minimal'.[70] He was right – only 6 per cent of the population had heard of her, but that was because she had been put on the blacklist by his state media as a person never to be interviewed on television and radio. The small liberal opposition in Russia grieved for her, but the ensuing international scandal, the overwhelming tributes, candlelit vigils and condolences from world leaders in her honour went a long way to blacken Putin's and Russia's reputation.

Because of Politkovskaya's articles and books, we know about the brutality, torture and catastrophe of Putin's war in Chechnya. In six years she wrote almost 600 articles on the subject. She worked on the ground, taking enormous risks, travelling to dangerous spots prohibited by the Russian army, so that she could talk to victims and record their personal tragedies. She was threatened, poisoned, arrested, detained and forced to flee abroad for a period when an army officer accused of crimes against civilians threatened to kill her. She was openly hostile to Putin – 'for his cynicism, for his racism, for his lies, for the gas he used in the *Nord-Ost* siege, for the massacre of the innocents … because he despises us … he believes he can do anything he likes with us, play with us as he sees fit'.[71] She was even more contemptuous of Putin's appointee in Chechnya, the 'coward' Ramzan Kadyrov, who some allege was the mastermind behind her murder.

Her passion and dedication to telling the truth made many of her collea-gues uncomfortable. When she died there were acrimonious comments: jour-nalist Maksim Sokolov, like Putin, dismissed her as someone whose 'citations were close to zero'; editor Vitaly Tretyakov announced irrelevantly that she had an American passport (she was born in New York of Soviet diplomat parents); Putin's spin doctor Gleb Pavlovsky called her articles biased; the blogosphere was often flippant. She had been placed on several nationalist internet lists as an 'enemy of the state'.

Eight years after Politkovskaya's death, following a retrial and numerous legal scandals, five men and a former policeman were sentenced to prison, two of them for life. It was revealed they were carrying out an order in what they believed was a $150,000 contract to kill. The case is not deemed to be solved by family and friends, because the mastermind has not been identified. *Novaya gazeta* colleagues believe the police's elite secret department and the FSB played roles in the murder, but none of the officers was brought to face justice at the trial.[72]

An ecological campaign to save an ancient oak forest claimed the life of the *Khimkinskaya pravda* ('Khimki Truth') editor, Mikhail Beketov (55) in 2013, five years after he had been savagely beaten with metal rods by two assailants and left to die in a pool of blood. His right leg had to be amputated, he lost several fingers, he was severely brain-damaged and unable to speak. Beketov had used his paper, which he financed himself, to campaign against corrup-tion and what he claimed were lucrative deals for the mayor and the local authorities of Khimki, an outer suburb of Moscow. The most publicised protests were against the building of a motorway to cut through a section of Khimki forest. Beketov was a well-known figure in the large protests, a battle that was eventually lost. He had been threatened numerous times before, his car had been set on fire and his pet dog killed. Other journalists and ecologists protesting against the motorway had also been attacked. Investi-gators failed to arrest anyone in connection with the assault on Beketov, but two years after he had been crippled he was convicted in a lawsuit for slander filed by the mayor and ordered to pay damages. The case was dropped on appeal.

TV critic Irina Petrovsksaya wrote on Facebook on the day of Beketov's memorial at the House of Journalists that not very many journalists had turned up. Two editors came, *Novaya gazeta*'s Dmitry Muratov and the *New Times*'s Yevgeniya Albats. The chairman of the Union of Journalists, Vsevo-lod Bogdanov was there, as was the old dean of Moscow State University's faculty of journalism, Yasen Zasursky, already more than 80 years old, who always came to honour his former students. An elderly woman, unknown to most of them but who had been seen at many protest demonstrations, spoke the most touching words. Many people come to pay their respect to famous actors when they die, she said, but they only play heroic characters; yet so few come to honour the real ones.

Notes

1   Interviewed by Anastasiya Uspenskaya, *BBC Russian Service*, 11 November 2010.
2   *Stanovlenie dukha korporatsii: pravila chestnoi igry v soobshchestve zhurnalistov*, V. I. Bakshtanovskii et al (ed), Izdatel'stvo Nachala Press, 1995. p. 243.
3   *Russia Journal*, 3–9 March 2001.
4   *A Russian Diary*, London: Vintage, 2008, p. 154.
5   Peter Kenez, *The Birth of the Propaganda State: Soviet Methods of Mass Mobilization, 1917–1929*, Cambridge: Cambridge University Press, 1985, p. 27.
6   'Bez maski', *Sobesednik*, November 1992.
7   *Against the Grain: An Autobiography*, London: Jonathan Cape, 1990, p. 156.
8   *Stanovlenie dukha korporatsii …*, p. 214.
9   'Grafomany', *Fantasticheskii mir Abrama Tertsa*, Mezhdunarodnoe literaturnoe sodruzhestvo, 1967, p. 80.
10 Fedotov interviewed by Vladimir Pozner, *First Channel*, 13 December 2010. *Eksperty dlya grazhdanskogo obshchectva*, http://www.4cs.ru/materials/wp-id_1320/ (accessed 29 October 2015).
11 *Stanovlenie dukha korporatsii.*
12 Ibid., pp. 166–7.
13 Author's interview, 27 May 2011.
14 Author's interview, 1 June 2011.
15 Author's interview, 30 November 2013.
16 'Russian free press under threat?', *Spotlight*, RT, 22 October 2009.
17 Sophia Coudenhove, 'ORT bias takes on new look', *Moscow Times*, 12 March 1996.
18 *Pravda*, 3 December 1987, in *SWB*, SU/0020, B/1, B/ 3, 8 December 1987.
19 Prezidentskoe poslanie, 12 December 2013 https://www.youtube.com/watch?v=J7vILudSgiU (accessed 11 November 2015).
20 Yuliya Savina, 'Animosity', *Novyye Izvestiya*, 8 September 2011, in JRL 162, 2011, no. 19.
21 Interfax, 11 August, 2011.
22 'Babushka – eto svyatoe', *Meduza.ru*, 29 December 2014, https://meduza.io/feature/2014/12/29/babushka-eto-svyatoe (accessed 29 October 2015).
23 'Televidenie u nas v strane – bol'she chem televidenie' *Izvestiya*, 17 April, 2002. http://izvestia.ru/news/260974 (accessed 20 October 2015).
24 Marcus Warren, *Daily Telegraph*, 6 March 2001.
25 'Nuzhna li "chetvertaya vlast'" rossiyskomy obshchestvu?', interviewed by Yevgeniya Albats, *Ekho Moskvy*, 22 October 2006 http://echo.msk.ru/programs/albac/46950/ (accessed 29 October 2015).
26 'Perestroika journalist from Radio Moscow', *Voice of Russia*, 22 September 2009. http://voiceofrussia.com/2009/09/22/1802807/ (accessed 29 October 2015).
27 'Teleekran i politika', *Izvestiya*, 11 September 1992.
28 *Stanovlenie dukha korporatsii …*, p. 101.
29 *Rossiya 1*, 10 August 2013. www.youtube.com/watch?v=4KGVUhdqsMQ (accessed 23 November 2015).
30 Laura Mills, 'Russia state news agency gets controversial chief', *Huffington Post*, 9 December 2013. www.huffingtonpost.com/huff-wires/20131209/eu–russia-news-agency/ (accessed 2 December 2015).
31 *812 Online*, 4 April 2014. www.online812.ru/2014/04/04/010/ (accessed 29 October 2015).
32 *812 Online*, 24 March 2014. www.online812.ru/2014/03/24/006/ (accessed 29 October 2015).
33 Brian Whitmore, 'Egypt plane crash: the Russian media veers into conspiracy', *The Atlantic*, 10 November 2015. www.theatlantic.com/international/archive/2015/11/russia-metrojet-flight-9268/415161/ (accessed 2 December 2015).

34 'Russia's search for itself', *International Herald Tribune*, 10 October 2013.
35 Svetlana Pasti, *The Changing Profession of a Journalist in Russia*, Tampere: Tampere University Press, 2007, p. 195.
36 Svetlana Pasti, 'A New Generation of Journalists', in Arja Rosenholm, Kaarle Nordenstreng and Elena Trubina (eds), *Russian Mass Media and Changing Values*, New York: Routledge, 2010, p. 67.
37 Ibid., p. 66.
38 Svetlana Pasti, 'Sovremennye rossiiskie zhurnalisty: otnoshenie k professii', *Vestnik Moskovskogo Universiteta*, seriya 10, Zhurnalistika, no. 4, July–August 2011, p. 31.
39 Ibid., p. 28.
40 Ibid., p. 30.
41 Pasti, *Changing Profession*, pp. 194–5.
42 Pasti, 'New Generation of Journalists', p. 61.
43 *Levada-Tsentr*, 6 June 2016. www.levada.ru/2016/06/06/smi-vnimanie-i-tsenzura (accessed 16 July 2016).
44 Levada-Tsentr, *Obshchestvennoe mnenie, ezhegodnik*, Moskva 2010, p. 172.
45 These figures and the data in the paragraph below for 2014 are based on two sources from the Levada Centre: Denis Volkov, Stepan Goncharov, *Rossiiskii Media-Landshaft: Televidenie, Pressa, Internet*, June 2014, http://www.levada.ru/sites/default/files/levada_report_media_0.pdf (accessed 29 October 2015); press publication of 18 June 2014, http://www.levada.ru/2014/06/18/internet-ne-smog-zamenit-rossiyanam-tv-v-kachestve-istochnika-informatsii/#main-menu (accessed 29 October 2015).
46 'Russian TV heavily dominated by national content', Digital TV Europe, 10 February 2014. www.digitaltveurope.net/145411/russian-tv-heavily-dominated-by-national-content/ (accessed 29 October 2015).
47 Author's interview, 14 June 2014.
48 *NoNaMe*. http://nnm.me/blogs/genav/rukopozhatnoe-selfi-moskovskogo-razliva-makarevich-peskov-leontev-venediktov-gozman-et-cetera/#cut (accessed 23 November 2015).
49 Dozhd' TV, 27 November 2014.
50 Yekaterina Vlasova, 'V sotssetyakh: Uskov protiv Kokha, chetvertaya seriya, rb.ru', 28 November 2014. http://www.rb.ru/article/v-sotssetyah-koh-i-uskov-chetvertyy-den-sporyat-o-rukopojatnosti/7414207.html (accessed 29 October 2015).
51 *Pervyi kanal*, 25 November 2010. http://www.1tv.ru/sprojects_edition/si=5817&fi=6319 (accessed 23 November 2015).
52 'Muchayushchiesya lyudi – eto svyatye', *Argumenty i fakty*, no.15, April 1996.
53 'Razgovor o sud'bakh Rosssii: Mikhail Shishkin vs Boris Akunin', *Afisha*, 29 July–11 August 2013. http://15.afisha.ru/2013/mihail-shishkin-vs-boris-akunin/ (accessed 29 October 2015).
54 For an analysis of these dichotomies in literature, see Daphne Skillen, 'Urban and rural images and ideas in post-revolutionary Russian literature, 1917–1924', Ph.D. thesis, School of Slavonic and East European Studies, University of London, 1985.
55 *Golyi God*, (*The Naked Year*), Letchworth: Bradda Books Ltd, 1966, p. 224.
56 Claire Bigg, 'Russia: scrutiny of foreign funds hurts democracy programs', *RFE/RL*, 15 February 2006. www.rferl.org/articleprintview/1065810.html (accessed 29 October 2015).
57 'Pinochet's "success" is unforgivable', *Moscow Times*, 13 October 1999.
58 'Pochemu vy molchite', *Novaya gazeta*, 21 August 2013. www.novayagazeta.ru/politics/59601.html (accessed 29 October 2015).
59 'Zakat intelligentsii', *Civitas*, 13 August 2013, http://vestnikcivitas.ru/pbls/3060 (accessed 29 October 2015).
60 Vladimir Magun and Maksim Rudnev,*Basic Human Values of Russians: Both Different and Similar to Other Europeans*, Working Papers BRP, 23/SOC/ 2013, p. 28.

www.hse.ru/data/2013/08/28/1290287129/23SOC2013.pdf (in Russian, see www.civisbook.ru/files/File/Magun_Rudnev_Bazovye.pdf) (accessed 2 December 2015).

61 Ibid., p. 13.
62 Lauren Wolfe, 'Corrupt Russian police are a "dark force" against press', Committee to Protect Journalists, 3 April 2009. http://cpj.org/blog/2009/04/corrupt-russian-police-are-a-dark-force-against-pr.php (accessed 29 October 2015).
63 The figures for 1993–2013 were taken from http://journalists-in-russia.org, a joint endeavour by a number of media-monitoring NGOs which held detailed information, but is no longer accessible. The 2014–15 figures come from Boris Timosheno, who monitors media rights at the Glasnost Defence Foundation (www.gdf.ru/monitoring), providing monthly statistics. The previous Memorium website founded by Oleg Panfilov's Committee for Journalists in Extreme Situations, with invaluable information, is also no longer accessible and the NGO has disbanded.
64 Committee to Protect Journalists. https://cpj.org/europe/russia (accessed 16 July 2016).
65 *Partial Justice: An Inquiry into the Deaths of Journalists in Russia, 1993–2009*, Belgium: International Federation of Journalists, p. 37.
66 *Pervyi kanal*, 25 November 2010, http://www.1tv.ru/sprojects_edition/si=5817&fi=6319 (accessed 29 October 2015).
67 Author's interview, 2 June 2011.
68 Catherine A. Fitzpatrick, 'A conversation with media activist Oleg Panfilov', *RFE/RL*, Media Matters, 4(14), 2 August 2004.
69 They are Igor Domnikov (2000), Yury Shchekochikhin (2003), Anna Politkovskaya (2006), Anastasiya Baburova together with Stanislav Markelov (2009) and Natalya Estemirova (2009).
70 'Prezident Rossii nazval ubiistvo Politkovskoi "omerzitel'nym prestupleniem"', *Lenta.ru*, 10 October 2006, http://lenta.ru/news/2006/10/10/putin/ (accessed 29 October 2015).
71 *Putin's Russia*, London: Harvill Press, 2004, pp. 282–3.
72 *Committee to Protect Journalists*. www.cpj.org/killed/2006/anna-politkovskaya.php (accessed 29 October 2015).

4 The normalisation of lying

> All this lying, even in its innocence, hints at our extremely important basic traits ... and, first and foremost, that we Russians fear the truth.
>
> (Dostoyevsky, *Diary of a Writer*, 1873)

I Living with lies

Free speech is meant to be about truth-telling, but Russians have always had a perverse relationship to the truth. When Gorbachev let the KGB float rumours that the United States had created the AIDS pandemic or when Putin claims that the internet is a CIA invention, do they believe these grotesque accusations? Do journalists knowingly violate their professional ethics in channelling them? Does the Russian public fall for it? Deception and falsification run deep in tsarist and particularly Soviet practice, and have plumbed these depths in the Putin regime. When Putin used Kremlin-controlled media to unleash a staggering scale of lies and distortions to annex Crimea and intervene in Eastern Ukraine, NATO declared it needed to find new resources outside conventional arms to combat Russia's 'hybrid' warfare. Lying as a weapon of war had achieved its goals with astounding success.

People all over the world lie, and so do politicians. One of the worst lies of recent history was the assertion by the United States, Britain and their allies that weapons of mass destruction existed in Iraq, a lie with enormous international repercussions. Since then, the leaders of that period have been removed by their electoral systems, and investigations into the war have not ceased. Russia's situation is systemic and exceptional, as Russians themselves and foreign visitors have observed over the centuries. Gogol, Dostoyevsky and Bulgakov have depicted the phenomenon in their work, the French traveller Marquis de Custine commented in 1839 that Russians of all classes possessed 'a dexterity in lying, a naturalness in falsehood',[1] while modern day diplomat Sir Rodric Braithwaite wrote in a secret missive that 'Russians lie when they feel they need to ... But they also lie without reason, by some inner compulsion, even when they know that their listener knows that they are lying'.[2] Another strong national trait is Russians' ability to laugh at their cultural waywardness. Everyone of a certain age has heard the Soviet anecdote: 'There's no news in *Pravda* (Truth) and no truth in *Izvestiya* (News)'. I myself am fond of the one about Waterloo. While watching a parade on Red Square, Napoleon turns to Brezhnev and says, 'If I had tanks like that, I wouldn't have lost the battle of Waterloo'. Brezhnev replies: 'And if you had newspapers like we have, no one would have known you'd lost the battle of Waterloo'.

The lack of a free press in Russia has made it easy to conceal truth and dupe people. Lying has been used extensively and effectively as a method of state control. Other communist regimes have also responded to crises in this way because of the vast disjuncture between goals and reality, which they need to justify. But the act of lying in Russia is also deeply entwined with questions of survival, freedom and identity which have evolved over centuries of coercion and tyranny. Fear is the central factor behind the bizarre relationship to lies. Russia's despotic rulers use lies as a tool because they fear their own people and the consequences of the demands they place on them. People who are unempowered are forced to accept lies and invent their own out of fear and a sense of survival. The grand schemes of despots to modernise Russia has had catastrophic costs on its people: Peter's Europeanisation, the Bolsheviks' proletarianisation, Stalin's industrialisation – all enforced leaps into an unknown future, without much prior rehearsal or organic evolution. Sociologist Yury Levada in his article on Russian 'cunning' and doublethink stresses a crucial factor in the relationship between ruler and ruled, that 'demands imposed on people were almost impossible to fulfil'. In adapting to social reality, the cunning person had to seek 'loopholes in its normative system, or ways of turning the current rules of the game to his own advantage while at the same time ... trying to find a way to get around those rules'.[3] Political scientists talk of informal networks, privilege, bribery and the black market as essential ways of getting around a system of arbitrary and personalised rule, selective justice and endemic corruption. In the sphere of information, lies are a useful way of promoting ideology, propaganda and alternative 'realities'.

Glasnost and the transition to democracy were attempts to change this historical trajectory, to tear down the veil of secrecy and fill in the 'blank spots' of the past. The media would create an open society and make the Kremlin accountable. It is true that the transition to democracy was yet another leap into an unknown future, but the significant difference was that it was not enforced. Nor was it built on lies and unfulfillable promises, even if it was misunderstood by the majority to be a quick fix for all woes. As long as pluralism of the media existed, the potential for a fairer life was there and even the dirtiest of lies and machinations were challenged and exposed. Although Putin repeatedly spoke of safeguarding free speech and democracy, by 2003 when the large television stations were in Kremlin hands, the truth that he had usurped the fledgling democracy became clear even to many who had believed his words. Opposition leader Boris Nemtsov called Putin a 'specialist in lying', a 'pathological liar'. In this instance he was referring to Putin's Ukrainian policy which had been built on lies. How could Putin be Commander-in-Chief of the Armed Forces and deny that Russian fighters were dying in Eastern Ukraine, when Nemtsov himself had seen their graves in Kostroma, Pskov and Nizhny Novgorod, where he had once been governor?[4] Nemtsov said this on the day in 2015 when he was assassinated. As a long-time Putin critic, Nemtsov was a scrupulous researcher in exposing the lies and corruption of the regime. In a 2005 article, 'The President, Simple and Lying', Nemtsov and Pribylovsky analysed ten main lying 'moments' of promises that Putin had betrayed.[5] Putin claimed otherwise. When Chinese journalists asked him for the secret of his popularity, he said:

> I always stick to certain rules. First, not to lie. To tell the truth, whether it's pleasant or not very. Our people deserve to be told the truth.[6]

Most of the lies are carried by the media; they are stated as fact without analysis. Television becomes glossier and glitzier all the time, swirling with graphics and new technology that cost billions of roubles. Newsreaders speak faster than they used to; and there seems to be more urgency to the news, the less truth there is, and the more contrived it becomes. Intense music accompanies the headlines. The form is what matters: to make the news look exciting and dramatic. Increasingly it begins to look like theatre, a staged production. To orchestrate this reality, teams of talented professionals were prepared to return to a system where the truth is not their responsibility. How much, then, has the Putin regime's media taken from the country's history of lies, and what innovations and digital technology have they brought to the culture of deception?

What impact does lying have on free speech? Free speech is the right to utter thoughts, it does not require that truth be told; however, its rationale as the centrepiece of democracy is telling truth to power. Pluralism is more important to truth than freedom, because truth is more likely to emerge in the multiplicity and collision of views than from any one free media source. The liberal democratic 'marketplace of ideas' stood in contrast to the Soviet party's three-quarters of a century monopoly on truth. Lying and duping the masses were justified on the grounds that the party knew what was best for the people. However naive or cynical the views behind the party's control of speech, its official aim was ideological, the re-education of the masses to achieve a glorious new future, axiomatically a higher truth – or the greater number of lies.

The goals under the Putin regime have little to do with truth. Destroying media pluralism was Putin's first political move. Postmodernist beliefs popular with the ruling elite were easily ingested from the Soviet Union's relativist morality where, as Lenin said, truth was subordinated to the interests of the class struggle. The postmodernist claim that there is no such thing as truth, only different views and interests which can be interpreted from different angles and perspectives, is a convenient position for Putin's PR gurus as it allows them to manipulate society's disenchantment with its lost communist and democratic ideals. Journalism can never be objective, they say. The fact that journalism can never be wholly free of its practitioner's political orientation and world-view is a truism, given that we do not live in a vacuum, but that does not mean that truth is unattainable. We need not delve into philosophical treatises on the objective foundations of human knowledge to argue simply enough that a proposition is true when it conforms to some fact or state of affairs in the real world. Putin's intellectuals, by questioning the existence of reality and truth, turn the argument into one of self-interest: what is in Russia's interest is good, so that citizens uphold their country on the basis of loyalty (one could say tribal loyalties) and not on universal values of right or wrong. Blatant lies issuing from the propaganda machine against Ukraine do not bother them much; what was important was to sustain the flow of highly charged disinformation that played on emotions and brainwashed minds and continued with only a few short pauses from February 2014 until suddenly full attention shifted to Syria, literally overnight in September 2015, when the weather presenter informed viewers that the weather in Damascus was excellent for Russian planes to fly out on bombing raids.

Let us look at a particularly abhorrent lie in the media propaganda war against Ukraine. This was a report on the state's First Channel that a 3-year-old boy had been crucified by the Ukrainian army. A woman talking to the reporter, Yuliya Chumakova, claimed to have witnessed the event, which she said took place in the town of Slavyansk in the main square, and described in grisly detail how the boy's mother had been forced to watch her child tortured, and after he had died, she herself was dragged by a tank until she was almost dead.[7] Independent Russian and foreign journalists in the area investigating the report found no evidence for the story, not one of the many dozens of people interviewed in the town knew anything about it, the square that was named did not exist, and the woman had a history of filing false police reports. 'Are they completely sick to be concocting this?', Aleksei Navalny asked on his blog. Outraged opposition figures condemned First Channel's incitement of hatred, and Navalny and Nemtsov called for the channel's management to be put on trial for broadcasting the falsehood. Deputy Minister of Communications and Mass Media, Aleksei Volin, was put on the spot by Dozhd' TV's Mikhail Zygar and asked why, given the information had been so roundly refuted, the channel had not apologised publicly for its misreporting:

VOLIN: You want your colleagues to be punished?
ZYGAR: Mainly we want to hear what your position is.
VOLIN: My position is that it's all normal The First Channel took an interview and showed what was said in the interview; that corresponds fully with all the norms, rules and criteria of journalistic ethics …

ZYGAR: After such an interview wouldn't you personally want to take a pistol and go to Slavyansk and shoot fascists?

VOLIN: I certainly don't want to take a weapon and kill people.

ZYGAR: It seems to me many would. For example, I would. If it's true that people are being crucified there, it's impossible for a person who's not indifferent to just sit and look at all this.[8]

An atrocity story of this magnitude would not normally be broadcast solely on the basis of one alleged witness's spoken account. Volin has had many years of experience in the media industry and was appointed in 2012 to manage a punitive media policy. His crude views reflect the cynicism of Putin-regime officials. Especially notorious was his definition of the function of journalism, which caused a storm in liberal and professional media circles. Speaking to Moscow State University's journalism faculty at its annual conference, Volin declared that journalists' only mission was to 'inflate their boss's wallet'. It would be 'criminal' if students were not taught what the real world was like:

> A journalist has to realise clearly that he has no mission to make the world a better place, to spread the light of truth and lead humanity along the right path. None of this is business ... The question is, do the media serve a propaganda function? Of course they do, to the extent their owners consider appropriate. Propaganda should not be obvious, propaganda should be concealed – it's only that way it can be effective ... We have to make it clear to students when they leave this auditorium that they will be working for some 'dude', and the 'dude' will tell them what to write and what not to write, and how to write about this or that. And the 'dude' has the right to do this because he pays them ... This is objective reality. Such is life and we have no other.[9]

To boos and heckles, Volin's replies to his audience sounded more like a mafioso talking, than a minister. To a professor who asked if he had considered the reaction to his speech, he replied: 'Why the hell should I care about your reaction?; and to the question of whether what he said was linked to the media law he replied, 'You work out which will get you further'.

In an essay on cynicism, sociologist Lev Gudkov explained its debilitating effect on society, how it erodes any sense of morality and optimism. He compares cynicism with nihilism. A nihilist rejects the moral value of an act; the cynic knows the difference between good and evil but consciously rejects and belittles people's most precious moral values, appealing to their:

> 'sense of reality', to an 'actual state of affairs', to 'the naked truth': that is, it strips them of their ideals and brings them 'down to earth'. They then end up coming across as inept, 'out of touch' 'moralists', impractical dreamers, idealists and so on.[10]

In the web of lies that is woven, it is hard to maintain any kind of logic. But, intellectually, Volin has got himself into a muddle. If journalists are meant to dish up the propaganda their private owners demand, how do these 'dudes' differ from Gusinsky and Berezovsky who have been excoriated by Putin, 'his' dude, for following their self-interest (business) and not the interests of society? Albeit what Putin really meant of course was the interests of the state or, more likely, the status quo. Volin knows that the view 'he who pays the piper calls the tune' is widespread, and one that basically makes sense when most people do not feel an unspoken contract with the state that free speech is an aspect of their culture.

Part of the effectiveness of lies is that it takes a lot of work to unravel them. Denials by Putin and top officials that Russian troops had intervened at the beginning of the Crimea crisis when suspicious-looking men – the so-called 'little green men' without insignia but armed to the teeth in the latest military hardware – had crossed the border to help pro-Russian separatists block Ukrainian forces, at first baffled western politicians and media. To lie so brazenly was simply not done. You get no kudos from it. And most people, if they remembered the cold war at all, thought Russia had become part of the sophisticated global community. By the time Putin admitted that the 'little green men' were Russian soldiers, the bubble of trust had already burst; and when more than a year later he denied that he had ever denied it, no one was listening. But lies need to be unmasked, and a war of lies needs round-the-clock mobilisation by media, bloggers and truth-seekers all over the world if the truth is not to be swamped. This battle has been ongoing. Websites have sprung up showing evidence that refutes many of Russia's claims: photos, videos, eyewitness reports, recordings of intercepted phone calls. Some sites are dedicated to uncovering falsehoods connected with Ukraine.[11]

Normalising the unnatural

In the various forms of thought control devised by Russian/Soviet propagandists, lies have usually played some part – small lies, half lies, outright lies. If no lie is involved (a lie is something that is invented), then the facts can be spun in such a way that the end product is meant to deceive. The most effective lies are those which have an element of truth to them, because they make the lie harder to unravel. Lies are also more effective if they touch on what people actually want, such as the feeling that 'Crimea is ours'.

Lying underpins different types of deception: cover-ups, disinformation, misinformation, concealment, façade, imitation, simulation, virtuality. It prevails under censorship, which limits the truth; propaganda, which distorts the truth; spin which manipulates the truth. In Russia everyone knows the power of these lies, they are a fact of life. Russians see the metaphor of 'the emperor has no clothes' as resembling their predicament: the collective denial of an obvious fact that each person knows to be false yet chooses not to recognise and participates in the ensuing charade. In 2008 Sergei Kovalyov in an open letter to Putin criticising the lies being disseminated before the elections spoke of the 'paradoxical chain' that forced everyone into the system of lies:

> You lie, your listeners know this and you know they don't believe you and are just pretending to believe you; and they also know you are aware they don't believe you. Everyone knows everything. The lie … has turned into an everyday aspect of life, an ordinary and obligatory rule of the game.[12]

The personal and political are intertwined. I have been lied to, even by eminent respected figures. When I first exposed a simple bare-faced lie I thought the liar would die of embarrassment to be found out, but there was no particular response, only a look of 'Well, I gave it a go'. In Russia's atomised society, where people mainly trust their families and a close network of friends, lying may be exploitative or it may be part of one's survival kit. When institutions do not work, as sociologist Boris Dubin explained to me, people have to depend on relationships, but:

> how you respond to truth depends on the situation, whom you talk to, what consequences might follow from it. Will telling the truth threaten you, will it be to your benefit or might it offend someone you may need later on or, the opposite, someone who is dangerous and might use the truth against you … so why not lie?

The act of political lying is tied to the process of normalising what is unnatural. It reconciles what is irreconcilable, moderates unresolved contradictions, and patches up Russia's fragmented identity torn, as we have seen, between Western and Slavophile dualities. To hold this vast and disparate country together has presupposed enormous powers of despotism and mythmaking. The historian Dmitry Furman in his article 'An Apologia for Simulation' argues that Russians' adjustment to social problems is based on the 'monstrous system of the universal lie':

> We live under a system of norms that contradict our customs and our psychology, norms that we are 'uncomfortable' with, ones that we cannot realistically follow … Our country has no deep internal need for the separation of powers. There is not even a special need for contested elections. They are the general norms of contemporary culture. These norms always arise in progressive countries and (or) in the top strata of society … You can hate these countries and these strata, but no matter how much you hate them, you acknowledge their norms, and if you cannot follow them, you are compelled to simulate them.[13]

Rubbing up for centuries against Europe's progressive values and freedoms has been a constant source of irritation. Starting as Europe's most backward country and the last outpost of a cruel serfdom has left feelings of insecurity and competitiveness. It has led to a love–hate relationship with the West, which Dostoyevsky observed in his own times. Russians will happily acknowledge the authority of a European, he said, until such time as the European falls off his pedestal or drops out of fashion, at which point 'no one is more severe with him than the Russian intelligentsia, there is no limit to its arrogance, contempt and mockery'.[14] Soviet bombast often carried this mixture of resentment and envy. Khrushchev's boast that the Soviet Union would 'catch up with and overtake America' when it could hardly feed or clothe its citizens was the kind of myth the masses loved. What is it that compels Russians to seek norms they cannot live up to? Furman's answer is to look to the roots of Russian history:

> In Kievan Rus' the boyars could certainly have driven the prince away or killed him. But the boyars never became princes. Let us assume that we ask a boyar why, when real power is in his hands, he does not declare himself the prince but instead follows the difficult path of looking for a new prince. What would he say? He would answer: 'But after all, I am not of princely birth'. Putin answers: 'But after all, that contradicts the Constitution'.[15]

What we see is a fetishisation of the Byzantine tradition of form over content, which turns rituals and customs that have been laid down over the centuries into the real objects of veneration. Façade and pomp are central to Russia's perception of itself. The atmosphere of the church contains in itself all that is satisfying to the senses: the scent of incense, the celestial music, the glint of gold and heavy embroidery: this is what entices church-going Russians rather than a study of the scriptures or theology. The schism in the seventeenth century articulated its main heresy as one of form, whether to make the sign of the cross with three or two fingers. Form and ritual have been used to incorporate different content, as Sovietologists noted in the rapid turnover of tsarist iconography into Soviet ones: the 'palaces' of the working class, the religious aura to cults of personality (Lenin's mummification). In this sense, the Constitution is a sacred relic of legitimacy. Stalin had no earthly need for a Constitution when he was conducting the terror in the 1930s, yet in 1936 he felt it necessary to have a liberal Constitution drafted for show. In the 1970s the dissidents' most reliable form of defence in court was to base their cases on articles of the Brezhnev Constitution, which the authorities were in awe of. Putin did not feel he could amend Yeltsin's Constitution to stand for a successive third term as president, but neither was he prepared to give up power. The usual Russian solution was to turn to deception, which he did by playing musical chairs with Medvedev. He let Medvedev fiddle with the Constitution by increasing the number of years of office, so that when he did switch places again he could stay in power longer. Form covers up deception and helps resolve problems, although it can sometimes produce new ones.

In this case the cynical presidential swap in 2011–12 led to massive street protests. Straight-talking opposition leader Aleksei Navalny's contempt for the Kremlin's 'confidence that any problem can be fixed with a con trick' was supported by the largest series of demonstrations in Moscow for a long time. 'The main thing', said Navalny, 'is that we don't have to lie to people. We can get through to them simply by telling them the plain facts about Putin, his billionaire friends, FSB generals whose children SUDDENLY all turned up working for state banks … The slogan "United Russia is the Party of Crooks and Swindlers" has stuck not thanks to some kind of technology, but because it's the truth'.[16] The truth that came with people's power was apparently so threatening that the combined total of police suppression, further media closures and new draconian laws was considered insufficient to protect the status quo. When Ukrainians chose ties that would bring them closer to Europe than to Russia, and exposed Ukrainian President Yanukovich's wealth and his enormous kitsch villa, through which thousands of weekenders with their families strolled aghast at the bling and the cost, the danger of exposure was too close for comfort. It was a snapshot backward to the army of workers and peasants rifling through the nobility's palaces.

The lie of the Putin regime from the beginning was its pretence to be a democracy. That its intentions were authoritarian from the start is discussed in Chapter 8, but to be accepted by the global community and maintain the goodwill initiated by the Gorbachev and Yeltsin leaderships meant it needed to maintain a façade of democracy, while at the same time chipping away at its institutions, first and foremost its free media. The lie enabled the regime to be what it is not. Putin needed to pretend that Russia's ideology was similar to that of western liberal democracy, but his goal was not to further it – it was to put a spin on it. Strictly speaking, to spin is not necessarily to lie: it is to manipulate, to be in control of the way a project is perceived, it is a politically motivated deception. Spin was Russia's twenty-first century contribution to its history of deception. By exploiting the fruits of digital technology, Putin's PR team built a 'virtual democracy' based on simulation: all the institutions of democracy are there – elections, parliament, political parties, market competition, civil society, media independence, etc., but they are not genuine because they do not fulfil the functions they were intended for. Virtuality creates an illusion, a hallucinatory quality that these institutions exist and you can even see them perform the motions. It is the big lie, so big it does not even ignore what is effectively denied.

II Two kinds of lying

Like freedom, which is expressed by two words, as we saw in Chapter 1, the dualities of Russian thinking affect other fundamental concepts such as truth and lies. Truth as *istina* represents a higher morality and tends to stand on its own. Truth as *pravda* is a general word with its opposite in falsehood or lies. There are two kinds of lies: *lozh'* – a deliberate straight lie and *vranyo* – a less serious lie, sharing some features with the Irish 'blarney'. *Vranyo* is a performance, a piece of theatre; played out face to face or for an audience. This kind of lie can be relatively harmless. The best-known exponent of *vranyo* in nineteenth-century Russian literature is Gogol's petty clerk Khlestakov, who is inspired when he is mistaken for the inspector-general and is able to live out his fantasies. The element of wishful thinking is part of lying, of pretending to be something you are not.

In his essay, 'A Word or Two about *Vranyo*', Dostoyevsky tried to uncover why 'everyone lied in Russia down to the last figure'.[17] True, he believed that women lied less, but among the intellectual classes 'a non-liar is an impossibility'; even completely honest people can lie in Russia, which he was convinced only scoundrels did in other nations. He noted that *vranyo* was greeted with 'delicate reciprocity' at all social gatherings of his day, making the lie a two-way collaboration; and as he felt *vranyo* and *lozh'* were largely interchangeable, the perpetrator and victim colluded in serious forms of lying as well. Himself a seeker after truth with ambivalent responses, Dostoyevsky believed Russians were too ashamed of themselves to want to know the truth, because they desperately wanted to be 'anyone, only not what they are'. By seeking for something that was not there or theirs, they missed out on the truth. 'Truth (*istina*) lies in front of people on the table for hundreds of years but no one takes it, instead they pursue the make-believe precisely because they consider it to be fantastic and utopian'.

What Dostoyevsky perceptively calls 'make-believe' (*pridumanyy*) is what we can understand today as 'alternative realities', inventions woven out of lies that present what is unreal as real. In the Soviet firmament there was 'Soviet reality', to be distinguished from 'bourgeois reality', which produced that reality's literary realism called 'revolutionary realism' and 'socialist realism'. It spawned such contradictions as the fatally flawed play *An Optimistic Tragedy*. Today we have Putin's various examples of 'make-believe' in managed, sovereign and majority democracy, all of which can be explained as 'virtual' realities, because they are make-believe versions of democracy.

The nature of the 'make-believe' and its level of ruthlessness depended on whether the lies were closer to *vranyo* or to *lozh'*. Under autocracy there was no special need for the tsars to lie because they felt divinely authorised to suppress dissent violently. The lying came from the population to avoid punishment and fool government officials – either the peasant's 'cunning' ways of dealing with landlords and masters, or local officials finding ways to cover up incompetence and venality. When Gogol's town officials are waiting for the arrival of the inspector-general, the judge tells the trustee of the town's charities he has nothing to fear: 'What's the worry? Give the sick some clean caps to wear and no one will be any the wiser'.[18] The clean caps are as much a façade as the famous apocryphal tale of Potyomkin's villages, only with the status raised to that of ambitious courtier ingratiating himself to his monarch. Anxious to please Empress Catherine that all is well in her empire, Count Potyomkin allegedly erected picturesque pasteboard villages at a distance from the river along which her royal barge passed on its way to Crimea in 1787. De Custine's reaction to the tale was contempt at the 'permanent conspiracy of smiles plotting against truth for the satisfaction of one person who is reputed to wish and act for the good of all'.[19]

The present clings to the raiments of the past with no newer plot than that of Putin the 'one and only'. I doubt most people would go to Dickens to find out what the English are like today (Russians remember reading him at school and are disenchanted when they visit). Time passes, yet the same unresolved and unchanged problems continue to suffocate Russia, because they have largely been papered over by deception. In 2011 Medvedev was complaining on television of Potyomkin villages being erected as soon as officials learned of his plans to visit a provincial town. He encouraged residents to send information beforehand to his blog and Twitter accounts. In one town, Lytkarino, not far from Moscow, local officials had wrapped buildings with construction mesh in an effort to imitate repair work; and a fence around a school had been painted only on the side of the road through which Medvedev's motorcade was to pass.[20]

The systemic lie began under the Soviet system in order to marry ideals with reality. In the early revolutionary years, although there were gross distortions of the truth, the horrors of civil war, hunger and death took place against a background of optimism for the glorious future. The utopian vision was expressed in the enthusiasm and brilliance of agitprop, poetry and art. It was more a period of mythmaking than lies. The main myth was the Bolshevik coup itself as seen through Sergei Eisenstein's eyes in his 1927 film *October*, the version that many Russians take to be the real account of the revolution. The luminous crowd scenes in the storming of the Winter Palace as choreographed by famous photo-artist Aleksandr Rodchenko was so effective that Stalin insisted it be included in Mikhail Romm's later anniversary film of 1937. In fact, the crowd scenes caused more damage to the marble tiles in the palace than the real event, at which there were far fewer people.

In the less restrictive periods of the Soviet regime *vranyo* was a factor of everyday reality. Ronald Hingley, writing in a 1962 article, 'That's No Lie, Comrade', gives an example of the kind of *vranyo* that existed at the time of Khrushchev's 'thaw'. He describes an official telling him how every summer tens of millions of Soviet workers and their families headed off to Baltic Sea resorts 'in their own cars'. When Hingley's face unwittingly betrayed disbelief, the official added, 'of course there are some workers who don't yet have cars of their own'.[21] Hingley felt it was tactless not to play along – 'it is all too easy to expose some harmless *vrun* (purveyor of *vranyo*) by implying that it was a piece of *lozh'* all along'.[22]

Vranyo was a part of Soviet reality from most of the 1960s to the mid 1980s. The lies were impossible to avoid and the social contract implied 'play along and you won't be hurt'. You talked to family and friends on a different wavelength, which meant living in parallel realities, one based on official lies, the other on personal relations. To live in a world of lies messes with people's minds, and allows those who benefit from and manage the system of lies to abuse their powers. One recommended way to maintain sanity was to compartmentalise one's private life and beliefs from the official world of compulsory lies. The more dangerous impact of lies on the psyche came under Stalinism in what Orwell called 'doublethink', a belief in both sides of a contradictory proposition, because the fear of not doing so could be fatal. The example Orwell gives is 'freedom is slavery'. In this world, the distinction between the official and the personal was obliterated because it might not be safe to divulge your thoughts to family or friends, and certainly not to your children, who might innocently blurt something out.

The mass hysteria whipped up by television over the Ukraine crisis shocked opposition journalists by its similarities with the terror of the 1930s. It is this historical repetition that horrified Ekho Moskvy presenter Kseniya Larina:

> When we were teenagers we asked our parents, how could you not have noticed that people were disappearing, that people were being shot, that thousands and millions of people were sent to prison for nothing, that neighbours disappeared in the night taking a suitcase with them? You even answered 'well, yes, we did know', or you hadn't really seen anything, or you didn't want to see anything, or that ugly secret feeling that people aren't thrown into prison here for nothing – there's no smoke without fire. All this has remained at the back of our minds.[23]

The big lie

Lozh' relates to false facts and disinformation. Unlike *vranyo*, it is conveyed by any means, personally or through television, publishing and other outlets. It is a strong word in Russian. *Lozh'* is the big lie. It is the word for Stalinism at its worst, when lies were invented and sustained by terror. Terror meant, according to the most recent estimate from Russian scholar Oleg Khlevniuk, that under Stalin between 1930 and 1952 about 800,000 people were shot; more than 26 million people were incarcerated in labour camps or imprisoned or deported, many dying in these barely habitable regions; up to five to seven million people died of manmade famine and, all together, about 60 million suffered from either 'hard' or 'soft' punishment.[24] Robert Conquest describes the kind of lies that were disseminated under Stalin's regime:

> After the disaster of collectivization, the leadership had two options: either to admit failure and change policy – perhaps even to relinquish total power – or to pretend that success had been achieved. Falsification took place on a barely credible scale, in every sphere. Real facts, honest statistics, disappeared. History, especially that of the Communist Party, was rewritten. Unpersons vanished from the official record. A spurious past and a fictitious present were imposed on the captive minds of the

Soviet people. To focus solely on the physical manifestations of the Communist terror – the killings, the deportations, the people who were driven to suicide – would be to overlook the larger context: what Boris Pasternak called 'the inhuman reign of the lie'.[25]

Lies combined with terror offered unlimited scope to control the narrative and deceive the population. Lies mounted upon lies. One of Stalin's terrible crimes which he attributed to the Nazis was the massacre of nearly 15,000 Polish officers in the forests of Katyn and nearby in May 1940. To add credibility to the lie, NKVD officers were later sent to exhume the bodies and plant documents that would make certain the blame was laid on the Nazis and not on Stalin. Although the Poles knew what had really happened long ago, it took 50 years for the Russians, under Gorbachev and the policy of *glasnost*, to admit to the atrocity. In 1992 Yeltsin sent documents to Poland with proof of Stalin's and Beria's guilt. In 2010, as a sign of goodwill to Poland, Medvedev ordered the online publication of the archives on the massacre, perhaps to show up Putin's encouragement of the Stalin myth.

Probably no other country has distorted its history in the way Soviet Russia has. The cinematic achievements of photomontage early in the century were put to the job of making lies credible. The tricks of retouching were used to airbrush Stalin's pock-marked face or to remove the image from photos of revolutionary leaders, who had once stood side by side with Lenin, but had fallen out of favour with Stalin.[26] Most of the main Soviet myths were based on lies: the impossible feats of Stakhanovite shock workers in the second Five Year Plan, the heroism of young Pavlik Morozov's perverse morality, the identity of the man who hoisted the hammer and sickle on top of the Reichstag in Berlin. That man was a young Red Army Lieutenant Aleksei Berest who, at the request of a war photographer, reached the top of the Reichstag roof against heavy German resistance. He died at the age of 49 keeping that moment of triumph more or less to himself. The official version was filmed two days after Berest's heroic act and gave the honours to two soldiers with appropriate looks and names: Yegorov (a good Russian name) and Kantaria (a good Georgian name and sop to Stalin). The true story about Berest came out in a documentary which was shown on NTV for the 55th anniversary of the end of the war in 2000.[27]

During the Gorbachev–Yeltsin years, many Soviet ideologically driven myths were exposed by the media, but in no way as much as one would have expected. I was surprised to learn that a small exhibition of faked photos, the 'Disappearing of People' that I saw in Moscow in 1996, probably the first of its kind in Russia, was actually a collection brought over from Paris – as if the Russians could not have done it themselves. Stories investigating historical lies make for thrilling reading and TV programming, as well as having educational value. The fact that there were relatively few of them, apart from a number of memorable documentaries, indicated an unwillingness to uncover the enormity of the crimes. Telling the truth was not as simple in Russia as it was in Germany as a conquered nation. The wonderful TV series, *Kino-Pravda*, devised by academic and TV presenter Georgy Kuznetsov, received bags of hostile letters and abuse every week. Kuznetsov showed old films from the Stalin era, usually beautifully made by masters of the cinema but ideologically distorted, followed by a 40-minute discussion with various experts. Broadcast in the early Yeltsin years, the plan was to pierce the myths of totalitarianism and show the real facts behind the cinematic cover-ups. Kuznetsov realised how wrapped up with the joys of youth and nostalgia these films were and how easily criticism could be counterproductive:

> These films were part of their lives; rubbishing these films to a certain extent meant doubting a person's worth. A person will never forgive that. It's no accident that a main slogan in our lives and many films is 'do you respect me?'. Our people need to feel respected ... You have to be very careful in hinting 'we've all been fooled, brother'.[28]

Russia's attitude to historical revisionism has been feeble. To confront its terrible past could never be easy, and would require all the support of government, the judiciary, education and media to handle the blows to the national conscience. Neither Gorbachev nor Yeltsin was prepared to tackle fully the lies of the system. Gorbachev tried to curb enthusiasts of *glasnost* in 1986 because 'if we start trying to deal with the past, we'll lose all our energy. It would be like hitting people over the head. And we have to go forward'.[29] Yeltsin always feared that a Nuremberg-type trial into the crimes of the Communist Party would result in civil war. Totalitarianism by definition meant everyone was involved, so where did one stop? The politician Galina Starovoytova lobbied to have lustration laws passed, as had been done in a number of post-communist countries. They worked especially well in East Germany and the Czech Republic with their purges after 1989, giving people affected by the secret police access to their files and screening officials for past collaboration with the security services so as to prevent them from gaining important government jobs. Such schemes held no chance of success in Russia: if they had, Putin, for one, would not have been able to stand for president.

As a result, there has been no healing process and no catharsis. Stalin continues to feature in opinion polls as the country's most prominent statesman, despite evidence of his crimes against humanity and genocide. In a TV show called *Name of Russia* in 2008, based on the British programme *100 Great Britons*, Stalin was the viewers' top choice, but was relegated lower down the scale out of embarrassment. Historical memory has been distorted by the difficulty of extricating victims from executioners, who later became victims themselves. This allows for such perverse situations to arise as the attempt to rehabilitate Beria, the notorious NKVD chief responsible for the death and torture of millions of people, on the grounds that he was accused and executed on false charges of 'counter-revolutionary activities' and being a British spy. Today, branches of Memorial, the organisation dedicated to revealing the truth about political repression, have been shamefully victimised and labelled by Putin's laws as a 'foreign agent'. Memorial's chairman, Arkady Roginsky, suggests that one reason why people are unwilling to face the truth is because 'unlike the Nazis, who mainly killed "foreigners": Poles, Russians, and German Jews (who were not quite their "own" people), we mainly killed our own people, and our consciousness refuses to accept this fact'.[30]

Who says sorry?

Russian journalists need sensitive antennae to catch changes in the political climate. How do they make the transition from one political system to another? As we have seen in Chapter 3, the transition from journalist-democrat to journalist-statist can be fairly seamless. The transition from Soviet communism to *glasnost* was also seamless for many journalists. It is hard to know the effect that adapting to the radical swings of the political seesaw has on people's personality, on their attitude to lying and on their defence mechanisms.

In the case of one of the leading lights of *glasnost*, Vitaly Korotich, the flamboyant editor of *Ogonyok*, the transition took place almost immediately. At the end of 1986, before the policy of *glasnost* had been fully confirmed, Korotich was still locked into a Soviet mindset. Presumably commissioned by his editor, Korotich denounced the BBC Russian Service's lies against the Soviet Union in the vitriolic tones required of the cold war:

> Sometimes BBC people behave like mongooses striving to destroy every-thing snakelike, like ferocious and exclusive exterminators of everything it is their job to combat. Nonetheless, in the absence of any snakes the noble little animal will probably not rush off and choke fire hoses. And whereas the mongoose's hatred is ultimately of use to people, the hatred of propagandists lacking objectivity engenders chauvinism, blinds people and urges them to overstep even fragile bounds at such an alarming time.[31]

Two months later, Korotich was on radio talking about honesty and honour: that Soviet citizens had got out of the habit of being honest. It was time to call truth and untruth by their real names and to sweep 'our house' clean:

> It's quite pathological the way a person, who has just criticised you from the rostrum, comes up and says, 'Well, you know, uh, I don't really think that way but, well, I had to … uh, do you fancy a coffee?'[32]

It was difficult to be honourable and at the same time behave as a mouth-piece. Korotich was one of those who tried to do both. He had adapted to the Soviet system: a USSR state prize-winner, head of the Ukrainian Union of

Writers, a practising doctor, poet and prose writer. Another prominent Soviet editor, Fyodor Burlatsky, used to say that people like them, who tried to use the system to make a career yet remain true to their own principles, were Soviet society's 'shock absorbers', because they took the flak for trying to make what small changes they could within the system. Korotich threw himself into Gorbachev's reforms, and was named the world's best editor in 1989 for his enormous contribution to promoting *glasnost*. He happened to be in America on the first day of the 1991 coup with a ticket to return home. Instead of returning to fight the putsch, Korotich gave in his resignation as editor of *Ogonyok* and stayed in America. He was accused by his colleagues of disloyalty. Perhaps another political trauma was too much for Korotich. He later explained that there were already disagreements between him and the staff about financial arrangements planned for *Ogonyok*'s future in the new conditions of the capitalist market: it was the young people's turn to struggle, he said. He stayed on in America for over 20 years as a lecturer, teaching at colleges.

Korotich agreed his behaviour had often been 'Pharisaical', but the Soviet Union was filled with 'contrite sinners and provocateurs'. He said: 'The majority of us are not saints and we know how we paid for our survival. But without exception, those who became executioners and informants did so voluntarily'.[33] It is a useful criterion to establish for Putin's proactive media professionals, who have gone beyond what many of their famous forebears were prepared to do by voluntarily becoming provocateurs in wars involving thousands of lives in Chechnya, Georgia and Ukraine. Journalists putting out the lies know what they are doing. They have access to the internet, they can read and watch foreign news sources and they are trained to do research. However difficult it is for journalists to leave their jobs on state channels which are whipping up the propaganda, they do not have the same justification that journalists could claim under Soviet conditions, because today journalists can simply walk away.

Russians tend not to apologise for wrongdoing, even if they are sorry. Most leaders do not either, except Yeltsin. He apologised when he retired for the things he did not do, and he apologised for not being able to save the three young men who died during the 1991 coup, although there was little he could have done. People apologise if they feel responsible. Without full independence, it is unlikely one feels fully responsible. As a result, only one journalist, Vladimir Pozner, appears to have apologised for the lies he disseminated, wittingly or unwittingly, during the Soviet period.

Pozner has apologised many times, and is particularly stricken for having made excuses for the 1968 Soviet invasion of Czechoslovakia. I remember hearing him on a programme with Scottish schoolchildren during a trip he made to the UK in 1985. When asked why Soviet citizens were not allowed to travel abroad, Pozner replied it was because the rouble was non-convertible – a standard Soviet half-truth that avoided mentioning politics, when politics was the main reason. Perhaps Pozner's apologies for his past have something to do with his unusual background. Born in France of Russian communist parents, Pozner went to school in New York and arrived in Moscow in 1952 at the age of 18. The young cosmopolitan Pozner, who had lived in a large flat in Manhattan, mixed in his parents' communist film circles and listened to the music of Pete Seeger, knew America well, its virtues and prejudices, and to this day is prickly about US political deviousness, often to the annoyance of more right-wing liberals. He was a committed communist, and as a foreigner he was probably more of a believer than his Russian colleagues. He worked happily as a propagandist in the North American department of Moscow Radio from 1973 to 1986. He began to have doubts only after the invasion of Afghanistan.

With *perestroika*, the trilingual Pozner became a hit at home and abroad. His star quality has not dimmed, and he has hosted a long series of his own current affairs programmes on the First Channel ever since. Pozner has managed to retain his reputation as a veteran liberal throughout the Putin regime, although he is not without critics. He can be slippery and seems to infuriate some people. He enraged historian Yury Afanasyev who in 2006 accused Pozner of being the 'fig leaf' covering the Putin regime. Afanasyev's anger was based on Pozner's sometimes woolly replies as to whether he is under pressure from broadcasting executives. Pozner will not give a straight answer, says Afanasyev; what he says goes something like yes, he is free, well not absolutely free, but then is anyone absolutely free?[34]

For some years now Pozner has been the only celebrity liberal from the Yeltsin years still broadcasting on mainstream television. All the other liberal names have fallen away or are no longer allowed to have their own programmes. If you see liberal journalists, they are usually online on Dozhd' TV or Ekho Moskvy. Having lasted so long, he is expected single-handedly to represent the liberal position, while at the same time adapting to a steadily growing authoritarianism. As a survivor, Pozner knows how to play the game. But he also puts forward views to the audience that otherwise would not be uttered at all. In 2012, during the massive street protests, he accused prosecutors of using KGB tactics against activists, with a rare reminder to people unconcerned about their history – 'There are hundreds of thousands, if not millions, of similar handwritten confessions in the KGB's archives, and we all know how they were procured'.[35] He regularly annoys parliament, especially when he made fun of its decision to introduce a ban on adoptions of Russian children by American parents in retaliation for the Magnitsky Act in 2012. Mischievously (he claimed it was a slip of the tongue), he called the State Duma, the State Dura ('Fool'). The Duma was so incandescent that they started writing a bill that would forbid foreign nationals (Pozner has three passports) to work on Russian TV.

Pozner is now over 80 years old and his programme, simply called *Pozner*, continues to be a sane and liberal voice in the ever increasing hysteria. He still rates as one of the most trusted journalists with state TV audiences. This is the second transition Pozner has had to make between a free and a non-free media. He has said that he is not bothered if they sack him – he has other countries to go to and other interests, having started a group of restaurants, one in Paris.

'An unpredictable past'

The prevalence of lying as a political strategy has created the feeling that one can never get to the bottom of things. The most insistent question is 'Who stands behind it?'. The lack of reliable information rarely produces an adequate answer, the perfect breeding ground for conspiracy theories and quirky obscurantist thinking. Itself paranoid, the Kremlin plays on paranoia. When Boris Nemtsov was assassinated in 2015 it was clear what the Kremlin would say (authorities have used it often before) and Putin said it – the murder was a 'provocation', that is, people from the opposition killed one of their brightest exponents in order to smear the Kremlin. Is this plausible? But then if millions of victims confessed, if poets preoccupied in intellectual pursuits turned out to be Japanese spies, if activists today are 'fifth columnists' – anything is possible. Such gross lies mean that nothing is sacred, and one can expect the worst from people.

Lies shake one's faith in reality, and if you believe in nothing, it means you could believe in anything. The audience that watches television is vulnerable, because society has left no established moral guidelines, only a morass of exploitative manoeuvres. Without a moral compass, people are more likely to swallow irrational beliefs and succumb to demagoguery. The result is an abundance of primitive beliefs, charlatanism, mysticism, prejudice, superstition, old wives' tales, folk medicine – echoes from Russia's ancient peasant and pagan roots which Putin's return to the values of tsarism have helped to legitimise. This has had consequences on the pursuit of inquiry and the standard of scholarship.

The ironic saying that Russia has an 'unpredictable past' continues today in the rewriting of history. As the Putin regime's nationalist ideology looks back to earlier centuries for legitimacy, a school of pseudo-historians has sprung up to reinvent history in a way that suits their imperialist fantasies. By mixing reality, myth and legend, this alternative history makes bold claims. It argues that the Mongols did not invade Russia, that Genghis Khan was a blond, that Russians were the Aryan progenitors of world civilisation and much else. Konstantin Sheiko's fascinating study of these writers and academics, whom he sees as searching for an identity that will make up for superpower humiliation, explains the process as steps in the transition from empire to nation state. Conventional historians, observing the enormous sales of these pseudo-histories, are uncertain whether to regard their authors as 'post-modern clowns or dangerous ethno-nationalists'.[36] Many critics are worried by the similarities to the Nazi regime in its run-up to power: humiliation at the loss of status, the embellishing of legends to pump up national pride and the focus on ethnic rather than civic concerns.

The Putin regime's endorsement of 'make-believe' history can be seen in the controversial appointment in 2012 of another fantasist historian, Vitaly Medinsky, as Minister for Culture. Medinsky became known as a popular author of books which alleged that negative myths about Russia – drunkenness, laziness, brutality, bad roads – were all European inventions to demonise his country and belittle its imperial greatness. He has claimed that Russians have an extra chromosome without which they could not have withstood the tragedy of their history in the last century.[37] Evidence is not Medinsky's strong point. Since becoming a minister he has claimed that the Soviet Union never occupied the Baltic states but only 'incorporated' them; that an infamous picture of a Nazi–Soviet military parade in Poland in 1939 was 'photoshopped' and that anti-Semitic pogroms in tsarist Russia have been 'greatly exaggerated'.[38] The Second World War historian Mark Solonin likens him to Goebbels and calls his appointment an insult to Russia's rich cultural heritage.

As it turns out Medinsky, with his three academic degrees, is a plagiarist. The website 'Dissernet', run by a group of journalists and lecturers who check for academic fraud and plagiarism, has found chunks of plagiarised texts in his dissertations.[39] Perhaps that is not a cause for resignation, since Putin has also been outed for plagiarism.[40] The use of plagiarism and the ghost-writing of dissertations and articles for money is widespread; another lie, another disguise along the way.

The Soviet Union had always considered winning at the Olympics and international championships a demonstration of the superiority of the Soviet state. With a sports-loving macho president eager to promote a bellicose nationalism, the most expensive ever Sochi Olympics 2014 was designed to show Russian muscle to the world, success guaranteed through the tried-and-tested method of cheating the system. Just as elections have to be rigged so that the right candidate is chosen, athletes need to be doped not to embarrass the country's presumptions. It was the unprecedented scale of the cover-up revealed just before the 2016 Rio Olympics and the systemic nature of the doping that shocked the world, exposed as 'state sponsored', controlled and enforced by the Russian sports ministry, the FSB, sports organisations, coaches and athletes involving hundreds of 'disappeared positives' and intricate ways to avoid detection. With lying and cheating revealed as a norm of the Russian sports world, the individual who wishes to win honestly is blackmailed into remaining silent by collective rules and the common sneer of, why, are you so special?

III The lies of censorship

One of the big lies under Soviet censorship was that there was no censorship. The organ of censorship, Glavlit, which lasted from 1922 until 1991, referred to the main administration for safeguarding military and state secrets, although its real function was political censorship. Its full name changed many times, but the word censorship was never employed. Nor did a 'censor' exist: he was referred to as an 'editor'. When I spoke to the deputy head of Glavlit, Nikolai Glazatov, in 1989 when the body was already on its last legs, he insisted that the word editor was the correct usage: 'even formally it was not censorship, because a censor controls ideas and thoughts and we didn't do that'. I asked him why then did children's books have to go through Glavlit, and he replied: 'in principle, there could be something about the Soviet army in them'.

Censorship was implemented at every step before the advent of *perestroika*. Nothing could be published in the Soviet Union without having first gone through Glavlit, not even vodka labels. The list of classified information called the Index (the same name given to the list of heretical books promulgated by Rome during the Inquisition) changed and expanded constantly, but it was never published in the press because officially it did not exist. Journalist Leonid Finkelstein revealed in the 1970s that as far as he knew one rule had never been violated: 'under no circumstances may there be any direct contact between the censor and the author … the rules of the game are such that the author is even supposed not to know that his work is censored'.[41] A censor sat in every outlet; he dealt with the editor or the 'responsible' assistant, and in a newspaper the presses rolled only after he had given his personal stamp of approval, which appeared as a letter and number somewhere in the newspaper or magazine.

As what was forbidden was not readily known, the area of censorship was made incomparably larger as journalists had to give a wide berth to any sensitive topic. The 'internal censor' was often harsher in anticipating problems than the external one. There were many examples of this under Soviet self-censorship, as in the case in 1981, for example, when the editor of *Izvestiya* was too scared to report a large earthquake in Central Asia because it might distract from the party congress that was taking place at the same time, even though the item had been passed by a censor at TASS, the Kremlin's wire agency.

Under the Putin regime, self-censorship has covered up the deception that enables officials to proclaim that censorship does not exist. Self-censorship is prior restraint by intuition. There is no need to block out words on paper physically. In the Soviet Union everyone in the industry knew very well what they could and could not say without being told, says Vladimir Pozner. 'It was a built-in reflex. So today there is a sense, something in the air, that tells you "Well, better not touch this subject". It is like a Pavlovian reflex, a form of self-preservation'.[42] The darling of Yeltsin-era news, Svetlana Sorokina, who has refused to work on mainstream television since 2006, describes how her comment in a programme on conscription, that she was happy she had a daughter and not a son, was cut. She asked the editor if he had been told to do so. He replied: 'Why wait for an instruction?'.[43]

There are many ways of getting the same results as censorship without having to change the Constitution's article prohibiting it: weekly discussions

TV executives and editors have with Putin's administration to receive instructions, the old Soviet use of the 'telephone law' (the practice of important officials ringing editors with demands of what should or should not be reported), libel suits, changes in legislation, excessive fines and the ubiquitous 'stop-lists' that everyone knows about but few have seen. Then there are all the forms of physical threat and danger, discussed in Chapter 3. Did Soviet censorship differ substantially from what is taking place today? One-time *Izvestiya* investigative journalist Andrei Illesh believed it to be different:

> What we have is not censorship but prostitution. These are different things. Soviet censorship … was tied to state secrets, even though the secrecy was catastrophically exaggerated … Today the taboos … are completely unjustified, dependent only on the interests of certain clans, and money – crazy money. This is not censorship but a distorted version of the Soviet 'telephone law'.[44]

Propaganda was also taught differently to journalists in the Soviet period. Prominent blogger Andrei Malgin says that when he was a journalism student in Moscow and Warsaw in the 1970s, propaganda was described as a glass half-empty or half-full. Both statements are true but they serve opposing propaganda purposes: one is made to be negative and the other optimistic. The authorities would interpret facts to suit their own purposes, but they did not necessarily lie, says Malgin. In his experience, having worked under four leaders from Brezhnev to Putin, 'this is the first time the authorities have lied so brazenly and shamelessly; they have truly reached a new low'.[45]

Malgin gives as an example the Malaysian airplane shot down over territory held by pro-Russian separatists in Eastern Ukraine in 2014. It was obviously an accident by the separatists and not deliberate, and they could have admitted as much. Malgin listed all the ridiculous lies Kremlin-controlled media preferred to invent rather than simply tell the truth:

> The plane was not shot down at all, but fell out of the sky by itself; a bomb exploded aboard the plane; the plane was hit by a Ukrainian missile fired from the ground; a Ukrainian air force fighter pursued and then attacked the plane; the US shot down the plane in order to damage Russia's reputation; no living people were aboard the plane as it flew on autopilot from Amsterdam, where it had been pre-loaded with 'rotting corpses'.[46]

Given the role played by lying in Russia's political history, we should not expect that even the most absurd lies will embarrass Putin or those who represent the regime. The purveyor of lies does not necessarily expect to be believed, but nor does he expect his listener to expose him. The game involves certain rituals, like the bargaining that is expected to take place in the bazaars of certain countries or the acrobatics conducted to avoid a person losing face. To foreigners who don't play the game, the last resort for Putin and his officials is to say that the lie is justified anyway, because of the inherent rightness of their cause – the old Soviet justification of ends over means. Habituated to the existence of one truth, they do not sense bigotry and dogma. The other resort is to accuse the opposing side of having been equally culpable at some time in history – the Soviet propagandist's technique of 'whataboutism', which avoids answering the question by asking another question, that is either irrelevant or *ad hominem*.

The most important factor for the regime is that the majority of viewers who watch television believe these lies or are collectively stirred by them even if they don't fully believe them. The lies need not be clever: after all, they don't fool the western audience. The Russian audience appears to be gullible, but it might be better to say it is cautious, inured to distortions of reality after a legacy of seventy years of lies, unverifiable information and isolation from the outside world. The theatre taking place is not only in the tableau of lies, but in the theatregoer, who knows he or she must respond 'with delicate reciprocity', as Dostoyevsky has already told us. Without psychological studies it is hard to tell what emotions and thoughts are running through the viewers' mind, but it might be a combination of pride, wishful thinking, anxiety, pleasure – and what Russians call 'fear in the genes'. The Russian public is volatile and unpredictable and rulers fear its nihilism precisely because its beliefs and emotions are not stable. Nor are the emotions of the propagandist, morphing, as we have seen, from one belief system to another. The issue of truth in a system of enforced lies will, by its very nature, be elusive and ambivalent.

Notes

1 *Journey for Our Time: The Journals of the Marquis de Custine, Russia 1839*, London: Phoenix Press, 2003, p. 108.
2 *Parting Shots: The Undiplomatic Final Words of Our Departing Ambassadors*, Matthew Parris and Andrew Bryson, London: Viking/Penguin, 2011 p. 170.
3 'Homo Praevaricatus: Russian Doublethink', *Contemporary Russian Politics: A Reader*, Archie Brown (ed.), Oxford: Oxford University Press, 2001, pp. 314, 313.
4 Ekho Moskvy, 27 February 2015. https://www.youtube.com/watch?v=ve6QBGB gUGQ (accessed 23 November 2015).
5 Vladimir Pribylovsky, *Chistka Vladimira Putina: Kto byvaet, a kto ostaetsya?* Algoritm Moskva, 2013 p.176
6 First Channel, 13 October 2004. www.1tv.ru/news/polit/73115 (accessed 23 November 2015).
7 First Channel, 12 July 2014. www.youtube.com/watch?v=rSCZQ0-V480 (accessed 23 November 2015).
8 Dozhd' TV, 15 July 2014. http://tvrain.ru/articles/zamministra_svjazi_aleksej_volin_ o_raspjatom_malchike_nepatriotichnyh_smi_i_samom_vlijatelnom_cheloveke_v_r ossijskih_media-372463/ (accessed 23 November 2015).
9 *Sibnovosti.ru*, 9 February 2013. http://fed.sibnovosti.ru/society/224089-vystuplenie-zamministra-svyazi-alekseya-volina-na-zhurfake-mgu-vyzvalo-skandal (accessed 23 November 2015).

10 'Russian cynicism: symptom of a stagnant society', *Open Democracy*, 22 October 2013. www.opendemocracy.net/od-russia/lev-gudkov/russian-cynicism-symptom-of-stagnant-society (accessed 23 November 2015).

11 See www.stopfake.org; some others include: http://maidantranslations.com/2014/07/03/enough-of-your-lies-20-of-the-most-disgraceful-russian-media-lies-about-the-events-in-eastern-ukraine/; www.kyivpost.com/content/ukraine/most-freakish-russian-lies-about-ukraine-now-listed-on-facebook-376725.html (accessed 23 November 2015).

12 *Prava cheloveka v Rossii*, 25 February 2008. www.hro.org/node/1293 (accessed 23 November 2015).

13 *Nezavisimaya gazeta*, 11 April 2007.

14 Dostoyevsky, 'Nechto o vranye', *Dnevnik Pisatelya: Polnoe Sobranie Sochinenii v tridtsati tomakh*, tom 21, 'Izdatelstvo 'Nauka', Leningrad, 1980, pp. 120–121.

15 *Nezavisimaya gazeta*, 2007.

16 'Akunin–Navalny interview', 11 January 2012. www.opendemocracy.net/print/63604 (accessed 23 November 2015).

17 Dostoyevsky, 'Nechto o vranye', pp. 117–25.

18 N. V. Gogol, *Revizor*, Letchworth: Bradda Books, 1964, p. 37.

19 Marquis de Custine, *Journey for Our Time*, p. 85.

20 Tai Adelaja, 'See-through make-believe' *Russia Profile*, 28 April 2011.

21 *Problems of Communism*, March 1962, p. 50.

22 Ibid., p. 53.

23 'Chelovek iz televizora', *Ekho Moskvy*, 17 May 2014. www.echo.msk.ru/programs/persontv/1321532-echo/#element-text (accessed 23 November 2015).

24 *Stalin: New Biography of a Dictator*, trans. Nora Seligman Favorov, New Haven, CT and London: Yale University Press, 2015, p. 38.

25 'Russia's election protests and the Soviet past', *Newsweek*, 19 December 2011. www.newsweek.com/robert-conquest-russias-election-protests-and-soviet-past-65957 (accessed 23 November 2015).

26 See David King, *The Commissar Vanishes: The Falsification of Photographs and Art in Stalin's Russia*, New York: An Owl Book, 1997.

27 Elena Ryumina, 'Victory real, but clouded in myth', *Moscow Times*, 12 May 2000.

28 'Menya vsegda vygonyali za delo', *Teleradio-Efir, Mezhdunarodnyi zhurnal*, 1, 1993, p.3.

29 'Aaron Trehub', Gorbachev meets Soviet writers: a *samizdat* account', RFERL, RL Research 399/86, 23 October 1986.

30 *Open Democracy*, 16 December 2008 www.opendemocracy.net/russia/article/The-Embrace-of-Stalinism (accessed 23 November 2015).

31 'Selection of facts with a certain slant', *Literaturnaya gazeta*, 24 September 1986, translated in SWB SU/8374/C/1 (A1, B), 26 September 1986.

32 Moscow Radio First Programme, 17 November 1986.

33 Vitaly Korotich, *Ot pervogo litsa*, Khar'kov 'Folio', Moskva 'ACT', 2000, p. 54.

34 'Fenomen Poznera', *Novaya gazeta*, 15–17 May 2006.

35 Jonathan Earle, 'United Russia deputy upbraids TV host', *Moscow Times*, 31 October 2012. www.themoscowtimes.com/news/article/united-russia-deputy-upbraids-tv-host/470796.html#ixzz2B0uYv7LA (accessed 23 November 2015).

36 Konstantin Sheiko, in collaboration with Stephen Brown, *Nationalist Imaginings of the Russian Past: Anotolii Fomenko and the Rise of Alternative History in Post-Communist Russia*, Stuttgart: Ibidem-Verlag, 2009, p. 17.

37 *BBC Russkaya sluzhba*, 21 January 2013. www.bbc.co.uk/russian/rolling_news/2013/01/130121_rn_medinsky_usa_interview.shtml

38 Tom Balmforth, 'Profile: Vladimir Medinsky, Russia's controversial new Culture Minister', *RFE/RL*, 3 June 2012. www.rferl.org/content/russia-profile-culture-minister-vladimir-medinsky/24602133.html (accessed 23 November 2015).

39 Sergei Parkhomenko, 'Delo Medinskogo, Zashchitit' nachal'nika okazalos' nechem', 26 May 2014. www.dissernet.org/publications/nothing-to-protect.htm (accessed 23 November 2015).

40 Igor Danchenko and Clifford Gaddy, *The Mystery of Vladimir Putin's Dissertation*, Washington, DC: Brookings Institution. www.brookings.edu/~/media/events/2006/3/30putin%20dissertation/putin%20dissertation%20event%20remarks.pdf (accessed 23 November 2015).

41 *The Soviet Censorship*, Martin Dewhirst and Robert Farrell (eds), Metuchen, NJ: Scarecrow Press, 1973, p. 54, fn. 89.

42 Peter Lavelle, 'Present perfect on Russia's media and Putin's politics', *National Interest*, 30 June 2004. http://nationalinterest.org/article/interview-with-vladimir-posner-present-perfect-on-russias-media-and-putins-polit-2699 (accessed 23 November 2015)

43 Arkady Ostrovsky, 'From freedom a return to pliant propaganda', *Financial Times*, 27 June 2006.

44 'Mne stalo interesno, smogu li ya protivostoyat' gigantskoi sisteme strany, ' 19 November, 2011. http://slon.ru/russia/mne_stalo_interesno_smogu_li_ya_protivostoyat_gigantskoy_sisteme_strany-607571.xhtml (accessed 23 November 2015).

45 'Putin's media lives in an alternate reality', *Moscow Times*, 30 July 2014. www.themoscowtimes.com/opinion/article/putins-media-lives-in-an-alternate-reality/504339.html (accessed 23 November 2015).

46 Ibid.

Part 2

5   The Gorbachev era: *glasnost*

> We are for *glasnost* without reservations or limitations, but for *glasnost* in the interests of socialism.
>
> (Gorbachev, 13 January 1988)

I The 'Gorby' phenomenon

Literally, *glasnost* means making things public. It is an old Russian word from *glas* meaning 'voice' and came to be used for Gorbachev's policy of loosening up the severe controls over the dissemination of information. Making things public has had different impacts in Russia's history. For Herzen in the nineteenth century the freedom to publish his accusations against the abuses of absolutist power from his émigré refuge in London was vital to winning the cause of emancipating the serfs. The freedom to 'make public' went along with 'being heard'. Herzen's ringing denunciations from his newspaper *Kolokol* ('The Bell') caused widespread panic among officials at home and even the tsar learned of scandals from Herzen's press. Today we can no longer expect that making a scandal public will provoke any reaction in Russia. But when Gorbachev came to power after three-quarters of a century of Soviet repression, even snippets of information were received voraciously.

Glasnost had a spellbinding effect on the Soviet Union and the world. For Gorbachev, it was the key to reforming the Soviet system and reviving an economy that he revealed was in a 'pre-crisis situation' after years of Soviet misrule. It was not intended to bestow greater freedom of speech as a concession to liberal democracy, but to breathe new life into the Soviet model of socialist development. By introducing what he called the 'human factor' he hoped to persuade ordinary people to participate in his reforms. He could not count on them if they were demoralised and discontented, nor could he expect improved labour productivity or discipline in the workplace. 'Wide-ranging, up-to-date, frank information is a testimony of trust in people, respect for their reason, feelings and capacity to work things out for themselves. *Glasnost* in the work of party and state organs is an effective means of struggling against bureaucratic distortions', he said.[1] *Glasnost* would help regain the party's authority based not on force but on consent, although Gorbachev did not realise how low the party's credibility was.

In the first years of *perestroika, glasnost* was linked to the policy of 'acceleration' (*uskoreniye*), to make the economy more efficient. To do this required eliminating the malpractices that had thrived under the Brezhnev system, where it was said that to fulfil the Five Year Plan was less important than to create the appearance of having over-fulfilled it. It was necessary to expose the rot in the system and tackle bureaucratic misdeeds, which consisted of a long list of sins: paper-shuffling, narrow departmentalism, inflated reporting, false accounting, fraud, absenteeism, wastefulness, window-dressing, bribery, etc. Media outlets were the most effective way of communicating ideological messages and television would put Gorbachev in touch with over 90 per cent of the population. Through the media he could appeal directly to the public, bypassing the resistance to change from bureaucracies and ministries, whose numbers would be reduced by reform. *Pravda*'s leader of 27 March 1985 puts it clearly: 'our press, television and radio are the instruments of *glasnost* and an important channel of information on the work of party, state and public organisations'.

At first, however, journalists had to be spurred on to embrace *glasnost* and overcome their well-founded in-built caution of a system that had punished initiative. In the first year, attempts at more openness had to be orchestrated by the party in leading articles in *Pravda*. But it was already clear that ostentatious photographs of the leader in the press and standard protocol appearances would not be taking place. Rumours made the rounds that Gorbachev had informed the editor of *Pravda* that he was no longer to be quoted simply to add weight to an important article; they could quote Lenin or Marx instead. The same story had been told of Andropov. It seemed to be the Kremlin's first stab at light-hearted public relations. In fact, neither the Kremlin, nor the media were clear about how to manage the entry of *glasnost*. A fairly unusual two-day tour Gorbachev made of factories and shops in Moscow, where he first rubbed shoulders with workers and ordinary people was a missed photo opportunity. To emphasise a new stage of history, the nation had to see Gorbachev behave in a different light.

This happened dramatically during Gorbachev's visit to Leningrad in May, two months after coming to power. It was here that his famous walkabout with the people took place, a thrilling experience for Soviet citizens who had become accustomed to inaccessible, geriatric leaders. It had been said that Gromyko, the 75-year-old master of Soviet diplomacy nicknamed 'Mr Nyet' ('Mr No') by the West, had not stepped out of his car to walk the streets of any city for 40 years. Here was Gorbachev, breaking away from his schedule, allowing himself to be surrounded by crowds, shaking hands with war veterans, smiling and exchanging comments. As an image-making exercise, the Leningrad tour had an enormous impact, but media chiefs were still hesitant: the walkabout received only a few minutes on television (but that was enough to dazzle viewers), while *Pravda* carried a dry summary of the three-day event. The real sensation came three days later when permission finally came from the Kremlin to broadcast Gorbachev's speech at the Smolny almost in full on television, so that viewers across the Soviet Union could see their new leader speaking with emotion, impromptu, and discussing problems with unusual frankness. This was to become Gorbachev's style: dynamic, spontaneous, open. It was in stark contrast with what had come before. Although Khrushchev had shown great gusto and energy with crowds, he was in power in the early days of television when only one in four people had television sets, while the last decade had only seen old and ailing general-secretaries unable to hold media attention. Gorbachev was aware of the power of television and the need for public relations, and his style promised to inject new life into news and current affairs.

To boost his reforms, Gorbachev brought friends and supporters into the top party hierarchy: Eduard Shevardnadze as Foreign Affairs minister; Aleksandr Yakovlev, known as the architect of *glasnost* and the person to whom editors could turn to most, heading the Central Committee Propaganda Department; and a few months later Boris Yeltsin, summoned from his post as First Party Secretary of the vast Sverdlovsk region in the Urals, to serve as Moscow city party boss. Reform was going slowly, mainly because appeals for greater freedom and initiative were bound up with demands for greater discipline and order. The unpopular anti-alcohol campaign was a case of the stick without the carrot. Based on an earlier Andropov disciplinarian programme which had the special support of Gorbachev's conservative second-in-command, Yegor Ligachev, himself a teetotaller, the campaign was run without subtlety and had disastrous consequences in practice. It led not to a decrease in work absenteeism but to a flourishing illicit trade in home-brewed liquor (*samogon*), and the destruction of vineyards in Moldavia and Georgia, causing unemployment and loss of revenue. The campaign bore all the hallmarks of bureaucratic indifference and lack of prior public consultation. As for *glasnost*, when *Pravda* took the bold step of publishing an article on party privileges and special elite shops for the *nomenklatura* in its issue of 13 February 1986, the paper immediately got into trouble. Entitled *Ochishcheniye* ('Cleansing'), using the device of readers' letters to criticise party privileges, it provoked heated debate within the party, engaging two sparring partners – Yeltsin, who claimed privileges were the cause of the party's decay, versus Ligachev, who publicly reprimanded the paper's editor and forced a public retraction. Ligachev was in no doubt about what *glasnost* really meant: 'All television and radio programmes must be subordinated to the single purpose of propaganda, explaining and putting party policy into practice. That is, they must be class oriented in essence'.[2]

The test case for *glasnost* came with Chernobyl on 26 April 1986. The instinctive Soviet reaction to major accidents had always been to conceal information; in fact, the first item on Glavlit's index of subjects for censorship was information about 'earthquakes, avalanches, landslides and other natural disasters on the territory of the USSR'.[3] Recent discussion in the press about such cover-ups had taken place after the earthquake that hit Leninabad at the end of 1985, and a letter writer caused public anger in pointing out that the Soviet press had reported the earthquake in Mexico in early 1986 in more detail than the earthquake in Tadzhikistan at about the same time.[4] Accidents which touched on human error were even more sensitive. Chernobyl elicited the expected response. No announcement was made for two days until Sweden's report that radioactive clouds were detected over the country. It was only on 28 April that the main news programme, *Vremya*, came out in its evening bulletin with a brief statement: 'An accident has taken place at the Chernobyl AES. One of the atomic reactors has been damaged. Measures are being taken to eliminate the consequences of the accident. Help is being given to the victims. A government commission has been established'. The world's worst nuclear disaster was reported in five short sentences. The report did not lead the news, but appeared as the seventh item.

Oddly enough, this was still a breakthrough. Once the accident was acknowledged, the story was followed up with video reports on the spot, aerial shots of the damaged reactor, critical commentary and human interest stories that had rarely featured on television. It allowed for the reporting of other accidents when they happened, such as the sinking soon afterwards of a passenger ship, the *Admiral Nakhimov*, due to criminal negligence. Chernobyl broke Soviet television's stereotype as a purveyor of good news. The Soviet reflex returned in Putin's accident-prone period in office, as the truth about each major accident or disaster was forced into the open only by persistent journalists or bloggers; while other accidents have not been reported at all.

'Us' and 'them'

Looking today at television's anti-western campaign, Russia's history begins to sound like a cracked record. Haven't we been through this before? In 1985 it was the other way round in the love–hate relationship as *perestroika* expressed the thrill of opening up to the West after decades of cold war hostilities. That was the exciting narrative conveyed by a sophisticated urban media, but it was a policy Gorbachev had to fight for against stubborn resistance from isolationist forces within the party and a suspicious public.

Perestroika brought Soviet citizens in touch with free speech western style. Its Soviet version, *glasnost*, was widening but Soviet journalists still knew instinctively when to stop. Therefore, they watched Gorbachev in Paris being grilled by foreign reporters on the persecution of political prisoners with amazement. No one expected anything other than Gorbachev's angry denials, the shock was in hearing him being questioned on human rights for the first time on their screens. Gorbachev's trips to Paris and the summits in Geneva and Reykjavik were relayed live so people could see for themselves Gorbachev's mesmerising impact on the West and the rise of the 'Gorby' phenomenon. They could also see Ronald Regan – the US president who had called the Soviet Union the 'evil empire' – and hear his New Year greetings to them in 1986 on Soviet television. On his visits abroad, Gorbachev included large numbers of people in his team – party intellectuals, writers, poets, academics – legitimising the exchange of information with western counterparts and the desire for 'mutual understanding'.

The breaking down of stereotypes between 'us' and 'them' took an innovative televisual form in more than 20 satellite links called 'space-bridges' between Soviet citizens and those of other countries. Much work and fanfare went into getting the ideological 'enemies' together. Sometimes participants in the shows were overly deferential, at other times sparks flew. The most interesting of the space-bridges were presented by US TV anchor Phil Donahue and the fluent English speaker Vladimir Pozner. In a Leningrad–Seattle space-bridge in 1986 there was this altercation:

DONAHUE: Why do 250,000 Jews want to emigrate from the Soviet Union?
POZNER: Where do you get that figure from? Have you carried out a referendum here or something? [*laughter in audience*]. Allow us to know better how many of us want to leave, or I will tell you now that 250,000 American Indians want to come to us ... surely you will not believe me?
[*applause in audience*][5]

There was the usual tit for tat, common in cold war sparring. There were complaints against Pozner for being either too pro- or too anti-American (the *Seattle Times* asking, 'Can we trust Pozner or anybody else to say what he or she truly believes ... if people on one side of the dialogue are not free to speak their minds, and simply echo government charges they may or may not believe?'),[6] while Donahue back home was being accused of being a 'red'. Despite these inevitable responses, the face-to-face contacts had a humanising effect, especially in the less political shows. Donahue and Pozner became close friends and presented a radio show together in the USA in the 1990s. At an anniversary show on television to celebrate the space-bridges ten years later, Pozner, when his reply to Donahue's question on Jewish refuseniks was played back, winced and responded that he was glad he had make-up on, 'so you can't see me blush' – 'we all knew what we could and couldn't say, it was an amazing game we played'.[7]

Tons of letters from Soviet viewers bombarded the media after the space-bridges with the USA. Pozner was shocked by the anti-Americanism, but it was an apt reminder that decades of cold war hostility could not simply vanish. One particularly virulent letter published in *Izvestiya* from a Leningrader about 'this filthy anti-Soviet spectacle' accused Donahue of being an 'ideological wrecker', assumed Pozner had got his job through cronyism, and expressed outrage that Soviet television was providing a sympathetic venue for 'an imperialist country, surrounded and nurtured by the country's ruling power of darkness, in the spirit of shameless anti-Sovietism and inhumanity, of animal hatred of all things Russian'.[8]

A survey of the letters revealed that many viewers showed double standards, separating what was for domestic consumption and what for export. A Soviet participant on the show, who revealed she had been on the waiting list for an apartment for ten years, got this response from an irate letter writer: 'Let her wait for another 100 years and may she rot in hell for telling that to an American. In our country everyone lives in good apartments'. The survey concluded that 'the authors of these letters are in favour of lying on television, they are against telling the truth to an American or to an American audience'. The main complaint was 'why did they tell him [Donahue] the truth?'.[9] Letter writers were also shocked by Donahue questioning people about their private lives, which they were not used to, on topics such as dating, teenage pregnancies, sex. The famous retort about sex came from one woman in the studio audience who replied: 'We have no sex'. The poor woman has been dogged ever since by this reply: she had meant to add 'on television'. The letters showed it was considered a matter of nationalism and pride not to wash one's dirty linen in public.

I asked Pozner a few years later what he thought was the main achievement of the space-bridges:

> We looked at the mirror and we didn't like our faces. We saw ourselves as dishonest, closed, uptight, defensive ... to my knowledge it was the first time the nation disliked itself. The other achievement was that for the first time they heard average, ordinary Americans expressing their prejudices, fears and dislike of the Soviet Union ... they began to see more realistically what Americans thought about them and they saw that Americans could criticise their own government and way of life but also be supportive.[10]

Another culture shock was the live interview with UK Prime Minister Margaret Thatcher on Soviet television on 31 March 1987, which caused a sensation and much soul-searching. In true combative form, Mrs Thatcher easily got the upper hand on her three top Soviet interviewers and provoked a crisis of confidence at the inexperience of Soviet journalists in handling western debating methods. For 50 minutes Thatcher harangued her interviewers, revealing sensitive issues about Soviet military installations (western diplomats were astonished at her boldness), defending the concept of nuclear deterrence, preaching the values of the parliamentary system, and discussing her work schedule. The reputation of the Iron Lady has never diminished in Russia.

At the time, one of the interviewers, Vladimir Simonov, a *Novosti* correspondent who had worked in Britain and the USA, was asked why Soviet journalists looked, in the words of one letter writer, like 'country chess players against Kasparov'. Thousands had written in with angry complaints: why was a propagandist for world imperialism given an open platform? Why were Soviet journalists so rude, interrupting a prime minister and a woman? Simonov tried to explain his position on an evening chat show:

Did the feeling of failure come from the fact that no international affairs lecturer stepped forward with his briefcase and pointer to explain: this point that Mrs. Thatcher made was bad; this point was good?[11]

It was time, Simonov insisted, to listen to what people had to say in an interview, even if you didn't agree with them. He admitted that it had been common practice to take an interview simply as a ploy to reject that person's view. The reason for an interview with Ronald Reagan, which had recently been published in *Izvestiya*, had been taken to insert an ideological critique, which was as long as the interview itself.

'No taboos'

The first two years of *perestroika* did not produce the economic acceleration Gorbachev had anticipated and he now turned to a radical transformation of the political system. In this second phase of *perestroika* the concepts of *glasnost* and democratisation (*demokratizatsiya*) dominated. Real change to the policy of *glasnost* came in a sudden rush, pegged to the 28–29 January 1987 party plenum at which Gorbachev pushed through ideas astonishing for the times of a choice of candidates at elections and secret ballots for party officials. We now know that the plenum was postponed three times and Gorbachev threatened resignation before he could get the support he needed. In the six weeks before the plenum, a TV watcher could guess that *glasnost* had been given the green light, as breaking news came thick and fast. TV's slogan was 'no more taboos'.

On 8 December 1986 on the anniversary of Brezhnev's birthday, the first critical article on him and the era that came to be defined as one of 'stagnation' (*zastoy*) appeared in *Pravda*; on 16 December, Dinmukhamed Kunayev, First Secretary of Kazakhstan and Brezhnev's old crony was released from his post; on 19 December, Andrei Sakharov was given permission to return to Moscow after seven years of internal exile in Gorky. About 140 dissidents convicted under Article 190 for anti-Soviet propaganda were pardoned, but only in exchange for agreeing not to seek rehabilitation or to engage in political activism, which some of the famous imprisoned dissidents refused to do and remained in jail longer. On 13 January 1987, jamming of the BBC that had taken place on and off for 40 years came to an end.[12] In the literary arena surprising events were also taking place that month: a decision was made to turn Pasternak's home in Peredelkino into a museum, acknowledging the petitions of a campaign that had been going on for a long time; appeals were heard to establish Bulgakov's flat in Moscow as a museum; the conservative head of Goskino for 21 years was finally retired, releasing the creative energies of film-makers in Dom Kino and Goskino, who were already among the most committed supporters of reform. Their immediate input was to write an homage to film director Andrei Tarkovsky, who had died in emigration in Paris; while Tengiz Abuladze's controversial film on tyranny and

Stalinism, *Pokayaniye* ('Repentance') opened in Moscow on the final day of the plenum.

For the media, there was the unprecedented Verkhin case when journalists took on the KGB and won. Viktor Verkhin, editor of the Ukrainian newspaper *Sovetsky Shaktyor* ('Soviet Miner') had exposed poor safety conditions for miners in the Donetsk region, which led to his uncovering corruption among law-enforcement officers in Voroshilovgrad. He was imprisoned for 13 days on trumped-up charges and tortured, while two friends who refused to testify against him were also abused and charged. Campaigning journalists in *Pravda* fought the case, compiling a dossier which succeeded not only in having a senior KGB official and several prosecutors sacked, but in getting a public apology out of KGB chief Chebrikov, published in *Pravda*. Two earlier cases of harassment against journalists had also been exposed: in February 1986 the Party Central Committee reprimanded the Ministries of Aviation and River Transport for bullying journalists who had criticised delays in building projects; and in June that year *Pravda* exposed local party officials in Strugi-Krasnyye for having copies of a local newspaper burned, because it had accused them of giving the town a cosmetic clean-up specially to impress a visiting government delegation. The uniqueness of the Verkhin case was that it was the first public exposé of KGB malpractice. Although the Verkhin dossier was never published (Verkhin died soon after from the consequences of his imprisonment), and no further reporting of KGB abuse followed, these cases indicated that the KGB and ministers could no longer be certain of impunity.

Glasnost was generally understood to mean greater autonomy and independence for the media. When the TV programme *Vzglyad* conducted a vox pop to see what people on the streets meant by *glasnost*, a young man put it succinctly: 'when people say what they want and remain alive' (5.5.1989). As political change speeded up after the January plenum *glasnost* began to be interpreted in a wider context. Jurists who had been asked by the Kremlin to draft a law on *glasnost* in 1987, which was never completed, planned to incorporate principles such as: open political activity; information to citizens to enable them to discuss and make decisions on matters of state and society; access to official organisations; and research into public opinion before decision-making.[13]

Gorbachev realised that if the media were to win people's confidence, they had to be shown to be telling the truth. In a speech to editors and broadcasters he admitted the problem: 'When you and I tried to deck everything in rosy colours the people could see through it all. They lost interest in the press and public activity, they felt degraded and insulted by being palmed off with a fake'.[14] After the plenum, those who had followed a wait-and-see policy felt more confident in Gorbachev's commitment to change. The media began to act not as anonymous vehicles for party instructions but as outlets with personalities and voices, some of which became identified as champions of Gorbachev's reforms.

Vitaly Korotich: Ogonyok

The most prominent flagships of *perestroika* were Vitaly Korotich's *Ogonyok* ('Little Flame') and Yegor Yakovlev's *Moskovskiye novosti* ('Moscow News'). These two weeklies set the pace for *glasnost*, taking Gorbachev's words literally, when he had said at the end of 1986 while talking to foreign journalists that there would be no more censorship. Two areas received most attention. First, the filling in of 'blank spots' (*belyye pyatna*), mainly a reference to the topic of Stalin and the purges, while not daring yet to touch on Lenin's role in the Revolution; in fact, the aim was to return to Leninist norms of public life. Second, issues that the media had been banned from divulging: organised crime, bribery, corruption, the sorry state of healthcare and education, the prevalence of drug use and Aids, and statistics on social issues. Gorbachev had personally asked Korotich to take over the reins at *Ogonyok*, a glossy magazine specialising in photojournalism, and it was there that sensational photos were published: troops in Afghanistan and the call for them to return home; and the photo that shocked the nation of a line of skeletons lying where they had been buried in shallow graves unearthed in the woods near Kuropaty in Belorussia. The public was used to seeing such atrocities documenting Nazi crimes, but these were victims shot by Stalin's secret police and there was evidence of many more graves. The magazine had many 'firsts' to its name, including literary excerpts from previously banned classics by Pasternak, Solzhenitsyn, Nabokov and Gumilyov.

A sensation was *Ogonyok*'s publication about corruption in high places, which led to the conviction of Brezhnev's son-in-law, Yury Churbanov. Korotich published an article entitled 'Confrontation',[15] which no other paper would touch, by two investigators from the USSR General Prosecutor's office, Telman Gdlyan and Nikolai Ivanov, and turned them into heroes, implacable in their pursuit of justice (although it was also alleged they had used unlawful methods to extract information). The two men were part of a team investigating the long-standing Uzbek affair of fraud and bribery in the cotton industry, involving millions of dollars, diamonds and jewels with links back to Moscow. 'No one wrote about such things at the time, high-ranking officials were above criticism and above suspicion', says Korotich. After the publication, Korotich added flames to the fire by agreeing to help Gdlyan and Ivanov with four cases of bribe-taking in the Party Central Committee, which were being blocked. The General Prosecutor's office could get nowhere because of a catch-22: Central Committee members could not be interrogated by prosecutors without permission from other members of the Central Committee, which members never gave. The idea was to bypass this process by appealing directly to Gorbachev during the proceedings of the 19th Party Conference. As a delegate to the conference, Korotich brought an envelope with the incriminating documents and in full view of members in the hall, handing the envelope to Gorbachev, he announced that there were bribe-takers sitting in their midst. The scandal was reported around the world. 'I wonder how many people watching in the hall wanted to kill me. Not a few, I think', Korotich says.

He published many more exposés of party corruption and organised crime in *Ogonyok* and was criticised for what his enemies called muckraking and sensation-seeking. 'We write about things that others are scared to write about ... how democracy was crushed after the revolution, how nationalities were destroyed, we try to struggle against injustice ... it's terrible when the truth becomes sensational', he told me. His scoops earned him many threats, but he remained buoyant: 'I can't both be Jewish and a fascist SS member', he complained about his enraged critics.[16]

Yegor Yakovlev: Moskovskiye novosti

Yakovlev set out to create a paper that would campaign for reform and independent thinking. Grigory Yavlinsky said of him after his death in 2005 that he had produced the 'first free newspaper since 1917'. All the issues and conflicts of *perestroika* can be seen by leafing through the pages of *Moskovskiye novosti*. Most of the progressive-minded intellectuals of the day wrote for it. Yakovlev was undoubtedly one of Russia's great newspaper editors, not only of the *glasnost* period but through to the post-communist era. Not only did he seize the moment when freedom was on offer, he understood the value of journalistic solidarity and had the organisational skills to bring the fragmented and individualistic journalist community together on many occasions to safeguard the media's newly found rights.

As editor of *Moskovskiye novosti* from 1986 to 1991, he turned its tiny circulation of 35,000 – it had been a tedious propaganda sheet for tourists, coming out in eight foreign languages, to be found lying abandoned in hotels – to 250,000 in the Russian edition; and it would have been more had the authorities allowed it to expand. On Wednesdays, when it came out, long queues of people would form to buy a copy or, as most of the copies sold out, read its pages spread out in glass boxes on the walls outside the editorial offices on Pushkin Square, in the heart of Moscow. On that January in 1987 when *glasnost* received its much needed boost from above, *Moskovskiye novosti*'s contribution was to remind the public of the once-secret document of Lenin's last testament with its disparaging remarks about Stalin. But every issue of the paper was an eye-opener – Soviet myths destroyed, questions of principle and ethics debated, issues of the day analysed from different perspectives, articles still memorable for opening up Soviet life, such as Yevgeniya Albats's harrowing account of women's experiences of giving birth in Soviet hospitals (17 July 1988 and 1 January 1989).

When I spoke to Yakovlev in his office in August 1989, he described *Moskovskiye novosti* as the light cavalry – 'we may not dig deep, but we are the first to raise issues'. He felt the task before him was intimidating, there was so much to learn: 'You can't go to bed a mute and wake up talking', he said.

'The first time we reported a train crash, it seemed so bold that we didn't think there was anywhere further to go'.

A passionate supporter of Gorbachev's *perestroika*, Yavkovlev was not averse to criticising Gorbachev or Yeltsin when he felt they were out of step. When major obstacles were raised against free speech, Yakovlev organised counter-responses: he was the first editor to respond in protest to Nina Andreyeva's letter; he flew to Tbilisi to investigate the massacre when government reports were unreliable; his board of directors at *Moskovskiye novosti* came out with the most damning response against Gorbachev to the bloodshed at the storming of the TV centre in Vilnius and, famously, he gathered liberal editors to form a paper for 'everybody' (*Obshchaya gazeta*), in response to the curfew against the press and electronic media during the coup. He resuscitated this emergency paper seven times during periods of crisis; the last, in 2001, to protest against Putin's victimisation of the independent television channel, NTV, which he called 'simple banditry'.

Yakovlev was alert to the responsibilities that came with greater freedom of speech. Earlier he had disagreed with Gorbachev's logic that the full reporting of ethnic conflicts, which had broken out in many areas of the Soviet Union, would be inflammatory and make the situation worse. Unlike many liberal journalists, he saw the need for tolerance and disagreed with colleagues becoming 'hysterical' whenever they came up against opposition. In dealing with the nationalist anti-Semitic group Pamyat ('Memory') he wrote:

> A few years ago I would not have objected if those people had been sent to Siberia to hold their meetings. Now I understand that if the Pamyat Society is sent to Siberia, eventually I'll be on my way there, too. Not everybody thinks this way ... The problem is, we just aren't used to normal debate.[17]

Always an independent figure, he rejected the tendency among his liberal colleagues to conform. In the 1996 elections when they campaigned almost en masse for the ailing Yeltsin out of fear of the communists returning to power, he chose to push forward Grigory Yavlinsky of the liberal democratic Yabloko party, as an alternative democratic candidate. For a while after the coup he headed Gosteleradio, where his first act was to throw out a number of KGB operatives embedded in the staff. Later, he turned *Obshchaya gazeta* into a regular weekly broadsheet, making it one of the most authoritative newspapers of the 1990s. Illness made him sell the paper in 2002. The oligarch who bought it exemplified the brash Putin years – the whole staff was sacked and the paper killed off, presumably as an offering to Putin to rid him of an inconvenience.

Yakovlev had always been interested in the problems of journalism. He had edited the professional magazine for journalists, *Zhurnalist*, and in 1991 he founded the first media freedom watchdog in Russia, the Glasnost Defence Foundation, which continues as one of the toughest and longest-standing

NGOs under Aleksei Simonov – today, in Putin's regime, struggling under the label of 'foreign agent'. The lessons Yakovlev had learned from the failure of Khrushchev's 'thaw' kept him on the alert. He was not an easy editor and had a foul temper, as his staff testify. It was no doubt his recalcitrance which had him sacked from many prestigious jobs during the Brezhnev years, but his friends usually found him somewhere else to work, even if it meant sending him to Czechoslovakia several times. A Marxist-Leninist thinker, he wrote numerous books on the subject and was one of the script-writers of a TV series about Lenin whose works, he said, he had been studying for 20 years. It was only after the Vilnius tragedy in 1991, when he predicted the end for Gorbachev, that he tore up his Communist Party card.

The Nina Andreyeva letter

The strength of the conservative backlash to Gorbachev's reforms became apparent in the Nina Andreyeva affair of 1988. It was only a mini coup or what Aleksandr Yakovlev called the 'apparat's revanche', but it presaged the big coup that would come three years later and its echo remains in the sentiments of Putin's nationalist allies. What was extraordinary about the affair was that it showed how quickly and easily the achievements of *glasnost* could be stifled, even in its third year in existence. It showed that *glasnost* was not irreversible, despite Gorbachev's insistence that there was no turning back.

The fast pace of change had unsettled conservative forces in the party. Not only were jobs and privileges threatened, but long-held beliefs were being revised, doubt was being cast on the historical achievements of a superpower, and values were changing: so many illusions were being punctured that hard-liners, as the saying went in a popular Soviet film, felt personally offended by the disrespect to the state (*za derzhavu obidno*). The future agenda envisaged even more terrible changes: multiparty elections, religious freedom, the right to emigrate. When I met Nina Andreyeva a year after her infamous letter, she had received 7,000 fan letters from around the country. Andreyeva complained to me about the 'elite intelligentsia' who only wanted money and privileges; and the liberal press that poured dirt on Soviet heroes.

The fuss started when the letter entitled 'I Cannot Give up My Principles' was published in the newspaper *Sovetskaya Rossiya* on 13 March 1988 under the rubric 'polemics'. The article was attributed to Andreyeva, a Leningrad chemistry lecturer. In fact, it was not wholly Andreyeva's letter but the product of an editorial collective at *Sovetskaya Rossiya* and was initiated and given the final stamp of approval in Ligachev's secretariat. The letter appeared in print just as Gorbachev was about to leave for Yugoslavia and Aleksandr Yakovlev was in Mongolia, a good time for a counter-attack. During the three weeks that Gorbachev was away, there was almost no protest or critique of the views stated in the letter. The pro-*glasnost* media were horrified, but cowed into silence. Only when Gorbachev returned did *Pravda* come out with an article on 5 April denouncing the article as an 'ideological platform and manifesto for anti-*perestroika* forces'.

Andreyeva was hardly the perfect role model to represent the conservative position. She and her husband had been expelled from their party branch for writing anonymous letters against colleagues (they were later reinstated on the recommendation of the KGB); and some of her views appear to have been too extreme for publication. The Moscow correspondent of the Italian Communist Party's daily, *L'Unità*, Giuletto Chiesa, obtained a copy of Andreyeva's original letter which he says had been completely reworked. Only five of her original 18 typewritten pages were used, because the views she expressed were considered too 'Stalinist, anti-Semitic, dogmatic and nationalist'. There were passages that spoke of 'nations of little importance, like the Crimean Tatars and Zionist Jews', and she accused Stalin's critics of writing 'in the language of Goebbels'.[18] But her paradoxical cocktail of Marxism-Leninism, Russian national chauvinism and anti-Semitism accurately represented the far-right's 'red brown' views, if softened for the article. Many of these views continue to represent communist and nationalist ideology today.

In the version published in the newspaper, Andreyeva argued that there were two ideological currents or 'classes' promoting *perestroika* and that both would lead to the death of socialism if something were not done. One current represented the 'conservationists', such as the 'imperialist' Aleksandr Prokhanov, who promoted a form of nationalism she espoused, but whose 'regression' to peasant socialism lacked an understanding of the October revolution's historical importance. The other current, which she rejected, belonged to the 'left-wing liberal intellectual socialists'. They were falsifying the history of socialism by claiming the country's past was 'nothing but mistakes and crimes', exaggerating Stalin's guilt and ignoring the part played by the 'trailblazers of socialism'. Scandalised by Mikhail Shatrov's plays, popular at the time with socialist reformers for taking a Leninist position, she condemned one of the play's 'biased' accusations that Stalin had been behind the assassination of Trotsky. Stalin should be given an 'objective assessment', by which she meant 'a historical assessment detached from short-term considerations, which would demonstrate ... the dialectics of the correspondence between the individual's actions and the basic laws governing society's development'. Elsewhere in the letter her explanation is more down to earth: 'when all is said and done, hardly anyone today is disturbed by the personal qualities of Peter the Great, but everyone remembers that during his rule the country became a great European power'.

Andreyeva went on to attack the class interests of 'left-wing liberal intellectuals', who pursued western consumerist aims, exchanging proletarian collectivism for individualism. Were they not, she asked, the spiritual heirs of 'Dan and Martov and other adherents of Russian social democracy, the spiritual followers of Trotsky or Yagoda, and the offspring of NEPmen, Basmachis and kulaks with grudges against socialism?'. She brings up the Jewish question by claiming that Trotsky's internationalism was a rejection of

Russia's own cultural heritage, and flings the derogatory term 'cosmopolitanism' at the liberals – a word used in Stalinist times to smear Jews. She also attacks the new informal organisations, early shoots of civil society, which showed no evidence of socialism, promoting unacceptable values such as the 'parliamentary system', 'free trade unions' and 'autonomous publishing houses'. Her aim, she said, was to prevent the threat to socialism. Fyodor Burlatsky argued a few weeks later that the crisis lay not in socialism but in the form of 'state socialism' that she espoused, which was more suited to the early period of war communism.[19]

What had so paralysed liberal editors from responding to the Andreyeva letter? They knew immediately that if a reader's letter was given a full page, on page three, written in neo-Stalinist tones, in a newspaper that was the organ of the Central Committee of the CPSU, the Supreme Soviet and the Council of Ministers of the RSFSR – it spelled trouble. Usually newspapers did not publish political articles the Kremlin did not agree with; if they did, it would go with an editorial comment, but there was none. The next day editors and broadcasters (except the two most radical, Yakovlev and Korotich) were summoned to a meeting, chaired by Ligachev, at which he promoted the article and instructed the official TASS news agency to send copies to provincial papers with a recommendation to reprint it. Many of them did (Andreyeva told me 936 local papers did), as well as the socialist press abroad, such as East Germany's *Neues Deutschland*. Although many meetings were being held by supporters of Andreyeva's letter and gleeful telegrams were being received by *Sovetskaya Rossiya*, there was no protest from the liberals.

A journalist, Ruslan Kozlov in *Komsomolskaya pravda* ('Komsomol Truth'), talks of his shame at the fact that they did nothing. His immediate reaction, as that of other journalists, was: 'So ... an article written in an instructive and directive tone, with no editorial commentaries ... such a major article of principle must surely have been agreed and perhaps even issued as a social imperative':

> We waited for a central party organ to speak out. Yet during those days, readers sent in letters expressing their bewilderment and disagreement with the stance of the anti-*perestroika* forces ... Surely it was the fear of accidentally being out of step which proved stronger than the desire to finally escape from the impasse? ... What actually happened? 'Three weeks of stagnation', during which we waited for decisions to be taken by those above us, or simply a continuation of the stagnation in our own souls?[20]

Only Yegor Yakovlev managed to break the collective conformism to publish a response in *Moskovskiye novosti* on 23 March. It came from the playwright Aleksandr Gelman, who spoke out at the radical Film-makers' Union on 23 March, expressing the 'potentially tragic consequences' in store for the country if Gorbachev's *perestroika* were defeated. He understood Andreyeva's concern that criticism of Stalin was a blow against the authority of the party but, he said, the party's future had to be laid on a 'purged foundation of truth'.[21] The union's board endorsed Gelman's statement unanimously and sent it as an official protest to the Central Committee.

When Gorbachev returned from Yugoslavia he called a session of Politburo members that lasted two days where, according to Aleksandr Yakovlev, he excoriated his colleagues' half-hearted response. Yakovlev himself thought the main point of the letter was to get control of the media:

> The media have been subjected to particularly harsh attacks. The most ruthless struggle is being waged to control every newspaper and every television and radio programme from the Central Committee. The front against *perestroika* has realised very well that its main opponent is *glasnost*. [22]

Yakovlev was put in charge of the reply to Andreyeva's letter. He confirmed the crimes of which Stalin was accused: 'not only did he know about (acts of lawlessness), he organised and directed them – that is now a proven fact'. Perhaps, he said, people had underestimated how hard it would be to get rid of the old authoritarian methods, but the only way forward was to have 'more democracy, more socialism'. *Glasnost* had given people the right to defend their views, he said, so why had there been no debate if the letter was called a 'polemic'?

It was a good question and caused anxiety among the liberal camp. 'What is the reason for such uncritical acceptance of a clearly dogmatic and biased article?', asked Nikolay Bodnaruk in *Izvestiya*.[23] Indeed, what did it say about the true scale of *glasnost* in the press if almost none of the powerful editors-in-chief had been prepared to take a risk without first getting permission? If freedom depended on getting instructions from above, then it was unlikely that freedom was what they had in the first place. *Glasnost* could not mean even partial freedom if it was no more than an instrument of propaganda to promote Gorbachev-inspired goals, however preferable they were to what had come before. Was this paralysis fatalistic, the result of decades of silence and an instinct not to rock the boat? If so, it boded no good for the cause of freedom. According to Yegor Yakovlev, *glasnost* failed to pass the test whenever the case was extreme, such as Chernobyl, Nagorno-Karabakh and the Andreyeva letter.

In the meantime, the silence of the pro-*glasnost* newspapers had allowed the conservatives to consolidate their forces in time for the 19th Party Conference on 28 June, 1988, probably the reason for Andreyeva's letter in the first place, so they could fight the increasingly radical reforms on the agenda. The backbiting between liberals and conservatives continued at the conference. On the one hand, the liberal writer Grigory Baklanov mocked the hardliners for fighting for their own enslavement: 'What kind of socialism will there be without *glasnost*? The socialism of the voiceless? How about it, comrades, have we taken one gulp of freedom and all choked on it?' (disturbance in the auditorium).[24] On the other hand, the conservative deputy chairman of the Russian Republic's Union of Writers, Yury Bondarev, was outraged by the immorality of the reformist press, which was perpetrating 'Ivan Karamazov's philosophy' (applause); raising doubts about everything sacred and terrifying people so that now 'both a fly and a man can be swatted by a newspaper'.[25]

The most significant speech on *glasnost* at the conference came from Mikhail Ulyanov, the famous actor known for his roles as Lenin, who put some hard questions to his pro-*glasnost* colleagues:

> It turns out we are still afraid 'to dare to have our own opinion'. Fine, you can understand people in the time of the cult [of personality]: they were afraid for their lives. It really must have been terrifying. You can understand people during the time of voluntarism: they believed in Khrushchev without reservation. You can understand people in the time of stagnation, when they did not believe in anything, seeing only universal lies and theft. But what are we waiting for now? What stops us taking a firm stand now, when our hands are not tied and our souls are open? Is it again that accursed fear in our genes?[26]

Ulyanov's question is one that can be put again in later episodes of the development of free speech when, as in the early Putin years, fear was not the ostensible reason for kow-towing to the state. It was easier to understand the Andreyeva affair when the repressive past was only recent and Gorbachev's views not always predictable. An exchange of views with Gorbachev at the conference brought out some of the ambiguities. Ulyanov pointed out the illogicality of demanding that the press intensify criticism but, God forbid, if it dares criticise anybody ('Some hack dares to criticise an elected worker!'); therefore, he said, the press should be independent and not someone's 'timid handmaiden'. Attempting to answer, Gorbachev tied himself in knots: *glasnost* and criticism were vital, he said, but if a man is insulted in our newspapers and magazines – 'is this permissible in a socialist society?'. Ulyanov tried to put him on the spot again: he wanted to know if Gorbachev would support the press even if it did sometimes make mistakes, so long as it was done in the interests of the people and the party. Gorbachev finally agreed: yes, if it is fair criticism. He then remarked that in a one-party system, no one group should monopolise the press – that way 'we shall have democracy such as has never been dreamed of by those abroad'; but he did not explain how that would be done.

What becomes clear is the uncertain nature of the policy of *glasnost*, inhabiting a framework that had not been properly defined and vulnerable to diverse interpretations. 'The press cannot exist by command – today for *glasnost*, tomorrow against *glasnost*' (Grigory Baklanov). It was also clear that the narrative had been conducted only with the one-party socialist system in mind. The conservative groups that were essentially against *glasnost* also paid lip service to it, limiting its sting by demanding the discussion of 'lofty' topics, criticism without 'nihilism' and historical facts that were not distorted. But if *glasnost* offended nobody, it would change nothing. Reformers at first spoke within the terms of democratic socialism, but their views were expanding towards freedom and democracy. Both groups appeared to be bursting at the seams of the political system they claimed to support.

II Central television

It could be said that Soviet television in the 1970s was dedicated to the service of one man: Leonid Brezhnev. That was the story recounted by the famous film and TV director Eldar Ryazanov about the lengths to which the gigantic structure of Gosteleradio was prepared to go to keep Brezhnev happy. Brezhnev was an ardent football fan and the problem arose when television executives realised that two popular football teams were playing in two different towns at the same time. No one knew for certain which match Brezhnev would prefer to watch on television. So they rang the party secretary of the Voroshilovgrad region, where one of the matches was to be held, and asked him to put the match off to another day. This was done promptly, although the tickets had been sold out. Brezhnev could now watch both matches live on television on different days if he wished. It could not be helped if thousands of fans were disappointed.[27]

There is a meeting point between Gorbachev's opening up of television freedoms and Putin's closing them down. Under Putin television has reverted to many Soviet stereotypes, ending genuine debate and giving the masses over to entertainment. In Brezhnev's time sports programmes were the most popular; it was what kept everyone happy. Gorbachev changed this trajectory, expanding the political arena to an audience so engrossed in news about their country that politics was more popular than light entertainment. This political appetite continued into the 2000s until the familiar signs of censorship returned. To understand just how much television began to change in the Gorbachev era it is worth remembering what TV looked like under Brezhnev.

Gosteleradio, the State Committee for Television and Radio, was the vast state monolith set up in 1967 to control the electronic media. Impressive as a technical achievement, its purpose was state propaganda. A complex satellite broadcasting network took Soviet television across 11 times zones[28] to reach about 250 million people. The country was divided into five television time zones, which meant that programmes that first came out in the Vladivostok region on the Pacific coast could always be censored before they were broadcast half a day later in Moscow and the European part of Russia. Gosteleradio embraced two nationwide (all-union) channels and all the republican and local stations in the USSR, broadcasting in 40 languages. The union-wide channels, called the First Programme and its adjunct the Second Programme, were known as Central Television, beaming from Moscow's Ostankino centre.

In 1986 the First Programme reached over 93 per cent of the population; the Second Programme over 67 per cent; both together could be watched by 82 per cent of the population.[29]

The chairman from 1970 until retired by Gorbachev in 1985 had been Sergei Lapin, a party stalwart who understood television well enough to provide an interesting diet of drama, game shows and quizzes, but kept anything to do with politics or news under a stranglehold. Lapin liked to remind people of his friendship with Brezhnev, and had his own quirks – men could not sport beards on television, women were not considered suitable as foreign correspondents; nor could they wear slacks. He closed the door to the freedoms that had existed during the 'thaw' and scrapped the audience survey department, as viewers' choices no longer determined output. People watched television anyway (the state didn't provide much entertainment in town), so TV held a captive audience.

In its role as organ of propaganda, television fulfilled ceremonial and ritualistic functions. The ideological focus was on the roughly 30-minutes news programme, *Vremya* ('Time') which came out at nine in the evening on both channels simultaneously, making it the only source of news on television. In the 1980s it was also repeated in full in the morning, supposedly for those working second shift at enterprises. There was a rigid agenda to its structure. Every bulletin started with domestic news no matter what world-shattering event might have taken place: first, matters of protocol to do with top leaders, such as visits with foreign dignitaries or Central Committee matters; next, the achievements of socialism in industry and agriculture, followed by foreign news, sport and the weather forecast. During the broadcast of the domestic news the supply of hot water from taps in flats would run out as most people used this interval to wash their dishes after the evening meal. This silent mutiny against tedium lasted until the foreign news. Gosteleradio's new chairman, Aleksandr Aksyonov admitted in 1986 that most people began watching the news at 21.15 when the foreign news came on.[30] But what the audience looked at was not what party officials intended. Although coverage of the West was usually negative, the audience disregarded the commentary and close-ups, instead scanning the background for the latest in cars, clothes, consumer goods and smart shops. The gleaning of truth from passing images and unverifiable facts brings its own irreality. Some of the disenchantment with the West in the 1990s had its roots in this disjuncture between the intended message and its perception. The émigré satirical novelist, Vladimir Voynovich described the consequences of this distorted mirror:

Every day Soviet newspapers, radio and television curse the USA, using colours blacker than black to describe American unemployment, racial discrimination, inflation and pauperisation. But thanks to that very propaganda, countless Soviet citizens assume that America has no serious problems; they imagine that in the USA money grows on trees, that you don't have to work and can spend your life gambling in casinos and driving around in Cadillacs.[31]

It was inevitable that the official news organ, *Vremya* would take a while to change its character, and much too slowly for many. After the January 1987 plenum, viewers could receive news and information from a variety of programmes. On 2 January the top *Vremya* commentator Aleksandr Tikhomirov announced that there were 'no subjects banned from discussion'. He gave two examples. Journalists no longer needed to fear tarnishing the country's reputation by revealing its faults, because even the Central Committee had criticised the Air Transport Ministry for covering up problems at Aeroflot and – 'did Aeroflot really lose its prestige on international lines? It didn't, did it?'. The second change was that 'things are being called by their names' – thus a bribe-taker is a bribe-taker irrespective of what position he holds.[32] That at least was the theory.

Many topics were being censored, particularly infighting among party members, Afghanistan, ecology and space missions: news of the last usually went something like 'the equipment is functioning normally, the cosmonauts are well'. In fact, as Vitaly Korotich revealed to the western press because it could not get printed domestically, a spacecraft had only recently been saved on its launch pad six seconds before countdown, which could have led to a tragedy on the scale of the *Challenger* disaster. Nevertheless, Tikhomirov was telling journalists to be tougher. From these confusing signals, journalists could be forgiven for not understanding which way to jump. However, conflicts within the party and between reformers and bureaucrats allowed for a space in which journalists could breathe. They might get caught in the crossfire, but those who accepted Gorbachev's initiatives and had the courage of their convictions began to take things into their own hands.

The new policy was confirmed by Gosteleradio's deputy chairman, Leonid Kravchenko, the television professional in the top party apparatus appointed to push through Gorbachev's *glasnost*. He reported that at the start of 1987 one-quarter of the old programmes had been replaced and 60 per cent revised. Already 13 per cent of programmes were being shown live[33] – a genuine loosening up of party control. Television had not allowed unedited footage to be broadcast since Khrushchev's 'thaw'. Many programmes now revolved around public discussion: phone-ins, debates, studio audiences, vox pops. Some programme makers no longer felt it necessary to infantalise their audience: viewers, they said, didn't need to be presented with 'pre-chewed food', they had to be aware themselves of the 'falsity of smooth answers', they could do without a moral at the end of a story. Programmes such as *Prozhektor perestroiki* ('Spotlight on *Perestroika*'), *Problemy, poiski, resheniya* ('Problems, Searches Solutions'), *Rezonans* ('Response'), Leningrad TV's *Obshchestvennoye mneniye* ('Public Opinion') were all in the new mould. This was no longer *glasnost* for the purpose of greater labour productivity but the beginnings of an engagement in free expression. The most watched programmes came out of the youth department headed by Eduard Sagalayev, gathering audiences of about 100 million.

One of the first was *Dvenadtsatyy etazh* ('Twelfth Floor'), in which ordinary teenagers had a chance to tackle officials and public figures, behaving not in the deferential way expected on Soviet television but as they wished to – in heated anger or sullen indifference. Using the experience of the space-bridges, the two groups were placed in separate venues and joined by satellite link. By distancing the teenagers from their targets in the studio, Sagalayev reduced the inhibitions they might have had in challenging established figures on the panel. The generational clashes were sometimes intense. One episode showed teenagers presenting novel ideas for dealing with a disused bit of land in the heart of Moscow, exposing the philistinism of officials in the planning departments. In another episode teenagers showed their own crassness in conversation with Uzbek writer, Kamil Ikramov, whose father had been shot in the 1937 purges:

YOUTH: When you were young why didn't you speak the truth – you, your generation?

IKRAMOV: At your age I was in prison. Anyway, today young people only seem great but they're terribly ignorant.

YOUTH: You didn't speak the truth because you were scared, because you lived with fear. We members of informal groups aren't scared of anything today.

IKRAMOV: That's easy to say. You can't compare us, we're in different weight categories. My whole family was shot. Twenty years ago I wrote the truth of what happened and all this time there hasn't been the slightest possibility of publishing what I wrote. I hid my manuscript ... You have no idea how savagely the countryside was destroyed

YOUTH: You think we should study what happened by reading books, the memoirs of your relatives. But we don't want to read books, we want to act.[34]

It was a period when anything might be expected to appear on television, a second's glimpse of Trotsky flickering across the screen, a long interview with Bukharin's widow, footage of the implosion of Moscow's Cathedral of Christ the Saviour (now rebuilt) replayed over and over again on their screens. People wanted to know about the past and how much of their pre-revolutionary culture had been destroyed. They worried about what they called their 'gene pool' if so many of the country's brightest talents had been murdered in the Stalinist terror; and could agriculture ever recover if collectivisation had broken the back of age-old traditions on the land? The number of people killed in the war against Nazi Germany kept rising. It had been fixed at 20 million ever since the war, but now it reached more than 27 million (the figure it remains at today).

At the same time as the 'blank spots' of history were being filled, Moscow's city spaces, previously used for national parades, began to open up for its citizens and would soon give room for the right of freedom of assembly that saw hundreds of thousands coming out into the streets to demonstrate support for reform. Moscow party boss, Boris Yeltsin was making the face of the capital more attractive by opening up the Arbat to buskers and street life; and his populist politics of riding on the Metro or making unannounced forays into shops to see whether food was hidden behind the counter made for good media coverage. Compared with Gorbachev, who had a tendency to waffle, Yeltsin was direct. Interviewed on television about the Komsomol, the Communist Youth organisation which had 37 million young members at the time, Yeltsin's answers were a breath of fresh air as he rejected the repressive attitude to young people (it was still a time when gauche remarks like 'western pop music distracts young people from serious problems' were being made on television regularly), saying they should not be banned from dancing as they wanted to or listening to music they liked, or 'standing on their heads' for that matter; while also tackling complaints from Komsomol members who were too scared to go on TV because they had to clear what they wanted to say with the organisation's hierarchy:

> I was told yesterday how speakers were prepared ... the secretary of the party committee of the factory block arrives, he sits the girl down next to him and says, 'Let's do some work on your speech'. And what is the upshot? How many ... ideas of the Komsomol girl remain in the speech and how many of the party committee secretary's? Well, probably 99 per cent belong to the secretary of the party committee, and just a word or two – 'hello' and 'goodbye' – belong to her ... The suggestion is this, therefore, let young people speak up boldly, frankly and openly.[35]

Late-night chat shows

The programmes that began to appear on television from 1987 spoke to massive audiences and were instrumental in turning *glasnost* into a far wider quest for information. The most popular were the late-night chat shows that emerged when television's closing time was extended after midnight, in particular the weekly shows *Vzglyad* (View) and *Do i posle polunochi* (Before and after midnight). They became an alternative source of news more important than *Vremya*. Serious political journalism embraced any topic that previously had been banned or denigrated or considered not for TV: pop music, for example, which had been the music of protest (called *magnitizdat*, as it was secretly circulated on magnetic tape). Producers began to stray from the rigid formats they had been used to and the divisions that had existed between genres, part of a stultifying bureaucratisation of content. The infotainment aspect of *Do i posle polunochi* was new and exciting for audiences because 'it turns out that it is possible to combine a live interview and a strict fact, fresh news presented by a political commentator and music by a rock group – they all get along perfectly well!', wrote a surprised television critic.[36] She was also impressed by the host, the tall elegant Vladimir Molchanov, not because of his rather mannered air of gentility, but because he talked, even 'stumbling at times'.

As an example of the show's range of content that made it such a hit, we can take an average evening: this one on 6 May 1987, which included the following items: a rehabilitation of the 1920s ego-futurist poet, Igor Severyanin, dubbed in Soviet annals as a bourgeois decadent; news from the Cannes Film Festival; a report on the death of Rita Hayworth with clips of her dancing in the film *Gilda*; a music video of the Soviet heavy-metal group 'Ariya' (Soviet music videos being a new phenomenon); an interview with the US journalist Grace Kennan, daughter of the prominent historian and initiator of the cold war 'containment' policy, George Kennan; an interview with Archbishop Pitirim on the availability of Bibles; and an interview with sociology professor, Igor Bestuzhev-Lada complaining that the youth of today were mindlessly aping western fashion, but blaming his generation for being 'too formalised', and praising young people for demonstrating against the demolition of historic buildings.

Vzglyad was more politicised and mischievous in its approach and probably holds the record for being the most popular television show ever in the country. Certainly its impact was enormous on the politics of the time. Every Friday at about 11 p.m. viewers would settle down before their screens to watch previously 'underground' material being brought out into the open in a live open-ended programme often continuing way past midnight because, as its deputy editor, Anatoly Lysenko told me, it wasn't in the Russian character to be too precise about time and they never knew what vital information might turn up at the last moment. When *Vzglyad* made its first appearance on 2 October 1987 it set out to break all Soviet genres by calling itself a 'weekly information-musical-publicistic-entertainment programme for young people'. But it was not just for young people, it appealed to an audience of 150 million. It played close to the bone but was light-hearted as well. Its humour ruffled bureaucrats' feathers when, for example, the *Vzglyad* team waited at the airport for the arrival of one of its more moralistic anti-western opponents in order to film him pushing a trolley packed high with western consumer goods from his trip abroad, or mocking the state agriculture ministry's claims of hygiene after displaying a sealed jar of pickled tomatoes with a condom in it. *Vzglyad* invited its auditorium to participate and send information from local areas, which made up part of the programme's scoops. Its phone lines were open during the show, viewers sent in information from all parts of the country and letters poured in for the hosts to solve all matter of personal and public injustice, as no institution could so effectively highlight a case as this programme.

Initially Lysenko had conceived a show called 'In the kitchen after 11', referring to the favourite room in people's flats during the Brezhnev years, where friends would gather to eat, drink and exchange the latest information. Meeting in the kitchen was not simply social, it was important to find out what was happening in the country from the grapevine, as official news might misinform or disinform. The kitchen was in effect the pleasanter aspect of survival politics. The show changed its name but its tone remained homely. Those who criticised it for its unprofessionalism missed the point, that its unruly nature was its virtue. Its young hosts were informal, wearing T-shirts and jeans. Its name, *Vzglyad*, was picked to mean 'a' view among many, and although the aim was to listen to a pluralism of views, the show made no bones about the fact that it supported *perestroika*.

Of the main trio hosting the show each had his own style, Vladislav Listyev (laidback); Dmitry Zakharov (serious); Aleksandr Lyubimov (extroverted) and the expert on pop music. Other journalists made their name on this programme, the two most politically acute being Vladimir Mukusev and Aleksandr Politkovsky[37] – in all, a male stronghold.

Vzglyad often shocked its audience. When the stage director Mark Zakharov suggested on the programme (on 21 April 1989) that the Christian thing to do would be to bury Lenin, the shock lasted several years (and Lenin is still in the mausoleum). Compared with its main rival, Molchanov's *Do i posle polunochi*, which was more refined and perhaps even too well-mannered, *Vzglyad*'s appeal was general and its spectrum social and political. When Molchanov did a polished piece on how the special militia were trained and groomed, *Vzglyad* followed up with a piece showing an Afghan veteran being beaten up by the militia in Gorky Park on Armed Forces Day. *Vzglyad* played its part in disclosing events that Gorbachev and hardliners were increasingly trying to cover up, such as the massacres in Tbilisi and Vilnius and the attempts to hound Yeltsin out of political life. One attempt to blacken Yeltsin's reputation took place during a television election debate for the Congress of People's Deputies (on Moscow television, 12.3.89), when questions were planted, ostensibly from viewers' letters, to discredit Yeltsin, while his opponent, Yevgeny Brakov, was treated normally. Yeltsin had to answer embarrassing questions about alleged privileges for his daughter and granddaughter. *Vzglyad* disclosed proof that the letters were faked, attributed to people who had not written them.

This ferment of creativity was replicated on Leningrad television, which was soon broadcasting its regional programmes nationwide. Different in style from Moscow, its most popular programmes, themselves in stark contrast to each other, were *Pyatoye koleso* ('Fifth Wheel') and *600 sekund* ('600 Seconds'). *Pyatoye koleso* was a show made by and for the intelligentsia. Leading among its hosts was Bella Kurkova. Reflecting on culture and history, it showed long interviews with writers and thinkers, meandering for two to three hours blissfully unaware of capitalism's logo that 'time is money', bathing in the luxury of spending as much time as possible on topics that had been taboo only recently and comfortable, as in all communist countries, with interminably long speeches. Its ironic title set itself up as superfluous, like a fifth wheel, because its aim was precisely to tell stories about people and ideals that had been considered superfluous by the Soviet regime, all those things about art and values. *Pyatoye koleso* dug into archives, broadcast documentaries that could find no other outlet, and showed comprehensive footage of the main protest events that after 1989 increasingly took reformers and Yeltsin in confrontation with Gorbachev's policies. In particular the programme excelled in its coverage of the dramatic events around Lithuania's bid for independence.

600 sekund, by contrast, was speedy, dramatic and sleazy, exposing the underbelly of Leningrad life. It looked as if it had been conceived as a travesty of *Vremya* with its rapid-fire talk, no protocol, and only bad news. It was headed by the dashing Aleksandr Nevzorov, previously a trick horse-rider and stuntsman, wearing a trendy black leather jacket and a permanently sardonic smile on his face. Most of the Soviet Union watched mesmerised to see whether in his race with the digital clock behind him (usually he would cover nine items within the 600 seconds of the show) he would manage to finish on the dot – which he always did, except when he missed deliberately to tease the viewer. Nevzorov was a colourful figure, and the first to practise tabloid television in the country. Speeding around in his minivan with the histrionics of a knight in shining armour he would scour the city's basements, squats and tenements. Indeed, travelling with him and the team on one occasion, you could see how popular he was with Leningraders who would wave him on, blowing kisses. Most of his scoops came from contacts he had in the KGB (his uncle had been in the service) or from the police, the ambulance service and fire brigade, and most of his stories centred on disasters – rape, murder, crime; and he would think nothing of shoving his microphone at people to ask personal or incriminating questions. Asked by journalists why he focused on the terrible and the bizarre, he would retort that he was only telling the naked truth, even if people complained. He gave the workers in Leningrad's crematorium as an example – 'I said on air that they were stealing flowers and slippers from graves. They were awfully indignant, as one lot only stole flowers and the other – slippers'.[38] When I spoke to his producer about this rather pat story, he said Nevzorov was exaggerating and had apologised on the programme. Nevzorov maintained that his methods enabled him to help victims and expose their plight – the many tramps, invalids and misfits who were most visible in his earlier reports:

> You can, if you want to, say that we're dealing with the seamier side of life when we talk about German and Soviet war invalids. How does the conquered invalid live and the invalid who has conquered? The former lives a normal life, has an enormous house, moves about in a Mercedes specially adapted for his disability. Our invalid, the conqueror, takes shelter God knows where and moves about in a handmade wheelchair ... Shouldn't someone talk about that?[39]

The programme, designed by Nevzorov and producer Aleksandr Bor-isoglebsky, fitted into a tradition of Petersburg urban tales, the 'fantastic rea-lism' of stories by Gogol and Dostoyevsky; and Nevzorov's use of Dostoyevsky's term 'the insulted and the injured' pinpointed that 'little man' of Petersburg's dark corners, humiliated by the city's bureaucrats. The literary tradition was only a reference point, however, as there was nothing high-brow about Nevzorov's programme: 'there's no talk of the intelligentsia here', he said himself: 'reporting is a terribly rough, soldierly profession'.[40] His focus on low-life had touched a sore point. Scenes of such ugliness and misery did not officially exist in the Soviet Union. What Nevzorov showed his viewers was a rotting welfare state and a bureaucracy callous to its duties, while the system on which it was based had eroded any natural acts of charity from ordinary people because to help, according to Soviet logic, was punishable as it highlighted the state's neglect.

But Nevzorov's 'soldierly' approach meant disregarding ethical standards, even as he was exposing himself to danger in uncovering mafia-run enter-prises, unhygienic food combines, prostitution rings, corrupt officials and small-time crooks. He was equally hostile to the party and to democrats, cynical about the Lensoviet, the city administration, whether run by a party conservative (Gidaspov) or a reformer (Sobchak). Nevzorov laughed off the numerous complaints against his methods of reporting, boasting that on one occasion there were 24 defamation lawsuits against him in one month.[41] In the summer of 1990 his popularity peaked as more than 90 per cent of view-ers watched the programme. But this was not to be for much longer. His behaviour had become erratic as he fell hostage to the darker arts of tabloid journalism and began to indulge in the gratuitous violence he was meant to be deploring. There were more corpses, bloody victims and the bizarre case of a man who had sex with a sheep and had his penis bitten off. On a personal level he began to see himself as a 'real' soldier; he was soon dressing in camouflage, sometimes carrying a gun. He was attracted to the tough gla-mour of paramilitary groups, he espoused nationalist sentiments and sup-ported and filmed the disparate and seemingly crackpot monarchist groups who liked to march in period uniform around the old imperial city.

There were many morally outraged party members wishing to set up supervisory controls on ethical matters, that were rejected by the pro-democracy media as simply a ploy to return censorship. Bringing in regulation by irate citizens before the institution of free speech had been established was not sensible. Nevzorov made use of the lack of regulation until his transgressions went too far. Hubris came in January 1991 when Soviet tanks rolled into Vilnius to put down Lithuanian separatists in a bloody confrontation. Nev-zorov dashed off to Vilnius to film his patriotic version of events, a 15-minute piece called *Nashi* ('Our Own'), in which he presented the paratrooper OMON unit as heroes, rejecting evidence that Soviet tanks had killed 14 civilians and run over a woman. Pouring all his dramatic intensity to extol 'our boys', he described them as bringing order to Lithuania and protecting the entrenched Russian-speaking population from 'getting their throats slit'. For many viewers it was a blow to see Nevzorov praising soldiers who had shot and killed civilians indiscriminately, but it became worse when it was revealed that he had doctored his footage. This was the conclusion reached by the Union of Film-makers, who studied the footage and claimed Nevzorov was responsible for 'staged falsifications'. Nevzorov's ratings dropped by almost half, to 40 per cent. Although he never regained his enormous popularity, he has left his legacy in Putin's youth movement, Nashi, which became known for thuggish behaviour and a eulogistic defence of the security services and the state.

Glasnost was an open door and the journalists who took up its call usually had one thing in common: the desire to change the current state of affairs. Mostly on television this was seen as 'democratising' society with a western thrust, but for some such as Nevzorov it meant an assertion of nationalism with its 'red brown' connotations. These two groups found themselves on different sides of the barricades as the conservative and reformist camps became more polarised in the remaining years leading to the breakdown of the Soviet Union.

'Socialist pluralism'

As his policy of *glasnost* expanded, Gorbachev held a number of meetings in 1987 and 1988 with heads of the media and creative unions to exchange views in 'comradely discussion'. Arguably the media might have been better able to safeguard their independence if there was more of a distance between them and the Kremlin, but in the Soviet context the fact that Gorbachev was encouraging discussion in decision-making was itself a breakthrough. To map out a timetable for *perestroika*, he suggested they 'synchronise their watches' in a relationship he called a 'partnership'. By this he meant that the criticism involved in *glasnost* should not be disruptive because they were all 'on the same side of the barricade' and therefore should maintain mutual respect. He went further in 1988 and called differences of opinion a form of 'socialist pluralism'.[42] This was a more radical approach because the term 'pluralism', so vital to the concept of free speech, was a dirty word in Soviet parlance. It is thought to have appeared only once in a non-pejorative sense since *perestroika* began, in a statement by Poland's minister of culture reported by *Ogonyok* in 1987. Otherwise, when the Italian Communist Party leader Enrico Berlinguer used the word 'pluralism' in his speech to the 25th Congress of the CPSU in 1976, *Pravda* refused to publish it and, to the fury of the Italians, substituted the word 'multiformity' instead.[43]

Just how toxic the idea of pluralism was for Soviet communists and Russian nationalists alike can be seen from a rant by Solzhenitsyn, in this case against fellow émigré dissidents of the likes of Sinyavsky, all of whom he branded 'pluralists' for believing in western liberal ideas and for being dazzled by 'myriad coruscations, the infinite spectrum of pluralist thought'. Solzhenitsyn finds it hard to get a grip on the concept, so redolent is it for him of immorality, uncontrolled freedom (*volya*), anarchy and chaos. If pluralism or diversity are considered the highest aim of mankind, he argues, it can only lead to a paralysis of thought, to relativism and the inability to distinguish truth from falsehood. How then can one find the 'one truth – God's truth'?, he asks, although he does not explain how this one truth will be revealed or why pluralism cannot be a means to that end. As far as he is concerned, the idea of 'Let's have as many views as possible – just as long as they're all different' is worthless, because 'if a hundred mules all pull different ways the result is no movement at all'.[44]

The problem of pluralism in Soviet thinking was that it entailed the concept of opposition. In a one-party state how did conflicting views fit in with maintaining the state's unity? It would mean the state relinquishing control over society and the citizen's right not to toe the party line. For orthodox thinkers this meant bringing society to the brink of chaos and anarchy. What if there was 'moral pluralism'?, asked the writer Valentin Rasputin. When the suggestion was put to the then head of Gosteleradio, Mikhail Nenashev, that Russia wanted its own alternative republican (non-union) television channel, he was horrified at the 'orgy of democracy' that would follow. The liberal old-hand Fyodor Burlatsky made sure when he was setting up his own alternative political group to reject any talk of a 'pluralism' of parties – instead, there were other words such as factions, platforms and fronts. Talk of multi-parties was completely rejected by Gorbachev as 'rubbish' and 'groundless' when the idea was first advanced.

Gorbachev had accepted early on that opposition was healthy and necessary for his reforms. *Glasnost* filled the absence in a one-party state of a loyal opposition. He said so discreetly to a group of writers in 1986, but his words were leaked to the western press. 'We don't have an opposition', he said. 'How then can we monitor ourselves? Only through criticism and self-criticism; and most of all through *glasnost*' – although he immediately qualified his words: 'at the same time democracy without limits is anarchy; that's why it's complicated'.[45] These sentiments were considered sufficiently heretical when he repeated them openly during a visit to Khabarovsk shortly afterwards for *Pravda* to remove them from its text, though they were reported on television. If Gorbachev thought opposition, criticism and self-criticism were necessary to lift society out of stagnation, the pivotal question was how much of each, and what was the price of dynamism against control?

Despite the vicious polarisation of views, Gorbachev insisted there was no 'antagonism' and no 'warring class interests' at stake as long as one criterion was obeyed: 'We are for *glasnost* without reservations or limitations, but for *glasnost* in the interests of socialism'.[46] Extreme views or sensationalist ones were quite acceptable, even desirable, because 'no one poses questions so deeply and acutely ... as your adversary'.[47] He sees no 'drama' in these polemics, the result of which will produce a more 'multilayered' society that will remain socialist. But if there is no drama to it, it is because Gorbachev assumed that a loyal opposition would develop under the control of the Communist Party;

he did not foresee 'real' opposition. His partnership with media reformers was successful while it was based on shared aims, but once they felt he was interfering with the pace of reform the sense of trust began to evaporate. Yeltsin's future press minister, Mikhail Poltoranin complained that every time there was a breaking story, such as a miners' strike or an ethnic conflict, editors would be gathered together and given instructions (*instruktazhka*) on what approach to take, which was nothing more than ideological censorship.[48]

If pluralism and opposition were seen as uncomfortable words unless they held tags like 'socialist' or 'loyal', the phrase 'criticism and self-criticism', often used together, was another form of both staying within a system while also being outside it. According to the CPSU Central Committee 'criticism and self-criticism are tried-and-tested instruments of socialist democracy'.[49] Criticism on its own is oppositional, but self-criticism keeps you within a system without being too assertive. *Pravda* performing self-criticism in editorial meetings would be an example. How far criticism could go in the end depended on how far the Communist Party let it go. When H. G. Wells interviewed Stalin, who asked if the newly formed PEN Club could also be set up in the USSR, Wells explained that the club insisted on 'free expression of opinion – even of opposition opinion ... I do not know if you are prepared yet for that much freedom'. Stalin replied: 'We Bolsheviks call it "self-criticism". It is widely used in the USSR'.[50] These modifiers allowed society to have it both ways, especially in Russia with its tradition of manipulating language and dissociating words from deeds.

The limits to *glasnost* were becoming increasingly clear. Although censorship had been semi-abolished by Gorbachev in June 1986 when he stated that Glavlit's role was now concerned only with state and military secrets, he did not define what 'state secrets' were. Indeed, much had been achieved. Yegor Yakovlev was fond of showing off his censor Misha, who sat in his office in the building, but did not interfere with editorial work. If there was prior restraint, it tended to come from party apparatchiks through the 'telephone law', but even that was becoming less common. Editors had learned to ask officials who still felt they were entitled to interfere in the work of the media to put their demands in writing, knowing that under *glasnost* they would hesitate to leave footprints behind. Responsibility had been placed on the shoulders of editors and journalists to take *glasnost* where they wanted to, but they were also getting instructions. And despite changes in the official attitude towards personal computers and videos, all photocopying and duplicating equipment were still under lock and key – a fear from the 1970s when dissidents had used older methods to copy and circulate banned documents.[51]

Of course censorship had not gone away. If the media were only 'instruments' of *perestroika*, as Gorbachev had stated, this in itself was a limitation. Nor were there any regulations to ensure access to information for journalists, all of which was determined in an ad hoc way. Prominent papers such as *Pravda* and *Izvestiya* had an easier time of it, *Izvestiya*'s Ivan Laptev saying: 'Dear comrade editors, it's up to you if you prohibit or permit, but everything you do should be determined by one thing alone, your conscience, your party commitment and your professionalism'. The reporter taking the interview for *Argumenty i fakty* ('Arguments and Facts'), N. Vityazeva disagreed, saying Laptev sounded like someone traversing a different orbit: 'Other newspapers, including ours, haven't changed that much from the past, we're hauled on the carpet and Glavlit prohibits us from publishing such "state secrets" as excerpts from Trotsky's book on Stalin', she said.[52] But Laptev was right that the onus was on journalists – on their conscience and courage. It put them in a difficult position. If they did not grasp the initiative themselves they were a party to self-censorship, because they had been given the green light; yet they would be in trouble if they published a story that was unacceptable to the powers that be. If the story became a point of contention within the Central Committee, they would have to rely on whatever pull and influence they had.

The less palatable consequences of a society that was beginning to thaw out was the flotsam and jetsam of prejudice and superstition that came up to the surface: racial discrimination, anti-Semitism, primitive religious belief, sexism, chauvinism, xenophobia. The emergence of Pamyat, which called itself a historical–patriotic society and was concerned with the restoration of old monuments, was better known for its anti-Semitic views, its paranoid discoveries of 'Zionist–Masonic conspiracies' everywhere and its mishmash of nationalism and mysticism which, *Izvestia* wrote, forced you to 'sink into a world of superstition and charlatanism'.[53] *Moskovskiye novosti* noted how aggressive these groups were during their marches and meetings: 'Their absolute intolerance of the opinion of others, and rejection of anyone else's beliefs, generate extremism not only in their assessments but in their behaviour as well'.[54] Many of these views were shared by pro-party conservatives and non-party nationalists.

Among the conservative forces were the Russophile members of the Russian branch of the Union of Writers and their literary 'thick' journals, *Molodaya gvardiya* ('The Young Guard') and *Nash sovremennik* ('Our Contemporary'), which confronted those of their liberal counterparts, *Novyy mir* ('New World'), *Druzhba narodov* ('Friendship of Peoples'), *Znamya* ('Standard') and others, the latter doing their utmost to print previously banned works or those that had sat on shelves for decades, which the right wing saw as 'literary necrophilia' (*Pyotr Proskurin*). Sometimes it came to fisticuffs as shown in a video clip on *Vzglyad*, when *Nash sovremennik* club members attacked the liberal writers' group April at the Moscow Writers' Club with Pamyat members hurling anti-Semitic insults. Many establishment writers from the different branches of the Union of Writers were no more than hacks who had climbed to the top of the party ladder and were scared of losing cushy jobs, but the right wing also included the talented school of 'village' writers, film-makers and artists whose conservative–nationalist views were not dissimilar to those of Solzhenitsyn. The split between the groups tended to follow the familiar duality between Slavophile and Westerner.

Yeltsin gagged

Yeltsin's ostracism by the party came after the 21 October 1987 Party Plenum. He wondered later whether he should have caused such an uproar in the party by attacking Gorbachev and Ligachev for stalling on reform, but he could no longer suppress his anger and frustration. He announced he wished to quit as candidate member of the Politburo – something that no one had ever done before. He had warned Gorbachev of this earlier and had planned his attack, knowing full well he would be 'slaughtered in an organised and methodical manner ... with pleasure'.[55] The trauma of confronting the party he had believed in all his life led to what Yeltsin called a 'breakdown'. In fact, as it became known much later, he had slashed the left side of his rib cage and stomach with office scissors. Because the wounds were superficial, Timothy J. Colton in his comprehensive work on Yeltsin, sees it more as a howl of anger than an attempt at suicide.[56] A few days after Yeltsin had been hospitalised, he was hauled from his sickbed by the KGB, barely conscious, to endure a Stalinist-style purge at the Moscow Party City Plenum. He was accused of Bonapartism and demagoguery and ousted from his post as Moscow party boss (without him it was all the easier for Ligachev to plot the Andreyeva letter a few months later).

Gorbachev presided over these vituperative denunciations directed at Yeltsin in the customary manner in which the partocracy treated members in disgrace. Poltoranin, who was in the hall, describes how Yeltsin was so ill and drugged he could hardly hold his head up. Several rows at the front of the hall had been fenced off for party members who apparently had their denunciations prepared for them beforehand – 'they came in serried ranks and sat in these front rows and then according to instructions they would leap up and each of them heaped dirt on Yeltsin's head', as described by Poltoranin.[57] Rumours of the October Plenum swirled around Moscow, as the minutes had not been published. One story circulated that Yeltsin had accused Raisa Gorbachev of undue influence on her husband's political decisions, which caused a frenzy of speculation. Poltoranin later admitted he had concocted the story because he thought it would go in Yeltsin's favour at a time when he desperately needed help.[58]

Poltoranin was asked by Yury Sklyarov, Ligachev's right-hand man, to sign a document saying that, as editor of *Moskovskaya pravda* ('Moscow Truth'), he had been forced by Yeltsin to write critical articles exposing corruption and mismanagement in the capital. Poltoranin refused and in an interview given to the Milan daily *Corriere della Sera*, he described how the entrenched networks in the region had attempted to sabotage Yeltsin's work:

> They tried to block any kind of initiative and tried to show that what the city secretary was saying did not correspond to the facts. We had lots of farm and garden produce brought in to fill the city's stores, but those responsible then kept it to rot in warehouses instead of distributing it.

There were also trainloads of foodstuffs that came from the Caucasus and were sent back without being unloaded. When we published these stories in *Moskovskaya pravda* [those responsible for distribution] made new threats against us. Our editorial office was an island under siege, as was Yeltsin's office.[59]

After the plenum the Kremlin placed a gagging order on Yeltsin's appearances in the media. 'It is psychologically extremely depressing to be gagged in one's own country, and to be unable to explain oneself or communicate with people except through the Western media',[60] Yeltsin wrote. Attempts to report interviews with him in *Ogonyok* and *Moskovskiye novosti* fell through, but when he gave interviews to the foreign media he was lambasted for disloyalty by the party, especially as his criticisms of Ligachev always caused a sensation. Yeltsin could not come to terms with his break from the party and at the 19th Party Congress in 1988 he recanted, asking to be rehabilitated. He was jeered and heckled and the request was rejected. In this ignominious way, the Politburo's most ardent advocate of *perestroika* was forced out into the cold, giving him the 'moral right', as Aleksandr Yakovlev put it, of heading the anti-Gorbachev opposition.[61]

Yeltsin slowly made a comeback during the elections to the Congress of People's Deputies in 1989, but Soviet propaganda was bent on smearing his reputation with bizarre incidents. It was not difficult to do this given his known drinking habits and bouts of depression. On one occasion Yeltsin turned up dripping wet and bruised at a police station during the election campaign and for years rumours circulated that he had got drunk, that he was on his way to see a woman, that an attempt had been made to drown him, and so on. Former KGB chief Vadim Bakatin conceded later that it was a KGB 'caper' to embarrass him.[62]

Although Yeltsin was increasingly admired and popular at home, his reputation in the West (until 1991) was overshadowed by Gorbachev's popularity. Western reports often reflected the Politburo's image of Yeltsin as demagogic and populist. It made no sense why Yeltsin's forays on public transport were smeared as cheap populist devices, while Gorbachev's walkabouts had caused such delight. During his trips to France and the United States he was cold-shouldered and had trouble meeting western leaders, who did not wish to aggravate Gorbachev. He often got bad publicity. He was falsely reported to be inebriated at a speech he gave at Johns Hopkins University on 12 September 1989 by the *Washington Post*,[63] and an even more lurid version came out in the Italian socialist newspaper *La Repubblica*, although Yeltsin's team and the US sponsor denied he had been drunk. *La Repubblica* claimed Yeltsin had left behind him 'a wake of catastrophic prophesies, insane expenses, interviews, and above all the perfume of Jack Daniels Black Label'. It was this story that was reprinted in the 17 September issue of *Pravda*. Poltoranin suspected that the story had originated at the Soviet wire service APN, which had a special department run by the KGB that paid in foreign currency for material to be published abroad, so it could then be reprinted at home and appear to be neutral. The Italian journalist who had written the article had spent some time on a training course at this department, Poltoranin told me – 'But I can't confirm the story, you know what the KGB is like'.

Yeltsin's expulsion from the party brought him new experiences: he travelled abroad, he visited a US supermarket and was stunned by its mountain of fruit and vegetables, he mixed with intellectuals of the Inter-Regional Group, such as Sakharov and Yury Afanasyev. He says his 'world-view' began to change. If Gorbachev had not initiated reform, perhaps the democrat in Yeltsin would not have struggled out, but his moment of truth came when distraught at his expulsion from the party, his aides took him to a bath-house where he was cheered on by the local lads. He realised, he says, that his views were broader than he had thought. 'I was a communist by virtue of history and Soviet tradition, by inertia, and by upbringing, but not by conviction'.[64] He no longer felt the Communist Party had any future in Russia.

III *Glasnost* breaks free

The democratic movement grew stronger as it came up against the conservative opposition. The Nina Andreyeva affair had presented the frightening prospect of a return to state socialism. Once liberal reformers realised they would have to fight their own battles to safeguard freedoms, the initiative to push forward the frontiers of *glasnost* broke out of Gorbachev's control and was taken up by a more radical media movement, increasingly frustrated by his cautious approach to change. They had a champion in Yeltsin. *Glasnost* had reached a point where it needed to speed forward or go into reverse. Aleksandr Yakovlev observed: 'what used to be forbidden is now becoming boring, what used to look shocking, sensational and unusual is now no longer so'.[65]

By 1988 most of what had been uncovered and discussed would have been unthinkable two years earlier or would have earned someone a prison sentence, yet once a subject had been aired it all seemed perfectly natural and long overdue. Very often it was no more than the media catching up publicly with rumours and half-truths gleaned by the population from the grapevine or discussed around the kitchen table. If people had not been given statistics on the health of the nation, they did not need them to know that healthcare was dire. If it was a sensation in 1987 to see a video clip of the Beatles for the first time taken from the early 1960s, it had still come 25 years too late, after several generations of fans knew the Beatles' lyrics off by heart. If revelations about Stalinism and the Terror were still hard for many to digest, and it appeared they had only skimmed the surface, something more systematic needed to be done. Public acknowledgement of partial truths did not lay the ghosts or bring a sense of closure. The question was: what next?

The logic of *glasnost*, once started, demanded more depth and analysis: the opening up of secret archives, massive publishing ventures for a country greedy for knowledge, free expression in media, theatre and film, all of which took place only after the collapse of the Soviet Union. The media began to reject *glasnost* in doses, rationed out by the authorities, and demand a law on the press which would protect their profession. Expectations were growing and not easy to stifle. Viewers and readers did not want to be infantalised by the media: the 'human factor' meant due respect for the public's intelligence and right to know. The study of public opinion, which had been restricted under Brezhnev, became the fastest growing academic discipline, laying down what has become almost a feeling of veneration for opinion polls. Even the KGB was playing to the tune and had opened a press centre. There was a sense of living betwixt and between different types of societies that either provoked a sense of existential doom or outbursts of euphoria. Negative views were fuelled by the almost banal range of consumer goods that could not be found in shops in the spring and summer of 1989: no toothpaste, soap, washing powder, rubber gloves, salt, matches, sugar, apples and that staple of every family – buckwheat. Shockingly, miners could not get soap to wash themselves after their shifts. It was one of the many reasons that turned the miners' strike into a massive political movement.

The refrain 'We can't live like this' (*tak zhit' nel'zya*), taken from the title of Stanislav Govorukhin's film, played to the mood of apprehension. With his trademark moralistic intensity, he took the debate on communism a step further: Lenin was no better than Stalin and infinitely worse than the tsar. Having created a communist experiment of such total amorality that the country might never have the resources to recover, the communist perpe-trators (cutting to footage of the Nuremberg trials) had managed to get off scot-free. He offered no solution: the USA had material prosperity but they were also suffering from a wave of criminality committed mainly by 'blacks', an expiation white America had to endure for the crime of slavery, he said.

The Congress of People's Deputies and the first session of the Supreme Soviet, the new parliament, held from 25 May to 9 June 1989, was a water-shed in the development of free speech. These first ever semi-contested Soviet elections were a learning curve in democracy. Not only was the congress the most diverse and outspoken forum since the 1917 February Revolution, it also spilled out into the streets and parks, beginning the massive street demonstrations and rallies that became a regular feature in Moscow. None of this could have been possible without the wall-to-wall live transmission of the congress proceedings on television and radio – a total coverage of 90 hours and 25 minutes – that kept people glued to television sets at home and work, and those walking in the streets to their transistor radios, to make sure they didn't miss anything. Poignantly, it was said at the time that television could never return to the past after such ground-breaking events.

The media experience became part of people's power. The political struggle had developed months earlier around democratic candidates seeking nomi-nation to the congress in a chaotic mechanism of indirect voting, which allowed nominations from 'informal' organisations, but presented obstacles at every step. Many journalist candidates managed to squeeze through – Yakovlev, Poltoranin; Korotich having a particularly hard time of it with anti-Semitic Pamyat members trying to break up his meetings. Throughout this period a campaign to undermine Yeltsin's candidacy had been continuing. The final blow came when party conservatives, whom Afanasyev had called the 'Stalinist–Brezhnevite majority', made sure Yeltsin was the only Moscow nominee in the election to the Supreme Soviet to be rejected, although more than 5 million Muscovites had voted for him, more than for anyone else. Popular outrage saw thousands showing up at the Luzhniki Olympic Stadium to protest. The party apparatus would have won if not for a fellow democrat, law professor Aleksei Kazannik from Omsk University, who gave up his seat in favour of Yeltsin: saying, as shown on the *Vremya* news bulletin as he and Yeltsin stood side by side smiling: 'Yeltsin is more important than me'.

The full live coverage on television and radio changed the nature of the congress. Gorbachev and people's deputies had to prove their worth to a watchful audience. Everything that was said was heard, and when Gorbachev turned off the microphone, as he did when Sakharov continued to speak on the need for fundamental change and insist that participants send a stronger message to China to reflect the full tragedy of events taking place in Tiananmen Square, people wrote down what he had said and copies of his full speech were run off and distributed. All the speeches were published in *Izvestiya* verbatim – with minor exceptions; and there was a fairly rounded coverage on the *Vremya* bulletins. The proceedings provoked a massive nationwide response with more than 10,000 letters and telegrams a day being addressed to deputies and floods of letters and calls to the media. Special hotlines were set up by newspapers – *Komsomolskaya pravda* called theirs 'Telephone on Pravda Street' (where their offices were). Over 1,000 Soviet journalists were accredited to the congress (it was the first time access had been given to journalists from the republics), and about 300 foreign journalists.

In Moscow there was feverish activity. At the end of each day pro-democracy deputies met supporters at meetings and factories, and regularly turned up at the Luzhniki stadium to give updates and discuss tactics (such as the attempt by party bureaucrats to end the live TV transmissions on the grounds that it was used by speakers to 'advertise themselves', but rejected by Gorbachev); people went in droves during intervals in the proceedings to talk to deputies at the hotels Moskva and Rossiya near Red Square where they were staying; on Sunday the 28th more than 100,000 people turned up at the Luzhniki stadium. For Yegor Yakovlev this experience proved the press still had much to learn:

> Why does the press, having done so much to establish *glasnost*, look so unmistakably bewildered today? Because it has not got the direct contact with the masses that the people's deputies have. Because it has not yet become as accountable to readers as the deputies are to their electorate. Because the press is still unable to speak the whole truth.[66]

The experience of participatory democracy was a turning point. It was the point when liberalisation turned into democratisation. Commentators ridiculed the rationing of *glasnost*. 'The mania of secrecy is still suffocating us – secrecy that is unwanted, stupid and harmful', *Izvestiya*'s heavyweight, Aleksandr Bovin wrote.[67] One of the incidents that had traumatised the media was the recent attempt by the Kremlin to stifle news of the massacre in Tbilisi on the night of 8–9 April that year. At a peaceful protest meeting, 19 people had been killed, most of them women, and several hundred injured by soldiers wielding trench-digging shovels and firing chemicals from gas canisters. Traditionally there had always been a close tie between Russian and Georgian intellectuals and the effort to find out what happened became almost a personal matter. It was even more outrageous when General Rodionov, who had been in charge of the troops in Tbilisi, was given a huge ovation at the congress from conservative deputies. Demands were made at the congress to condemn the incident and ascertain exactly who was responsible. Who ordered shovels to be issued to the paratroopers? Why were chemicals used in great concentration? The instinct to quash information had been the same as at Chernobyl. It meant Georgia and the whole world knew of the massacre in Tbilisi before Moscow and the rest of the Soviet Union. Bovin thanked Voice of America in print for revealing the truth, defying the censor who had warned him not to.

In fact, TASS, *Pravda* and *Vremya* had lied – the story they told was that people had died in the ensuing crush at the protest, not that they had been battered to death by troops. Alternative information came from the well-known Moscow photojournalist Yury Rost, who happened to be in Tbilisi at the time and went to the protest that night. He seems to have been the only media professional on the scene. Before he was searched, beaten and his camera broken, he had managed to hide two rolls of film in his jeans pocket under a bunch of keys. Rost sent his report to his newspaper, *Literaturnaya gazeta* ('Literary Newspaper'), which did not run it. He also passed it on to a small local Tbilisi paper with a print run of no more than 60,000, *Molodyozh Gruzii* ('Georgia's Youth'), which was determined to print it, even though the editor had been instructed by the Georgian Central Committee and the censor not to do so. Accidentally, the van distributing copies of the paper was stopped by a military patrol in the middle of the night and the military then took the decision to confiscate the whole issue – but not before part of the print run had already been distributed. After negotiations, the rest of the issue came out a day late.

Moscow reformers took things into their own hands. A five-man team, including Yegor Yakovlev, flew to Tbilisi to carry out their own independent inquiry as parliament's deputies. Their report came out in *Moskovskiye novosti*, on 23 April, two weeks after the event. Even then, Yakovlev had to slip the issue past the censor, who said he would complain to the Central Committee. Yakovlev retorted – no, it is I who will complain that you want to censor a people's deputy. He wrote:

Who is it who always decides that, during such clashes, it is expedient to switch off *glasnost* like some electric power supply? And why? ... Facts witnessed by tens of thousands of people were brazenly distorted ... The Republic's Minister of Health said in an interview with Vremya that the troops used shovels and chemicals to break up the meeting. This was edited out of the interview. Everything was being done to conceal the tragedy.

Again, how did this happen? There had been no formal ban against printing alternative information about the event and Glavlit was not meant to interfere with these matters anymore. Igor Golembiovsky, then deputy editor of *Izvestiya*, tried to explain to me why journalists felt paralysed. *Izvestiya* had four correspondents in Tbilisi, but none of them had been at the protest meeting and their information was vague. 'Naturally it would have been correct to report what they did know', Golembiovsky agreed, 'that people had been killed, but they didn't know how many, that special troops had taken part and perhaps even army units ... and then inertia took over' – as well as the usual fear that reporting rumours could lead to pogroms, as had happened in Sumgait and Baku only recently. Golembiovsky had told Rost he would try to get his report in the newspaper, but doubted he would be allowed. He was in touch with all the details of what was happening at the Tbilisi newspaper, as his son worked there:

> In Moscow TASS came out with the first piece of information. We printed it and it turned out to be the most terrible disinformation. It was a shock. We found out a week later that it had been falsified in Tbilisi by the Georgian government through their channels. There had been no official ban but traditional taboos remained. On the next day, however, when a state of emergency was called, the Georgian government did declare this topic censored and set conditions on all journalists of the central press to show them their reports.

How could the Georgian republic set conditions on journalists in Moscow? I asked:

> Well, it was so unexpected we were all confused. In fact, I know that the Central Committee was insisting that as much as possible should be published, but the traditional idea of what a paper should or should not print is so strong that even that did not succeed ... Earlier, the military also did not have the right to confiscate the distribution of the Georgian newspaper. The first full information came out only a week later in Shevardnadze's speech on the 16th, which the papers printed.

Golembiovsky said, 'you can justly ask, what kind of *glasnost* is this if we can't read about such an event in our central papers!'[68]

With the politicised mood in the streets and the new status some journalists had gained as people's deputies, most of the media no longer felt committed to Gorbachev's attempts to bridge what seemed an insurmountable gap between conservative and pro-democracy forces. Yeltsin had called Gorbachev an 'eternal' proponent of half measures and his balancing act, however complex, was going nowhere. A master of intra-party politics, having negotiated the treacherous currents of Kremlin intrigue to successfully replace half the hardliners in the Central Committee, Gorbachev could not make the final break from that legacy. He had been an *enfant terrible* by comparison with them, but did not have the will or the flexibility to manoeuvre radical systemic change. The party was moving slower than society. It was the liberal sectors of the media that pushed *glasnost* forward and fought to extend its influence in opposition to the party hierarchy and to Gorbachev himself.

The changed attitude of journalists to authority was particularly evident when Gorbachev tried to sack Vladislav Starkov, editor-in-chief of the weekly *Argumenty i fakty*. Perhaps it had been unwise to pick on a media outlet with the largest circulation in the world, soon to peak at over 30 million copies. Starkov believed the cause of Gorbachev's ire was the result of a popularity poll of people's deputies published by the weekly, which Gorbachev said was 'erroneous'. The ratings showed radical democrats topping the bill, with Andrei Sakharov first on the list, followed by Gavriil Popov and Yeltsin. Gorbachev was omitted from the publication because of his low rating.[69] Because the list was based on 15,000 readers' letters from different parts of the Union, the weekly admitted the poll was not scientifically representative and apologised, but the journalist collective was not prepared to accept the resignation of their editor. Starkov was summoned to the Ideological Department of the Central Committee three times but refused to resign. Theoretically the Central Committee could not sack him, as legally this could be done only by the board of the weekly's 'founder'. This was the Znaniye ('Knowledge') Society, an eminent public organisation crammed full of academicians and scientists who were unwilling to take on this unpleasant task.

Starkov remained in his post but one thing had become clear: Gorbachev could not be relied on to support *glasnost*. Starkov argued that *glasnost* could not be compartmentalised: '*Glasnost* as a right is an indivisible concept. I therefore believe that a blow against *Argumenty i fakty* is a blow against *glasnost*'.[70] The frustration reformers felt took a more sensational form six months later when pro-democracy deputies simply seized Leningrad television to ensure a programme would not be censored. Television executives had refused to allow an interview to be broadcast with Nikolai Ivanov, the famous prosecutor in the Uzbek affair. To make sure it was broadcast, 30 deputies took over the studio and remained there until the four-hour programme had ended.

Although *glasnost* had been introduced as a policy 'from above', it was now being advanced 'from below' by the media and their supporters. The demand was no longer for *glasnost* but for free speech. Once Article 6 defining the guiding role of the party in the Soviet Constitution had been abolished in March 1990, *glasnost* was dead. The word '*glasnost*' had already largely gone out of currency, people now talked about a free press and independent media. Free speech was pursued not as an instrument of government policy, but in its Enlightenment connotation of the spirit of critical inquiry, without any attempt to find new 'socialist' forms of improving it. Of all the democratic reforms Gorbachev had initiated, *glasnost* was the most successful and tangible, laying the foundations for the new Russia that would emerge under Yeltsin. In extending the parameters of *glasnost* the media now had to oppose Gorbachev, whose brainchild it was. If up to 1990 the pro-democracy media were often critical of Gorbachev's actions, they were not hostile to him; but after what came to be known as Gorbachev's 'turn to the right' in the winter of 1990 he began to be seen as an opponent.

In early 1990 changes in political structure benefited the democratic movement, narrowing Gorbachev's powers. The end of the party's monopoly of power entailed the acceptance of a multi-party system and a pluralist society. The parliamentary victory of the democrats at the local and republican elections placed well-known radicals in leading positions and made Yeltsin, elected as chairman of the Russian Republic's Supreme Soviet, one of the most powerful men in the country. Heading the largest and most significant of the 15 republics in the union, Yeltsin had established a rival power base to that of Gorbachev's, whose new role as President of the Soviet Union would become irrelevant if Yeltsin's proclamation of sovereignty for all the republics was put into effect. Yeltsin threatened that he would not tolerate the squandering of Russia's wealth to support the imperialist ambitions of the Soviet Union. He was not proposing that Russia leave the union yet, but he was emphasising its powerful new status.

In this radical climate the much-awaited USSR Law on the Press and other Mass Media finally came into force in August 1990. Under the provisions of the law, any organisation or individual could start a newspaper or media company. A plethora of newspapers of different political groupings and opinions came out, mostly democratic in orientation. Some quality outlets, such as *Stolitsa* ('Capital') and *Kuranty* ('Chimes') did not last through the 1990s, while others became permanent fixtures, such as *Kommersant* and *Nezavisimaya gazeta* ('Independent Newspaper') – although with changing ownerships. The conservatives were not as concerned about starting new outlets because they could still rely on such established pillars of society as *Pravda* and TASS. As the opportunity arose for a free press, the problems of the market made themselves known. The shortage and price of paper increased and the race for subscriptions began. The press now had to determine the cost of independence; as one headline said '*glasnost* needs more paper'.

In the electronic media, some of the best known programmes became independent production companies with the idea of buying air time from Gosteleradio. *Vzglyad* formed its own company, VID, while another group of well-known TV figures formed ATV. A new private wire agency, Interfax, gained a reputation for being more up to date than its state-run rival TASS, especially in reporting reliable leaks – a new phenomenon for a formerly air-tight society. An independent radio station, Ekho Moskvy ('Echo of Moscow') began its career with a group of young enthusiasts. At the same time there was a demand that the Russian Republic have its own television channel. All the union republics had their own television and radio stations except Russia which, as always, had the dubious honour of being represented under the Soviet banner. The idea was for Gosteleradio to allocate air time on the second channel for Russian television and a frequency for Russian radio, which would be under the control of the Russian (RSFSR) Supreme Soviet. The technology involved in broadcasting studios and expensive equipment bought with foreign currency meant that Russian republican television could work only if Central Television was willing to share its facilities. In the increasingly aggressive political climate this became a problem. No sooner had outlets come to life as independent entities, when they found themselves facing fierce censorship again in the conservative clampdown that took place in the winter of 1990–1.

After the party

The shift of power favouring the democrats had unexpected consequences. The party, which had gone into a state of shock after the abolition of Article 6 was now, in the words of one of its opponents, 'coming out of the trenches'. Gorbachev's power base as President of the Union was shaky and he chose to make tactical allies not with the democrats but with the most reactionary elements in the conservative camp: militarists, the KGB and hardline communists, men who later plotted the coup. The conflicts of dual power between Gorbachev and Yeltsin, the union and republics, were reflected in the media, as both camps vied for outlets which would become their mouthpieces. The newly found independence of the press posed a challenge to the Kremlin at a time when Gorbachev was fighting to control the republics and their demand for sovereignty. The concessionary politics that had given birth to the Law on the Press, with its emphasis on pluralism, no longer suited Gorbachev. If the press had become unruly, television had not yet been dismantled. Gorbachev's officials took the position that the Press Law did not relate to television, and the earlier promise to give air time to Russian television was left up in the air. A number of Yeltsin's appearances on TV had been cancelled, putting the radicals in a vulnerable position.

Gosteleradio's head, Nenashev, complained he had no peace with calls from Gorbachev and Yeltsin for air time and from the new radical mayors of Moscow and Petersburg who had been swept to power. For the purposes of democratisation, he said, it was necessary to renounce the existing monopoly the union held over all television channels and set up a new structure to replace rigid centralisation. But while Nenashev was mapping out the future of television at a press conference, he had not been informed that he would be sacked the following day. Gorbachev had no intention of losing his monopoly of television and appointed Leonid Kravchenko as Gosteleradio's new chairman. On 14 November 1990, Kravchenko made his position clear: 'I have come to fulfil the president's will'.[71]

Kravchenko could be relied on. A protégé of Ligachev and an establishment figure, he had held high positions in the press and television and had just been poached from TASS. He had already spoken out at the first congress of people's deputies against the democrats who were trying to 'intimidate us' with the label of Stalinism; in fact, he asked, what sort of democrats were they if they were intolerant of the 'dissenting majority' of party activists whom they called Stalinist–Brezhnevite?[72] Kravchenko set about curbing television freedoms almost immediately. The biggest scandal came when he closed down *Vzglyad*. On 28 December 1990 an announcer explained that the programme would not be transmitted because of the presenters' 'assessment' of certain events. The reason was Shevardnadze's resignation as Foreign Minister on 20 December. *Vzglyad* knew that Shevardnadze would not speak to the media, so they intended to interview two of his assistants. Kravchenko would not permit it.

Shevardnadze's resignation had the effect of a bombshell, as did his cryptic statement to parliament that 'dictatorship was approaching'. That this man who had been so respected at home and in the West, who with Gorbachev had been co-author of the ending of the cold war and the withdrawal of troops from Afghanistan and Eastern Europe, was abandoning Gorbachev's team was an ominous sign for the country's democratic reforms. Shevardnadze had raised the anger of right-wing military circles and the 'black colonels', conservative deputies opposing the secessionist movement in the Baltics, with whom Gorbachev had formed an alliance and who were now calling the tune on television. Apart from a report on *Vremya* on the day of his resignation, which was passed only because Molchanov happened to be the presenter of the news that evening, there was no coverage of this momentous event. (Molchanov resigned from *Vremya* soon after.) Reports in the democratic press pointed to Gorbachev's betrayal of his old liberal colleagues – Shevardnadze, Aleksandr Yakovlev, Vadim Bakatin – 'who will be next?', asked *Kommersant*.

On 9 January 1991 *Vzglyad* was formally closed down with a written ban. This was the first time in Soviet TV history that a written ban had been issued. On all other occasions bans had issued from nowhere, based on the 'telephone law'. Was this an improvement? Throughout the three years of its life *Vzglyad* had often been threatened with closure, but had always bounced back, and in the heyday of *glasnost* it would have been difficult to suppress it. Now *Vzglyad* and ATV were off the air.

The next independent organisation to suffer was the private news agency Interfax, which was unceremoniously kicked out of its premises at TV Centre on 11 January. Gosteleradio's collegium had met that morning and by the afternoon all the equipment had been seized and the doors barred by militia. That evening, Valery Komissar, the general-director of Interfax, had a personal meeting with Kravchenko, where he said he would file charges against Gosteleradio for the loss of their equipment. An agreement was reached whereby Gosteleradio returned their equipment and Interfax returned borrowed computers. Komissar then went to Yeltsin for help and was promptly given a room by the Moscow City Executive Committee. Interfax was back in business a day later, but without the wide journalistic network or the facilities it had been able to use at TV Centre. Gosteleradio looked to legal means to explain its thuggish behaviour, arguing that Interfax had not registered as required under the Press Law. Interfax, however, was able to make use of a loophole in the law, which had not taken into account the existence of fax – in effect, there was no law against the use of conveying information by telephone!

With Kravchenko in tow, Gosteleradio's programming policy changed dramatically. Kravchenko's approach was well known: less politics and more entertainment. 'People are tired of talking heads whatever channel you happen to switch on', he said.[73] He had a point, because television had begun to transmit all parliamentary proceedings to make sure no side would start complaining. Channel One broadcast sessions of the USSR Supreme Soviet, Channel Two sessions of the Russian Supreme Soviet, the Moscow channel sessions of the Mossoviet and the Leningrad channel sessions of the Lensoviet. This was extravagant, but it was also a part of the learning process of democracy in a society that did not feel wholly confident of relying on the media to interpret information for it. There was no evidence that the public wanted these transmissions stopped or an end put to the familiar studio discussions *glasnost* had introduced.

All the signs pointed to a crackdown in the Baltics, where we now know preparations were under way to impose direct presidential rule and dissolve the elected councils and parliaments. This conspiracy on the part of the army and hardline communists had two aims: to preserve the Union on which Gorbachev's authority rested and to oppose the bid of other republics, particularly Russia, for independence. In January 1991 events in the Baltics reached a climax. The 'black berets' or OMON – special paramilitary troops under the Soviet Internal Affairs Ministry – were sent to Lithuania and on 7 January the printing house in Vilnius was seized. Ostensibly the issue in dispute was Communist Party property. When the Lithuanian party had broken away from the union parent organisation, all that remained of it was a small Russian-dominated group whose interests OMON was now claiming to protect. This small group of the old Lithuanian Communist Party had set up a Committee of National Salvation, an unelected and unconstitutional body, which announced on 11 January that it was taking power in Lithuania. Gorbachev later said he had known nothing about it, but nor did he do anything to punish the perpetrators. He was in a weak position and his only recourse, he said, was to 'zigzag'.[74] The build-up of events culminated at 2 a.m. on 13 January in the storming of the Lithuanian TV Centre by the OMON troops.

Unarmed crowds that had gathered around the TV Centre to prevent the buildings being taken were shot at by Soviet troops. In this tragedy 14 Lithuanians were killed and more than 800 wounded.

Among the many eyewitness accounts of what happened early that morning, this statement is from Egidijus Zickus, a member of the Lithuanian Union of Journalists:

> I was one of those who joined hands and stood around the TV tower. With searchlights blazing, the column of tanks approached, beginning to crush the cars that had been parked to create a barrier. Then paratroopers arrived. Without warning they rushed at us and began to beat us with their rifle butts. Then shots were heard. With my own eyes I saw a paratrooper open a burst of machine-gun fire at the crowd. Five people fell to the ground. My colleague and I lifted up a man lying close by, but he didn't show any sign of life. I swear that none of those shot at were armed. It was a kind of madness. Right up to the last moment we did not think they would open fire.[75]

Reports and TV video clips from Lithuanian and foreign sources of the carnage were seen around the world, but this did not deter *Vremya* from fabricating its own version of the news. According to presenter Dmitry Biryukov, fire was opened outside the television centre not by Soviet troops but by Lithuanians on the orders of the Lithuanian president and Sajudis, the Lithuanian independence movement. TASS reinforced the lie in its reports.

Gosteleradio then turned heavy-handedly to the late-night news, TSN – a news group set up by the TV journalist Aleksandr Gurnov and modelled on short US-style news bulletins. With a team of young journalists, TSN had gained a reputation for impartial news coverage. The popular young presenter, Tatyana Mitkova had 30 minutes before going on air when Gosteleradio's first deputy chairman Pyotr Reshetov scrapped the bulletin they had planned, which was to be a special film of the bloodshed by Latvian TV and footage from CNN and Swedish TV. Instead Reshetov handed her his own hastily scribbled text with the official Soviet version of events. Mitkova rebelled and refused to read it:

> 'If you don't read it, we'll close down TSN', Reshetov said.
> 'Bring in your own announcer then', Mitkova replied.[76]

After that the rebels at TSN (Mitkova, Dmitry Kiselyov and Yury Rostov) had censors assigned to watch them, and soon after were sacked.

Aleksandr Nevzorov's notorious fabricated film of the events, *Nashi*, was a godsend to Gosteleradio, which broadcast it three times on nationwide television. As defender of the 'black berets', Nevzorov's nationalist approach fitted well with Gosteleradio's message, if at the price of further discrediting the channel and Gorbachev's position:

If there is even a grain, a drop of justice, in this world, then in years to come, by the foot of this tower at the TV centre, these 160 maligned and spurned paratroopers … should be cast in bronze. They saved Lithuania, they saved it from bloody disgrace that can never be washed away … these 160 embattled, unshaven lads. [the Wagner soundtrack reaches a crescendo as the so-called documentary turns into pure agitprop and we see Kalashnikov after Kalashnikov in slow motion, each one labelled with the word Nashi in bold letters][77]

Many newspapers expressed outrage at the army's brutality against peaceful Lithuanian demonstrators and, later, at the four deaths in Latvia. Particularly damning was the front page of *Moskovskiye novosti* with its heading 'Bloody Sunday' and a statement from the newspaper's board of directors, framed in funereal black and headlined 'The crime of a regime unwilling to leave the stage'.[78] The members of the board were all prominent cultural and media figures who had at one time taken up the banner for Gorbachev. Yegor Yakovlev, as editor, felt justified in giving the board's statement front-page coverage, but he himself did not sign it. He never lost his loyalty to Gorbachev for initiating *glasnost*. Although many suspected that Gorbachev had become a hostage of the conservatives, he had made his choice to stand with them and not with the democrats. Earlier, when he became USSR President, he had rejected a proposal to make Yeltsin his vice-president.[79] He had rejected an even earlier proposal, after the 1987 Plenum, to keep Yeltsin as an ally. Had he done so, Yeltsin later said, 'history might have veered in a different direction'.[80] As it was, Yeltsin had become the most popular man in the country with his commitment to transform Russia into a democratic society and give the republics the right to self-determination.

The demand to kill off *glasnost* when it was in full swing showed the same lack of awareness among the ministers Gorbachev had put into power, as they later showed when plotting the coup. Simply giving orders no longer had any effect on large swathes of the population. The massive demonstrations and political meetings that were taking place in early 1991 included calls for a free media and the demand of 'Kravchenko – out!'. There were demonstrations in support of *Vzglyad* outside the Ostankino TV centre and on 22 February on Manezh Square, at the time an enormous open space by the Kremlin walls. Crowds cheered *Vzglyad*'s Aleksandr Politkovsky when he jumped onto the podium and welcomed the masses with the words 'Hello comrade anti-communists' – typical, Kravchenko said, of *Vzglyad*'s hooliganism. There were cheers as well for Radio Russia, which had been given a frequency that only one-third of Russia could access, and for TSN with its rebellious presenters.

The party bias against Yeltsin was so severe that it brought him even more sympathy than he already had. At this point Yeltsin would accept only live broadcasts from Kravchenko for fear that his speeches might be edited to his disadvantage. When Yeltsin wanted an hour live on the first channel he had to negotiate with Kravchenko for weeks and finally received 40 minutes on 19

February only with the help of the RSFSR Supreme Soviet. His speech caused a storm, and even shocked his supporters. Gorbachev had deceived him and the people and was now taking the country into a dictatorship, said Yeltsin. He had made his choice, from which he would not deviate. He dissociated himself from Gorbachev and called on him to resign immediately, transferring powers to the federation council, the chamber for representatives of the Republics in the Union. Criticism against Yeltsin on the first channel was fierce: he was attempting to overturn the constitutional order and bring the country to the point of civil war, all because of his political ambitions. What the first channel did not report was support for the speech from the overwhelming majority of the RSFSR Supreme Soviet. On 23 and 24 February two large demonstrations were held on Manezh Square: the first organised by military leaders which got massive publicity on the first channel, the second, held by the Democratic Russia movement, which was not reported but was attended by about 100,000 people, far more than on the previous day.

The largest demonstration in the history of the Soviet Union was held on 10 March with half a million people in Manezh Square in support of Yeltsin; and another half a million in the provinces as reported by TSN, but not by *Vremya*. It called for Gorbachev's resignation and rejected the referendum in support of the Union to be held on 17 March. As Kravchenko now really feared what Yeltsin might say on television, he refused to give him live air time before the referendum. After a public outcry, he offered him ten minutes. Yeltsin refused the offer and spoke on Radio Russia instead. Central Television unleashed a propaganda campaign 'unprecedented since the death of Stalin', according to one article, urging people to vote 'yes' to the union. Except for occasional rebellious TSN reports, no opposition voices were allowed on the first channel. Two days before the referendum, programmes were interrupted every two hours with a video clip instructing viewers on how to cast a Yes vote. No information was given on the No vote. TSN, on the other hand, displayed a sample ballot and advised people to think for themselves. That evening the three rebellious presenters were dismissed.

After the Lithuanian events, Gorbachev was stung by the barrage of criticism he received. But he shocked liberal deputies in the Supreme Soviet even more when he suggested out of the blue that the Press Law should be suspended. In its place, he said, the Supreme Soviet should take control of television, radio and all the newspapers to ensure that all points of view were expressed. (Noise in the hall.) He understood his mistake as soon as people's deputy and Dostoyevsky scholar, Yury Karyakin, questioned his proposition:

> The president says that it's necessary to suspend the Press Law even if only for a month. Does he remember that we suspended it once before in 1918 [1917 – DS] and after that it took us over 70 years to restore it?[81]

Karyakin later pondered at the offhand way in which Gorbachev had introduced such a dramatic move:

He made a suggestion – and what a suggestion! – and immediately revoked it. What does that mean? Was it a slip of the tongue or did he let the cat out of the bag? Was it carelessness or calculation, or was he trying it on, as it were?[82]

Karyakin wondered if *glasnost* had failed to make an impact on the Soviet Union. Surely, as Anna Akhmatova's *Requiem* and Solzhenitsyn's *The Gulag Archipelago* had been published – the works that had so demystified the Soviet regime – it wasn't possible that nothing had changed? As one of the 'people of the 1960s', he was nervous the clock would turn back. If repression returned, how would it be done? 'Through censorship? Kravchenko? Bringing Ligachev back from retirement? Jamming foreign radio stations? Putting photocopiers under surveillance?' He concluded positively, that the process of *glasnost* had changed people's perceptions irreversibly. Gorbachev had no chance of rolling back his own policies because 'hundreds and thousands of bottles have been uncorked and no force can fool the genies to get back and be recorked'.

Karyakin was right that things had gone too far. After six years of *glasnost* many people had become accustomed to speaking their mind, they wanted democratic change and had a powerful leader in Yeltsin. On 12 June 1991 Yeltsin became President of the RSFSR in Russia's first ever presidential elections, where he gained more than 57 per cent of the vote. He had scored a personal victory against Gorbachev with his reformist politics. The Russian republic finally got its own Russian TV channel, which was allowed to go on air regularly from 12 May 1991, broadcasting six hours only a day at first. There was no lack of presenters to work for the channel, as many of the best journalists refused to work under Kravchenko on the first channel or had been sacked for disobeying orders or had been removed from appearing on the screen. In fact, the crème de la crème was on the Russian channel. Many of the TV journalists and presenters who later became household names in Yeltsin's Russia got their first journalistic experience in this political milieu. At the Congress of the Russian Union of Journalists a decision had been taken not to participate in certain programmes on Central Television. An underground version of *Vzglyad* was coming out occasionally in video cassettes, put together by Aleksandr Politkovsky from a private flat and distributed in some provinces. There was greater solidarity among journalists and pro-democracy supporters than ever before. They showed they could fight for free speech and democracy against reactionary forces. It was in this upbeat mood that pro-democracy supporters confronted the coup plotters in August 1991.

Notes

1 'Zhivoe tvorchestvo naroda', speech to the All-Union Scientific and Practical Conference, 10 December 1984, *Izbrannye rechi i stat'i* , Izdatel'stvo politicheskoi literatury, Moscow, vol. 2, p. 95.

2 *Pravda*, 21 November, 1985.
3 *The Soviet Censorship*, Martin Dewhirst and Robert Farrell (eds), Metuchen, NJ: Scarecrow Press, 1973, p. 56.
4 *Sovetskaya Rossiya*, 5 January 1986.
5 First Programme, 19 February 1986.
6 Holt Ruffin and Judy Ballnt, 'Vladimir Pozner, a propagandist', 26 May 1986.
7 'Most Vremeni', ORT, 12 June 1996.
8 Letter from G. N. Bochevarov, *Izvestiya*, 14 March 1987.
9 *Pravda*, 16 April 1987.
10 Interview with author, 31 May 1989.
11 Soviet Television, 4 April 1987, SWB, SU/8535/A1/7, 6 April 1987; Viktor Yasmann, 'Reaction of Soviet Television viewers to Thatcher interview', RFE/RL, 135/87, 10 April 1987.
12 BBC external broadcasting reported that after jamming began Soviet listeners of the Russian service rose to 17 million a month, *Guardian*, 22 April 1988.
13 *Glasnost' kak predmet pravovogo regulirovaniya*, M. A. Fedotov (ed.), Moskva, 2009, pp. 31–2.
14 *Pravda*, 15 July 1987 and First Programme, 14 July 1987.
15 Telman Gdlyan and Nikolai Ivanov, 'Protivostoyanie', *Ogonek*, 26 June 1988.
16 Author's interview, November 1989.
17 Stephen F. Cohen and Katrina Vanden Heuvel, *Voices of Glasnost: Interviews with Gorbachev's Reformers*, New York and London: Norton, 1989, pp. 210–11.
18 Kevin Devlin, '*L'Unità* on "secret history" of Andreeva letter', RFERL RL 2165/88, 26 May 1988, pp. 4, 6.
19 'Kakoi sotsializm narodu nuzhen', *Literaturnaya gazeta*, 20 April 1988.
20 21 April 1988.
21 *Sovetskaya kultura*, 9 April 1988.
22 *Omut pamyati*, Moskva, Vagrius, 2000, p. 275.
23 10 April 1988.
24 *Pravda*, 2 July 1988.
25 *Pravda*, 1 July 1988.
26 *Pravda*, 30 June 1988.
27 'Pochemu v epokhu glasnosti ya ushel s televideniya', *Ogonek*, no. 14, 2–9 April 1988.
28 Medvedev changed the division into nine time zones in 2011.
29 'Here in Ostankino', First Programme, 7 July 1987, SWB SU/8619/C1/1 (B) 14 July 1987; and *SWB* SU/W1389/B/1. 9 May 1986.
30 Televidenie i radioveshchanie, no. 1, 1988.
31 *The Spectator*, 24 August, 1985, p. 10.
32 Soviet Television, 2 January 1987, SWB SU/8457/B/2 5 January 1987.
33 TASS 31 January 1987, SWB SU/8482/ii, 6 February 1987; TASS, 15 March 1987.
34 Quoted in L. Parfenov and Ye. Chekalova, *Nam vozvrashchayut nash portret: zametki o televidenii*, Moskva 'Iskusstvo', 1990, p. 139.
35 Soviet Television, 17 December 1986, SWB SU/8448/B/1, 22 December 1986.
36 Lidiya Pol'skaya, 'TV and viewer: meeting each other', *Moscow News*, no. 20, 1987.
37 He was married at the time to Anna Politkovskaya, who later became famous for her reporting on Chechnya and was assassinated in a contract killing.
38 Aleksandr Nevzorov, *Pole chesti*, Sankt–Peterburg, 'Shans', 1995, p. 60.
39 Ibid., p. 68.
40 Ibid., p. 67.
41 Ibid., p. 60.
42 *Pravda*, 11 May 1988, SWB, SU/0149 C/1, 3, 12 May 1988.

43 Elizabeth Teague, 'Gorbachev answers his critics', RFE/RL, RL, 289/87, 15 July 1987, p. 4.
44 'Our Pluralists', *Survey*, vol. 29, summer 1985, pp. 1–2.
45 Aaron Trehub, 'Gorbachev meets Soviet writers: A *samizdat* account', RFE/RL, RL Research 399/86, 23 October 1986.
46 Meeting on 8 January 1988, Tass (also *Pravda* 13 January 1988), *SWB* SU/0048 B/5, 14 January 1988. There were four main meetings with the media: on 14 February and 14 July 1987; and 8 January and 11 May 1988.
47 Soviet Television, 14 July 1987, SWB, SU/8621/B/3, 16 July 1987.
48 Ibid.
49 'Criticism in the press: how well argued it is and how people react' (leader), *Pravda*, 9 March 1987, SWB, SU/8515/B/5, 13 March 1987.
50 *New Statesman and Nation*, 27 October 1934, in Christopher Silvester (ed.), *The Penguin Book of Interviews: An Anthology from 1859 to the Present Day*, London: Penguin, 1994, p. 341.
51 Viktor Yasmann, 'Photocopiers in the era of *glasnost*', RFE/RL 371/87, 21 September 1987.
52 No. 36, 9–15 September 1989.
53 G. Alimov and R. Lynev, 'Where memory is heading', *Izvestiya*, 3 June 1987, SWB, SU/8592/B1, 12 June 1987.
54 Quoted by Tony Barber, 'Unofficial "patriotic" group marches in Moscow, weekly says', Reuters, 14 May 1987.
55 Boris Yeltsin, *Against the Grain: An Autobiography*, trans. Michael Glenny, London: Jonathan Cape, 1990, p. 147.
56 Timothy J. Colton, *Yeltsin: A Life*, New York: Basic Books, 2008, p. 148.
57 Author's interview, 15 June 1990, taken for Brian Lapping Productions.
58 Colton, *Yeltsin*, p. 153.
59 Kevin Devlin, 'Soviet journalist describes El'tsin's struggle against party "mafia"', 20 May 1988, RFE/RL 206/88, p. 3.
60 Yeltsin, *Against the Grain*, p. 170.
61 *Omut pamyati*, p. 273.
62 Colton, *Yeltsin*, p. 176.
63 Ibid., p. 175.
64 *Zapiski prezidenta*, Izdatel'stvo 'Ogonek', Moskva, 1994, p. 181.
65 *Pravda*, 3 December 1987, *SWB*, SU/0020 B/2, 8 December 1987.
66 'The Congress and political reform', *Moscow News* (in English), no. 25, 18 June 1989.
67 '*Glasnost* rationed out', *Moscow News* (in English), no. 19, 7 May 1989.
68 Author's interview, 19 May 1989.
69 *Argumenty i fakty*, no. 40, 7–13 October and no. 42, 21–27 October 1989, SWB SU/0594 B/2, 23 October 1989.
70 Soviet Television, 25 November 1989, SWB SU/0634 B/1, 8 December 1989.
71 V. Arsenev, 'Ya prishel, chtoby vypolnit' volyu prezidenta', *Izvestiya*, 4 December 1990.
72 Soviet Television, 27 May 1989.
73 *Izvestiya*, 12 February 1991.
74 Bridget Kendall, 'New light shed on 1991 anti-Gorbachev coup', *BBC*, 18 August 2011. www.bbc.co.uk/news/world-europe-14560280 (accessed 17 December 2015).
75 *Moscow News* (in English), no. 3, 1991.
76 *Moskovskie novosti*, no. 3, 20 January 1991.
77 Soviet Television, 16 and 20 January 1991.
78 *Moskovskie novosti*, no. 3, 20 January 1991.
79 The proposal was put forward by Georgy Shakhnazarov; see Archie Brown, *The Gorbachev Factor*, Oxford: Oxford University Press, 1996, p. 287.

80 A suggestion by Gorbachev's foreign policy adviser, Anatoly Chernyaev; and Yeltsin's response on hearing about it from Timothy J. Colton as recorded in his *Yeltsin: a Life*, New York: Basic Books, 2008, p. 147.

81 'Prezident predlagaet i otkazyvaetsya', *Moskovskie novosti* , no. 4, 27 January 1991.

82 'Snova zagnut' dzhinna v butylku? K debatam o svobode pechati', *Moskovskie novosti*, no. 4, 27 January 1991.

6   The coup: give freedom a chance

> The peoples of Russia ... are becoming masters of their fate.
>
> (Yeltsin, August 1991)

I Tragedy or farce?

The coup lasted only three days – 19, 20 and 21 August 1991 – but its impact was huge. During those days there was no image more iconic of defiance to the coup than Yeltsin standing on top of a tank outside the White House, the seat of the Russian republic's parliament, surrounded by supporters – an image that was flashed all over the world. The other iconic image was when television went blank, and came on with a film of the ballet *Swan Lake* that was played and replayed endlessly between news bulletins. It was a bleak forecast of what awaited free speech if the coup succeeded. But what can one make of the symbolism 20 years later in 2011, when to mark the anniversary of victory over the coup the state channel Kultura broadcast the same film of the ballet *Swan Lake*. Was it mockery? A bad joke? Or a derisory comment on the days of freedom when people went out into the streets to take control of their own lives?

The fact is that after two decades, perceptions of the coup have changed. In the Levada Centre's opinion poll in 2011, 39 per cent saw the coup as a tragic event that brought disastrous consequences to the country and its people. This was higher than ten years earlier in 2001 when 25 per cent saw the coup in this way. In 2011, 49 per cent thought the coup had taken the country in the wrong direction. Most respondents in 2011 saw the coup in terms of a power struggle among political elites which had little to do with them. A mere 10 per cent in both 2011 and 2001 viewed the coup as a victory for democracy that brought the Soviet regime to an end.[1] This tells us that most Russians, looking back at the Yeltsin years after the coup, see them as a time of economic disaster and cultural disorientation; and only the more socially aware talk about receiving basic freedoms and self-realisation. Added to that, public hostility to the 1990s has been consistently stoked by Putin's media, which describe the decade as a period of unremitting chaos.

Another significant fact to emerge from these surveys is that over the last two decades people have lost the confidence they had in themselves as political actors. When asked why the coup failed, only 15 per cent (2011) and 20 per cent (2001) replied that it was a result of resistance by the people; although 57 per cent had given this as their answer in September 1991. In 1991 as well 55 per cent said the coup failed because of decisive action by the Russian leadership. Two decades later people presumed the coup failed not because of their or Yeltsin's actions, but because the plotters were badly organised (28 per cent), while 26 per cent did not know.[2] Sixteen years of political apathy had made itself felt under Putin's stated objective to 'manage' society. It was not like that in 1991, as Masha Lipman remembers: 'people believed in democracy against oppression, they believed in Boris Yeltsin and most amazing of all they believed in themselves. Never in Russian history was "we the people" so meaningful and so peaceful'.[3] The human rights advocate Lev Ponomaryov adds: 'money played no part at the time. Muscovites knew that the putsch was not directed solely against Yeltsin and people's deputies, but against each one of them. That's why they went out on the streets. Not because Yeltsin called them or instructed them to come out, but because they wanted to, heart and soul'.[4]

The anniversary replaying of *Swan Lake* on state TV reflects the ambivalence today to an event which truly did have enormous consequences. The coup led to the end of 74 years of communist rule, the ousting of Gorbachev and the demise of the Soviet Union. It was called the August Revolution and equated with February 1917, only this time it brought an end to the grand and devastating experiment that started with a coup in October 1917. By comparison with this gravitas, the coup itself was a farcical misadventure. No wonder so many newspapers quoted Marx's sardonic comment that the first time is tragedy, the second time is farce. Not only was the coup mishandled, there was an element of Soviet surrealism about the way the plotters never felt they needed to do much more than say the word, bring out the troops and people would fall into line, as they always did. It was as if the past few years of political struggle had meant nothing. The plotters launched military intervention, bringing an estimated 20,000 troops with armoured vehicles into Moscow and could have provoked bloodshed on a massive scale, but they continued to give the impression of normalcy. The attempt at deception, a stock in trade as we saw in the different ways of normalising lies in Chapter 4, was to enforce change without taking responsibility if things went wrong. It might have worked if Yeltsin and the Russian government had not immediately exposed it for what it was: a 'right-wing reactionary anti-constitutional coup'. It was only public resistance and the determination of protesters who faced the tanks that stopped the plotters in their tracks. Otherwise, as Yeltsin put it in his appeal to the armed forces, the country would have been 'wrapped in eternal night'.

Fewer and fewer people remember what was at stake. The coup plotters or GKChP, the Russian acronym for the USSR's State Committee for the State of Emergency, which they called themselves, were all ministers and officials that Gorbachev had brought into his government. The first thing they should have done was arrest Yeltsin, as they had planned to do. But in their eyes the main opponent was 'Michael', the derogatory name they gave Gorbachev for succumbing to flattery from the West, whose reforms they planned to thwart and save the multinational Soviet Union, 'one and indivisible', as it was once known but now tearing apart at the seams. The timing of the coup was no accident as the union treaty between Gorbachev and the republican leaders, which would have taken power away from the union bureaucracy, was to be signed on 20 August. This, to the plotters, was a betrayal of the Soviet Union. The day before the coup, five of the conspirators had flown to the Crimea, where Gorbachev was in his holiday villa in Foros on the Black Sea, to ask him to resign. When he refused, they decided to say he was ill and incapacitated.

Yet Gorbachev was also the person they called their 'friend' throughout the coup and to whom they rushed when it failed, rather than fleeing to Cuba or Iraq, the only two countries that had approved the takeover. This strange dependence fuelled heated speculation that Gorbachev had collaborated in their plans and would, after they had done the dirty work, return to power. Yeltsin made no comment at the time, but in 2006 he said Gorbachev knew all about the coup from the beginning and waited to see who would win, knowing that whatever the outcome it was a 'win-win' situation for him.[5] Gorbachev maintained he would never reveal 'the whole truth', but in 2011 he made an admission of sorts: 'People said Gorbachev knew – and how could he have not known? ... they rang me from everywhere, warning me – a coup, a coup, a coup ... my entourage informed me ... but the main thing was to prevent much bloodshed ... and we did ... there might have been a civil war'.[6] This disjointed jumble of words is not unusual of the way Gorbachev speaks, but it seems to confirm Yeltsin's statement. It also shows the abysmal level of journalism in 2011 that no one at the press conference asked Gorbachev to explain himself.

No doubt, there was a hidden game. Although the coup plotters put Gorbachev under house arrest, they later claimed they had never intended to depose him or to seize power. 'I never meant to deprive the president of his power', said Marshal Yazov, USSR Minister of Defence. 'We wanted him to delegate his powers temporarily to the vice-president', said Vladimir Kryuchkov, KGB chief. 'There was no coup', said Valentin Pavlov, USSR Prime Minister – who drank himself into such a stupor that he had to be hospitalised and thus claimed he was not responsible for the events that took place.[7] The charade of innocence was hard to sustain when troops had been summoned, plans to obliterate the White House and everyone in it had been found and stashes of handcuffs and arrest warrants had been prepared beforehand. It so exasperated the prosecutor during their interrogation that he expostulated to Kryuchkov: 'The way you talk, you would think a few youngsters had got together and decided to play a game'.

In effect, the coup was an act of entitlement by members of the communist *nomenklatura* confident of impunity. This old school of Soviet politics was jolted out of existence by the new political culture of direct action that had developed in the pro-democracy movement. Yeltsin did not mince his words when he defined the act immediately as a state crime. The Russian government at the time swiftly and efficiently dealt with all eventualities, from General Kobets's plans to counter military intervention, to Moscow deputy mayor Yury Luzhkov's management of the city to ensure the Metro was running and goods were on the shelves to prevent panic; while pro-democracy supporters knew they were fighting for their freedom when they manned the barricades. Even if Gorbachev was ill, and there was deep concern for his fate, they were aware that the right-wing offensive was against democracy.

The plotters, thinking in the old way, had assumed that everything stood or fell on the fate of the party general secretary. In their eyes the coup had probably succeeded the moment they had secretly arrested Gorbachev. In earlier days when Beria and Khrushchev were deposed in palace coups society had absorbed these events seamlessly. The plotters' focus on Gorbachev may explain why they made so many mistakes. As well as failing to arrest Yeltsin, they did not cut Moscow's city telephone network, the media were only partially closed down, parliament was not dissolved, the White House was not cordoned off, and although a blacklist had been drafted of people to be detained during the coup, only three were arrested and they were released a day later. The list of 69 names, with Yeltsin as the last name, reads like an honours list of democratic activists and campaigning journalists.[8] The GKChP had been plotting for almost a year and, between them, they had all the information the state could offer. In fact, Kryuchkov had been involved in massive wiretapping, from Raisa's hairdresser to Gorbachev himself, an unprecedented act. Valery Boldin's office in party headquarters held vast safes crammed with secret files of bugged conversations. Nevertheless, with all this power at their fingertips, as soon as they were confronted by popular resistance they faltered and began blaming each other for having been dragged into this fiasco. Nor did they expect to pay for their actions: the party had always looked after its own. Most of them were surprised when they were arrested after the failure of the coup. The KGB's Kryuchkov asked: 'Why, was it so terrible?'[9]

The first thing the plotters did was to muzzle free speech. Gosteleradio's TV centre was seized by the military and most newspaper buildings were surrounded by armoured vehicles. Throughout the day, interspersed between *Swan Lake* and concerts, there were announcements from the GKChP. People knew that whenever classical music replaced normal programmes something serious had happened, usually the death of the party general secretary. What was happening now was unclear: was Gorbachev really ill? Was he dead, or were the rumours true (General Varennikov's story) that Gorbachev had gone mad because the birthmark on his head had seeped into his brain? With TV centre in their hands, the plotters could invent whatever story they wanted.

This was the peak of many years of struggle for the liberal media and pro-democracy reformers. They had crumbled before when hardliners had tried to sabotage reform. This time, having experienced several years of full-throated freedom, the very thought that they could be throttled at a stroke seemed inconceivable. Although the danger on the streets was real, it was the sense of being pinned down while in full flight to a freer life that made resistance almost automatic. Many people said they didn't stop to think. Suddenly solidarity was not a problem: the aim was simple and unanimous, to defeat the coup and protect democracy. Journalists cooperated with each other to use every device up their sleeves to overcome the media quarantine.

What followed resembled an operetta or a blockbuster, three days of intense political activity and moral fervour. Today, in the climate of an obedient media and a population happy to be fed on propaganda, it has almost been forgotten that thousands fought for Russia to be a democracy. The most tangible way of describing the drama is through the words of witnesses. There are many facets to this story (political, military), but for our purposes it is a story of how free speech was successfully exercised to expose the lies behind the coup. My account is based on a variety of sources: descriptions in the Russian media, memoirs and books, the Public Prosecution's interrogations and extensive interviews I took soon after the coup.[10] The first day was the most decisive, determining the future success in defeating the coup.

19 August

The head of Gosteleradio, Leonid Kravchenko was woken up in the early hours of the morning and called to the phone. He was told a KGB car would bring him to Communist Party headquarters on Staraya Ploshchad. The fact that the conspirators were plotting from party offices was no surprise. The traffic between party headquarters and the Kremlin was as active as it had always been despite the fact that the party's leading role in state affairs had been abolished in March 1990.

The plotters were preparing to broadcast their announcement on the six o'clock early morning news. Kravchenko was told to wait and take the documents at 5 a.m. to the TV centre at Ostankino. Kravchenko was Gorbachev's man, but he says he had no reason to question the GKChP about Gorbachev's supposed illness. He had tried to phone him in Foros, but the lines had already been disconnected. When 20 years later at a studio discussion with some of the main players Kravchenko claimed he was a 'hostage' to the GKChP, it received hearty laughter from an old-time opponent, Aleksandr Lyubimov, who reminded him of how he had facilitated Gorbachev's 'turn to the right'. Like many functionaries who were not privy to the GKChP's plans, Kravchenko played a wait-and-see game. When Russian government leaders tried to solicit his assistance to use central television to denounce the GKChP and find out what had happened to Gorbachev, Kravchenko told them there was nothing he could do as he was under military supervision at TV centre.[11] Other TV professionals, however, were not deterred.

That morning, Kravchenko phoned Gennady Shishkin, who was in charge of TASS while the director was on holiday. He was told there was urgent news to put out. The KGB car that came to collect him rushed through the empty streets, ignoring traffic lights. Shishkin was apprehensive. As they drove up to Lubyanka Square there were two buildings in front of him, the KGB building on the left and the Party HQ on the right. Shishkin breathed a sigh of relief when it turned to the right. He received the documents and was driven to TASS. A phone call from the KGB told him to expect two men, who would be arriving to 'assist' him. These KGB officers took seats in his office and monitored his movements for the rest of the day.

Earlier still that morning, at 3 a.m., the order came from Kryuchkov to surround Yeltsin's country dacha in the stylish suburb of Arkhangelskoye, outside Moscow. Paratroopers from the crack anti-terrorist unit Alpha were to keep the dacha under surveillance and monitor Yeltsin's movements.

When Kravchenko arrived just before 6 a.m. at TV centre, the building was already surrounded by armoured vehicles and he himself had trouble getting inside. Over a thousand people on the nightshift were held back from leaving the building, while the morning shift could not get in, until he had made the necessary phone calls. KGB officers and soldiers were patrolling the corridors and, according to staff, they must have been generously paid on the eve of the coup, because during the day they frequented the cafés and bars in the building using crisp 50-rouble notes. Unidentified men sat in Kravchenko's office, where they remained the rest of the day.

That morning the Soviet Union woke up to the startling news that Gorbachev would not be able to perform his duties as president due to 'reasons of health' and would be replaced by vice-president Gennady Yanayev. The news was coming out simultaneously on Soviet television's first channel and radio. Yeltsin's Russian government channels had been seized. A news reader read out the decrees. A state of emergency was declared for six months in Moscow, Leningrad, the Baltics and the Transcaucasus. The country would be run by an eight-man State Committee – the GKChP.[12] The state committee's 'Message to the Soviet People' was emotional: 'A mortal danger hangs over our great Fatherland! The policy of reform initiated by M. S. Gorbachev ... has come to a dead end ... the country has in effect become ungovernable'. It went on to talk of 'extremist forces' that were seeking the collapse of the state, provoking an 'explosion of egoism'; never in its history had the 'propaganda of sex and violence seen such scope', the pride and honour of the Soviet Union were at stake.[13] The language is familiar in Putin-propaganda rhetoric today. At the time, the information was confusing. If the GKChP was simply taking over because of Gorbachev's illness, the implication that he had been the cause of the crisis indicated power was being usurped. The plotters had been uncertain whether to use Gorbachev's name negatively, but the sentence was inserted at the last minute anyway.

At 6.45 a.m. on the orders of the Commandant of Moscow tanks, armoured vehicles and armoured personnel carriers began to move on Moscow. Marshal Yazov gave the signal to General Pavel Grachev, commander of the paratroopers, to move some of his 106th Tula airborne division to the Tushino airfield, while others would take positions around all the major buildings in the capital. Grachev put Major General Aleksandr Lebed in charge of the battalion that was later sent to the White House. If these two generals of the airborne troops had not decided to go over to Yeltsin's side, the coup might well have succeeded. In the post-Soviet government, Grachev became Yeltsin's Minister of Defence and Lebed, head of the Security Council.

At 6 a.m. Yeltsin's daughter, Lena, woke him up and said: 'Papa, get up, there's been a coup'. She had just heard the news on the radio.

At 6.30 Yeltsin rang Grachev and asked him what was happening. They had met only a month before when Yeltsin had visited Grachev's paratroopers and they had got on well. Grachev was surprised: 'Didn't you know anything about it?', he asked. 'Of course not, this is a provocation. Can you set aside any security forces for me?' Yeltsin says there was a long pause before Grachev replied stiffly that as an officer be could not disobey orders. Yeltsin said that he understood he was placing him in a difficult position, but Grachev quickly added that whatever happened, he would send troops to protect him. Yeltsin put down the phone and told his wife – he's 'one of us'.[14]

Most of Yeltsin's cabinet and high-ranking members of the Russian parliament were staying in government dachas scattered around Arkhangelskoye, and it didn't take them long to rush over. Ruslan Khasbulatov, chairman of the Russian Supreme Soviet, was the first to arrive. Before long Yeltsin's living room was bursting at the seams: the State Secretary and Yeltsin's right-hand man, Gennady Burbulis; the Commander-in-Chief of the Russian forces, Konstantin Kobets, who had taken the precaution a few weeks earlier to draft a plan to defend the White House; the Russian Foreign Minister, Andrei Kozyrev, who flew to Paris to represent the Russian government; the Leningrad[15] mayor Anatoly Sobchak, who rushed back home apparently to take charge of the opposition (with his little-known deputy, Putin, at his side), among others.

Despite the magnificent speech Sobchak made on Leningrad television against the plotters, his unreserved support for Yeltsin has been put in doubt by well-known political observers, who believe he was playing both sides to be safe. According to Masha Gessen, Sobchak spent much of the time hiding in a bunker with Putin. This has been recently confirmed by then Commandant of Leningrad, Viktor Samsonov, who many years after the coup punctured another official myth, that Sobchak and Putin had negotiated with him during the coup not to bring tanks into the city. That, he said, was an agreement he had made solely with his deputy. Yet another strange revelation was Sobchak's call to Kruchkov on 20 August to ask him to cancel Putin's membership of the KGB because, Putin said, his first letter of resignation had been lost. One can assume they feared that if the plotters won, and if Putin was still a KGB lieutenant, he may have been put on trial as a traitor.[16]

Yeltsin's team in Moscow was fully behind him. Mikhail Poltoranin, the Russian Press Minister and Yeltsin's close friend since his Moscow party days, had woken at 5 a.m. to go mushroom picking. He knew nothing of what was happening until Yeltsin's bodyguard knocked on his door and told him to go immediately to Yeltsin's dacha, 300 metres away. When he arrived Yeltsin was on the phone in his dressing gown and slippers. Poltoranin noticed the tulle curtains on the windows and the apples Yeltsin's wife Naina had spread out on the windowsills to dry for making pickles. He noticed that during the morning people kept going up to the windows and eating the apples.

Khasbulatov was at the table writing the appeal 'To the Citizens of Russia' by hand, while everyone chipped in. The appeal came straight to the point: it demanded that Gorbachev be allowed to address the nation, it called on people to take part in a general strike and urged the army not to support the coup.[17] The document now had to be typed. Some people have wondered why it took Yeltsin and his team so long to leave Arkhangelskoye, but the reason was mundane. They had no typewriter. The bodyguards were sent to search adjoining dachas and brought one back, together with an elderly woman typist. Poltoranin began to dictate the appeal, but when the typist realised what was happening her hands began to tremble. They brewed her a pot of tea to calm her nerves, but it was no use. In the end Yeltsin's daughter sat down and typed the appeal. The next problem was to photocopy it. This time the bodyguards broke into a dacha, whose owner used it as an office, and threatening the caretaker with their rifles commandeered the photocopier. Copies were made and distributed to each person on the principle that if any one of them was arrested when they left the dacha at least some copies would get through. In the meantime, Yeltsin's daughter had managed to find a working fax machine in a dacha and had sent out the appeal.

Yeltsin insisted on going to the White House and some of his aides agreed. Others felt it would be too dangerous and it would be best if he issued instructions from the dacha. Both sides argued forcibly and Yeltsin threw up his arms in perplexity. At that point Yury Ryzhov, an expert on the military–industrial complex and a much-respected intellectual, rang from Burbulis's office in the White House, where others from Russia's government were gathering.

Ryzhov says:

> I asked Burbulis what they planned to do, but before I could get an answer Yeltsin had grabbed the phone and said they were finishing an appeal to the people. I told Yeltsin: "I'm switching on the tape recorder right now. Read out the text. We'll hold a press conference and invite diplomats and journalists". Yeltsin said not to switch on the tape recorder, he would send a car with the text instead. I expressed doubt that the car would reach the White House. Yeltsin asked someone else's advice

and it seemed to me that he had not yet decided whether to go to the White House, but during our conversation he made up his mind. He said "We'll come ourselves". I said that was even less likely to succeed. "No, we'll come", he said. Yeltsin told me to organise the press conference, which I suggested we fix for midday. It's only forty minutes from Arkhangelskoye but I gave him two hours. Yeltsin said: "No, for eleven". I told him that if he got here, which was unlikely, eleven was too early. "No, eleven", he said. His voice was quite decisive. I was amazed when they all showed up at eleven'.[18]

Yeltsin got dressed and had to be persuaded to wear a bullet-proof vest. He was exasperated that his supporters were fussing over his safety. He got into his black Volga car with Burbulis, protected by his security guards in cars driving in front and behind them, their machine guns just showing through the open windows. As they sped along the Kaluzhsky road they passed the tanks moving on Moscow. The soldiers glanced curiously at them, but no one tried to stop the cavalcade.

All morning the convoy of tanks and armoured vehicles had been moving through the outer suburbs, watched in astonishment by passers-by and people hanging out of windows. The convoy rumbled down Kalinin Prospekt, converging on the Kremlin at 11 a.m. Another column moved along Kutuzovsky Prospekt heading towards the White House – a relentless stream of hardware so vividly caught by CNN TV cameramen perched high up on a roof where they remained for several hours, transmitting on screens all over the world the steadily encroaching military machine moving along the eight-lane highway. CNN had offices opposite the White House and were able to film Yeltsin standing on the tank and the crowds in the square, contributing substantially to information for those with satellite television, which included the Kremlin and most institutions, plus those who could rig up an antenna.

There was public bewilderment and anger, but no panic. Some shrugged cynically. Women shouted at tank drivers: 'Go back or you'll never be able to wash the blood off your hands'. Others placed carnations and roses in the barrels of machine guns, pleading with soldiers not to fire on people. 'We don't want to shoot', came the reply from many young men who looked no more than 17. The army didn't give the appearance of a disciplined war machine as so many were youthful conscripts. Many of them had never been to Moscow and those who were not accompanied by traffic police had difficulty finding their way, having to consult tourist maps of the city. And if this really was a coup, who had ever heard of tanks stopping at the lights?

At the press conference Yeltsin spoke briefly, telling the audience they had just received information that 50 tanks were moving on the White House – 'so save yourselves if you can', he said. This was greeted with laughter and derision – 'let the junta save itself'. Part of the public anger came from contempt that such mediocrities were forcing their will on the country. A radical people's deputy, Vitaly Urazhtsev, one of the three men detained during the coup, burst out laughing at hearing the names of the plotters. 'I knew that people with so little authority would get nowhere', he said.

At the same time as Yeltsin's press conference was taking place, Khasbulatov was chairing a meeting of the presidium of the Russian Supreme Soviet in another part of the building. A resolution was adopted to convene an emergency session of parliament in two days. In the meantime, people began gathering in all the main city spaces already surrounded by troops and hardware. Tanks rumbled onto the embankment facing the White House, taking positions at the base of the wide steps leading to the ornate front of the building, their engines revving noisily and belching fumes.

Yeltsin and his team were inside by a window, looking at the tanks below. It seemed as if the first move to arrest him had begun. 'At first we didn't pay any attention', says Poltoranin, 'but Yeltsin started getting agitated and suddenly jumped up and said "How can we sit here? Let's go down". He picked up a copy of the appeal and strode decisively to the door. Everyone rushed after him and by the time he got downstairs a large crowd was following him'.[19]

Yeltsin confidently descended the steps, surrounded by his bodyguards and friends, although the building was undefended. There were no more than 500 people gathered in the square at the time. Tank no. 110 was standing in front of them. Without hesitation, Yeltsin clambered onto the tank, and when the surprised soldier poked his head out of the turret, warmly shook hands with him and the other soldiers. Standing on the tank, Yeltsin read his appeal to the people calling for resistance.

It was a spectacular act of defiance, the defining moment of opposition to the coup because, as it happened, Yeltsin's appearance was broadcast to the whole Soviet Union on the official news, *Vremya*, that evening. A young TV journalist, Sergei Medvedev had been sent to report on what was happening in the city. As he says in his piece to camera, he had little hope of his footage getting through. But Gosteleradio's first deputy chairman Valentin Lazutkin decided to risk it. *Vremya* was the only news programme allowed on air. Medvedev had not been at the White House when Yeltsin was standing on the tank, but Lazutkin had managed to get footage from foreign colleagues. The team viewed the report while a KGB operative stood by: he did nothing to stop them, only noting that they were asking for trouble. That morning at the editorial meeting Kravchenko had said nothing about having to support the GKChP, just to show restraint. In the evening Kravchenko had disappeared to his dacha. Lazutkin phoned him and got his okay to use the item, but no more than two and a half minutes. It was in fact four minutes and probably changed the course of history. From the news item people all over the country learned that Yeltsin was opposing the coup, and Muscovites found out where to go if they wanted to join the resistance. That night more than 10,000 people turned up to defend the White House.

The report showed footage of Yeltsin outside the White House beginning the appeal: 'Because television won't let us speak and radio won't let us speak …'. The team decided that if they broadcast any more of Yeltsin speaking, it would be less likely to get through. Instead, Medvedev reported Yeltsin's demand that Gorbachev be allowed to address the nation, his appeal for people to take part in a general political strike and his call to the army not to be drawn into a reactionary coup. Medvedev continued: from what he could see on the streets people were preparing to defend the city; volunteers, he said, were 'not especially difficult to find', as footage showed people dragging paving stones and blocks of cement to build barricades around the White House. Others were showering leaflets of the appeal from balconies. He asked a group of men how they knew what to do, and one replied: 'Vilnius taught us'. There were no provocations between soldiers and the people, he reported; the two sides seemed to understand each other.

As soon as the item went out, there were outraged phone calls to Lazutkin and Kravchenko from the GKChP. Lazutkin was warned that he would be dealt with in due course, Medvedev was sacked (and reinstated after the coup as Yeltsin's press secretary for a time). Kravchenko was also in trouble: not only had he left TV centre early, the plotters were still annoyed with him for not having found a better metaphor to adorn blank screens than a dying swan. Kravchenko later explained that the film had simply been on the schedule that day. In his memoirs he shows resentment that the coup plotters had him hauled out of bed, without giving him adequate warning to have orchestrated the television coverage of the takeover. Certainly their ignorance of the way television worked did not help their cause. For one thing, they had ignored the Soviet Union's different time zones. While Moscow and central Russia had received the breaking news at 6 a.m., the rest of the country east of the Urals and Central Asia had started their day earlier with no knowledge of the takeover. Inevitably there was confusion and panic in the rest of the country, but as the telephone system had not been switched off it was possible to exchange information. Some regional leaders were demanding to appear on television to show their loyalty to the plotters.

Yeltsin confirmed that the coup's failure had much to do with the plotters' ignorance of new technology, which had only recently been introduced into the country with the setting up of business enterprises. 'The elderly putschists simply could not comprehend the breadth and depth of the information reality that was new to them', he said.[20] Photocopiers were prohibited but, with the usual disregard for unreasonable laws, there were plenty of them around. Businesses, banks and the stock exchange, fearful of what would happen to them if the GKChP won, were particularly helpful to protesters in making their resources available.

Kravchenko believes that if TV centre had been put in the hands of supporters of the coup, he could have ensured that television worked in their favour. He would have integrated the country with its different time zones, from Kaliningrad to Vladivostok, in a massive tele-marathon where 'politicians, workers, academics and cultural leaders would support the state of emergency ... creating a picture of universal support'. This Soviet-style propaganda exercise, he thought, would have achieved 'what all the tanks and armoured vehicles could not'. Given the circumstances, however, he did not see why he should stick his neck out. 'To be honest', he writes, 'it would have turned out that Kravchenko personally was the main ideologue for the putsch. And he would have been the first to have his head chopped off, wouldn't he?'.[21] In the end Kravchenko was sacked by both Yeltsin and Gorbachev. He was particularly upset that Gorbachev did not stand up for him when he was questioned by the Public Prosecutor.

The third iconic image on television was the man-who-would-be president's trembling hands. It happened at the GKChP's press conference in the afternoon, the plotters' first and only public appearance. Yanayev, who had replaced Gorbachev, was in the chair. The conference was packed with Soviet and foreign journalists, most of whom were highly sceptical of the coup plotters, whose answers to their questions were sometimes received with loud laughter. Tatyana Malkina became famous for her questions to Yanayev: 'Do you realise you've carried out a coup?' she asked; and do you think its historical parallel is 1917 or 1964? – when Khrushchev had been deposed. All the questions were broadcast. The production team at TV centre was told to edit out Yanayev's trembling hands, the laughter and images of him wiping his brow and blowing his nose before broadcasting the item on *Vremya*. The team ignored their instructions. The editor, Yelena Pozdnyak's response was: 'too bad, let everyone see!'.[22] It was the image of Yanayev's trembling hands that became the butt of many jokes and dented any pretensions to the throne. Gorbachev said later that when he saw the trembling hands he knew the plotters could not succeed.

Pro-democracy journalists mobilised very quickly. The constant struggles of the last few years meant they were experienced in fighting back; and most of them were not prepared to lose their hard-won rights.

A public address system was rigged up in the White House, manned by popular TV personalities. Leningrad's Bella Kurkova got the ball rolling with her fiendish energy, with Vladimir Molchanov and the young presenters Aleksandr Lyubimov and Aleksandr Politkovsky from *Vzglyad* quickly taking up the call. The makeshift studio at the White House, situated in the basement, soon filled up with the anti-coup intelligentsia, journalists, actors, comedians, film-makers, poets; all of them willing to display their support for Yeltsin. Regular news broadcasts were transmitted to the public; Yeltsin's appeals and decrees were read out and frequent information was provided by Russian leaders. The news kept coming in from the republics and from the Russian provinces, where on the first day 60 per cent of regional Soviets had already declared the coup unconstitutional. In Leningrad there were mass demonstrations and Anatoly Sobchak had spoken on the city's television station, which defied the plotters and refused to close down.

'We had constant ties with Leningrad, Sverdlovsk and all the cities', Lyubimov says. 'People from the Baltics were sending us news. Six armoured personnel carriers were moving from Riga towards Moscow to defend Yeltsin. All the telephones and airports were open. Sasha [Politkovsky] and I worked round the clock. We kept repeating the refrain "everything's fine, we're breathing normally" to keep people's spirits up. At about 4 or 5 a.m. we'd stop broadcasting, it was safer when it got light'.[23]

Before coming to the White House, Lyubimov had made hurried plans to protect *Vzglyad* property from the KGB. Now a private company with its own equipment, he organised *Vzglyad*'s reporters to film everything happening in the city. It was history in the making. At 10 that morning he had rented two flats, one for himself – to avoid being arrested at home, the other to store equipment. Their archives were removed to a place outside Moscow, where they left cash and a getaway car with enough petrol to reach the Finnish border. They had four cameras filming, and a rota system so that if one TV crew got arrested, another would take its place. It was essential to conceal the footage in secret hideouts. Altogether the *Vzglyad* crew shot 70 hours of film by the end of the coup. It is mainly this footage that was shown all over the world after the coup, and remains as a historical record.

The White House's radio was also used to help defend the building and ensure the safety of protesters. When ten tanks from the Taman division defected to the White House, only assurances from the radio by known prodemocracy journalists managed to convince protesters that they were friendly. It was not hard to spot KGB provocateurs mingling with the crowds, the 'men with sports bags', as they were called, in their usual disguise of tracksuits and trainers. Food appeared miraculously sent by owners of expensive cooperative restaurants or simply brought by women who had baked pies, wrapping them in newspaper and distributing them to the crowd. Taxis in the nearby depot gave their services free. The dreaded bikers of the Hell's Angels variety proved to be good couriers. Businessmen donated money and the stock exchange stopped working; even gangsters were there, Lyubimov remembers, with their wallets bulging with money ready to help.

There were three centres of operation in the White House: Kobets's defence headquarters, Burbulis's and vice-president Aleksandr Rutskoi's offices. Here there was a continuous flow of movement and information, planning the defence, sifting information, receiving informants and maintaining links with the provinces and republics. Yeltsin's office was filled with advisers and colleagues coming and going; anyone who wanted to could drop in.

That evening Yeltsin again came out to speak to the defenders, this time protected by metal shields. After his flamboyant behaviour on the tank, some 30 snipers had appeared on the high-rise buildings around the White House and in the Hotel Ukraine which faced the window of Yeltsin's office across the river. The metal blinds in Yeltsin's office were lowered and even at night the ceiling lights were not switched on, so that no shadows would be cast by the figures inside. There were constant fears that the White House would be stormed that night. It was raining, but people remained outdoors, huddled around bonfires. At 11 p.m. Grachev sent Lebed, in charge of 20 combat vehicles of the 106th Tula paratroopers, to guard the White House. But the next morning they were withdrawn by Marshal Yazov, who became suspicious of troops fraternising with protesters.

20–21 August

To defeat the coup plotters, the role of the military was crucial. Grachev was aware that any official refusal to obey Yazov would have been futile, as a more zealous commander would have been put in charge of the paratroopers. Instead, he bided his time.

Preparations for Operation 'Thunder' were under way – the name given to the plan to attack the White House and arrest Yeltsin. The assault was timed for 3 a.m. of 21 August. The operation was designed to take out the first and second floors of the White House with the aid of helicopters and paratroopers; while special forces, such as Alpha, would break into the building and take over the fifth and sixth floors, where Yeltsin and the government's offices were. There was little chance of survival for the defenders of the White House. Lebed had done a reconnaissance of the White House that day and came back to the Ministry of Defence visibly shaken. He said there would be significant casualties if the plan was implemented. General Varennikov cut him short and told him not to be a pessimist.

One of Alpha's chiefs, Leonid Gummenoy, spoke of the madness at the heart of the assault. 'According to the plan of action, Group "B" (from Moscow's KGB) would "work on" the first and second floors with secret weapons of enormous destructive power. After this "working out" both floors would have ceased to function. The plan to arrest Yeltsin, which … was assigned to us, was unrealistic for the very reason that after this "purge" everyone, including the President of Russia, would have been dead'.[24]

At midday a demonstration rallying support for Yeltsin had swelled into a huge display of solidarity with more than 50,000 people chanting Yeltsin's name, and luminaries of the democratic movement out in full force: Shevardnadze, Mstislav Rostropovich, Sakharov's widow Yelena Bonner, speaking out against the supreme insult of tyranny – 'we'll show them, we'll prove that we are people, people and not cattle'.[25] Spirits were further lifted when hundreds of supporters arrived carrying over their heads a huge Russian tricolour flag, almost 100 yards long, which was fixed on the balcony of the White House as an emblem of resistance.

While journalists continued to slip information about the resistance into television broadcasts on *Vremya*, the banned press also refused to be muzzled. Under GKChP's Resolution No. 2 'On the output of central, Moscow, city and regional newspapers' all newspapers had been banned except for six central ones, such as *Pravda, Sovetskaya Rossiya* and *Trud* ('Work'), as well as *Izvestiya*, to the chagrin of its journalists and printers who did everything they could to prevent the newspaper coming out and giving credibility to the plotters. When their conservative editor Nikolai Yefimov arrived from his dacha, they insisted that if the GKChP's statement was not printed together with Yeltsin's appeal, they would wreck the printing presses. The former was printed on page one, the latter on page two. Journalists were actively engaged in countering official propaganda, photocopying documents issued by the Russian government and using the manually operated printing machines made available by *Izvestiya*. That morning some banned newspapers had come out in shortened photocopied versions. *Kuranty*'s headline read: 'A doomed takeover'.

At midday Yegor Yakovlev was gathering the editorial staff of 11 of the country's mainstream banned newspapers[26] in the offices of *Kommersant*, the only newspaper with computer facilities that did not belong to the state. The idea was to collectively bring out an emergency newspaper called *Obshchaya gazeta*, which was produced as a four-page tabloid with the headlines: 'Democracy must defend itself: Statement from editors-in-chief of periodicals whose banning is a violation of the Press Law':

> Our Obshchaya gazeta is born of our common misfortune ... The first thing the plotters did on taking over supreme power was to ban the central and Moscow newspapers that don't suit them. The aim of the putschists and the reason for these events is to liquidate freedom of information – the most substantial achievement of perestroika. There is no doubt they intend to impose a punitive regime on the country ... Today they have attacked the press, tomorrow, when there is no freedom, it will be each one of you.

The paper printed an appeal from Yeltsin, details of troop movements around the city, the first bits of information coming out that Gorbachev's villa had been blockaded, and the Russian government's list of demands to the USSR Supreme Soviet: to produce a medical certificate of Gorbachev's illness, to arrange a meeting with Gorbachev, to call off the state of emergency, to withdraw the troops and end the takeover. Local versions of *Obshchaya gazeta* came out in many regions. Yegor Yakovlev and journalists at *Moskovskiye novosti* also produced a special issue of their newspaper, which they managed to get printed in Tallinn and which came out on 21 August in Moscow and other cities.

What is today the most important independent radio station, Ekho Moskvy was only a small operation then, one of many stations that received licences in the expanding private sector, but its young journalists and amateurs, including Aleksei Venediktov, now the radio's director, then a journalist who was still working as a history schoolteacher, proved to be the most persistent at getting the opposition's views out. It aired the most reliable up-to-the-minute information nationwide, although it was constantly being closed down. At 7.40 on the first day, eight KGB men arrived and cut off their early morning broadcast but did not seal the building, as they had threatened to do. Every time the station was cut off, journalists received help from the dissenting USSR Deputy Minister of Communications, A. Ivanov, to get it back on air. After their report of the three young men who had been killed defending the White House, the radio was switched off again, and this time a fake radio calling itself Ekho Moskvy began broadcasting inflammatory statements, that hundreds of people had been killed outside the White House and that snipers were everywhere. This provocation was done convincingly by using genuine reports from earlier radio broadcasts. Venediktov believes they were allowed to go back on air each time precisely so that the station could be used for this purpose.

Negotiations were taking place all day in different parts of the military, conspiring with or against the GKChP. Vital to Yeltsin's success was the phone call between the USSR Commander in Chief of the Air Force, Yevgeny Shaposhnikov, and Grachev. It was the first discussion between two of the military's top men who had taken the risk of revealing their opposition to the GKChP. They understood that if Operation 'Thunder' was implemented, it would mean large-scale slaughter. They agreed they would not allow their forces to take part in the operation. Grachev understood the mentality of the coup plotters. 'I get the impression they want me to do their dirty work. The bastards want me to give the order'. What would he do, asked Shaposhnikov. 'I'll tell them to go to hell'. They agreed that if the GKChP gave the order to attack the White House, they would give the command for two fighter planes to bomb the Kremlin.[27]

Opposition to military action was growing among the top brass and the rank and file, as well as among Alpha on which the assault depended. In the White House, preparations were being made for its defence, and gas masks were distributed as there had been warnings that Alpha might use nerve gas. The White House radio was broadcasting instructions. Women who wished to leave the area should do so while the Metro was still operating. Everyone had to move 50 metres from the building, leaving a space that was lit up so that intruders would be seen. The Russian Vice-President Aleksandr Rutskoi, an Afghan veteran, was barking orders with a pistol by his side. Yeltsin was taken to a bunker in the depths of the White House, but did not stay there long. He was looking tired, but by all accounts his suit was neat and unwrinkled and he appeared to be in control of the situation.

The rain kept pouring down and at one point there was an order to close all umbrellas, which prevented detecting suspicious movements in the crowd. Aleksei Venediktov watched from the fifth floor as, at the order, all the umbrellas closed in one graceful movement. Roaming the corridors, he found Khasbulatov's office, blocked by armchairs, with the pipe-smoking Khasbulatov sitting at his desk with five pipes smoking simultaneously in ashtrays so that he didn't have to spend time lighting them. Half an hour after Venediktov's interview with him went out on Ekho Moskvy, the radio station was taken off the air again. The broadcasts infuriated Kryuchkov, sitting in the Lubyanka. He gave his staff a dressing down for being unable to stop a group of amateurs from defying their plans.

Venediktov was in the White House that night. The maze-like building is bewildering at the best of times and now most of the lights had been switched off; everyone seemed to be talking in whispers: 'People were walking with machine guns expecting the assault any minute, everyone was drinking tea and complaining that there was no sugar, the lifts had stopped. Some corridors were completely dark and you had to find your way feeling along the wall saying "'anyone there?" so as not to bump into someone with a machine gun. Everyone's nerves were frayed'.[28]

According to the Prosecutor's office there were 50,000 to 100,000 people around the White House that night. During the day the total number of people taking part in the resistance – building barricades, pleading with the troops, distributing leaflets, preparing for the defence of the White House – was estimated at more than a million. To take the country as a whole, it was closer to two million.

At about one in the morning of 21 August tragedy struck in an underpass not far from the White House, when three young men were killed fighting a column of armed combat vehicles that came crashing through heavy barricades. It was an accident that could have been averted, except for the high tension in the streets and the enormous number of troops the coup plotters had brought in. The convoy had arrived to enforce the curfew, not to start the assault on the White House, but no one knew when or how the assault would be carried out.

'We only told two lies over the White House radio', said Lyubimov. 'When the three men were killed … we were scared people might go against the tanks, so we said there had been a confrontation but we had no news of victims. The second lie was when we said hundreds of people's deputies had come to the White House, when in fact there were about 200. We wanted to give the impression that everyone had come'.[29]

It was soon after these deaths that Yazov called off the assault. 'I did not want to be a Pinochet', he said later. Some of the other coup plotters (Baklanov and Shenin, in particular) were furious. 'What, lost your nerve?' asked Baklanov.[30] Burbulis phoned Kryuchkov at about 2 a.m. to demand he stop the operation. Kryuchkov replied gruffly that there would be no assault – they could 'sleep peacefully'. Although he was telling the truth, it was only at dawn that the defenders of the White House could breathe a sigh of relief.

In effect the coup was over. After that it became a race to get to see Gorbachev in Foros, a cat-and-mouse game played by the two groups wanting to get there first. Yeltsin feared the plotters might harm Gorbachev; the plotters wanted to get to Gorbachev before Yeltsin blackened their name. Although the plotters reached him first, Gorbachev refused to talk to Kryuchkov until his phone lines were reconnected. He then rang Yeltsin, who told him the

Russian delegation was on its way and stressed that he should not talk to the plotters until the group arrived, concerned that Gorbachev might succumb to the entreaties of his previous allies. Raisa writes in her diary that her husband had spoken to Yeltsin, who had said: 'Dear Mikhail Sergeyevich, are you alive? We've been fighting to the death these 48 hours'.[31]

Gorbachev returned to Moscow unharmed, but he had lost touch with political realities. His first precipitous remark, that he was 'in full control of the situation', did not bode well. He did not listen to his advisers when they suggested he go straight to the White House, where tens of thousands were celebrating and waiting to hear news of him. He did not especially thank Yeltsin or the pro-democracy protesters, but talked incessantly about his and his family's ordeal. The coup's defeat had rung the death knell for the party, but Gorbachev continued to urge its renewal and reform, ignoring the fact that members were giving up their party cards in droves and Yeltsin had confiscated its vast property. Gorbachev began to replace ministers and officials with hardliners again, not checking their roles in the coup, many of whom Yeltsin vetoed – not that he had any right to, but there was already little doubt about who was the dominant partner in post-coup politics. Finally, at the Russian parliament, after a welcoming ovation, Gorbachev was booed and hissed when he began to defend his union officials and republican leaders for their stance against the coup, showing he had not updated his information. When he tried to defend his cabinet of ministers, virtually all of whom had betrayed him, it caused an uproar in the house – with cries of 'truth! truth!'. At this point, Yeltsin, who had been behaving in a fatherly manner, swooped without ceremony. He had given Gorbachev the minutes of the cabinet meetings, but Gorbachev had not read them. As seen on television, Yeltsin strode up to the lectern where Gorbachev was standing, waving the incriminating document. 'Read it out', he said, to applause and laughter. Gorbachev tried to turn away but Yeltsin, wagging his finger at him, insisted: 'Mikhail Sergeyevich, read out this document'.

It was the final iconic moment recorded by television of events brought about by the coup. The spectacle of the president of Russia forcing the USSR president to face the indictment of his own government was Yeltsin's *coup de grâce*. Gorbachev had threatened Yeltsin in 1990 that he 'would never let him back into politics', but the tables had turned. Four months later the Soviet Union collapsed. Gorbachev resigned on 25 December, 1991. Yeltsin was rude and ungracious in having him bundled out of the Kremlin.

II Freedom and national identity

There is no doubt that the struggle against the coup was a triumph for freedom and democracy. The exercise of free speech had enabled that triumph to happen. Why then wasn't this high point of freedom – the highest point since the February Revolution – celebrated as a national holiday or honoured in any way? We know that people looking back at this period through the prism of Yeltsin's eight years in office see more of what was lost than gained, but that does not explain why the event was not honoured during the euphoria that prevailed immediately after the coup. One reason often cited is the trauma of the Soviet Union's collapse as a consequence of the coup. The GKChP's claim that they were patriots, not traitors, who had wanted to preserve the Soviet Union, found a response in party and nationalist circles. We know that for Putin the breakup of the Soviet Union was the 'greatest geopolitical catastrophe of the century', because it brought a superpower to its knees. The trial against the plotters was never concluded and although they spent some time in jail, they were amnestied by parliament, to Yeltsin's anger, although he did not veto it, in 1994[32] Since then, both Putin and Medvedev have decorated Marshal Yazov.

There are some critics who see Yeltsin's secret negotiations with Ukraine and Belorussia to declare their independence from the Soviet Union as on a par with the GKChP's plot. According to Vitaly Tretyakov, then editor of *Nezavisimaya gazeta*, 'Yeltsin and the leaders ... in the union republics staged another coup ... and stole power from Gorbachev'.[33] This argument, that because both acts were unconstitutional and led to the union's collapse they *ipso facto* bear the same weight, has done much to take the sheen off the courage and camaraderie of the struggle. Yeltsin's supporters fought the coup not because it was unconstitutional, but because it was reactionary. The GKChP's mismanaged coup reflected the bankruptcy of the USSR government; while Gorbachev's democratic credentials had been tarnished by his 'turn to the right'. Although the referendum to preserve the USSR of 17 March 1991 had shown 76 per cent of Soviet citizens in its favour, it was not a plausible survey as six of the 15 republics had refused to take part in it. Yeltsin's secession from the union, even if it allowed him to attain supreme power, was a logical progression from Russia's struggle as the largest member of the republics to gain independence. Unlike Gorbachev, who had never stood in direct elections, Yeltsin had a mandate as Russia's first freely elected president. Whatever one thinks of Yeltsin's part in breaking up the Soviet empire, it was not an undemocratic move to give the union republics their independence (even if not all of them wanted it).

But the urge to minimise the achievements of freedom seems strong. Tretyakov continues: 'People thought they were fighting for freedom (but without the union) or for the integrity of the country (but without freedom), while the elite groups were fighting for power and control of national property'. Even the liberal pollster Yury Levada argued in this way: 'The people were witnesses to rather than participants in the events. Apparently the real rivals met on other levels, in complicated intrigues and negotiations between Yeltsin's team and the security structures ... actually this is what enabled the outcome to be peaceful'.[34] The negotiations were vital, but it is unlikely they would have been successful if one million Muscovites had not acted as 'participants' in the events. Yet there is a public reticence in accepting that protesters acting freely and spontaneously can produce positive results.

The oddities of the coup have thrown up more than the usual plethora of conspiracy theories. Richard Sakwa analyses some of these, including the 'crudest' version put forward by Boris Kagarlitsky, which sees Yeltsin in league with the plotters. This theory claims that Yeltsin later betrayed his alleged co-plotters and used the coup as a pretext to whip up democratic forces in order to stage his own coup, the 'real' coup, which projected him into power.[35] The upshot of such conspiracy theories is to darken all political players, however blameless, with Machiavellian misdeeds. Along the way it discredits people's power and protesters as an easily manipulated mob. In 1994 Yeltsin wrote about how the August Revolution had become an 'ideological cliché': 'People are irritated when they remember these events. Whereas before they were proud to tell their friends about the nights they spent at the barricades, now they boast sometimes that they didn't go anywhere, they didn't decide to return from their holidays and that generally they took no part in events. It seems this has become more fashionable'.[36]

A day that minimally honours victory is Flag Day on 22 August, although it is not a public holiday. The spectacularly large tricolour that was paraded through the streets during the coup became Russia's official symbol replacing the hammer and sickle; it was the flag adopted by February 1917 during its nine-month existence. But celebrating a flag is not the same as honouring a nation's freedom or making freedom part of a country's emotional heritage in the way that the Declaration of the Rights of Man has seeped into France's consciousness or Americans talk of a land of the free and home of the brave. The modern struggle for freedom as a value in itself or the commemoration of people who were part of that struggle has not become attached to Russia's identity. Nor have Yeltsin's rousing words in his appeal to 'the peoples of Russia who are becoming masters of their fate'. As a result, people have forgotten that some of the freedoms they still enjoy in Putin's Russia (if not freedom of speech) were won after the coup: the freedom to travel, to acquire consumer goods and possess property, none of which was possible under the Soviet Union. If at a general level there is suspicion of acts of freedom and their ennobling, the spirit of struggle has not died out. The large-scale anti-Putin protests of 2011–13 showed the same creative determination to succeed until they were one-upped by the audacity of the annexation of Crimea – according to Putin, not a coup, although breaking all international laws.

Why was it so difficult to make freedom part of Russia's national identity? Most countries have their creation myths rooted in some symbolic narrative, which might not be entirely plausible but touches a deeply meaningful chord. There were many moments during and after the coup that could have struck that chord. The sense of liberation in the tumultuous crowd the day after the coup when cranes pulled down the imposing (and aesthetically rather impressive) statue of 'Iron Feliks', the Soviet Union's founder of the Cheka secret police, Feliks Dzerzhinsky, looming over the KGB's headquarters in

Lubyanka Square, with searchlights illuminating the sky, courtesy of the Moscow mayor's office, was as splendid a symbol of the defeat of totalitarianism as anyone could have hoped for. Instead of this event incising Dzerzhinsky from Russian history's honours roll, there have been eight attempts since the coup to restore the statue to its former plinth.

To the liberal intelligentsia there may be a fear of inauthenticity to myth-making, given the history of lies pumped by politically dubious propaganda machines. It is also understandable that an element of distaste may accompany any expression of revolutionary fervour that brings up memories of collectivist allegiance enforced by the Soviet state. But the roots of caution may go deeper than that. The French have been able to dissociate the guillotine from the liberties of the French Revolution in a way Russia has not been able to, partly because these rebellions did not lead to liberty. They are seen more as the product of *volya*, the opposite of 'my freedom is your freedom'; a time when the mob or what Russians call the 'lumpen' display their merciless savagery.

Yeltsin also connected social upheaval with nihilism and feared things might get out of control after the coup. For all his turbulent nature, he did not like the term 'revolution', softening what had happened with the prefix 'quiet revolution' (*tikhaya revolyutsiya*). Yeltsin was proud of his record of not seeking revenge Bolshevik style against the Communist Party or his enemies. He wrote in his diary that he had witnessed ugly scenes in the change-over from Khrushchev to Brezhnev, and did not agree with those who reproached him after the coup saying he should have automatically sacked all senior party workers from the government apparatus. What he had wanted to do immediately after the coup was to set up a western-style parliamentary system but here, he said pointedly, it was not the communists who obstructed him but the comrades who had fought against the coup with him. He had sensed the urge to tear down and destroy, when he had driven past crowds outside the buildings of the Central Committee of the CPSU in Staraya Ploshchad after the coup as people started breaking windows. He wrote:

> I could see the spectre of October before my eyes – pogroms, riots, looting, permanent meetings, the anarchy with which this glorious revolution started. I could have turned August into some kind of October '17 with a flick of the wrist, a single signature. But I didn't do it and I don't regret it. During those 70 years we got tired of separating the 'clean' from the 'unclean'.[37]

Quite soon after the coup, Yeltsin vanished from the public eye, leaving Moscow for several weeks. It was not the first time for such vanishing tricks. Understandably, he was exhausted and had not slept for days, but it was not the right time when he had the rare opportunity to take action that may have had long-term positive consequences. It was probably the only time he could have dismantled the KGB properly, or closed Lenin's mausoleum without riots, sending Lenin's mummified corpse to St Petersburg to be buried next to his mother. There were many iconic possibilities celebrating the end of tyranny. Yury Afanasyev and Yevgeny Yevtushenko lobbied on behalf of the Memorial Society, which Yeltsin had joined in 1988, to turn the Lubyanka KGB headquarters into a museum dedicated to the party's millions of victims. Aleksandr Yakovlev suggested a monument to the casualties of Stalinism to replace the spot emptied by Iron Feliks. Yeltsin was not interested in any of those ideas. Only later did he tell Yakovlev that he should have 'squeezed' him a bit more.[38] I remember being impressed by an idea from a letter writer in the newspaper *Sobesednik*, who suggested that all the triumphalist statues of party leaders from the whole Soviet Union (granted the vast majority would have been of Lenin as the only one to survive the whole 70 years, most statues of Stalin having been pulped to make more Lenins) should be brought to Moscow and erected on the island in the Moskva river. It could have been a pop-art version of a cemetery to the cult of personality.

Out of all the possible material that could have been used to create a liberal–democratic ritual of national bonding, Russians, as children of their history, found no natural reflex to imprint freedom onto their national identity. This ideological vacuum was filled by Putin, returning to regressive but familiar mythmaking in the trappings of monarchy. He has made the presidential inauguration ceremony very much his own. Started by Yeltsin in 1996 after his re-election, it attempted to do what was not done spontaneously after the coup, to create 'a ritual of national significance', as state television put it on the day, except this celebration would provide 'lofty meaning to the first president of sovereign Russia' and 'symbolise Russian statehood', not freedom. This state pageant started off with enormously pompous plans, and a celebratory ode which *Nezavisimaya gazeta* thought so execrable that 'it is impossible to write a parody of the composition because it is parodic in and of itself'.[39] As Yeltsin was known to be quite ill, most of the bombast and the ode were thrown out for a fairly simple and short ceremony in the Kremlin.

The ceremony, as fulfilled three times by Putin, has become a fanfare occasion, watched by thousands of guests, as he walks endlessly to the blare of trumpets through the golden confines of St George Hall into St Aleksandr Hall and into St Andrew Hall, the former imperial throne room, all in his distinctive streetwise gait (his old schoolteacher said he had to do something about that way of walking, when he visited her). At Putin's first inauguration, the political climate in the country was so different from what it is now that this footage was often replayed on television as the stuff of satire. Now it is often inserted on television when it is necessary to emphasise power and might. To the monarchical trappings, Putin has added a whole host of Soviet insignia to implant onto the national consciousness.

If Yeltsin feared disorder and lawlessness after the coup, he might have found some other adequate symbol of freedom to express the 'quiet revolution' which he and his supporters had made. It is no surprise that bewilderment and doubt about the coup remain, if the winners could not provide an icon of triumphant freedom. Without it, the chance of making freedom a bonding ritual was missed, to the detriment of the mission to turn Russia into a democratic country.

Notes

1 Rossiyane o sobitiyakh avgusta 1991-go goda. Rezul'taty oprosa (Levada Tsentr). Intelros. www.intelros.ru/subject/ross_rasput/10814-rossiyane-o-sobytiyax-avgusta-1991-go-goda-rezultaty-oprosa-analiticheskogo-centra-yuriya-levady-levada-centr.html (accessed 14 November 2015).
2 Ibid.
3 'Twenty years later, communism's effects linger', *Washington Post*, 18 August 2011. www.washingtonpost.com/opinions/twenty-years-later-communisms-effects-linger/2011/08/17/gIQASQt8LJ_story.html (accessed 14 November 2015).
4 'Avgustovskii putch. Kak eto bylo'. http://www.ntv.ru/novosti/236682/ (accessed 14 November 2015).
5 Victor Yasmann, 'Yeltsin accuses Gorbachev of complicity in 1991 coup', *RFE/RL*, 2 February 2006.
6 'Gorbachev znal o planakh GKChP ...', *RIA Novosti*, 17 August 2011, http://ria.ru/politics/20110817/418879844.html To listen to Gorbachev's speech on You Tube, go to: https://www.youtube.com/watch?v=rgHTYqf2gJE (accessed 16 December 2015).
7 *Izvestiya*, 10 October 1991.
8 For the list of names see *Krasnoe ili beloe? Drama avgusta-91: fakty, gipotezy, stolknovenie mnenii*, M.K. Gorshkova, V.V. Zhuravleva, (ed.) "Terra" – "Terra", Moskva, 1992, pp 95-6. The list was destroyed by the KGB in the last hours of the coup and was pieced together by the Public Prosecutor from evidence supplied by KGB operatives of the people they had been instructed to follow and spy on. Among the journalists on the list were Yegor Yakovlev, Vitaly Korotich, Mikhail Poltoranin, Yury Shchekochikhin, Fyodor Burlatsky, Oleg Poptsov.
9 *Izvestiya*, 10 October 1991, p. 7.
10 I flew into Moscow with a BBC Panorama film crew the day after the coup; and several months later returned to take interviews for a proposed docudrama for Granada Television, which was never completed.
11 Kravchenko: *Kak ya byl televizionnym kamikadze*, Moskva: AiF print, 2005, pp. 243–4.
12 The eight men were Vladimir Kryuchkov, Marshal Dmitry Yazov, Gennady Yanayev, Valentin Pavlov, Boris Pugo, Oleg Baklanov, Vasily Starodubtsev and Aleksandr Tizyakov.
13 'Obrashchenie GKChP', published 18 August, 1991. http://www.agitclub.ru/gorby/putch/gkcpdocument.htm (accessed 22 November 2015).
14 *Izvestiya*, 4 September 1991; *Soyuz* , no. 36 September 1991; Boris Yeltsin: *Zapiski prezidenta*, Izdatelstvo "Ogonek", Moskva, 1994, p. 84.
15 With Sobchak's election as mayor, Leningrad returned to its original name of St Petersburg on 12 June 1991 two months before the coup, but because it took time before people began to refer to the city by its old name, I continue in this chapter to refer to it as Leningrad, as also seen in a quote.
16 For more information, see Gessen's, *The Man without a Face: The Unlikely Rise of Vladimir Putin*, London, Granta, 2012, pp. 104–18; Timur Olevsky, 'Gde zh byl Putin vo vremya GKChP. Tri dnya shag za shagom', Dozdh TV, 20 August 2015. https://tvrain.ru/teleshow/lobkov_vechernee_shou/gde_byl_putin-393005 (accessed 22 November 2015).
17 *V avguste 91-go: Rossiya glazami ochevidtsev*, compiled by Viktor Maslyukov and Konstantin Turevits, Moskva, Sankt and St Petersburg: Limbus Press, 1993, p. 235.
18 Author's interview, November 1991.
19 Author's interview, February 1992.

20 *Zapiski prezidenta*, Izdatel'stvo "Ogonek", Moskva 1994, p. 83.
21 Kravchenko, *Kak ya byl televizionnym kamikadze*, pp. 245–6.
22 *V Avguste 91-go*, p. 18.
23 Author's interview, November 1991.
24 V. Stepankov and Ye. Lisev, *Kremlevskii zagovor: versiya sledstviya*, Izdatel'stvo "Ogonek", 1992, p. 172.
25 Yu.S. Sidorenko, *Tri dnya, kotorye oprokinuli bolshevizm: ispoved' svidetelya, pokazaniya ochevidtsa*, Izdatel'stvo, Periodika Dona, Rostov-na-Dony, 1991, p. 30.
26 The newspapers were *Megapolis Express, Moskovskii komsomolets, Rossiiskie vesti, Rossiiskaya gazeta, Stolitsa, Kuranty, Argumenty i fakty, Nezavisimaya gazeta, Komsomolskaya pravda, Kommersant* and *Moskovskie novosti*.
27 *Soyuz*, no. 36 September 1991; *Krasnaya zvezda*, 31 August 1991; *Nezavisimaya gazeta*, 12 September 1991, p. 4.
28 Author's interview, 12 December 1991.
29 Author's interview, November 1991.
30 Stepankov and Lisov, *Kremlevskii zagovor*, p. 183.
31 *Komsomolskaya pravda*, 20 December 1991.
32 Boris Pugo and his wife committed suicide on the morning of 22 August. In his suicide note he asks his family to forgive him and says 'It was all a mistake. I have lived honestly all my life'. There were a number of other prominent suicides.
33 'Why the state of emergency committee lost in 1991', *Rossiiskaya gazeta*, 19 August 2004 in JRL 8333.
34 'Why isn't August Revolution day a national holiday?', *Obshchaya gazeta*, no. 33, 16 August 2001.
35 'The Revolution of 1991 in Russia: Interpretations of the Moscow Coup', *Coexistence*, 29, the Netherlands, Kluwer, 1992, p. 347. Sakwa quotes Kagarlitsky's argument from *New Statesman and Society*, 6 September 1991, pp. 18–20.
36 *Zapiski*, p. 67.
37 Ibid., p. 166.
38 Timothy J. Colton, *Yeltsin: A Life*, New York, Basic Books, 2008, pp. 252–3.
39 Patrick Henry and Jonas Bernstein, '25-minute Yeltsin inaugural renews health worries'. www.friends-partners.org/oldfriends/spbweb/times/185-186/25minute.html (accessed 22 November 2015).

7 The Yeltsin era: free speech

> Don't fall into temptation, don't exchange it for economic gain … Remember,
> freedom comes from a free press; that's not an exaggeration, the freedom of our
> society depends on it.
>
> (Yeltsin, 12 June 1993)

I Transition to democracy

In the eight years Boris Yeltsin was president, the country enjoyed a degree of
free speech unprecedented in scope and duration. Yet to talk of Yeltsin's
legacy invariably provokes strong emotions about the extent of his commitment to freedom and democracy. His huge and controversial impact in
changing almost every aspect of Russians' lives as they moved through seis-
mic economic, political, cultural and imperialist changes has laid him vulnerable to all sorts of criticism. Some are well deserved: he was a colossal but
flawed figure, while the task before him was Herculean. His goal, as he saw it,
was clear: to bury communism and take Russia along the road to democracy.
If he was not a pinup democratic leader all of the time, he was the most
democratic the country has ever had. His motivating principle, and one he
often expressed with anguish, was to create what he said Russians deserved
after so many years of suffering: a prosperous and democratic society out of
the debris of the Soviet system. It did not go smoothly. 'People expected
paradise on earth', he writes in his memoirs, 'but they got inflation, unemployment, economic shock and a political crisis'.[1] Yet, despite the constant
turbulence of these years, Yeltsin was presiding over and facilitating the most
dynamic and liberated period of Russian history.

If there is disagreement about Yeltsin's legacy, even his opponents agree
that the free rein Yeltsin allowed the media and political opposition during
these years was his greatest achievement. By promoting free speech Yeltsin
did what seemed impossible: he freed society from fear. Archives were opening up, books were being published, public records were becoming available.
The daily *Nezavisimaya gazeta* said of him in an obituary (though notably
not during his lifetime when events were too frenetic and hopes vied with

ignorance about what could be done) that it was precisely because he had 'removed fear from people's hearts' that people took out their frustrations on him. 'Citizens interpreted their own difficulties in adapting to a new way of life as the blunders of the country's leader. And as people no longer had fear, the head of state was ostracised by just about everyone'.[2] By raising the sluice gate on speech, it is probably true to say that Yeltsin became the most trashed leader in Russian history. The free flow of speech was not only of the respectable kind, but a cacophony of noises, pushing the boundaries of convention, sometimes inflammatory and odious, expressing a need not always to learn so much as to vent feelings, to speak and give voice. The arsenal of criticism against Yeltsin was large because the range of possibilities that opened up was even larger.

Yeltsin's contribution to freedom and democracy has to be measured not against the exaggerated hopes of citizens brought up on communist utopian politics, but against the real dangers the country faced from total economic collapse and civil war. What was amazing within the context of Russian history was that he managed to avoid its worst excesses. Yeltsin's role model was Peter the Great, but to implement reform Peter took his people 'kicking and screaming' into the new world, as did almost every other leader of revolutionary change in the country. Yeltsin tried to find practical solutions. In negotiating the collapse of the Soviet Union he managed to maintain peaceful relations with his 'near abroad' neighbours, a success for which he has won little credit. Within Russia he devolved power from the centre, trying to create a flexible federal system while keeping regions such as Tatarstan and the Ural republics from seceding. He made endless compromises to avert tribal conflicts in the tinderbox of the North Caucasus. Only quick and skilful intervention prevented a worsening of the situation in the first post-Soviet ethnic conflict between North Ossetia and Ingushetia in 1992, where more than 450 people were killed within the space of five days. 'In other words, far from being a time of "chaos and failure", Yeltsin's Russia managed to avert a number of conflicts', says historian Sergei Markedonov, pointing to Yeltsin's policy of making complicated arrangements to accommodate disparate interests in a whole list of conflicts that was erupting.[3]

Yeltsin's big mistake, and the first act to disappoint his liberal supporters, was to send troops into Chechnya rather than continue the difficult negotiations. Earlier, his bombing of the White House to put down the nationalists' parliamentary revolt was also shocking, but the fear of a bloody civil war was real. The most disastrous failure for many Russians was the privatisation programme which saw the country's vast natural resources being sold off at auctions for a fraction of their real worth. The squandering of the country to the benefit of a small elite on the basis, as Anatoly Chubais constantly reiterated, that property had to be taken out of the hands of the state as quickly as possible to prevent a communist return to power, has led to today's corrupt, corporate, bandit state. The Chicago and Harvard schools of free market economics were at their peak in the early 1990s, dominating international lending bodies such as the IMF and the World Bank, but this is no excuse for the policies adopted by Yeltsin's economists, who were far to the right of their western neoliberal colleagues in Russia's usual maximalist spirit of leaping to the opposite extreme. Many had chosen to get their first crash course on western economics by going to Chile in 1991, a year after dictator Pinochet's retirement. The economy was not Yeltsin's area of expertise and he put his trust in these young modern economists. Press secretary Kostikov recounts how Yeltsin was sure that things would soon get better for ordinary people, saying frequently with a gesture of his hands – 'you just have to wait a wee bit [*chut'-chut'*]' – showing a small gap between thumb and index finger.

Yeltsin took unpopular decisions and acted in the early days with the determination of a 'bulldozer', as people called him. To establish democracy, he enshrined in law and in practice liberal values such as free speech, free elections, civil society and the rule of law. He laid out the basics for the market that enabled the country to prosper economically a decade later under Putin. With such credentials, it is odd that many commentators refuse to accept him as a genuinely democratic leader, honouring only Gorbachev with the title of 'father of democracy'. 'A wave of historical amnesia' has swept over commentators who have forgotten that it was Gorbachev who launched democratic reforms (Katrina vanden Heuvel)[4] or a 'vast amount of nonsense' has been talked about Yeltsin introducing freedom and democracy to Russia (Archie Brown).[5] There is no doubt that Gorbachev was the first to initiate reforms and democratise the party, but he was hampered by his belief that the Soviet Communist Party was reformable. Like Khrushchev, he opened up society but got cold feet when it began to spin out of his control. He was never willing to go far or fast enough. Although some of the new democratic laws came out in the last 18 months of his rule, he was largely pushed into adopting them by the pro-democracy movement at the head of which was Yeltsin.

The transition from a Soviet to a democratic state was nothing short of revolutionary, and Yeltsin's use of rule by decree rather than consensual methods was often the only way of breaking the advantages of incumbency in favour of the emerging democracy. But when he was advised to take seriously undemocratic actions – halting elections in 1996, as proposed by Berezovsky and Korzhakov, or abolishing direct elections of regional governors in 1999 as suggested by Primakov (and later implemented by Putin), he confirmed his democratic instincts by refusing to do so. There were many facets to Yeltsin's personality that made it hard to pin him down. He could be brilliant or awkward or boorish. His anarchic personality, so stereotypical of the Russian 'wide soul', inspired hundreds of thousands to march for democracy and contained the brazenness to shake up an entrenched state that seemed set in stone. Different virtues were expected from him as president, and personal failings and illnesses interfered with running the ship of state. He embarrassed his country by openly drunken behaviour and vanished from office at crucial periods, his absences usually excused as 'Yeltsin is working on documents'.

Sometimes you could not tell if he was drunk, ill or simply slurring his words, as he was prone to do. In fact, according to his aides, he practically stopped drinking after a heart attack in 1995, but reports of drunken behaviour continued to dog him. There were different Yeltsins: the career opportunist and apparatchik, the over-achiever, the charismatic rebel, the shameless drunk, the imperious 'tsar Boris' and the ailing man of the last years, whose powers were increasingly transferred to oligarchs and the so-called 'family', with his daughter, Tatyana Dyachenko, acting as a conduit between him and the outside world.

One of his aides, Georgy Satarov described Yeltsin to me as introspective, an 'introvert', who took matters close to heart, churning over problems in his head – 'he might not sleep all night before government sessions, walking and thinking. He had a file on his desk where he would slip in notes about things he needed to sort out for himself. All that talk of his political instinct was the result of constant, hard work'. There was more of the intellectual to Yeltsin than is thought; an awareness of his society, the psychology of its culture and his place in it. The Yeltsin era up to its last breath felt free, much of which depended on his personality. He felt the responsibilities of power strongly and probably, uniquely, is the only Russian leader to have asked the Russian people for forgiveness 'for not fulfilling the hopes of people who believed that we would be able to jump from the grey, stagnating totalitarian past into a bright, rich and civilised future in one go. I myself believed in this'.[6]

The real dissatisfaction with Yeltsin was entangled in the hopes that the transition to democracy raised. Some of these hopes were dashed by opportunities Yeltsin missed, but many of these hopes were unrealistic in a society that had not changed overnight. It was still a corrupt elitist Soviet state with a strong gangster element caused by a brutal and punitive heritage. A society of 'victims' of this history was demanding a rapid improvement to its lifestyle without any real understanding of how to get it. When their expectations were not fulfilled, they blamed democracy. Or they blamed Yeltsin, because the Soviet state was expected to provide welfare in exchange for an acquiescent citizenry. Everything was now turned on its head. Citizens were not required to salute the state but to get on with building their own lives. The emerging world of civil society with its non-governmental organisations (NGOs), funded by international donors (USAID, UK's Know How Fund, EU's TACIS, etc.) to provide technical assistance and 'know-how' on what it meant to live in a participatory democracy, often based on ideals which the West fell short of themselves, was producing slogans such as 'show initiative', 'be enterprising', 'realise yourself', words that sounded weird translated into Russian. The nanny state was eroding before the citizen had come of age.

We are led to believe that the 1990s was a time of unmitigated chaos and disorder, crime and poverty. It was a mixed period, part of which evoked the Wild West in its lawlessness and avarice, as the controls of a repressed and impoverished state loosened. Contract killings took place and in one period it seemed that so-called bankers were being liquidated at a fast rate, but many of these killings took place in the world of business and organised crime. Nevertheless, ordinary people were sensible to invest in strong steel-padded front doors. The early years were painful and disorientating for people in other ways as well. After the liberalisation of prices, they lost their savings, wages went unpaid, workers suffered. It was particularly unfair for pensioners, world war veterans and *afgantsy* (those who had fought in Afghanistan). The Soviet state had left behind a bankrupt economy, and there was no let-up in political struggles for power. But there were time-honoured ways of getting around austerity through barter and moonlighting, part-time work, making use of a car or a private vegetable allotment out of town, and many Russians as usual proved resilient.

The exciting side were the new freedoms that opened up: not only to speak freely, but to create projects, engage in business, make money – acts which were criminal offences in the Soviet Union. Many who went abroad came back with videos and computers to sell. People with enormous black plastic bags made the regular shuttle service across the Black Sea to Turkey to bring back leather goods which were sold in markets all over Russia. For a country which had known decades of deficit in food and consumer goods, these products on sale in street kiosks and underpasses and any available space that could be found were like manna from heaven. In the block of flats where I lived, the residents' collective unearthed a disused basement, painted it and rented it out as offices, using the proceeds for improvements to their flats – what was called 'evro-remont' (European-standard improvements). This energy was replicated in one form or another all over the country. Individuals and collectives in all walks of life were beginning to organise their lives. It was a rite of passage not everyone sailed through, but it marked a person's progress to a more mature and engaged role in society. There was no one out there to tell you what to do, to 'impose' an ideology or enforce a way of living. That Russian word 'impose' – *navyazyvat'* – with its unpleasant connotation of 'tying you up' – expressed the malaise that Russians had never before been able to escape. They were now in charge of their lives, but living in difficult market conditions.

As a liberal reformer, Yeltsin removed constraints and allowed people to get on with their own lives; in J. S. Mill's sense, to pursue their own good in their own way. In Radishchev's words, the 'leading strings' were removed from the infant. Yeltsin provided 'negative' freedoms, on which society could build. The genuine absence of censorship allowed the media to decide their own fate. Yeltsin was a hands-off leader, giving government and ministers a long leash. He saw himself as the final instance: a father figure above the fray, the type-cast mythical tsar above unruly interests, quick to intervene when he felt things were going wrong and to dismiss ministers and advisers at will. It was a benign position, but traditionally its underpinning is despotic. Burbulis and others argued that one of Yeltsin's gravest mistakes was not to have formed a political party, which would have provided a centre for participatory democracy and perpetuated his legacy. Yeltsin felt that once the Constitution and laws were in place, it was up to people to get on with their work and lobby for their political interests. In the atmosphere of the times, it would have been presumptuous to tell people what to do or lay down any line. If anything even smacked of ideology in these early years, it was spurned with almost visceral distaste as a reminder of hollow communist slogans.

The buck had passed from the state to the individual or collective. This was the main distinction between the Yeltsin and Gorbachev eras for journalists. What people expected from *glasnost* was the truth about the crimes of the party and the right to publish. In the post-Soviet era these obstructions had largely been removed and journalists were safeguarded by law. Theoretically they were in the same position as journalists in the West in so far as almost any material could be published if there was the will and the money to investigate abuse by the government or private sector. In practice, of course, Russia's legacy of chronic secrecy in government and the bureaucracy made it hugely difficult and in many cases unsafe, but journalists had acquired the right of accreditation and access to information.

Democracy is a two-way street. The right to vote needs voters; the right to free speech needs people prepared to speak freely, if the possession of 'rights' is to make sense. It therefore depended on journalists to make use of their freedoms and build democratic institutions that would support their work. Because the media were immediately plunged into a market economy that threatened their very existence, free speech did not develop in the squeaky clean way they had envisaged. But there was no inexorable reason to kowtow to the state or private owners, if they valued their profession.

Yeltsin and the media

In a round-table discussion on television about Yeltsin with his former liberal advisers, the presenter Nikolai Svanidze asked a famous Tolstoyan question. Tolstoy, reflecting on his heroine Natasha Rostova, asks: how was it possible that the young countess, who had been educated by a French governess, simply knew how to move to the spirit of a Russian folk dance? The question in the Yeltsin puzzle was: how did a first secretary of the Regional Committee of the Communist Party of the Soviet Union pick up such a refined understanding of the value of free speech?[7]

This was in 2001, more than a year after Yeltsin had retired. The advisers agreed it could not simply be attributed to Yeltsin's much-vaunted political instinct. 'It's not right to say that he knew intuitively that free speech was sacred. His understanding of free speech was more a world-view, which didn't depend on who was exercising it or what form it took or what impact it had', said Gennady Burbulis. Originally an academic from Yekaterinburg, Burbulis recalled how Yeltsin as Sverdlovsk's regional first party secretary would invite sociologists to public discussions where, even if 10 per cent of the questions were planted, the remaining ones were allowed to be asked freely. 'He learned to listen to these questions and answer them', says Burbulis. Was he a convinced free speech advocate or a pragmatist? Both, said Georgy Satarov. 'He knew he was dependent on public opinion and considered a free press his strategic partner with whom he could not quarrel, he simply had to put up with it'. Lyudmila Pikhoya described how upset Yeltsin would get at unjustified or offensive attacks, but whenever she suggested he take a journalist to court for defamation, as Moscow Mayor Luzhkov had done successfully many times, Yeltsin always refused.

His attempts to get used to criticism are well documented. He was particularly wary of journalists he thought were loyal to Gorbachev. Press secretary Kostikov described an incident to me when Gorbachev criticised Yeltsin in the western press while he was abroad, which Yeltsin saw as a stab in the back. He asked Kostikov to make a public statement that Gorbachev's behaviour had been unacceptable. *Izvestiya* immediately ran a front-page heading to support Gorbachev's right to say what he wanted – 'Speak, Mikhail Sergeyevich, speak!'. Kostikov says that his bodyguard, Korzhakov, did much to stir up Yeltsin's suspicion of journalists. Although he held all the levers of power to control the media had he wanted to, he did not do so, nor did he manipulate the press by playing games of favouritism, as Putin has done with his special Kremlin pool of approved journalists.

As for the vituperative communist and nationalist newspapers that never spared him for having banned the party and broken up the Soviet Union, Yeltsin was more libertarian than the liberal journalists who supported him. His willingness to listen to different and even repellent views was part of what made him a good negotiator. He had been lambasted before when as Moscow Party boss he received the anti-Semitic group Pamyat' in his office to hear out their views. As president, he angered liberal editors by not banning nationalist and pro-fascist literature:

I. GOLEMBIOVSKY (EDITOR, IZVESTIYA): In St Petersburg alone 31 newspapers of an openly fascist orientation are being printed. They violate the Constitution. Why doesn't the president take *Den'* to court? The president is insulted in every issue.

B. KURKOVA (CHAIRPERSON, ST PETERSBURG TV): Not only the president. They are calling to overthrow the system.

I. GOLEMBIOVSKY: They're getting away with it all ... this is a very dangerous tendency

YELTSIN: I understand. Your proposition is logical. But then practically any newspaper or editor sitting here could be caught out for distortion and caricaturing the president. I consider it an enormous victory for Russian democracy that after the August coup we did not respond in kind by announcing terror to the communists ... therefore to announce a campaign now to prosecute a newspaper ... that is not a president's job. [noise in the hall][8]

Yeltsin had given a perfectly Millian response. It was important to listen to all sides. He had sufficient nous to understand that laws prohibiting hate speech could be used far more broadly than for their ostensible purpose. This was still the early period before media lawyers began to argue the finer points of regulating the media, and demonstrates how clearly Yeltsin understood the value of accepting a pluralism of views. If they were uncomfortable and inflammatory ones, they had been stirring in the pot for so many decades under a ban of silence that they needed to be released. In this approach, Yeltsin showed himself to be ahead of the international development agencies that provided advice to countries in transition to democracy. It was only much later that office bearers such as the UN Special Rapporteur on Freedom of Expression laid down the importance of tolerating hate speech as part of encouraging the development of a robust democratic media, so long as it did not directly incite riot. The preferred antidote to hate speech these days is to encourage the development of many voices rather than to ban the few.[9]

Despite Yeltsin's 'hands-off' approach with the media, he realised the press required state assistance to allow it to survive the onslaught of market forces, and decrees were passed on state subsidies and other means of financial support. This was accepted by needy newspapers with caution, as it meant they were once again in thrall to the state; while the new proudly capitalist press, such as *Kommersant*, with strong neoliberal attitudes, scorned such overtures. The press minister, Poltoranin, had Yeltsin's ear whenever problems arose. If Poltoranin is to be believed, he put a stop to Yeltsin's plan to hand over the first channel to Italy's Berlusconi which, with hindsight, may not have been quite as ridiculous as it sounds.[10] In the early years some 15 meetings were held between Yeltsin and editors. These were not meetings to get 'instructions', as editors confirm, but a forum where issues could be thrashed out and complaints made. In one of these meetings, Yeltsin clearly set out his position on free speech:

> If a leader, a ruler, a president begins to put pressure on the press, that means he is weak. A strong ruler will not put pressure on the press, even if it criticises him. This criticism is needed. If we don't criticise now, we will roll back into that bog we lived in for many decades. We can't let that happen and I, as president ... state once again that I will defend and support the media.[11]

Yeltsin shielded the media from the bureaucracy which to his mind, as an ex-party man, was the main obstruction standing in the way of freedom and democracy. If journalists had also obstructed oligarchic interests in the name of free speech, the media might today be a totally different entity. Decades later, Pavel Gusev, editor of *Moskovsky komsomolets*, who had started his career in 1983 under Andropov and had a panoramic view of the development of the media in modern Russia, was emphatic about the opportunities Yeltsin had opened up:

Under Yeltsin a bureaucrat would have been afraid to even hint that he wanted to influence the media. Boris Nikolayevich had made it clear that the media were free from the bureaucracy's abuse of power and could on no account give journalists instructions. It was a golden time for Russian journalism, when we really were the fourth estate. They listened and responded to us. Of course, some hated us and some liked us, but to threaten to close us down or something else – that simply was not on the cards.[12]

On the few occasions that Yeltsin publicly interfered in media affairs, they were connected with violent conflict. He dismissed Yegor Yakovlev as chairman of Ostankino TV in 1992 over a documentary on the ethnic conflict between North Ossetia and Ingushetia, accusing Yakovlev of 'serious mistakes'. Yeltsin was responding to the rage of the North Ossetian leader, who claimed the documentary was one-sided; in fact, the TV crew had not been given permission to enter North Ossetia. In that month he also sacked Poltoranin (and his closest allies Burbulis and Gaidar) to appease his parliamentary opponents before the Seventh Congress of People's Deputies. It was what Yeltsin called the 'logic of life',[13] as he scrambled to hang on to power and continue market reforms. Yeltsin apologised to Yakovlev and offered him an ambassadorial posting, but Yakovlev rejected his offers. Thus one of the most innovative democratic figures was lost to broadcasting at a time when television was waiting, like a *tabula rasa*, for a new imprimatur.

On two occasions Yeltsin banned *Pravda*: after the 1991August coup and after the storming of the White House in 1993. With the coup, his supporters persuaded him to lift the ban on *Pravda* three days after the coup ended. In 1993 Yeltsin removed the ban against *Pravda* and other newspapers a few weeks later, except for those newspapers that were taken to court for inciting riot.

In the old days, Yeltsin as Moscow Party boss had treated the media in the way all Soviet leaders did, as an instrument of the state. The party paper *Moskovskaya pravda*, however admirable its crusading courage in pushing for radical change against the party's attempts to sabotage it, was Yeltsin's mouthpiece and not a free agent. Yeltsin admitted it took him some years to accept this loss of entitlement, but in discussions in 1999 with his then Prime Minister, Yevgeny Primakov, a reformer of the old school, he was surprised at just how difficult it was for Primakov to rid himself of neurosis 'at the sight of a newspaper'. Primakov had come to him with a file he had put together of every article that had been written in the newspapers about his new cabinet. He had read all the articles and underlined sections in coloured pencils. Behind every article Primakov suspected 'complicated intrigues, subtexts, or threats from his political opponents. The reality of a free press was impossible to explain to him', Yeltsin writes:

A directive had been given (by Primakov) to the 'apparat': Conceal information from the press; give a minimum of interviews; all contacts with journalists must be strictly supervised. Primakov's many years in closed institutions – the Central Committee of the Communist Party, the Foreign Ministry and the Foreign Intelligence Service – had taken their toll. But in the last few years, government operations had become transparent. Journalists had grown accustomed to discussing various steps taken by the cabinet. Now, suddenly, they found that Soviet-style controls had been slapped on them ... 'Yevgeny Maksimovich', I began. 'I got used to that long ago. They write about me every day; they've been doing it for years. And you know the tone they use. But what can I do? Close down the newspapers?'[14]

It would be wrong, of course, to say that Yeltsin never interfered in the media behind the scenes, or that certain ministers and state television executives did not know where his and their interests lay or that there was no bias or propaganda on television, of which there was a great deal, especially during elections. But blanket propaganda was never imposed, there was no particular use of the 'telephone law', and on many occasions Yeltsin interceded to assist the media. He tolerated the barrage of media criticism over the first Chechen war, a high point of holding office bearers to account, and influential in ending the war two years later. It shows the media could exercise their right to speak freely. What is more doubtful is whether this right was exercised appropriately or frequently in the public interest.

II Soviet television dismantled

The collapse of the Soviet Union hastened the privatisation and redistribution of media property that had started with the abolition of the Communist Party's guiding role in society. The old stranglehold of Soviet television was dismantled and decentralised. It was the end for Gosteleradio. The main two state nationwide channels changed status. The first channel, which had been the mouthpiece of Soviet Central Television, now called Ostankino, lost its official position but, as the largest channel that covered most of Russia and the 'near abroad', it has never lost its place as the channel most people turn to. The second channel, Rossiya (or RTR), which had been the former Russian republic's channel, now received priority replacing Gosteleradio as the All-Russia State Television and Radio Broadcasting Company (VGTRK in Russian). RTR had been the opposition channel during *perestroika* and most of Yeltsin's supporters had moved over to it.

These channels no longer saw themselves as state instruments but as 'independent' in spirit, a word frequently employed at the time. To be independent usually meant not being under the control of the state. Private or commercial media outlets were called independent in the belief that if they were not state-affiliated they must be impartial. In this early transitional stage, television was neither truly independent, nor in the grip of the state. It represented the general political confusion of the times, hovering somewhere between glimmerings of independent broadcasting and Soviet-style propaganda.

With the abrupt change to the free market and the dire economic situation, the state budget could no longer bear the crippling costs of maintaining its previous vast television empire. RTR remained fully state-owned and subsidised, but it soon needed to seek advertising as well. Ostankino became a hybrid state–private joint stock company, with 49 per cent of its shares up for grabs to private investors. Its state funding dried up by 1996, but it had studios and equipment to rent and had become both a programme maker and publisher broadcaster. Private production companies, which looked to advertising and sponsors for financing, rented equipment and facilities from Ostankino and depended on it for a slot on its channels.

Advertising was becoming big business, an activity that hadn't existed a few years earlier. One of the first advertisements on Soviet television had been the Don harvester, directed at large agro-industry. In 1991 there was no need to advertise consumer goods: all you had to do was set up a stall on the street and everything would be sold out. By 1994 there were already 2,000 private advertising agencies in Moscow with some of the world's largest foreign multinationals wanting to break into the new market. Competing with them were two Russian companies, Premier SV (headed by Sergei Lisovsky) with about 1,000 employees and Video International (founded by Mikhail Lesin). 'Russia is like a black hole, it's sucking up everything into the market', said Vladimir Yevstafyev, then head of an agency with international clients such as Cadbury Schweppes.[15] In 1994 a 60-second advertisement in prime time cost $25,000, already six times higher than the year before. Such potential wealth in advertising, at a time when state funding for television was breaking down meant that an unhealthy relationship developed between journalists, advertisers and PR companies.

What was becoming a murky advertising world contrasted with some of Yegor Yakovlev's idealistic ventures as head of Ostankino before he was sacked. He brought in respected sociologist Vsevolod Vilchek to organise a department for the measurement of audience ratings, acknowledging for the first time the demands of viewers and their value as targets for advertising. With the transformation of the former republics into a Commonwealth of Independent States (CIS), Yakovlev planned to turn Ostankino into a shared CIS television space. There was reason to believe it could work. Vilchek's opinion poll showed that seven out of eight viewers in the CIS valued Ostankino TV more than any other station, including their own republican ones in their own language.[16] Yakovlev conducted negotiations with the former republics, charting a procedure by which they could agree on the reporting of ethnic conflicts and even considered forming a corps of foreign journalists – a kind of UN blue beret corps – that might be acceptable to all sides. After he left, there was no one authoritative enough to push through the idea. The question of financing, as well as intra-republican conflicts and fears of Russian imperialism, managed to bury the idea, leaving only a small block of programmes on the channel in the afternoons.

With market forces at work, television lightened its load by buying mainly cheap Latin American soap operas to fill their schedules. The most popular were Mexico's *The Rich Also Cry* and America's *Santa Barbara*, which played up to fantasies of how people lived in democracies. As far as I know, no thorough surveys were done on the effect these soaps had on people's expectations and hopes; certainly the theme of rags to riches, particularly servant to mistress, was highly appealing, and some of the extravagant forms of dressing that Russians became addicted to may have had their model here. Criticism of the dumbing down of standards had little effect on viewers, many of whom were sick of the constant politics on television. One letter writer retorted that for all the primitiveness of slave girl Izaura (another Latin American soap) it was better than 'the crap we were offered about blood-sucking kulaks and noble Chekists [secret police]'.[17]

The survival of the press

The economic crisis hit the press much harder than it did television. After the liberalisation of prices, the cost of running a newspaper soared. Ironically, the press was able to indulge in free speech when it was on the point of economic extinction.

Izvestiya's print run fell from 10 million (1989) to 4 million two years later (1991) to 800,000 (1994). *Argumenty i fakty*, the most widely read newspaper, went from 33.2 million (1990) to 5 million (1993).[18] *Komsomolskaya pravda* had a print run of over 20 million in 1990; yet on its front page on 20 February 1992 it explained that it had not come out the previous day, the first time ever in its history since 1925, because it was bankrupt. An issue of the paper was selling at its old price of 8 kopecks at a time when it cost 70 kopecks to produce. During this rough patch, many newspapers were unable to publish issues every day. While newspapers had freed themselves, the ministries they depended on for printing, paper and distribution were still part of corrupt state monopolies, demanding prices that far exceeded their actual cost. The paradox was that the more copies a newspaper sold, the more broke it became.

A decree passed by Yeltsin in February 1992 granted subsidies to newspapers to keep them afloat during the transitional period. At least 300 newspapers received subsidies, including opposition papers such as *Sovetskaya Rossiya* and *Pravda*, until the latter was bailed out by a Greek communist businessman. But, as media expert Andrei Richter pointed out, Poltoranin did not hesitate to favour papers that promoted the 'rebirth of Russia'.[19] Mass circulation newspapers, *Trud* and *Komsomolskaya pravda* (Yeltsin's favourites) were singled out. Yeltsin issued a decree ordering paper producers to sell 70 per cent of their output at a fixed price; and provided subsidises to the agency dealing with distribution, to bring down the cost. The government promised the monopolies would be privatised, but did nothing about it, and private printing houses were slow to set up.

Newspapers tried to bypass the monopolies and sell directly to local kiosks or hire people to sell newspapers with a 'negotiated' rather than a set price. New sources of newsprint were sought at home and in Finland. Subscription rates had to increase, which meant fewer subscribers than before, but by European standards newspapers still had high print runs. The press found diverse forms of financing. Some newspapers joined foreign media companies to bring out joint supplements. *Argumenty i fakty* bought a construction company, a telecommunications business in Nizhny Novgorod and started dealing in shares and securities. *Moskovsky komsomolets* created several trade companies and began to provide high-interest loans to different businesses.[20] When asked how ultra-nationalist *Den'* ('Day') found money for its publication, Poltoranin speculated that it was probably using illegal Communist Party money that had not been returned to the taxpayer.[21]

The curious situation in the years to come was that although the press could not make ends meet, more and more newspapers started up. By the law of the market, if supply exceeds demand, at least some of the less popular newspapers should have gone broke, but this did not happen. As in the case of television, the value of newspapers as an instrument of politics and business became a dubious saviour. 'Newspapers are bought not to make profit, but to fight for steel, oil, a governor's post or whatever', said the Union of Journalists' secretary Pavel Gutiontov.[22] The overcrowding of the Moscow market, with 12 national dailies in 1997, put journalists in an even weaker position to fight for editorial independence.

President versus parliament

Apart from the economic crisis, the deadlock between president and parliament, known as the constitutional crisis, took the country to the edge of civil war. It was prompted by what one commentator called parliament's 'strange ambition' to usurp Yeltsin's political dominance, attained through his popularity as Russian president and hero of the defeated coup. Parliament had been elected in March 1990 to serve the Soviet system which no longer existed. Formally, according to the Brezhnev Constitution, it had supreme power, but it failed the test of legitimacy.[23] Yeltsin held the mandate of public support and was committed to democratic reform – credentials which parliament on the whole, with its large conservative and nationalist factions, lacked.

The principles of free speech were being tested in volatile conditions when profound choices needed to be made about what a future Russia would look like. Was legality more important than legitimacy? In a country setting out to be a law-governed state, many felt that legality was the only answer. Legitimacy required making refined political judgements, something they were not used to. Were personalities more important than constitutional issues? Yeltsin promised democracy, but if he received broad powers what would happen in the long term if xenophobe and nationalist Zhirinovsky became president? As it happened, Yeltsin's popularity pushed ultimate power resolutely towards the president, which was to benefit President Putin's authoritarian rule. Was free speech more important than democratic reform? If this was a struggle between democrats and reactionary communist-nationalists, to what extent was television airtime parity simply a nicety? Hadn't Hitler slipped in through parliament?

The crisis began in November 1992 when parliament refused to extend Yeltsin's emergency powers to push through unpopular reforms. Gaidar's shock therapy had caused hardship and suffering, and many deputies were hostile to market reforms. Some of Yeltsin's most prominent allies, who had stood with him during the coup, now turned on him in a naked struggle for power. His rebellious Vice-President Aleksandr Rutskoi called Yeltsin's liberal intellectual economists 'little boys in pink shorts', while parliamentary speaker Ruslan Khasbulatov simply dismissed members of the cabinet as 'worms'. Parliament's centrists were drowned out by raucous groups on the far right, a collation of communists, militarists, ultra-nationalists, Cossacks, monarchists and racists. Everyone wanted free speech, which the far right often turned into a space for mudslinging and brawls.

Tensions had arisen in the summer of 1992 when tens of thousands of hardliners, led by the firebrand ex-TV correspondent Viktor Anpilov, staged a two-week picket outside Ostankino TV centre, camping in tents across the street from the television tower. Brandishing red Soviet flags and anti-Semitic posters, they demanded an hour of airtime daily on television to voice their views and put an end to 'tele-drivel'. Every day TV workers had to run the gauntlet of heckling demonstrators, putting up with verbal abuse and anti-Semitic taunts. The protest that there were too many Jews on television was a constant refrain, although some of the most popular and professional television presenters were Jewish. The view blazoned on posters of 'Russian TV for Russians' played its part in scuppering plans to make Ostankino TV a CIS channel.

Liberal-minded journalists did not want to be told whose side to take by Kremlin officials, but neither were they willing to let nationalists walk over their democratic revolution. Parliament's complaint that it did not have parity with the Yeltsin media was true, as media professionals overwhelmingly supported democratic change, but it did not mean parliament was left without a voice. It had its own newspaper, *Rossiyskaya gazeta* ('Russian Newspaper'); and hardline factions could rely on their privately acquired press network of *Pravda, Sovetskaya Rossiya, Den'* and a plethora of small badly printed papers written by the 'red-brown' contingents and sold outside the Kremlin walls, in underpasses to the Metro or in army and workers' circles. Despite parliament's repeated complaints about not getting airtime on Ostankino, Yegor Yakovlev calculated the opposition had taken part in about 25 programmes by summer 1992 and had multiple access to radio.[24]

Parliament also had RTR under its jurisdiction, but the channel had less audience reach and was only beginning to develop its base. It had instructed RTR to transmit all sessions of the Supreme Soviet and the Congress of

People's Deputies, its full body, which was part of the reason it was receiving bad publicity. The spectacle of constant political bickering at parliament's sessions and its inflexibility, more intent on sabotaging Yeltsin's power than reaching consensus for the sake of national stability, was not inspiring. As well, RTR's chairman, Oleg Poptsov, was personally affiliated to the democrats, having been appointed at a time when president and parliament were firm friends. Poptsov recalls the hardliners' hatred of Yeltsin, his democratic goals and the economic aid packages he was negotiating with the IMF. He quotes the well-known ex-KGB officer Aleksandr Sterligov at a meeting of the Joint Council of Patriotic Forces, whose threats against Yeltsin were received with an ovation from the hall – 'we don't need a jury, we have the experience of our fathers, the experience of purges and bringing about order. We don't need a jury for enemies of the people'.[25]

In an audacious move, parliamentary forces attempted to seize the pride of the liberal press, *Izvestiya*. The building was surrounded by members of Khasbulatov's 5,000-strong private army, which had appeared as out of nowhere. *Izvestiya* had been the organ of the Soviet parliament, but after the collapse of the Soviet Union in 1991 the journalist collective voted to become its 'founder'. As the flagship of democratic reform, it was the least likely newspaper to give in. *Izvestiya* appealed to Yeltsin, who upheld the paper's right to independence, as did the Constitutional Court. But it was television that parliament wanted, which became the battleground of struggle. Parliament was temporarily appeased with a programme, *Parliamentary Hour* on RTR, wholly under its editorial control, but it had its eyes on Ostankino. The coup had shown how important television was for success.

Yeltsin had sacked Press Minister Poltoranin as a peace offering to parliament, but Poltoranin popped back a month later as head of a vast new body called the Federal Information Centre (FIC), which put the activities of television, radio and the wire services under the president's jurisdiction. Independent-minded journalists criticised FIC as the Ministry of Propaganda with Poltoranin as 'chief censor'. Poltoranin's empire-building annoyed Poptsov, especially his suggestion to bring together RTR and Ostankino into one large channel. 'Why not join up all the opera theatres into one to simplify administration?', Poptsov asked sarcastically.[26] Programme makers at Ostankino complained of increasing directives from the FIC, but Poltoranin was adamant about making political capital out of television.

The fight for television

By this time Yeltsin had consolidated his power over the media by providing subsidies to keep newspapers afloat, and ensuring directors loyal to him were in charge of the state channels. To sabotage Yeltsin, parliament began to write new laws in its favour. Tit for tat followed as parliament and president attempted to upstage each other by drafting competing laws. The decision by parliament's full body at the Eighth Congress to take control of Ostankino, RTR and ITAR-TASS was only just defeated by a shortfall of 28 votes. As a result, Yeltsin's office passed several special decrees to forestall parliament's perceived aggression. The decree on the media of 20 March put television and radio under the protection of the president as 'guarantor of the rights and liberties of the individual' and called on the Interior Ministry to take 'necessary measures to guard state television'. Although this point worried democrats, the possibility of something like the *Izvestiya* scandal being repeated caused greater alarm.

Parliament retaliated with an attempt to introduce censorship through the back door. Ostensibly 'to ensure freedom of speech on state television', its resolution of 29 March abolished the FIC, made itself a co-founder of state television with the government, gave itself a say in the appointment and dismissal of TV chiefs and set up 'supervisory councils'. The greatest threat to free speech were the supervisory councils, which stated that the supervisors' job was to 'ensure' freedom of speech rather than 'supervise' what had been shown on television. That entailed prior restraint, allowing supervisors to censor and cut programmes, which is exactly what happened immediately in the provinces, in Volgograd and Novosibirsk, where supervisory councils were rapidly set up and began to dictate what was shown on television. In Saratov, on the Volga, local deputies who opposed the president simply marched into the local television station and seized the microphone from a surprised reporter. He retorted angrily: 'With the old regime, we were told not to show empty fields, or to show workers on their knees so that the wheat looked taller. Maybe that will happen again'.[27]

The new Press Minister, Mikhail Fedotov, co-author of the Media Law, objected strongly to the resolution: 'This will create a gigantic monopoly instead of the semi-monopoly we have today, when television belongs to different branches of power' – Ostankino under the president and RTR under parliament.[28] The whole purpose of their game, Fedotov said, 'was to call freedom censorship and censorship freedom'.[29] The next motion passed by the Ninth Congress of People's Deputies, which called for Yeltsin's impeachment, was only narrowly defeated. Terms were finally agreed for the 25 April 1993 referendum, which Yeltsin had promoted as an opportunity to reconfirm his personal mandate. He promised that if he did not win, he would resign. His popularity was flagging but he was still seen as the only valid leader. The campaign's famous pro-Yeltsin 'Yes Yes No Yes' leaflets were distributed all over the country. Voters were asked to tick 'yes' to questions that asked if they trusted the president, approved of his socio-economic policies and considered it necessary to hold immediate parliamentary elections; 'no' to an immediate presidential election.

Television showed little impartiality during the campaign. When Yeltsin received a vote of confidence at the referendum, Khasbulatov claimed the victory was due to 'Poltoranin–Goebbels propaganda'.[30] An opinion poll showed that in the run-up to the referendum 80 per cent of reporting on the two main TV channels was pro-Yeltsin,[31] but ratings also showed that the pro-Yeltsin vote had much to do with parliament's rowdy behaviour during the last three congresses, especially at the Seventh Congress when a brawl broke out between rival factions with fisticuffs flying – all broadcast live on television at parliament's behest. Journalists were also giving Khasbulatov a hard time. A sophisticated and articulate lawyer, he had once happily socialised with them, but they now found him arrogant and aggressive. Cameramen liked to annoy him by filming the heels he wore to enhance his height, while newspapers needled him about Brezhnev's former lavish apartment which he had managed to grab for himself.

Despite Ostankino's pro-Yeltsin bias, there had been no single propaganda machine organising the Yeltsin campaign to win the referendum. The TV documentary *A Day with the President's Family* was state commissioned, but the idea and financing came from the independent company REN TV, and although the film was guaranteed a slot on Ostankino, the film's distinguished director, Eldar Ryazanov, got little assistance and no pre-publicity from Ostankino or from its new chairman, Vladislav Bragin. REN TV's producer said there were no special favours:

> Bragin rang me before the shoot, asking what we planned to film and what questions would be asked. I made it very clear to him that Ryazanov would not allow any interference in his work and that we would bring the prepared cassette on the 20th, the day it was to be broadcast. Bragin offered to help with equipment and editing facilities, but when I actually began to ask for the necessary equipment it turned out that they didn't have this and that and could only provide an editing suite for one night. So I gave up and as usual rented everything we needed, including the three cameras.[32]

Press Minister Fedotov had asked the Constitutional Court to assess parliament's March 29 measures to amend the Media Law, which it did two months later. Basing its decision on the outdated Constitution that gave all power to the Soviets rather than the president, the Constitutional Court upheld parliament's right to establish supervisory councils on the two state channels, and declared the FIC illegal. The councils would take office by mid August. On August 21 Fedotov resigned from his post in protest: 'All my life I've tried to provide for a free press and now I'm being asked as minister to pass a reactionary law. I won't ruin what I created with my own hands', he told me. By the end of that year the scene would change completely. Fedotov would leave for Paris as Russia's UNESCO ambassador and not return until 1998; Poltoranin and Bragin would be out of office; Yeltsin would abolish the harmful amendments to the media law, and close down the FIC. All that happened after the bloody events of October 1993.

Bloody October

On 21 September 1993 Yeltsin seized the upper hand and dissolved parliament, calling for a new Constitution and elections to a new parliament in December. Parliament's constant obstructions and refusal to accept any of his compromises made it impossible for him to move forward with reform. A state of emergency was imposed for a month. The Russian Federation's Council of Ministers was named the legal successor of the Supreme Soviet until the elections and took control of parliament's media,[33] including *Parliamentary Hour*, which was suspended. Yeltsin's Decree 1400 called for stage-by-stage constitutional reform. Yeltsin appeared on TV looking a bit awkward and sipping tea. He was not unaware of the ironies of the situation, as he explained later:

> The president formally violates the Constitution and takes anti-democratic measures to dissolve parliament so that democracy and lawfulness are established in the country. Parliament defends the Constitution to topple the freely elected president and establish Soviet power in full force. How did we get so tangled in these contradictions?[34]

In this situation, both Ostankino and RTR announced their support for Yeltsin, defending his position and seeking international confirmation. John Major and Bill Clinton were understanding, Clinton with the proviso that the forthcoming elections should be free and fair. Some of Yeltsin's opponents were banned from television, and Bragin was heard saying: 'We don't need the whole truth now; when we need it I'll let you know'. Rutskoi was refused airtime officially, but he was interviewed anyway, as well as by VID presenter Aleksandr Politkovsky's *Politburo*. Politkovsky complained that Ostankino's managers would not let him interview other opponents. Another VID programme, *Red Square*, was banned when presenter Aleksandr Lyubimov planned to invite the controversial Constitutional Court chairman Valery Zorkin. Although *Red Square* was banned in Moscow, it was broadcast in other regions of the country, which confirmed journalists' suspicions that the Ostankino management was scared of getting into trouble with senior Kremlin officials. Conservative member of the presidential council, Andronik Migranyan, confirmed that Yeltsin had not known about the ban on *Red Square* until several days later. The press ministry assured journalists that only 'soft temporary' censorship would be introduced, but they were rightly alarmed. They had been deprived of accreditation to parliament, even as clashes with the riot police were taking place there.[35]

In response to its dissolution, parliament voted to impeach Yeltsin, appointed Rutskoi as acting president and called on the army to disobey Yeltsin's decree. Khasbulatov and Rutskoi repeatedly called for mass insurrection. Many of their followers on the streets were armed volunteers and paramilitary groups from private armies, such as those remaining in

Khasbulatov's guards and Aleksandr Barkashov's neo-fascist Russian National Unity organisation. Pitched gun battles erupted in Moscow on 3–4 October. Riot police who had been told in preceding weeks not to use their weapons or aggravate the situation, now found it hard to deal with the violence. Yeltsin says he sensed the beginning of civil war, and was uncertain that the army would come to his defence. With rioting on Smolenskaya Square and in the mayor's building nearby, where rebels had managed to breach all seven floors and set parts of it on fire, the only way to get Yeltsin into the Kremlin was by helicopter. Khasbulatov and Rutskoi, intoxicated by their success, could be seen on the White House balcony calling on their followers to take arms and storm the Ostankino TV centre.

The shooting and firefights outside Ostankino started after 17.30. Paramilitary forces that had returned from the separatist struggle in Transdniestria were the main aggressors outside the television station, commanded by retired General Makashov, known for his anti-Semitic views and support for the 1991 coup. As shown later on RTR television, the scene in this familiar part of Moscow was terrible, with corpses lying on the street and on the marble floors just within the building. It is thought that 62 people – opponents, journalists and bystanders – were killed in the clashes at the TV centre.[36] A band of armed men also set out for ITAR-TASS and held up the director and staff of the wire agency, demanding they announce Rutskoi as the new president. They refused.

Poptsov, waiting at RTR television in a different part of the city, was in constant contact with Bragin at Ostankino. Bragin, who had been hired as a Yeltsin loyalist and not for his television expertise, was completely out of his depth. At 19.40 Poptsov received a desperate call from him that they were closing down Ostankino – 'they're on the fourth floor!' he exclaimed. In fact, the rebels had only just breached the ground floor outer walls, but Bragin was terrified they might get on air. This was a humiliating defeat for mighty Ostankino, as viewers saw a nervous presenter announce that the station had been forced to stop broadcasting and that RTR would take over from a reserve studio outside Ostankino's technical centre. At that point all national broadcasting at Ostankino went dead.[37]

At exactly 20.00 RTR came on air. Yeltsin later wrote it was the Russian television channel that had saved Moscow and Russia.[38] Its emergency broadcasts became the only source of information for the whole country about what was taking place in the armed struggle between pro-democrats and the 'communist fascist rebels', as Yeltsin now called them in his TV address. Poptsov, a professional to his fingertips, had foreseen what might happen and had made preparations at RTR and at the ministry of communications. Although the address of the back-up studio was supposed to be a secret, Poptsov was amazed at the number of people who turned up to voice support for Yeltsin that night: politicians, artists, businessmen. Poptsov says he kept looking over his shoulder to see whether the rebels had also found out the address and were coming to get them. Gaidar spoke on RTR calling people to come to the Moscow City Council building on Tverskaya Street and defend democracy, so that their children 'wouldn't have to live in one big concentration camp'. VID presenter Aleksandr Lubimov took exception at what he saw as Gaidar's irresponsibility in asking people to go out onto the streets at night to risk their lives. It was not so much this comment that upset viewers as the indifference Lyubimov and some of the former *Vzglyad* team showed, which Poptsov characterised as 'lock your doors, have a drink and spit on politics'.

It was symptomatic of how much Russia had changed during the past three years. This shambolic group of young men from *Vzglyad*, the very icons of *perestroika*, were now executives in smart suits, owners of what would become one of the most powerful media companies in the country. Poptsov's contempt for these 'Russian-style future Murdochs' who had turned 'information, political views, poverty, laughter and even compassion into consumer goods'[39] was reflected in the flood of protests that came into RTR. The most memorable response was from the much-loved comic actor Liya Akhedzhakova who, among those at the reserve studio, vented her full wrath against those who quibbled about constitutional issues instead of defending Yeltsin; they really only wanted to ensure their privileges were safe, she said – 'this is the Constitution that threw people into insane asylums, and you talk about legitimate or not, people are being killed!'.

The final act was held in the White House. Attempts had been made to evict deputies and their supporters: electricity, heating and hot water had already been cut off. The deadline to give up weapons, stacks of which were stored in the building, was 4 October. Yeltsin tried to reach a last-minute compromise through the mediation of the Constitutional Court and the Orthodox Church, as well as seeking Grigory Yavlinsky's help, but about 200 of the rebels refused to budge or give up their arms. The siege of the White House by troops and tanks, the shoot-out with smoke and fire billowing from the building as the concrete of its walls was blasted, could all be seen on CNN, filming from its offices opposite the White House, just as it had filmed the coup two years earlier. Officially the total death toll was 187, although this is probably a low figure. None of the dead were parliamentary deputies – 'they entrusted this onerous duty, to die, to others', Poptsov commented dryly.[40]

Like the 1991 coup, there had been a suspended sense of reality to the events. When the siege of the White House began, crowds stood watching it as if it was a spectacle, exposing themselves to the crossfire. The BBC's Bill Turnbull reported: 'Russians are killing Russians in front of a grandstand audience'. Soviet society's fragile grip of reality turned events into theatre, while inflammatory words were flung about by opponents as if they had no consequences. Rutskoi and his followers later showed little remorse for inciting people to riot, which had ended with so many deaths. Some comments in the quality broadsheets were also out of proportion. Vitaly Tretyakov compared Yeltsin's actions 'with those of Nicholas II and Lenin, both of whom destroyed elected assemblies and moved towards authoritarianism and repression'[41] – when Yeltsin was calling for parliamentary elections in two months' time. Tretyakov's *Nezavisimaya gazeta* fuelled emotions further with a front-page headline alleging that 1,500 corpses had been found inside the White House, a story which was based on the words of one officer of the interior ministry.[42] Such rumours remained for a long time, although it would have been well-nigh impossible, with reporters sniffing around, to conceal so many corpses being removed from the White House. It was said that more people had been inside the building than came out, but it was also thought that many had made their escape through underground tunnels in the basement, which had first been discovered by defenders of the White House during the coup.

In this first post-Soviet conflict in Moscow when people were able to say and do pretty much whatever they pleased, the situation had ended in bloodshed. The Media Law prohibited incitement to riot in Article 4, but there was reluctance to impose any kind of restraint on media freedoms. Journalism professor, Sergei Muratov lamented that 'we have learned to hold meetings, but not to talk to each other'.[43] Attitudes in the press were muddled and unrealistic. Yeltsin was damned for what he did and didn't do. He was criticised for not being decisive enough, yet when he acted forcefully he was accused of being dictatorial. Yeltsin himself feared taking harsh action, bending backwards to accommodate the opposition; then overreacting and allowing blood to be spilled.

Revulsion at the carnage was expressed in an open letter published in *Izvestiya* on 5 October 1993 by 42 members of the liberal intelligentsia, who demanded the government take decisive action in dealing with political parties and organisations that had brought the violence to a head. One of their demands was that legislation against the propaganda of 'fascism, chauvinism, racial hatred, calls for violence and brutality' should be taken seriously by the courts:

> Organs of the press, which from day to day inspired hatred, called for violence and are, in our opinion, one of the main organisers and perpetrators of the tragedy (and potential perpetrators of a multitude of future tragedies), such as *Den'*, *Pravda*, *Sovetskaya Rossiya*, *Literaturnaya Rossiya* (as well as the television programme *600 Seconds*) and a number of others, should be closed until judicial proceedings start.

Newspapers connected with the armed insurrection were suspended, pending criminal proceedings and decisions to be taken by the press ministry. On 20 October the ministry made its statement on outlets that had acted with 'aggressive amorality'. More than a dozen of the small hardline nationalist newspapers that had 'assisted in the destabilisation of the situation during the mass disturbances' were closed down.[44] *Den'* and *Sovetskaya Rossiya* had been 'virtual ideological headquarters in preparing the uprising', said the ministry. Others papers, such as *K toporu* ('Take up the Axe') and *Russky poryadok* ('Russian Order') propagated fascist ideology. The ministry apologised to the public for not stopping their publications before the bloodshed had taken place. Its statement that 'leaders of these newspapers, including the sacked editors of *Pravda* and *Sovetskaya Rossiya*, should and could have foreseen where one or the other publication could push readers. They did foresee this, moreover made their own contribution ... in preparing the violence, blood was spilled, tens of human lives sacrificed'.[45] On Petersburg television, Aleksandr Nevzorov's *600 Seconds* was shut down for fomenting 'national, class, social and religious intolerance'. He was offered a weekly crime show instead, but rejected it.

The right's flagships, *Pravda* and *Sovetskaya Rossiya* were not banned but suspended and their editors sacked. They had the option of re-registering their newspapers. *Pravda* reappeared on 2 November 1993 after reaching a compromise with the ministry, but because of financial problems did not reappear again until 10 December. *Sovetskaya Rossiya* took legal action against the government and won a ruling in November that the ministry had failed to obtain a court closure as required by the Media Law. It was not until mid December that it reappeared. *Den'* was simply registered a month later as *Zavtra* ('Tomorrow') by the son-in-law of the editor, Aleksandr Prokhanov, who continues as its editor to this day.

The activities of the red-brown contingent, who preferred to call themselves nationalist-patriots, remained a force in strong opposition throughout Yeltsin's period in office and found their moorings under Putin. At a meeting of Kremlin analysts in 1994 on the threat of fascism and extremism, 90 organisations under various names, headed by men such as Barkashov, Zhirinovsky and others, were considered to be fascist in nature. On this basis, as well as on the results of sociological surveys, Otto Latsis predicted in *Izvestiya* that 'if a fascist turned up who did not seem to be a fascist but a strong leader capable of imposing "order", he would have a strong chance of success'.[46]

A few days after the storming of the White House, on 6 October, the press was shocked when a number of newspapers came out with blank spaces in places where critical articles had been removed. *Nezavisimaya gazeta* had four articles censored; while the editor of *Segodnya* complained that two reports had been removed: one advocated the need for an opposition press, the other was Sergei Parkhomenko's report on his visit to the Kremlin where he found total confusion. Fuming editors called a press conference, but Kostikov intervened, saying there had been a misunderstanding. He explained that the newspapers had been censored on the orders of the commandant in charge of the state of emergency which, according to the relevant law, allowed for restrictive measures to be taken. This had been done in the first and most dangerous day for democracy after the riots. Yeltsin spoke later in the day of 6 October, revoking the censorship.

At Ostankino, a few programme slots were discontinued, such as Lyubimov's *Red Square*. More controversial was the decision by Ostankino's board of directors to ban Lyubimov and Politkovsky from appearing on television on the grounds that they had dishonoured their profession. Most journalists felt this had gone too far and Yelena Chekalova, who had found their attitude on television insulting, wanted to know if 'persecuting people for their opinions had started again, even when they do not call for violence'.[47] About a year later, Lyubimov was back as the star of Ostankino's current affairs programme.

The first multiparty elections 1993

The eyes of the world watched to see whether Russia would fulfil its democratic obligations in the first free multiparty parliamentary elections in Russia's history, held on 12 December 1993.[48] In 1917 the provisional government had held free elections, but that history was brief. The Bolsheviks had failed to gain a majority to the Constituent Assembly, so when the assembly convened a few months later in January 1918 it lasted 13 hours before the Bolsheviks dissolved it. The 1993 election then was a historic moment, and coming in the wake of bloody October it had much to prove.

There is no doubt that in these elections Kremlin officials made a great effort to provide the necessary framework for free and fair elections, although their actions were sometimes ill-conceived.[49] On the one hand, they could not resist the Soviet habit of controlling information by giving the democrats more airtime on television than their rivals. On the other hand, they bent backwards to be neutral to such an extent that they largely contributed to the success of Zhirinovsky's ultra-nationalist deceptively called Liberal Democratic Party of Russia (LDPR). This result came as a shock not only to the Kremlin but to the pro-Yeltsin broadcasting executives, who appeared on television on the night of the polls in a self-congratulatory celebrity-hosted extravaganza, only to bring the show hurriedly to an end as the results showed that the democrats had not achieved an outright majority. It meant that conflict between Yeltsin and parliament over democratic reform was not resolved.

Officials learned a number of lessons about the power of television, which would have a profound effect on the future administration of elections. First, the influence of television on the electorate surpassed all expectations, showing for the first time how telegenic politicians such as Zhirinovsky could radically change public opinion in a short space of time. Second, it showed how gullible and easily swayed public opinion was. Third, journalists had been so concerned not to offend candidates and parties that they failed to ask probing questions, letting them get away with self-aggrandisement. Fourth, the results showed that 'PR' had arrived and it was possible for an irresponsible politician like Zhirinovsky to become a star and attract 23 per cent of the electorate. The democrats' professorial leaders, Gaidar and Boris Fyodorov, could not compete in this populist contest. In later elections, a whole industry would grow around what came to be called 'black PR', making use of paid campaign advertising, public relations, concealed advertising and dirty money.

An arbitration court dealt with 159 complaints, many of them expressing the bitterness felt from the recent 3–4 October tragedy. Gaidar accused Zhirinovsky of being a Hitler, Zhirinovsky and Nikolai Travkin hurled insults at each other, Travkin and film-maker Govorukhin repeatedly labelled Gaidar a 'swindler' and Nevzorov branded Yeltsin a mass murderer. Govorukhin was a repeat offender. He included lurid and dubious images of the democrats in his election commercials, and stirred up conspiracy theories over the October events, alleging that Gaidar had paid one billion roubles to get supporters out on the streets (this figure increased a few days later to 11 billion), leaving seeds of doubt which, foolishly, the democratic party Russia's Choice considered beneath its dignity to refute.

The new electoral regulations that had just been drafted ensured there would be no accusations from the 13 parties and blocs in the race that they had not been given free and equal access to television and radio to air their campaign videos and political broadcasts in the three weeks before polling day. More than enough time was allotted – one hour on each of state-owned TV and radio stations. Additionally, the regulations allowed parties to buy time on all TV and radio channels without limit, provided each party that wanted to pay was equally served. This enabled richer blocs to buy more airtime and, inevitably, gave the pro-government bloc an advantage. The price of paid time on state media for candidates was high: one minute of airtime on Ostankino cost 707,000 roubles ($578); a little less on Russian TV. The amount on private channels was negotiable. When *Moskovskiye novosti* appealed to all parties to reveal their sources of financing during the campaign, only Yabloko complied. What was known from the arbitration court was that some parties received preferential treatment from television companies, while others were forced to pay in advance. Zhirinovsky appears to have benefited from such favouritism.

The introduction of big money into the elections, especially when stashes of murky money were known to be readily available, should have been a matter of concern, but it was not highlighted as an issue in the media or by the Central Electoral Commission. There had been no good reason for the commission to turn to the USA as a model for paid advertising. On many issues Russia looked to Europe, especially France and Britain, as its democratic guide. Paid advertising was not common in democracies at the time, although the US, Canada, Australia and Israel allowed it. Only in the USA was there no free time and no limit to the amount of time that could be bought. In the USA, however, the source of income had to be declared to enable the electorate to judge what interests lay behind a candidate. Such a mechanism had no way of being realistically applied in Russia, with its resourceful ways of concealing 'black cash' (*chernyy nal*). Yet money and political advertising dominated the elections, with paid time on television far exceeding free time. As usual with Russia, the façade was important – a total of 94 hours of free and paid party campaigning on television – even if much of it was unbalanced because of the issue of affordability.

One of the most serious failings of media coverage was the passivity of journalists. This was not because they were biased, but because they were scared of being accused of bias. The European Institute for the Media's monitoring results showed the problem was 'not one of partiality, but of failing properly to inform and to represent the electorate'.[50] Partly journalists lacked experience in non-Soviet 'balanced' reporting, partly they were keenly aware that in Soviet politics disagreement was taken as personal animosity. Oleg Poptsov explained the pressure felt by state TV executives: 'Don't think we stood with our heads bowed. We were consulted, everything was explained and discussed, but there was more apprehension than trust. The Central Electoral Commission was scared of making a mistake and having to confront the parties'.[51] Only the private channel NTV held a fairly lively series of interviews. Bland reports in the media made in good faith were hard to distinguish from those made in bad faith by journalists paid by parties. Yeltsin condemned this well-known practice: 'The corruption of journalists and editors can be explained by their miserable salaries. But still I cannot consider the press "free" if journalists receive money – sometimes exceeding their annual pay – for covert advertising, the favourable presentation of a party line or the hushing up of criticism'.[52]

With facts hard to come by and a plenitude of rumours, it was unavoidable that voters would make choices based on emotion and mood. A dramatic change in public opinion ten days before the elections testified to the spontaneity of voting responses and to Zhirinovsky's success. According to VTsIOM, at the start of the campaign LDPR had garnered only 1.3 per cent of potential voters. Of the 23 per cent of votes that Zhirinovsky received at the polls, 40 per cent of those who voted for him decided to do so during the last few days. Almost one-fifth of those who made up their minds to vote for Zhirinovsky said they were influenced by television and other media.[53] For attracting attention, Zhirinovsky was unbeatable, exploiting nationalist sentiments and populist solutions. With journalists too cautious to challenge him, he was free to make outrageous promises. He offered free vodka to everyone if he won; he would 'nuke' Japan if it tried to acquire more of the Kurile Islands; he would return Russia to its tsarist borders by annexing parts of Finland, Poland and virtually all of Ukraine and Alaska. Instead of the western politicians' ploy of kissing babies, he offered the orgasm. Bullishly looking into the screen in his neat burgundy jacket, he explained his sex/pol version of Soviet history (in Wilhelm Reich style), scattering words like 'masturbation' and 'orgasm', which had never been heard on Soviet/Russian television before.

It seemed like a bad joke, except for the method to his madness. Whereas many politicians continued in the Soviet tradition to appeal to the 'people' (*narod*), Zhirinovsky divided his electorate into gender and interest groups, devoting short segments of airtime to each. He singled out women and arranged to meet them later in a park without their husbands, discussing cooking and underwear and playing the role of agony aunt. He appealed separately to Cossacks, the army, the legal profession (he was a lawyer) and spoke to the Islamic population in Turkic (he had also graduated in Oriental languages). He was helped along by a last-minute gambit by Bragin at Ostankino TV to discredit him. Breaking the election law that banned campaigning after midnight on 10 December, Ostankino broadcast Pavel Chukrai's documentary *The Hawk* (*Yastreb*), a seemingly accurate but damning report on Zhirinovsky a day before the polls. Either because it was already too late or as a protest against the government's bias, the film spurred votes in Zhirinovsky's favour.

During this first democratic election, with its free political atmosphere, there was more fun and honesty to be had than in elections to come. Some journalists, frustrated at the strict regulations against commentary imposed on them, ridiculed editors and the electorate's gullibility. The TV programme *Press-Express* in tandem with *Komsomolskaya pravda* conducted an experiment on the streets in which they offered free beer to anyone who would vote for their candidate, who changed from day to day, their posters showing various famous faces such as Chancellor Kohl's, and proved they could easily get a promise of votes. A documentary about a spoof party called *Sub-Tropical Russia* described its aim to canvass support for raising the temperature of Russia's climate, with a sly dig at Zhirinovsky's dream, via Alexander the Great, of Russia's conquering troops washing their boots in the Indian Ocean – not all that outrageous when we look at Russian imperialist fantasies conveyed on television today. In the press, one of the most stylish articles came from *Izvestiya*'s Sergei Mostovshchikov, who mocked Russia's lack of understanding of pluralism and free speech as evidenced in the Zhirinovsky phenomenon:

> Pluralism is dear to the hearts of Russians, especially as the *Great Medical Encyclopaedia* defines the term as group sex, in which no fewer than three citizens participate. It really is good of Vladimir Vol'fovich to promise to provide this quickly, in the course of the first three months of his rule. It's true that at first we will have to destroy 5,000 criminal gangs, halt supplies of anything and everything outside the borders of our motherland, sell arms to India in return for food and clothing, take back all the debts we owe the world and pay nothing in return and get housed in cottages, but then, oh then, we'll have pluralism.[54]

III Television and cash

The main problem for the media in the Yeltsin years was to create free and honest journalism in conditions of post-Soviet capitalism. As it was, television had already become a hostage to politics and money. The main source of financing was advertising and sponsorship. Even the 100 per cent state-owned

RTR on the second channel rarely saw all the money that the government had budgeted for its operational costs. Ostankino TV received less in the way of government subsidies and its employees were not always paid. There were 18,000 people working at the Ostankino centre, of whom 6,000 were called 'creative' workers. Revenue from advertising that should have been going towards salaries for the general staff was being ripped off by advertising brokers, advertising agencies, production companies and shadowy criminal organisations. Officially a broadcaster with the state as majority shareholder, Ostankino was being looted to make private fortunes.

Journalist Irina Petrovskaya, who became the most authoritative commentator on television affairs, started her career at the same time as the enormous changes taking place on TV. She called the channel the source of all types of corruption: 'According to the most modest calculations, Ostankino failed to receive more than 60 billion roubles – they vanished without a trace in people's private pockets. The average price of a minute of advertising time today is $5000. There are up to 100 such minutes a day on Ostankino. Therefore, it should receive about half a million dollars *a day*, but it gets 600–700 thousand dollars *a month*!'.[55] For many people working in Ostankino, it had become their private cash cow. The setting up of a body that brought together six of the largest advertising brokers, called Reklama-Holding, did not settle the matter. But it introduced powerful players who wanted to break into television, men such as Sergei Lisovsky, on his way to becoming an advertising tycoon, and the now infamous Boris Berezovsky, who became the channel's virtual owner, both in the money he paid into it and the political influence he got out of it.

Ostankino's head of audience ratings, Vsevolod Vilchek wrote in *Izvestiya* on 6 January 1995 that he was resigning 'with a heavy heart' because of the channel's corruption. According to the statistics he had gathered as an insider, Reklama-Holding was paying Ostankino an average of about $4,000 for one minute of advertising time, but was taking in $12,000 (sometimes up to $20,000, he told me). When he tried to gather information about concealed forms of advertising, he was inundated with anonymous phone calls and threats. He was warned by a top executive that if he worked at Ostankino he would have to stop criticising it. No one sacked him, but they took away his car, then they moved him to distant offices, then they took away his computer.

An Ostankino whistle-blower gave some idea of the way income and concealed advertising were generated. First, it could be done through advertising brokers, who had a franchise to buy time from Ostankino and sell it to advertisers, but were defrauding the channel of its real earnings. The second way was through sponsors' money allocated for special events and programmes, where part of the payment would be officially paid to Ostankino's accounts office and part would go in 'black cash' to programme makers and administrators. The third form was bribery. Anytime a camera lingered on a person or product it was probably paid for. A close-up in 1994 cost between $100 and $150. 'There are virtually no "free" programmes on TV. I don't want to preach morality, but the result of the many layers of corruption on television is upsetting ... Creative ambitions have long been discarded. Competition exists only on the level of money'.[56]

A dramatic overhaul was called for. In November 1994 Yeltsin passed a decree to privatise the first channel and transform it into ORT, the Russian acronym for Public Russian Television. Although it has never been a public service broadcaster, its name shows that the idea was compelling at the time. A plan for the full privatisation of ORT was put forward by the most successful television production companies that had formed after 1990, VID, ATV and REN TV, but they pulled out when Yeltsin agreed only to partial privatisation. ORT became a joint stock company, 51 per cent of its shares owned by the government and 49 per cent parcelled out to private investors, mainly financial structures. This suited Yeltsin: it was the business community who had the money to finance ORT and he knew they would support him. Boris Berezovsky was made chairman of the board of directors. The person named general director of ORT was superstar Vlad Listyev, one of the talented *Vzglyad* team and co-founder of VID, as well as creator and presenter of the most popular shows of the time. After his appointment, Listyev unexpectedly announced that he would impose a temporary moratorium on all advertising on the channel to deal with corruption – 'until strict rules are set up to regulate advertisements in the interests of the economic development of society and ethical standards', Reuters reported.[57] This was not what most businessmen wanted: they stood to lose millions of dollars, the stakes being in excess of 35 billion roubles ($7.7 million) per month.[58] In this affair, Listyev seems to have been a figurehead. It is generally regarded by insiders that Berezovsky and his financial assistant Badri Patarkatsishvili were behind the moratorium, to clean up the advertising sector and bring it under their control. But the shock was electric when the news broke that Listyev, the nation's favourite, had been assassinated in a contract killing on the day the ban on advertisements started, 1 March 1995.

People said: if Listyev has been murdered, no one is safe. All day ORT screens showed only news bulletins, interspersed with the words: 'Listyev has been killed'. Who stood to gain from it? – the perennial Russian question. Quite a number of people, it seems. Big names circulated on the grapevine and in publications – Berezovsky, Patarkatsishvili, Lisovsky, Gusinsky and names close to Listyev's inner circle.[59] The murder has never been solved. The latest versions of who killed Listyev come in two accounts. The first is from an acclaimed biography by one of the VID–Vzglyad group, Yevgeny Dodolev. He says Listyev's murder was an accident, which went terribly wrong. It was ordered by Patarkatsishvili, to give him a scare.[60] This was told to him by Aleksandr Litvinenko, who died of polonium 210 poisoning, and Patarkatsishvili has also died in suspicious circumstances, so it is not a story that can be verified. The second version caused a scandal in 2013 when Konstantin Ernst, general director of the First Channel who eventually replaced Listyev, is alleged to have told a journalist (the dictaphone was turned off) that it was advertising magnate Sergei Lisovsky.[61] The article was immediately taken off the portal snob.ru and denied by Ernst. What most people are certain of is that Listyev was not killed because he was a TV journalist, but because of some shady business deal.

Could free speech breathe in air polluted by murder, sleazy machinations and criminal commercial deals? Did this *ipso facto* tarnish the nature of the information? It was the golden youth of *perestroika* television that was expected to create an independent and liberating culture for post-Soviet broadcasting, and recreate the intense focus on social concerns that had captivated viewers. But this was not the kind of television being broadcast on the national channels. More of a picture emerges by looking into the murky world that Listyev inhabited. 'We had never seen anything like it', writes a TV critic. 'We couldn't even imagine that money could do such things to people. Big money and small people. It overturned our perceptions of good and evil, friendship and work, power and passion'.[62]

Big money brought envy and intrigue. Listyev had been president of VID since companies had gained the right to work as commercial structures towards the end of Gorbachev's rule. VID received a head start as the first to receive the right to negotiate with and receive profits from advertisers directly. Yevgeny Dodolev describes the kind of atmosphere that existed around the team. Listyev had been pushed out of VID's current affairs programmes by Lyubimov and turned to light entertainment, where he found instant success. He introduced the first US-style games show, *A Field of Miracles*, which awarded consumer goods as prizes. He had adapted it from the US show *Wheel of Fortune*, which he saw one night in a Paris hotel. There was no show more popular in Russia. It was pure gold as a slot for prime-time advertising. Listyev discovered he had a talent as a talk-show host, stylish and light, a new genre for Russians, as was the tuxedo he wore. When his shows began to rake in money, the VID team feared Listyev would abandon the company and take his programmes with him, which were now financing most of VID's operations and keeping its current affairs programmes afloat. To take the reins out of his hands, Listyev was pushed out as president of VID and replaced by Lyubimov. At that point a strange incident occurred. Listyev's friend Leonid Yakubovich, who had taken over as host of *A Field of Miracles* was 'kidnapped' and held incommunicado for several days on the orders of three of VID's board of directors. The apparent intention was to make him sign away his contract with Listyev, get the programme out of Listyev's hands and push him out of the company. Yakubovich refused to be intimidated. When Listyev was appointed head of ORT he made it clear he would not allow any of VID's shows, other than his own, on the channel.

One of the original *Vzglyad* team, Vladimir Mukusev, suggested Listyev leave these intrigues behind and join him in Novosibirsk, where he was helping to create an independent television station, away from the corruption of the capital. Listyev, he says, was not impressed. 'He took an unopened pack of one hundred dollar bills from his pocket and asked rhetorically: "Do you want me to give this up for Siberia?" At the same time, he looked at me over his glasses ... as if he was looking at an idiot ... who didn't understand the most elementary things about life'.[63] Mukusev reports that when Listyev died, he held $17 million in his personal account, not including property he owned. Such was the life of the young lads from *Vzglyad*, who started off in 1987 on a contract of 40 roubles between the three of them. Apart from Lyubimov, however, most of the famous names from *Vzglyad* have not seen the profits VID has enjoyed.

Acknowledged as one of *Vzglyad*'s creative directors, Vladimir Mukusev subscribed to another type of journalism, one that was not stuck on the get-rich-quick mentality. His vocal criticisms of corruption on television have made him *persona non grata* on national networks to this day. He could have been a top broadcasting executive, had he compromised. Press Minister Poltoranin asked him to head Ostankino in 1993, which Mukusev agreed to only if the documents about corruption at the channel were handed to the Prosecutor General's office. Mukusev had spent three years, from 1991 to 1993, as a deputy in the Duma and had chaired the parliamentary commission examining corruption at Ostankino. He knew these documents contained evidence of large-scale fraud: 'To put it bluntly, the monstrous looting of resources from sponsorship, advertising and the state budget; the uncontrolled letting of studios as warehouses, the sale of expensive machines and technical equipment'.[64] He says Poltoranin seemed to agree with him. However, not for the first time, Mukusyev was smeared. Several newspapers reported that he was an alcoholic, suffering from cirrhosis of the liver and on the point of death, information that was passed on to Chernomyrdin, who rejected his appointment. Another smear took place when he was offered the post of deputy chairman of RTR. On the day before the interview a story appeared on the internet that he had Aids. Still, he says, he was happy not to have become an executive. 'I'm proud to have been involved in creating more than 20 regional companies, mainly in Siberia, making real Russian television and not today's department of propaganda for brainwashing'.[65]

He played an impressive role as people's deputy representing the Union of Journalists in parliament. In 1993 he filed a lawsuit against Yeltsin and the government in the Constitutional Court to win index-linked compensation for people who had lost their savings as a result of Gaidar's economic 'shock therapy':

> I won the case against Yeltsin and Gaidar, but as a result I lost my career prospects as a journalist. They didn't forgive me for that. I was told that when Yeltsin saw my name [on the candidates' list for director of ORT] he crossed out Mukusev with such anger that he broke the pen. Nevertheless, in 1996 Yeltsin made a campaign promise to return money stolen from depositors with the Savings Bank. Even now I think it was worth it.[66]

Mukusev had a penchant for upsetting important people. One of his TV offerings asked the question, 'Why are there so many Tsereteli monuments in

Moscow?' – a subject guaranteed to fire up Muscovites outraged by Tsereteli's kitsch works, especially the gigantic monument to Peter the Great. Mukusev expressed publicly what everyone presumed privately, that the sculptor shared 'material interests' with Moscow mayor Luzhkov. Another of his areas was investigative journalism, especially the years he spent tracking down the killer behind the murder of two Russian TV journalists in Yugoslavia[67] – the murderer now sentenced by the Hague International Criminal Tribunal.

Public service journalism never became part of the mainstream of Russian journalism. One can ask, what was the point of free speech, if the public was ignored? A humane and publicly focused journalism would have explained to ordinary people the extraordinary things that were happening in their lives, things which they could hardly comprehend on their own. Perhaps journalists did not understand them either, but that was part of their homework. What was the privatisation voucher, what was a pyramid scam? Public service announcements about Chubais's voucher privatisation scheme between 1992 and 1994 that theoretically entitled all citizens to an equal share of state property, abounded on television, but the scheme was not going according to plan. People were told that in time their 10,000-roubles voucher ($1,660) invested in their factories and places of work would produce dividends. Chubais promised that these vouchers would one day buy everyone two Volga cars. In the bulk of cases these investments proved to be worthless, while insiders who knew where to invest bought up vouchers from gullible people and made fortunes. Were journalists napping?

Then there was the MMM advertising campaign, one of the cleverest PR series of advertisements viewers had ever seen, with lovable peasant Lyonya Golubkov dreaming of getting the money to buy a pair of boots and a flat in Paris. The MMM investment fund, which crashed in July 1995, was a classic Ponzi scheme.[68] It was a disaster for ten million investors, many of them pensioners and innocents who did not know the first thing about capitalist investment. The advertisements promised wealth overnight, sometimes offering 3,000 per cent annual dividends. For the media, however, MMM was a godsend, reportedly spending 10 billion roubles a day on advertising alone. By not exposing the huge risks that MMM posed, the media became its accomplice.[69] A July decree by the government banned the advertisements from being shown, but they continued to appear in the media in slightly disguised forms.

The goal to inform, educate and entertain were Reithian principles that Russian journalists knew lay at the heart of the BBC. They quoted them regularly, admired them and wanted to follow them. Many had participated in workshops and exchange programmes provided by British and EU funding to support media development in the transition to democracy. The dream of some media professionals and academics was to create a public service broadcaster free of advertising and the state, but the likelihood of citizens adding to their annual utility bill or paying a separate licence fee was nil. Soviet citizens had always received television free of charge; the only payment had been a small tax added to the purchase of a TV set; while now, if you bought a set, it was most likely to be made abroad. Soviet television, if ideology was ignored, had been serious and informative, with an audience that did not suffer from attention deficit, and much that was entertaining and educative could have been built on these foundations.

A programme in 1997 on REN TV with Vladimir Mukusev had public interest in mind, asking a range of questions of obvious interest. 'Why aren't wages being paid?', 'Why are teachers on strike?', 'Who are Russians?', 'Can a woman be president?' The format was a bit rusty but the content and interactivity with the audience were as pertinent as ever. The show was called *Explain This to an Ordinary Person* (*Ob'yasnite prostomy cheloveku*), which was precisely what was needed in a Russia turned upside down. Nevertheless, there were few debates on topics such as health, education, childcare, civil rights, at a time when these public institutions were being reorganised. It was precisely this kind of public service offering in print that made *Argumennty i fakty* the highest circulation newspaper ever in Russia. Its simple question–answer format on everyday problems, politics and history gained it huge ratings. If it has not repeated its *Guinness Book of Records* peak print run of 33 million copies in 1990, the newspaper still outstrips its rivals by selling more than 2 million copies today. Young journalists who do not want to work on Putin's television, such as Andrei Loshak and Yekaterina Gordeyeva have started their own public service ventures online on the website *Takiye Dela* ('That's the way things are') which will bring 'the person back into journalism'. Launched with a charity called *Nuzhna Pomoshch'* ('Help is Needed'), it concentrates on social issues ignored by mainstream media.

The power of television

Trust tends to focus on personalities rather than institutions in Russia. Just as media professionals trusted Yeltsin rather than the system of government to guarantee their exercise of free speech, so the public trusted TV personalities more than channels. There was a period, however, when people thought NTV, as the first non-state broadcaster of news and current affairs in Russia, would change this state of affairs.

NTV had no trouble competing in the big league with state channels ORT and RTR. It had talent and money. Its owner, Vladimir Gusinsky, had made a fortune with his bank MOST under the patronage of Moscow mayor Luzhkov. The team that left Ostankino with Yevgeny Kiselyov after October 1993, fed up with editorial interference and tempted by the idea of creating 'independent' television with money made available by Gusinsky, consisted of some of the brightest stars on television.[70] NTV became the most creative and professional channel that Russia has ever had. Its news and current affairs, especially Yevgeny Kiselyov's *Itogi* ('Summing up'), were required watching, its satire brought fun to politics (*Puppets*) and its innovative cultural experiments such as Leonid Parfyonov's *Namedni* ('The Other Day') were much admired.

The money Gusinsky put into the channel made its media professionals the elite of television. As well as generous salaries, more than a hundred of the staff received cash or interest-free loans or 'bonuses' in tens and hundreds of thousands of dollars to buy flats or luxury homes in Moscow's leafy outer suburbs for the top executives. This was not that unusual within the Soviet system of patronage in the past with its special shops, the best flats and other privileges for high officials and party members. Moreover, it was a time of economic crisis and mortgages had hardly been heard of. But it meant that from the start NTV journalists were whisked into a privileged class and beholden to their patron: hardly conducive conditions for free speech. A less personalised system could have been developed, if time had been given to it. Some paid back their loans to retain their independence, others did not. The question remains: how does one relate to a patron, even in a situation where patronage is not abnormal? Would you turn down the offer, if you were lucky enough to be given the opportunity in a corrupt unequal society? Was it better or worse than the 'stealing' taking place on state channels and, for that matter, in one form or another all over the country? These moral questions were not openly debated, and have remained unanswered. The effect on television, however, was felt.

As a result, NTV punctured the myth believed in so strongly after seven decades of state totalitarianism that media under private ownership would be free and independent and would tell the truth. NTV told the truth, when it suited it. The state did not interfere with NTV's editorial content, but Gusinsky *qua* owner did, using his media to further his business interests, and as they were inevitably tied to government connections, his interests were played out between different political factions. Because NTV could be so professional, its flaws were all the more disappointing. Because it was so unfairly targeted in 2001, its own unpalatable methods were dwarfed by Putin's ruthlessness. But NTV was always part of the Kremlin game. Its studio debates were not to be missed, but they were mostly about Kremlin intrigue and political power games, not about what mattered to ordinary people in a society in transition. It often fulfilled its commitment to the principles of free speech, holding political players to account and illuminating dark corners of the Kremlin, but in numerous cases, as we shall see, its obfuscations prevented the process of democracy. NTV focused on the Kremlin, rather than the public, because its own interests of power and influence were tied up with the Kremlin.

NTV started humbly enough, broadcasting a few hours a day on the Petersburg channel, but very soon gained the evening slot on the reorganised national fourth channel. In getting this slot, it pushed out the Russian universities' programmes, successors of the old Lenin University of the Millions, connected with further education. For many this was a terrible loss of a channel that could have been developed along the lines of an open university.[71] Although aiming to be the serious quality channel, NTV was prepared initially to broadcast late-night Playboy shows, pornographic adult viewing and violent B-movies to finance its productions. Its attempts to gain a foothold on television meant fighting off rivals with the dirty methods that were used on television. The REN TV production company's director Irena Lesnevskaya, angered that Yeltsin had allocated a piece of the fourth channel to NTV, but had rejected her plans with other production companies to create the full privatisation of Ostankino, persuaded Yeltsin to freeze the decree he had signed in NTV's favour. Lesnevskaya was a friend of Yeltsin's wife, Naina, which sometimes gave her insider privileges. Lesnevskaya relates Gusinsky's behaviour that made her take back her request:

> He ran around the room, shouting and screaming, shouting that he hadn't taken into account one stupid wench ... that he had been pushing through this decree for half a year and now the decree had been stopped ... He told me: 'You have one son. What could be more important for a mother than that her son should be alive and well? But on the 101-st kilometre mark of the Moscow Highway there are always some kind of incidents. He could be accidentally hit by a car, his car could turn over, burn up'.[72]

As well as his media outlets, Gusinsky felt the need to invest in protecting his assets. He hired former high-ranking KGB boss General Filipp Bobkov to train a squad of private bodyguards, made up of more than 800 former KGB agents, to be at his disposal and sometimes loaned out to allies. Bobkov had been trained under Beria and had been appointed by Brezhnev as deputy chairman of the KGB's Fifth Directorate, whose task was to fight 'subversive ideological activities', which meant to intimidate and punish dissidents. This was one of the ironies of transition without lustration: NTV, which proudly regarded itself as the freest-speaking television channel in the country, chose to be protected by one of the most notorious former persecutors of free speech.

NTV could be a brilliant broadcaster. It was at its best in covering the first war in Chechnya. This was an unpopular war, and most of the media was against it, but NTV led the way by its high standards, its reports from the front and its battle footage. Figures show that NTV's ratings doubled during the crisis, as did RTR's by 30–40 per cent, because the channels were seen to be trustworthy.[73] It was these channels that gave a voice to Yeltsin's adviser on human rights, Sergei Kovalyov, and parliamentary deputies returning from Grozny with descriptions of the savagery and destruction waged on the civilian population. This contrasted with Ostankino's war propaganda and the showing of patriotic documentary films made by Nevzorov in the style of his earlier *Nashi*. Of the journalists in Chechnya, 83 per cent mentioned the hostility of official and military personnel to them.[74]

Yeltsin angrily accused journalists of being in the pay of Chechen leader, Dzhokhar Dudayev. Editor of *Moskovsky komsomolets* Pavel Gusev explained how the story had originated. It was true that several months before the war Chechens sent by Dudayev had been visiting editorial offices offering money, but as far as he knew no one had accepted the bribes. It seemed to him more like a provocation, either by the FSB's Chechen agents or by Dudayev in case the media turned against him, leaving a convenient slur of 'did they or didn't they?'. The media, Gusev said, were not unaware of the negative side of the Chechen separatist movement, but they could not accept the same faults in the federal army who 'don't have the right to act like bandits, to beat up journalists, to kill civilians and torment people'. He said that journalists' attitudes had changed sharply after witnessing the atrocities committed by the army and, above all, its military commanders.[75]

The first Chechen war is so far the only war in Soviet and recent Russian history to have received open and pluralistic coverage. Even the government's own official channel RTR was not prepared to be used as an organ of propaganda. A story did the rounds that Poptsov would suffer for it: a story that came from Sergei Kovalyov, who had seen a signed decree dismissing Poptsov on Yeltsin's desk, after a meeting with him on his return from Chechnya. In a rare show of solidarity, RTR and other sympathetic journalists protested that they were ready to go on strike, which helped Poptsov keep his seat for another year. RTR's sense of independence came from its origins as the rebellious Russian republican channel that had supported Yeltsin against Gorbachev, and its maverick spirit remained intact until Putin came to power. Its news bulletin *Vesti* was much praised for its even-handed reporting. Its presenter from 1991 to 1997, Svetlana Sorokina, the viewers' favourite, whose special signature of a few friendly words to the audience at the end of each bulletin, where she voiced her own take on the news as if talking around the kitchen table, may not have been objective journalism, but it gave the channel a warm homely touch. NTV, for all its polish, never gained the public's affection as did RTR.

On the day he declared his intention to run for a second term in office in 1996, Yeltsin sacked Poptsov, describing RTR as consistently putting out 'negative' news. Either Yeltsin does not watch TV, wrote critic Irina Petrovskaya, or once again he is listening to malicious informants: 'If there is a channel today which by some incomprehensible means opposes unrestricted commercialisation and gives some sense of what is rational, good and eternal it is [RTR]. Only it shows what life is like in Russia's rural depths; only it allows itself to speak of the problems of old people and children; only it spits on ratings, that lever of commerce, and laments the destruction of our culture'.[76] If Poptsov had to go, said RTR news editor Mikhail Ponomaryov, he should have been heaped with honours. It was mainly he who had done so much to save democracy in Russia through his role on television after 1991 and in 1993,[77] but Yeltsin was no sentimentalist in politics, and quite ruthless in discarding old allies.

By contrast, ORT on the first channel was permeated with its Soviet legacy as the official tool of the Kremlin, and its vast premises and bureaucracy kept it locked within its traditional conservative framework. Even as a hybrid state–private company, it was the channel used to run propaganda, whether for the Kremlin or Berezovsky. Although it has had many interesting slots hosted by independent-minded presenters, it is also the channel that has aired, to this day, the best-known hacks. But, by tradition, it continues to be the most watched channel; under Putin simply renamed First Channel.

With these three channels, the Yeltsin years saw a flourishing of news and current affairs programmes and an appetite for them from viewers. It seemed that there were more news bulletins on television in Russia than in any other country in the world in the 1990s. On the first channel, news bulletins came every three hours from 6 a.m. to 1 a.m.; on RTR there were four bulletins from 7 a.m. to 23.20; NTV, when it received its full channel, ran a series of bulletins. At different periods during the 1990s you could also watch BBC and EU news dubbed into Russian. For those who could afford it, there was CNN and other broadcasters on satellite television. During the day bulletins ran usually for 15 minutes; in the evening they were 30–40 minutes long. It resembled the rolling news we have today. Additionally, there were the prestigious one-hour 'information–analytical' programmes on Sundays on different channels, presented by top anchors such as Yevgeny Kiselyov's *Itogi*, Nikolai Svanidze's *Zerkalo* ('Mirror'), Sergei Dorenko's *Vremya* ('Time'); other one-hour political talk shows with well-known presenters such as Vladimir Pozner and Dmitry Kiselyov; and lighter daily news shows, such as *Vremechko* ('Little Time'). Most of the programmes covered national politics; much less was done on social and cultural affairs, and not much at all was reported from the vast provinces, which ran their local stations, except in cases of big corruption scandals. If the news was not always trustworthy, there was a plurality of it. In 1996, however, the media ganged up against the communists to re-elect Yeltsin as president.

Presidential elections 1996

The 16 June 1996 presidential election was a turning point in the liberal media's use of their free space. Instead of covering the election campaign 'freely and fairly', they played at politics, a mistake that contributed to the demise of their independence. Most of the liberal media voluntarily collaborated with the Kremlin to have Yeltsin re-elected as president. ORT's vice-chairman Grigory Shevelyov said: 'You can only refer to pressure if there is resistance, but there was none'.[78] The liberal media were prepared to do whatever was needed to prevent the communists from returning to power.

It meant manipulating and concealing news, collaborating with oligarchs to mystify voters, and denying the public the right to know. The stage was set: the intractable Poptsov had been removed from RTR, and Berezovsky's allies were in charge at ORT. The odd one out, private channel NTV, which could have stayed out of it, was even more involved. As the liberal media had been criticising Yeltsin unstintingly and, as far as Chechnya went, with good reason, why did they see no alternative to him for president and why were they prepared to go to such lengths to keep him in power?

The Communist Party leader Gennady Zyuganov had recently made a good impression with international financiers at Davos, but for Russian democrats this was Zyuganov's social democratic face 'for export', while behind the scenes at the Communist Party congresses the old faces threatened a 'maximum programme' and a settling of accounts. For ordinary people there was anger at Yeltsin over the drop in living standards, but turning to the communists was also a leap into the unknown. What changes might take place if the communists returned? Would privatised industries be re-nationalised? Would the flat you had bought for a nominal price return to the state? Would there be a clampdown on travel abroad? Communist parties had returned to Estonia and Poland without any repetition of the horrors of the past, but Russia had been the cradle of communism and such a return aroused serious foreboding.

Yeltsin's popularity ratings at the start of the presidential year were as low as 3 per cent, with Zyuganov racing ahead in the polls. The solution proposed by the so-called party of war, the circle of Yeltsin's hawkish advisers who had dominated politics since October 1993, was to cancel the elections. This circle consisted of First Deputy Prime Minister Oleg Soskovets, KGB chief Mikhail Barsukov and Yeltsin's bodyguard and close friend, the chief of the Presidential Security Service, Aleksandr Korzhakov. General Korzhakov had been taking liberties far beyond his position, even after Yeltsin had publicly reprimanded him on television for meddling in politics. On 23 April the so-called Group of 13, consisting of top oilmen, bankers and two of the country's emerging media tycoons, Berezovsky and Gusinsky, had a letter published in all the main newspapers in which they also proposed calling off elections and forming a coalition between Yeltsin and the communists. On the verge of putting off elections for two years, Yeltsin decided instead to agree to the deal of an alliance between business and the media to organise his campaign. It was their initiative, Yeltsin writes in his memoirs, referring to the group of seven bankers who became involved: it was the first time he had met them.[79]

The party of war that had been organising Yeltsin's electoral campaign without success was now pushed aside and Chubais was brought back into Yeltsin's team to head the campaign. Into the inner sanctum came Igor Malashenko, president of NTV, to spearhead Yeltsin's presidential campaign. Such an arrangement would be seen, some said, as a crude abuse of the media's objectivity in most countries in the West. Malashenko retorted this was not the West. Observers had already noticed that NTV's attitude to Yeltsin had softened considerably in the last few months. Malashenko expressed what he saw as a catch-22:

> If we work strictly according to objective, professional, unbiased, non-party laws and Zyuganov wins tomorrow, we would know that we had

dug our grave with our own hands. To avoid this, if we support Yeltsin and try to get round it, it means the media become a medium of propaganda. Either way it's bleak.[80]

Had Malashenko been offered a sweetener for his professional services? NTV had been broadcasting six hours in the evenings on the much sought-after nationwide fourth channel, which it had received without a tender. Commentators speculated that NTV was attempting to beat its competitors and receive the right to broadcast on the entire channel as a reward for Malashenko's work. This is in fact what happened. Malashenko's management helped to win the elections and two months later, in September 1996, the entire fourth channel was transferred to NTV for national broadcasting. Gusinsky had already made a move at expansion earlier when, on 13 April, he made a deal with the state gas monopoly Gazprom under which Gazprom bought a 30 per cent stake in NTV to help it develop a satellite pay TV network. Before this, NTV had been the only news broadcaster with no ties to the government. Now, NTV had put itself into a vulnerable position in relation to the state, but its 'reward' was to be well on the way to building a media empire under Gusinsky, its tycoon owner.

Yeltsin's electoral campaign organisers had learned from the 1993 and 1995 parliamentary elections that overt propaganda did not necessarily bring the expected results in democratic conditions. With the combined talents of all three channels, a clever campaign was designed. The solution was to make public messages more anti-Zyuganov, than pro-Yeltsin. The idea was to scare the electorate with the spectre of communism's return. Yeltsin was left out of most of his promotion videos. They were lyrical and rather schmaltzy set pieces – an old babushka, a rural hut, a church, old family portraits – showing that people were still living well and preferred the status quo to changes that might traumatise their lives. The clips gave a warm feeling, ending with 'I believe, I love, I hope' (*Veryu, lyublyu, nadeyus'*). Yeltsin's slogan was 'Let your heart choose' (*Vybiray serdtsem*). There were special US-inspired slots for young voters – 15 minutes on RTR every day of the week called *Golosuy ili proigraesh'* ('Vote or Lose'), which were not directly connected with Yeltsin but continued the theme of the dangers of returning to the past. A bus with the name of the TV programme travelled to rural settlements and 22 cities, big rock concerts were held in the cities, celebrities made appearances (ballet diva Maya Plisetskaya: 'I will vote for Yeltsin. The party killed my father and put my mother in the gulag. I don't want to see a second communist paradise').

Another reason for omitting Yeltsin from most of the election broadcasts was the fear of overburdening the ailing president, although in moments of crisis Yeltsin, as usual, excelled, throwing himself into the campaign. He travelled to a dozen regions: he was seen on a swing with a child in Arkhangelsk, going down the mines, energetically dancing the twist, visiting hostile 'red' country in Krasnodar, travelling to China. With these trips around the country and breaking news – a list of the regions that had received money from the budget to pay salaries, an attempted peace settlement in Chechnya, a visit to Grozny – Yeltsin showed enormous energy. The only thing he refused to do was engage in debate with Zyuganov. He said he had spent 30 years in the Communist Party and had heard enough 'demagogy' to last him a lifetime.

The press was more pluralistic and diverse than television, and most of the newspapers gave broad coverage to other candidates in the field. *Izvestiya* said after the elections it had 'tried to be honest but did not promise to be impartial'.[81] It stressed that the communists had not changed and their ideology did not allow for it. This they could often prove. Zyuganov's remarks to *Der Spiegel* that 'today there are more victims of repression in camps than under Stalin' and 'in my village in those times they arrested two people and they were both criminals' were enough to frighten many people. *Izvestiya*'s response was a full page devoted to Central Committee documents under Stalin ordering batches of people to be rounded up and shot, with zealous local officials asking that the numbers be increased.[82] *Komsomolskaya pravda* played dirty in one of its issues, publishing alleged excerpts from the current Communist Party's economic programme that called for the expropriation of property and wage and price freezes – a document that was faked.[83] A pro-Yeltsin newspaper that suddenly appeared and vanished after the elections was *Ne day Bog* ('God Forbid'), a lurid propaganda rag, expensively produced in colour on Finnish paper with a free circulation of 10 million, which ran articles such as 'Zyug-Heil' and was distributed free. As it was published by the Kommersant Publishing House it could be traced back to its Stolichny Bank owner, Aleksandr Smolensky, who also had shares in ORT. The project cost $13 million, an enormous amount at the time.

There was no doubt about the pro-Yeltsin bias on the three television channels ORT, RTR and NTV. According to monitoring by the European Institute of the Media (EMI), in the first round of the elections Yeltsin received 53 per cent of airtime to Zyuganov's 18 per cent. But in votes it was still close: Yeltsin – 35.28 per cent, Zyuganov – 32.04 per cent.[84] Malashenko said many years later that it was always assumed Yeltsin would not win in the first round. For all the discrepancy in airtime, it would not be correct to say the communists were not seen or heard. They had their newspapers, they made great use of regional papers, they ran political advertisements on television for the first time, Zuganov was seen dancing on television rather more sedately than Yeltsin, and they were interviewed on the main current affairs programmes. Part of the problem with Zyuganov and other communist leaders was that their culture came from a different era. Their slogan remained the old one of 'Russia, Motherland, the People' (*Rossiya, rodina, narod*). Their video clips showed marches, red flags, little girls with red ribbons in their hair. Sometimes they were their own worst enemies, as in Zyuganov's faulty timing in visiting Novocherkassk on the 34th anniversary of the Communist Party's massacre of protesters. There was little new energy in the ranks, no trendy scriptwriters to produce stylish advertisements and no money or desire to pay for upmarket PR companies. In Kiselyov's interview with Zyuganov they seem to speak different languages:

KISELYOV: Gennady Andreyevich, if you lose the presidential elections will you accept the fact that you've lost?

ZYUGANOV: I want to say that the country is not a casino. Everyone plays games, this is immoral in a country that has been shattered ...

KISELYOV: You're not answering my question.

ZYUGANOV: Yes, I am.

KISELYOV: No, you're not.

ZYUGANOV: Yes, I am. I don't want to play games with the elections, voters are being pressured, I want them to vote calmly. After we've supervised the polling stations, received a copy of the votes and calculated them, what is expressed by the will of citizens will be our supreme law and we will observe it strictly.

KISELYOV: Who do you mean – radicals, such as Messrs Anpilov, Terekhov and Makashov?

ZYUGANOV: Why radicals? The greatest radicals are those who ripped off the population and destroyed the economy and today in fact don't want to hold honest elections.

KISELYOV: You know, my colleague Svanidze said a wonderful phrase in summing up his interview with you recently, that if one asks you what time it is you will say thank you, I've already had lunch.

ZYUGANOV: Excuse me, instead of asking questions Svanidze broke the law on the presidential elections and started explaining ... Incidentally, journalists ask questions and I answer, but they are obliged not to make comments, that's the law.[85]

Kiselyov is rude, Zyuganov waffles: they exasperated one another. Kiselyov's question about the radicals is fair enough – they had incited the crowds to violence in October 1993; Zyuganov's reply is clever. Zyuganov gets the election law wrong: it is only on candidates' free time on air that journalists were not allowed to make comments; and such instructions did not apply to commercial stations such as NTV.

The liberal media had an almost visceral terror of the communists returning to power, which perhaps explains why they blindly followed the campaign team rather than seeking other options. Why should the new communists be any different from the old ones, since they had never renounced past errors? Although Zyuganov refused to comment on any ministerial posts, journalists felt, especially after a leak in the press from alleged party documents, that Viktor Anpilov could become the minister of the press. That was quite possible, given that Zyuganov would have to repay him for the support given by his party, Working Russia. Nothing worse could be imagined: the scourge of democrats, the main protagonist against Ostankino TV centre and an unabashed anti-Semite. Kiselyov's interview with him on *Itogi* was not comforting. What would he do if he were put in charge of television? Anpilov replied:

> I would put an end to the anti-nationalism we see on television – I mean musical programmes, serials which don't reflect our lives and make people look at television as a kind of religion ... I think a lot of people don't have the right to appear on the screen. They have speech defects, they can't pronounce their r's – Lenin couldn't, but then he didn't appear on TV as a journalist, he wrote. I think we should have those who represent our indigenous nationalities, who are born in the language, speak the language and more accurately reflect the basic layers of our society. I'm an internationalist, but why do we only see people of Jewish nationality? You know, this is insulting, it's unacceptable.[86]

Many years later, President Medvedev, talking to a group of opposition leaders in 2012, let slip that the 1996 elections had been rigged ('Hardly anyone doubts who won the 1996 presidential elections, and it wasn't Boris Nikolayevich Yeltsin'). He has since refused to elaborate.[87] If ballot rigging took place, it makes the enormous amount of money, airtime and manipulation of public consciousness all the more futile. The first scandal came in the form of an alleged 'coup' – known as the case of 'cash in the Xerox box'. Anyone who was awake at one o'clock in the morning of 20 June – I was, and many people watched late television in those days – when programmes were interrupted on NTV with an ominous announcement that a special bulletin would be broadcast within the hour concerning a plot – Kiselyov called it 'coup no. 3'. A pale newsreader came on air at 2 a.m. to report that two leading officials of Yeltsin's campaign team, Sergei Lisovsky, the advertising tycoon connected with Berezovsky and ORT, and Arkady Yevstafyev, close aide of Chubais, had been detained on the personal instructions of Barsukov and Korzhakov. 'It is obvious', read the newsreader, referring to the latter two, 'that these actions were directed at wrecking the president's election campaign in the critical period before the second round of the presidential elections. It is obvious that these actions were intended to provoke a state of emergency in the country and to cancel the presidential elections, which Korzhakov publicly spoke about on 1 May'.

But nothing was 'obvious'. The two men had been detained by presidential security guards at the checkpoint coming out of the White House carrying a photocopier-paper box with $538,000 inside, for which it was alleged they had no corresponding documents. This was later understood to be cash that came from illicit campaign funds. Anatoly Chubais, however, defended the men in his team, claiming there was no cash in the box and the detention bore all the marks of KGB-style provocation. The men had been picked up at 17.00 the previous day and interrogated for 11 hours. According to NTV, Chubais had nipped a coup in the bud. Yeltsin's recently appointed national security adviser, General Aleksandr Lebed, was already on air at 4.20 a.m. confirming that 'those people who want to plunge the country into the depths of bloody chaos do not deserve pity'. The call for journalists to be ready to interview Lebed that morning came, significantly, from the offices of Logovaz, Berezovsky's car sales company, where those steering the campaign had gathered – Chubais, Gusinsky, Malashenko and Yeltsin's daughter, Tatyana Dyachenko. It was from here that the story emerged that Korzhakov and the security ministers were plotting a coup to cancel the elections, which they denied.

The affair makes more sense if we look at the internal power struggles taking place within the Kremlin. Yeltsin's liberal advisers explained that everyone knew candidates were topping their campaign funds with additional money, because the law regulating campaign financing had placed the ceiling very low at $3 million. Because the candidates were all doing it, no one had accused anyone else of it. The fact that Korzhakov and the security ministers chose this moment before the second round to try to incriminate Chubais and the campaign team meant their intentions had been to regain Yeltsin's favour – not that they were planning a coup.[88] Chubais's story was blown a year later when a taped conversation was leaked by the tabloid journalist Aleksandr Khinshtein in *Moskovsky komsomolets* in an anti-Chubais campaign.[89] A US journalist on the *Moscow Times*, Jonas Bernstein, also caught Chubais out some years later. Chubais was asked what had happened to the money in the Xerox box, and he replied that it had been returned to the state budget.[90] He had forgotten that he had said the money did not exist. In fact, the episode had been a useful invention by Chubais to remove unwanted hardliners from Yeltsin's apparat and make it possible for the liberals to replace them. It was undoubtedly a victory for the democrats to be rid of the party of war which had caused such a fiasco in Chechnya, but the methods that ORT and NTV used were not all that different from the Soviet behind-the-scenes manipulations that they so feared would return with the communists.

The cash in the Xerox box was only a small part of Yeltsin's illicit campaign finances. To cover the massive campaign with its rock concerts, car rallies, billboards, television advertisements ranging from $10,000 to $20,000 per minute, tours around the country and bribes to newspapers and public officials would have exceeded the permissible maximum of $3 million. Then there was the payment to the California-based advertising company that Dyachenko had hired to provide state-of-the art publicity, which had been kept secret from the public eye. Then, as Gorbachev revealed, Yeltsin's team was paying for Lebed's election promotion to raise his chances in the first round (it did, to third place, with a large 14.52 per cent chunk of the votes), and to gain his votes in the second round. In all, according to Paul Klebnikov's calculations, the campaign cost more like $1–2 billion.[91] The Central Electoral Commission was powerless to keep track of breaches of the law, especially as the law conveniently specified that the auditing process was to be carried out after the elections, by which time abuses of the law would have no effect on the outcome. The secret funding, which was coming from financial–industrial structures depending on Yeltsin's future goodwill, was coordinated by Berezovsky.

For support from the business world the nation would have to pay dearly, much of it in the loans-for-shares auctions organised by Chubais as a way of acquiring funds for Yeltsin's campaign. In this privatisation scheme the bankers who lent money to Yeltsin's campaign became fabulously rich by getting stakes in huge lucrative companies, such as Norilsk Nickel, as collateral. As the state never paid back the loans, the major banks involved were permitted to organise auctions and sell the shares to themselves at derisory prices. As an example, Mikhail Khodorkovsky and his Menatep Bank bid $309 million for the Yukos oil company, whose market value soon after was $15 billion.[92] Berezovsky was sufficiently brazen to tell the *Financial Times*: 'We hired Chubais and invested huge sums of money to ensure Yeltsin's election. Now we have the right to occupy government posts and enjoy the fruits of our victory'.[93]

The media largely knew the coup was a concocted affair. The election team had gathered editors of the main liberal newspapers to swear them to secrecy until after the elections. By their complicity, the media covered their eyes to the massive public embezzlement that was taking place. State borrowing for campaign funding was happening at the same time as schoolteachers, doctors, workers and miners were not receiving their salaries. The communists were quite right in their accusations when people's deputy Vladimir Semago scornfully reported that 'We are constantly assured that Yeltsin's ratings are growing. Lies. The only thing growing is the expense of his electoral campaign ... Moreover, a part of this gigantic sum is taken from the state budget, that is, out of taxpayers' pockets'.[94] The loans-for-shares scheme deprived the nation of its natural resources for a pittance, creating a class of billionaires whose fortunes were made not by investment in the country but by wheeling and dealing. By not doing their job, the media perpetrated a number of sins: they collaborated in the impoverishment of the country, they abdicated their duty during elections of providing accurate information to voters and they conspired to convey false information for political purposes.

Even worse was the media's complicity in covering up the fact that Yeltsin had suffered a massive heart attack between the two rounds of the elections. This happened on 26 June, a week before the second round on 3 July. A veil of silence hung over the truth. Kremlin advisers produced vague answers to explain Yeltsin's absence – he had lost his voice, he had the flu, he was tired. I happened to leave Moscow for London on 1 July and was amazed to hear the British media discussing Yeltsin's heart attack at great length. Having come straight from the horse's mouth, I knew less than the British public. In his memoirs Yeltsin describes how he managed in those last few days to cover up his illness. Because he was adamant about keeping a meeting with Lebed on 28 June to push forward negotiations on a peace settlement in Chechnya, the room at his dacha in Barvikha where he was staying had to be rearranged to look like an office, the piano and other give-aways removed, and only a Kremlin cameraman allowed in. As he could barely stand on voting day – his heart was constantly seizing up – he went with his wife to the ballot box in Barvikha rather than Moscow and just about managed a smile and a few words to the crowd of reporters and TV cameramen waiting for him.[95]

What was the point of this farce and the media determination to prop Yeltsin up at all costs? The 65-year-old Yeltsin was suffering from serious health problems and had had a severe heart attack in late 1995, which was not publicly known. Only three months after winning the elections, he had to undergo major heart surgery and endured five bypasses. It was a period when the country stood still: nothing could be done until it was certain who was in charge. Yeltsin was always supremely confident of his capacity to overcome fate and was not prepared to give up the leadership, but those around him knew the catastrophic state of his health. The stern rules of deference to a patron-benefactor no doubt played its part. As Yeltsin never fully recovered, many of the decisions in the last few years were influenced by the 'family' – Dyachenko and her future husband, one-time *Ogonyok* journalist and ghost writer of Yeltsin's memoirs, Valentin Yumashov, in alliance with Voloshin, Berezovsky and Roman Abramovich. The media had collaborated to install unelected representatives to influence national policy, and although no important decisions were taken without Yeltsin's okay, the choices presented to him would inevitably have been selective.

Yet the media went along with the myth that there was no alternative to Yeltsin: it was either continuing Yeltsin's economic reforms or a fate worse than death. Individual journalists, such as Aleksandr Minkin, objected: 'To be against the Communists does not mean to be for Yeltsin. Before the first round, we really did have other options'.[96] There were many other politicians committed to supporting democracy: the Prime Minister Chernomyrdin and Nizhny Novgorod governor Boris Nemtsov, as well as other presidential candidates such as Grigory Yavlinsky and the eminent eye surgeon and businessman, Svyatoslav Fyodorov. Even Aleksandr Lebed had shown himself amenable to democratic politics. Hardly had there ever been so many competent pro-democracy presidential candidates. In fact, if Zyuganov had won, democracy would have triumphed and it is unlikely the future would have been apocalyptic – a view that many liberals now concede. Zyuganov had shown himself to be timid in the face of national and international pressure; and the party's vast property had gone into the state's coffers. He had never spelled out the Communist Party's programme, because the party may not have had a clear understanding of what its policies would be if it were in power. The communists may not even have wanted to win, any more than they wanted to in 2000, when they preferred to make a deal with Putin to be paid as the opposition. Most importantly, they would have had to face a society with a robust media, business community and NGOs; a society which was more politically active and raucous in its demands for democratic rights than at any other time in its history, and unlikely to be cowed at attempts by the communists to repeat the restrictions and horrors of the past. In opposition, these democratic forces would have created a more energised democracy than the society that emerged, and one with a less rapacious financial elite. In fact, this was the media's last chance to cover elections freely and fairly. The example of 1996 changed the political elite's attitude to elections, especially once Yeltsin was no longer a player in 1999.

The media's naivety comes out starkly in the Gusinsky-owned newspaper *Segodnya*'s headline a few days after the elections: 'Today the fourth estate moves over to where it belongs – in opposition to the government'.[97] It was not that simple. The media landscape had changed and emboldened media tycoons. The way the media could easily be exploited for commercial and political purposes showed the bankers, now much wealthier from the loans-for-shares scheme, that it was expedient to buy media outlets. Media rights advocate Aleksei Simonov saw the collaboration as 'suicidal', leading to a loss of credibility and dignity: 'the principles of professionalism cannot be put aside temporarily, not even when it seems politically expedient'.[98] There was not much remorse or analysis at what had happened. When, before the 2000 presidential election, TV critic Irina Petrovskaya reminded Yevgeny Kiselyov that NTV had lied about Yeltsin's health in 1996, he agreed it had been a mistake: 'We should have looked not at tomorrow or after-tomorrow but a bit further into the future; it seems we created a power monster'.[99] However, it is unclear what Kiselyov really thinks. In 2009 he said that if they had not helped Yeltsin to win 'We'd be living in a better version of North Korea'.[100] Many professionals have conceded that their conduct in 1996 was a mistake, but I do not get the feeling that this has been a lesson learned; people often end with: 'but who knows?'. In contrast to Putin's hack propagandists, some of the top players in 1996 are seen today as heroes, forgetting the role they played in tarnishing journalism and its devastating legacy.

Gusinsky gave a strange reason for the role played by his media some years later, saying 'journalists defended their right to practise their profession. Bias was a form of such defence'.[101] He expressed this opinion at a Freedom Forum seminar at Moscow State University's faculty of journalism in 1998, which I attended. When the audience was asked whether they thought NTV was impartial, no one put their hand up – except Kiselyov – which provoked a great deal of giggling.

The logic that dominated thinking at the time was that to pursue free speech now would be to forgo it for ever. But if the democrats lied to demolish the communists, because the communists could never be trusted, why would we, the public, believe the liars? Put in another way: if the media believed that a communist victory would threaten their free speech, did they want free speech as a means to truth-telling or for the acquisition of political power? If it was the latter, then the democrats were playing the same game their Bolshevik ancestors had played.

IV Media empire-building

The use of the media as a political tool in the 1996 elections spurred on bankers and industrialists, now called 'oligarchs' as their wealth and influence seeped into the political landscape, to acquire media outlets in time for the next elections, when Yeltsin would be out of the picture. The media needed cash investments and journalists had shown their willingness to cooperate in dubious schemes. Berezovsky recalled the intense competition that existed between oligarchs who were making billions, but were still 'unhappy that others were getting more'. The unity that had prevailed between politicians and oligarchs in re-electing Yeltsin was now fragmenting into power struggles among the elites for power and property in a capitalist free-for-all. Accusations and counter-accusations were hurled in political ping-pongs that came to be known as the 'information wars', which characterised the behaviour of the media in the latter part of Yeltsin's rule. The two noisiest camps revolved around media tycoons Berezovsky and Gusinsky.

Berezovsky had been rewarded for his part in the elections by being appointed deputy secretary of the Security Council, bringing him close to the heart of government. His main weapon was the influence he held at ORT. Despite the state's 51 per cent control, it had withdrawn from the daily management of the company; while out of the original 49 per cent owned by private investors only three shareholders remained by March 1997: Berezovsky's company LogoVAZ – 8 per cent, Gazprom – 3 per cent and a consortium of banks (Stolichny, Menatep, Alpha-bank, Obyedinenny bank) – 38 per cent. Although the consortium held the larger number of shares, Berezovsky was the most powerful figure.

Named by Forbes in 1997 as one of the world's richest people, in the 97th spot, with an accumulated wealth of $3 billion, Berezovsky had made his fortune through car dealership (LogoVAZ) and had interests in oil (Sibneft) and aviation (Aeroflot). Notorious as a Machiavellian fixer, he was later called a kingmaker for helping Yeltsin and Putin win elections. As the most powerful oligarch in the second half of the 1990s, his political adventurism did incomparable damage to the fledgling democracy. 'I am absolutely convinced', says one of Yeltsin's former ministers, Alfred Kokh, 'that no one caused more harm to the democratic movement than Berezovsky'.[102] He was largely responsible for destroying the media's independence and sense of purpose, and acknowledged this himself a year before committing suicide, repenting on Facebook for his part 'in the destruction of independent journalism'. The other two things he repented were his greed and bringing Putin ('a greedy tyrant') to power.[103]

Berezovsky was without doubt a colourful character, and people were carried away by his ebullience, charm and money. Many top journalists were rewarded generously for their contributions to his various self-serving causes. Viktor Shenderovich describes what it was like being in his presence. 'It's not that getting close to him was risky, it's just that everyone knew that he would use you and discard you at the first convenient moment. Nothing personal, that was the way things worked'.[104] When Berezovsky became Putin's bogey-man for all ills, Vladimir Pozner found it disturbing to watch the hypocrisy of those vilifying Berezovsky after his death: 'It was shocking how some of my colleagues insulted the dead Berezovsky ... let's say, those presenters of TV shows and the guests they invited. I tried to imagine how they would have behaved if Berezovsky had been alive and well. How they would have been bowing and scraping, and kissing different body parts'.[105]

For a man with such influence on politics, it is surprising that he only man-aged to get an audience with Yeltsin a total of two or three times. Part of his talent was to bamboozle people into believing he was constantly dancing attendance on Yeltsin and his daughter. Dyachenko exposes some of his devious ways of pre-tending to be a part of the inner sanctum; but she did not reveal this at the time, furthering his influence and other members of the 'family' on Yeltsin.

With Berezovsky and major banks in control of ORT, the channel had little sense of itself as a public broadcaster. The president's Council of Trustees was meant to be a guarantor of 'free speech, justice, objectivity and humanism', but it hardly ever met. Although Yeltsin had appointed Aleksandr Yakovlev as chairman of the board of directors because of his moral authority, Yakovlev was holding other positions and writing books. Members of the board were divided equally into top government officials ignorant of television and bankers who had their own agenda. No one from the arts and sciences. That fitted well with Berezovsky's plans to show that market reform was 'in the interests of the state and therefore of society'.[106] By March 1998, Berezovsky had acquired a number of new media outlets: a majority share in TV6, the news-papers *Nezavisimaya gazeta* and *Novyye izvestiya*, magazines *Ogonyok* and *Matador*; and by 1999 the prominent publishing house Kommersant, which included the daily of the same name, a favourite with businessmen.

By contrast, Gusinsky's stated aim was to run a business which would be profitable because of its journalism, audience ratings and good management practices. His ideal was Rupert Murdoch, whom he visited in London and New York. Murdoch's business acumen and political influence impressed Gusinsky, who also saw political machinations as part of the business of being a media mogul. Resigning from his post as president of his bank, Gusinsky gave all his time to building his media-holding company, Media Most, into which he assembled the diverse parts of an integrated media empire: the NTV Plus satellite network, NTV International that broadcast abroad, NTV Kino that acquired films to serve television channels, the TNT network that served the regions, and so on. A one-time theatre director, Gusinsky knew how to bring in talent and create an artistic concept, which saw NTV's news and current affairs peaking in popularity ratings. Media Most acquisitions included the fiercely independent radio station Ekho Moskvy, the newspaper *Segodnya*, the magazine *Itogi* and the radio and TV listings *Sem' Dney* ('Seven Days').

The economic giant Gazprom (40 per cent state-owned at the time), the world's largest gas company, also launched into the media market with a subsidiary, Gazprom-Media. Its media arm would defend its political interests and provide it with a better image, as it was being roundly criticised for tax evasion. It wanted to be available as a mouthpiece for Prime Minister Chernomyrdin, former boss of Gazprom and main defender of its interests, in case he stood for president. Gazprom had stakes in NTV and ORT and had a project to develop small regional TV stations in oil and gas-producing regions. All in all, it had 29 newspapers and television stations by 1998. It had a reputation for not interfering with editorial matters in the early days, until pushed by the government. In due course Gazprom-Media would become one of the largest media corporations, increasing in strength in the Putin years.

The fourth emerging media empire was potential presidential contestant, Moscow Mayor Yury Luzhkov, who was building his media base through the Moscow city government bank's acquisitions. Particularly important was the bank's 67 per cent stake in the third national television channel, TV Centre. The bank provided start-up capital for REN TV, the production company owned by Irena Lesnevskaya and her son Dmitry, who had acquired a television licence for what became known as the intellectual's TV, for a while running on a UHF channel. In 1998 Luzhkov gained control of the large *Moskovskaya pravda* printing press. Like Gazprom, TV Centre did not ram its politics down the public's throat.

Some of these acquisitions did not go without a fight. In buying into major newspapers, Oneximbank had trouble in snapping up *Komsolmolskaya pravda*, provoking vicious infighting between editorial staff and senior management. The staff rebelled because it feared the bank's known aggressive tactics. It preferred to be bought by Gazprom, which was offering less money in the sale. Management, headed by chairman of the board Vladimir Sungorkin, won and approved the sale of 20 per cent of the company's stock to the bank in exchange for $20 million in investment over the next two years. It had carried the day by tempting journalists to sell their shares, which had risen from $150 to between $500 and $1000, causing dissension within the ranks. Oneximbank's ownership put the newspaper squarely into the Chubais camp, because of his friendship with the bank's founding president, Vladimir Potanin. This defeat sealed the newspaper's fate, which is now a sensationalist tabloid and a pro-Putin ally under Sungorkin.[107]

By the middle of 1998 there was hardly a media outlet that was not incorporated into one of the media empires. Other banks were involved to a lesser degree, but their share could always be bought up by richer media magnates for their political purposes. Preferring to guard his independence, Yegor Yakovlev allowed several banks to have small stakes in *Obshchaya gazeta* and retained his trustworthy reputation.

Kompromat

The struggle for power burst into open media warfare almost immediately Yeltsin returned from hospital after heart surgery towards the end of 1996.

The manipulative politics of the 1996 elections developed into a dirtier game called *kompromat*, in which compromising material was used to incriminate political and business opponents. Finding *kompromat* did not involve the hard slog of investigative journalism; it was usually handed over to journalists from a source in the FSB or one of the other security services. It could involve sleaze or sex or corruption, it could titillate the senses and shock moral scruples; but its primary aim was directed at business and politics. There were enough former KGB operatives on the streets, demobbed in the early days of cleaning up the security services, who needed work and were willing to sell their services and knowledge.

The first victim was Aleksandr Lebed, which showed just how fickle media struggles were. Only four months earlier Lebed had been hailed as a hero over the alleged Korzhakov plot. Lebed had become so popular as the strong and honest soldier who had successfully ended the 20-month Chechen war that he threatened the ambitions of Chernomyrdin and Chubais. After a smear campaign probably plotted by Chubais, Lebed was sacked as national security chief by Yeltsin. When Lebed chose to join forces with Korzhakov, he came into the immediate line of fire of NTV, Korzhakov's long-standing enemy. A media campaign was orchestrated through NTV's flagship programme *Geroy Dnya* ('Hero of the Day'), where Yevgeny Kiselyev and Interior Minister Anatoly Kulikov read out documents claiming that Lebed was plotting an armed coup. Lebed pointed out that NTV was playing to the same script as the 'cash in the Xerox box' affair: a dramatic warning of a coup, followed by dismissals.[108]

It was a pathetic spectacle. In June 1996 Lebed had been so useful to NTV in getting rid of Korzhakov that TV observers mocked the constant interviews on NTV with Kiselyov as a love affair. The enmity between Korzhakov and Gusinsky went back to an earlier conflict in December 1994, which the papers had dubbed 'snow falls in Moscow'. An extraordinary and at the time inexplicable event had taken place when Korzhakov's presidential guard, armed and clad in combat jackets, their faces hidden by balaclava masks, had chased Gusinsky and his cavalcade of cars across Moscow, sealed off Gusinsky's headquarters in the MOST bank building in central Moscow and forced some of his bodyguard to lie face down in the snow for several hours. This had been Korzhakov's warning to Gusinsky (and, beyond, to his ally Luzhkov) not to think of supporting anyone but Yeltsin in the 1996 elections. Since then, having been sacked by Yeltsin, Korzhakov's feelings for his old boss had soured. It was widely believed that Korzhakov had bugged the offices of the Kremlin administration and was well stacked with *kompromat* to use on old enemies and ex-friends. His scandalous revelations made for shocking news. He claimed that although Berezovsky and Gusinsky were now allies, Berezovsky had once asked him to kill Gusinsky, as well as Luzhkov. Korzhakov now called his exposés 'hunting geese' ('gus' is the word for 'goose', the root of Gusinsky's name). In response, there were damning allegations that Korzhakov had taken part in a Kremlin racket to extort $40 million from the national sports fund, which he denied.

Needless to say, it was almost impossible to untangle these webs of intrigue. Along the way, moral issues got lost. The focus in the media was not on the allegation as such: was it true or false? Did it affect the normal work of the office holder? How outrageous was the moral offence? Press interest lay more in the political motivation: who stood behind the *kompromat*, who was stabbing whom in the back? Definitive answers hardly ever emerged, as most of these cases turned into an unfathomable sludge of endless conjecture. The impact of such allegations depended largely on the basis of 'where there's smoke there's fire'. But neither could they be ignored, as corruption was everywhere and people were making fabulous fortunes overnight. Cases of *kompromat* usually had decisive impacts on the running of government.

The first western-style sex scandal brought down the Minister of Justice Valentin Kovalyov. The journalist Lydia Kislinskaya was handed a video cassette by a member of the Interior Ministry, showing a man resembling the minister in a sauna romping with three female prostitutes. Three pages of the monthly *Sovershenno sekretno* ('Top Secret') were covered with these grainy shots (no. 6, 1997). Sex scandals had never played a part in the Russian media before. In fact, when a female journalist wrote an article about her affair with Khasbulatov, it improved his image. The compromising information in the Kovalyov story lay in the fact that the sauna belonged to the Solntsevo mafia and Kovalyov was head of the commission fighting organised crime.

The most sensational *kompromat* of 1997 was when Chubais was nailed by journalist Aleksandr Minkin for taking a bribe in a shady book deal. It was a complicated affair and took years to unravel. Known as the 'Writers' case', Chubais and top privatisation officials were accused of accepting a $450,000 honorarium for a book that had not been published.[109] Each of the authors had been paid $90,000 for his contribution. The accusation was that the fee was a bribe for rigging the major privatisation auction of Svyazinvest, Russia's giant state telecommunications network, which two of the oligarchs were fiercely competing for: Gusinsky and Vladimir Potanin of Oneximbank. Gusinsky had not been involved in earlier privatisation deals and felt it was his turn to benefit from the sale of state assets. The *kompromat* linked the publisher to Oneximbank, that won the auction. The book was eventually published, but the fact that the authors had apparently been paid such a high fee in advance caused a scandal. The privatisation team was fired by Yeltsin; Chubais remained in office but lost his portfolio as finance minister.

The main privatisation chief who had lost his job, Alfred Kokh, had another story to tell. The 'Writers' case' was concocted by Gusinsky, who knew the money was not payment for writing a book, but Chubais's bonus for managing Yeltsin's election campaign, which he had divided up with privatisation officials who had helped. The money had come from illicit campaign funds which Gusinsky knew, says Kokh, but it was to Gusinsky's advantage to have them sacked from their job in the government's finance department: 'They wanted to teach all of us in the government a lesson: either you do what we tell you or you'll be out on the street. We refused to do that and we were out on the street'.[110] NTV had made a lifelong enemy in Kokh, which was the reason he was made head of Gazprom-Media in 2000 when the first blows against NTV struck. Kokh has little sympathy for those who defend NTV's good journalism: 'It does not mean it was "democratic and free journalism"', he says. 'Goebbels also had highly qualified and talented journalists, you've got Leni Riefenstahl to show for it ... Stalin did too'.[111]

The *kompromat* that revolved around the Svyazinvest auction was the most serious case of interference with government policy by oligarchs fighting for their commercial interests. The sale of a 25 per cent stake in Svyazinvest had sent the oligarchs into a competitive frenzy quite unlike any of the other sales. By contrast with the loans-for-shares insider deals, the sell-off of Svyazinvest was set up to go to the highest bidder, in effect the first auction of state property that was sold close to its market price ($1.875 billion). The so-called young reformers, Chubais and newcomer, Boris Nemtsov, vowed there would be no more covert deals: the federal budget needed to pay its debts to the army, teachers and doctors and the pair had made a pledge to Yeltsin that money would be found. Chubais, who had been the bankers' friend, now refused to negotiate an insider deal, while Boris Nemtsov insisted there would be no more 'bandit capitalism'. Although all the bankers had gained their wealth at the expense of the state, Potanin's Oneximbank presented a different model for the Russian economy, opening up the market and working with foreign investors (George Soros was part of his winning consortium; Soros later said he had never made such a bad mistake as to get involved). Crucially, Potanin had been a deputy prime minister in Yeltsin's government and was a close friend of Chubais, which infuriated those on the losing side. As a warning to the government and to show who was the boss, the Berezovsky-Gusinsky team joined up to unleash a war of *kompromat* through their media outlets. Nemtsov also became a target, thus maligning a man who had been Yeltsin's favourite as successor at one time and who, as he became better known, was seen to be one of that rare breed of politician in Russia who was honest and intelligent.

Cases of *kompromat* left the public up in the air. Journalists themselves may not always have been aware of what lay behind a story, happy to be given a scoop. It was not always possible to tell the motives behind *kompromat*. When Central Bank chief Sergei Dubinin accused Oneximbank of embezzling more than $500 million in federal funds, was he doing his job as the country's top banker, or doing a favour for rival bankers?[112] ORT (Berezovsky) gave the story top billing; NTV (Gusinsky) played it down. Speculation had it that at the time Gusinsky was negotiating with Oneximbank in the bid for Svyazinvest. It was full-time work on a daily basis to establish who had concocted what, who had lied, who had outwitted whom. It was usually necessary to refer to the Fossato – Kachkaeva updates on media empires which were coming out regularly at the time.[113]

Izvestiya *and Igor Golembiovsky (1991–7)*

More than any other newspaper, *Izvestiya* embodied the spirit of new democratic Russia. Under Igor Golembiovsky – the first editor in the country to be elected by the journalists' collective and, also rare, unanimously – *Izvestiya* was proud of its radical roots and its reputation as the Soviet Union's second newspaper, never the first, because that would have meant being the official mouthpiece of the party, *Pravda*'s job, and not theirs. As *Pravda* sank, *Izvestiya* rose. It had a distinct view of how it could support Russia's liberal reforms and could turn to its legendary reformist editors, Stalin's main opponent, Nikolai Bukharin (1934–7) and Aleksei Adzhubei (1959–64), Khrushchev's son-in-law, who had thrust *Izvestiya* to the forefront of the attack against Stalinism.

Izvestiya's moral core was linked to the 'generation of the sixties', to Adzhubei's reforms and the progressive intelligentsia's concern for the 'insulted and injured', at the same time as it accepted the brash new ideology of the free market and its harsh economic realities. When *Izvestiya* fell to oligarchic capitalism, the rival media gleefully mocked its lofty ideals. But the demise of the editorially independent *Izvestiya*, the country's main national quality broadsheet with a circulation of over half a million at the time, meant the loss of commitment to public interest values and human interest journalism.

Izvestiya's privileged history, the list of prominent figures who had trained in its school, and its vast facilities on Pushkin Square in the centre of Moscow, extending from its iconic 1925 constructivist premises, made it a natural home for new ideas bubbling to the surface. As Yegor Yakovlev's *Moskovskiye novosti* across the square had been the flagship of *perestroika*, so Golembiovsky's *Izvestiya* identified with Yeltsin's democratic goals. When critics attacked him for being too close to Yeltsin he retorted that it was ideas, not people, the paper supported. In fact, he was often a thorn in Yeltsin's side as chairman of the club of editors-in-chief and uncompromisingly against the first war in Chechnya. *Izvestiya* organised the press conference for human rights advocate Sergei Kovalyov when he returned from Grozny to report on the atrocities of the war. Like much of liberal Russia, Golembiovsky and his team sincerely believed in the market liberalism espoused by Gaidar and Chubais, and despite the miseries these policies were bringing, saw it as necessary to cure Russia's economic ills.

Izvestiya's old guard had been formed by Adzhubei's principles. Chief political writer Otto Latsis said the lessons they had learned from him were startling for their times: to maintain professional standards, to make articles interesting to readers – no one cared before, he said, it was only the party line that counted – and to understand that the state did not overwhelm the interests of 'people, their personalities and inner worlds'.[114] These were the principles that guided Golembiovsky, the paper's respected editor who, with the special charm he had retained from living in Georgia, was always accessible to staff and visitors who came to see him in his spacious office. Golembiovsky was proud that no one took bribes on his paper, a rule applied so firmly that journalists joked it was better not to write a positive piece as it might be construed as concealed advertising. When other newspapers in the 1990s were speculating on sensational political intrigues, *Izvestiya* could be trusted to give a sober analysis of events and not to be distracted from what it saw as its public duty of investigating injustice and lawlessness in Moscow and the far-flung regions, where it was rich enough to maintain its own correspondents.

Let us take two months in 1996, to see its investigative focus. A soldier dies in the Far East of hunger, while generals spend millions. The small town of Zavolzhsk in the Ivanovo textile region along the Volga has 'no gas, no hot or cold water, no pigeons and few dogs' – they have been eaten, because the chemical factory has not paid wages and the director hides behind closed doors. The old communist elite has robbed shareholders of a once flourishing clock factory in the Penza region. The overcrowding of Moscow's notorious Butyrka prison has seen its death rate grow as cells built for 30 people now house 100, and those ill with Aids and TB live side by side with those who are still healthy.[115] It was campaigning journalism, and it tried to be scrupulous in its reporting and research. A model was the years Andrei Illesh spent uncovering the true story behind the Korean airline 007 flight which was shot down by the Soviet Union in 1983, killing over 200 civilians – a story Golembiovsky risked his career to break.

Uniquely, in a situation where newspapers showed little solidarity, Golembiovsky had the loyalty of *Izvestiya*'s journalists, who were prepared to defend him and editorial independence, some of them three times on three different newspapers, in what they saw as a defining struggle for free speech in the new Russia. Journalists of the 'sixties' may not have been dissidents, but they valued their self-respect. Golembiovsky already had a history of struggle: he had been 'exiled' to Mexico during the Andropov regime, he was passed over as editor when nominated by the staff in 1990 ('the party does not know him', said the media minister), and he was almost sacked when he signed Yegor Yakovlev's petition calling Gorbachev's policy in Vilnius a 'crime' (but, fatefully, saved at the last minute when the then editor fainted at the meeting at which Golembiovsky was to be sacked). Throughout this period the staff considered him the de facto editor, but he came into his own after the coup. Latsis had also suffered for his principles, forced out of journalism for 11 years and out of *Izvestiya* for 20. These men were not easy to bully, as Khasbulatov found out when he tried to take back *Izvestiya*. In the court case that followed, the *Izvestiya* team fought to win its name and premises, but lost its printing house and special workers' dachas.

Izvestiya followed a democratic model. In privatising the newspaper, all members of the journalist collective received shares in the new company, which was rare in the industry. Although Golembiovsky had to whittle down the staff to below half, mainly through redundancies, *Izvestiya* was doing well, the staff was well paid, it was the first paper to take advertising, and Golembiovsky entered into profitable joint ventures with foreign companies such as

We/My, a dual-language weekly with the American Hearst corporation, and a venture between *Izvestiya* and the UK's *Financial Times*. This was normal business, but when it came to dealing with the dirty financial world of oligarchic business, the team proved to be out of its depth. The troubles began when *Izvestiya* decided to expand its regional issues and turned for capital to Lukoil, the country's largest oil corporation, 36 per cent of which was owned by the state. Lukoil acquired 22 per cent of shares in the paper and pledged it would not interfere in editorial matters.

The scandal erupted on 1 April 1997 when *Izvestiya* reprinted an article from the French daily *Le Monde* alleging that Prime Minister Chernomyrdin had amassed a personal fortune of $5 billion through his ties to Gazprom. The article caused a furore in the government. The prime minister earns only $715 a week, said his spokesman. An outraged Chernomyrdin responded by refusing to approve a government decision awarding Lukoil a profitable share in an international oil consortium. Lukoil held a press conference, rejecting *Izvestiya*'s article and calling for Golembiovsky's resignation. Instead of apologising, as *Le Monde* had done, *Izvestiya* hit back, publishing articles on alleged criminal activities involving Lukoil.

When asked why the paper had not apologised, many of the journalists were convinced that the oligarchic structures had to be confronted if they were to win their independence. They warned of the danger to free speech: 'Censorship has been reanimated' ran a headline; corporate interests are trying to 'break defiant journalists' and turn the paper into a 'bastardised propaganda rag'.[116] Attempts were made to get Chubais's help, and through him to reach Yeltsin, but Chubais refused, and Yeltsin tended not to interfere in business matters. *Izvestiya* had only recently celebrated its 80th anniversary, when it had been swamped with congratulations from public officials and Yeltsin himself, but now it was shunned. Golembiovsky's phones no longer rang. 'We realised we were alone with this oil giant intent on crushing us without the slightest pity', wrote a younger member of the paper, Valery Yakov, later to become editor of *Novyye izvestiya*.[117]

Next, Lukoil began to buy up shares from *Izvestiya* journalists to seize control of the paper. *Izvestiya* responded by making what they thought was a friendly deal with Vladimir Potanin's Oneximbank. The deal was verbal, based on a gentleman's agreement, although Oneximbank had already acted in a predatory way in acquiring *Komsomolskaya pravda* and *Trud*. Oneximbank would provide the capital to buy enough shares to allow the newspaper and Oneximbank to hold 25.1 per cent each. Again, a pledge was made that editorial and financial matters would be kept separate. Yakov says they did not sense any danger; the old guard was used to the Soviet style of doing business, which was based on trust and not on the law or money.

The scramble for shares began, with the editorial team working all hours with Oneximbank to find *Izvestiya* journalist-shareholders, past and present. It was a race which left behind emotional traces, tales of friendship and betrayal, although I was amazed when talking to Golembiovsky at how unjudgemental he was. Colleagues had to decide whether to give in to the highest bidder for their shares or save the old Alma Mater. The last 98 shares, which would decide the balance, belonged to *Izvestiya*'s foreign correspondent in the USA, who accepted Lukoil's offer. When he arrived in Moscow, his colleagues connived to get him away from his Lukoil keepers and talked him out of it. He passed on his shares to *Izvestiya*. It is said he was offered a million dollars.

But it was all to no avail. Oneximbank, which held the newspaper's shares, betrayed the paper and did a deal instead with Lukoil to oust Golembiovsky. The banks understood one another. 'We were set up in every way', says Yakov. 'We lost. We'd been so terribly and brazenly duped that we could not even believe it'.[118] Golembiovsky was offered various figurehead positions, but was sickened by the whole 'cynical show'. He had been at *Izvestiya* for 31 years. On his last day at work he gathered his papers into his briefcase, took his umbrella with its *Izvestiya* insignia and left alone.

The *Izvestiya* battle had been a test case in the struggle for free speech. Certainly *Izvestiya* had made mistakes, but surely its downfall would be treated with sympathy? It was not. There was the usual element of envy: glee that the prestigious *Izvestiya* had fallen and inflated rumours about how much everyone had made out of their shares. One could expect the worst from Dorenko: 'There are two versions of events. One is that Lukoil is bullying *Izvestiya*. The other is that *Izvestiya*'s people wanted to make some money, made their money, but then fell out with their paymasters and passed themselves off as the Joan of Arc of the Russian press'.[119] The liberal intelligentsia wrote appeals to save *Izvestiya*, but the media were aloof. Many newspapers refused to join a petition to the president signed by 13 editors and printed on 22 April in the paper. If the petition had been accompanied by demonstrations of support and journalistic solidarity, some of its demands might have been implemented to the benefit of the media community as a whole: that Yeltsin come out in support of the paper; that the Media Law that gave journalists editorial freedom should be taken as seriously as the law on shareholders; that bureaucrats should stop meddling in the media.

Instead, a Darwinian spirit prevailed in the media's arguments that the competitive market was predicated on natural selection. *Izvestiya* was accused of pitiful whingeing: if you want to live in a market economy, put up with the consequences, stop these feeble-minded appeals to the president, grow up, this is the way it's done in the West. The comparisons with the West were invariably wrong, ignoring Russia's lack of similar practising institutions: laws that worked, media regulations, cross-ownership media laws. Oligarchic monopoly was growing, but journalists in good jobs treated it with complacency, reminiscent of a pearl of wisdom by Rupert Murdoch that 'monopoly is a terrible thing until you have it'.

One of the more acute commentators on the paradoxes of Russian life, Leonid Bershidsky, sympathising with *Izvestiya*'s old guard against the brash new breed of journalists, asked: 'Who knows? If these excellent writers had done their apprenticeship at the *Young Stalinist*, they might be less inclined to compromise now'. What irritated the young 1990s journalists was *Izvestiya*'s view of itself as the conscience of the nation. In an age when ideology was anathema, they insisted their function was to inform readers and keep an ideological distance. In practice, however, they were manipulating the truth on behalf of their proprietors without even *Izvestiya*'s do-gooding. Academic Ivan Zasursky represented this new approach:

> *Izvestia* is a bad newspaper, extremely bad. It is very old-fashioned; it is very engaged in politics. Lots of journalists from *Izvestia* still think that a good journalist is an agitating journalist ... They are very old-fashioned in terms of selecting one political line, and then fighting for it, like communists ... It's not professional ... Democracy or totalitarianism. People's capitalism or monopoly capitalism. You can't do anything with these abstractions! They're not good for judging the situation any more.[120]

Having lost the battle in *Izvestiya*, Golembiovsky and some of the old team did not give up and fought two more battles with the oligarchs to try to gain editorial independence. On both occasions, the forces against them were too strong, and the media environment too complacent. A group of about thirty top journalists and printers left *Izvestiya* with Golembiovsky to launch a new full-colour broadsheet which they called *Novyye izvestiya* ('New *Izvestiya*'). The finances came from Berezovsky, a rival of Lukoil and Oneximbank. He did not interfere with Golembiovsky as editor, but in 2001 Berezovsky was pushed out of the country by Putin, and new pressures emerged. Berezovsky agreed to sell the paper to a businessman that *Izvestiya* had nominated, but in the lawless spirit of the times, the new owner, Oleg Mitvol, seized the paper and sacked Golembiovsky. He did so after the paper had published a critique by analyst Vladimir Pribylovsky on the growing cult of personality around Putin, an article with the resonant title '... plus the Putinisation of the whole country' (from Lenin's famous slogan 'Communism is Soviet power plus the electrification of the whole country').[121] As the paper had been publishing articles critical of Putin for some time and Mitvol had not interfered, Berezovsky surmised that he had 'got the nod' from the Kremlin. Once again the team defended Golembiovsky and its independence. They went on strike and shut down the paper. They were out on the street again.

As the options narrowed, the tight-knit group began to split. Yakov received the intellectual property that was *Novyye izvestiya*, but not the building or the equipment and turned it into a newspaper that continues today to maintain a balanced position. Golembiovsky, Latsis and others in the team started a new paper, *Russky kuryer*, with a small circulation of 35,000, 'one of the best papers in Russia', according to the Union of Journalists' secretary Igor Yakovenko, who worked on it.[122] When its owner decided to go into politics in 2005, however, he sacked the team. It closed in 2005 without stirring much interest.

A complicated court case that Oleg Mitvol brought against Golembiovsky for financial mismanagement at *Novyye izvestiya* seems to have been devised as punishment by the Interior Ministry's investigating committee. It was 'absurd', said Yakov. 'Mitvol himself was responsible for our finances'. The case dragged on for five years to harass Golembiovsky, now a sick man, and was dropped for lack of evidence only a few months before he died in 2009. Yakov believes the court case was linked to articles in the newspaper critical of Putin.[123] Golembiovsky was underestimated, wrote *Moskovskiye novosti*'s then editor, Viktor Loshak, because he did not court self-publicity. But the obituaries remembered Golembiovsky as a newspaperman of the 'romantic' period, a 'legend', a man who transcended his epoch (*chelovek-epokha*), representing its higher aspirations.

Izvestiya sank into tabloid obscurity, owned by different pro-Putin proprietors. As Russians like to say, the 'brand' had gone. For a while, when Raf Shakirov was appointed editor, it sprang to life and then died again when he was sacked for his graphic coverage of the Beslan school siege. The final blow came in 2011 when the much diminished staff was removed from its famous premises, which were then rented out as offices. As the *Izvestiya* old guard predicted, it has turned into a propaganda rag.

It's a dog-eat-dog world

Unlike most western countries, the media in Russia lined up according to ownership and not political allegiance. Financial issues were what mattered. It was unclear what the media's political or moral allegiances were, other than to defend their owner's vested interests. As these interests were business, the goal was usually connected with reform and democracy, so long as not too much thought went into the ambiguities of these vast concepts or into the differences between liberal social values and capitalist economic ones. Were they defending free speech, or the free market? Journalists used their respective outlets to accuse each other of muckraking and perfidy. Having broken the story of Chubais's book deal, Aleksandr Minkin was the unnamed target of the new RTR chairman Nikolai Svanidze's wrath. Such reports, said Svanidze, usually had a rich master behind them with a journalist who got paid between $300,000 and $500,000 a year.[124] It was widely assumed in journalistic circles that Minkin had been in Berezovsky's and Gusinsky's pay for some time. The description of the book deal, complete with secret bank account details, indicated an FSB source and probably the two tycoons. Minkin, a combative and talented investigative journalist, maintained he had got his information from a confidential source. He could not be faulted when he argued that stories he had written about Chubais's financial dealings had been ignored until ORT and NTV had turned against Chubais.

To get to the bottom of many of the clashes, it was often more illuminating to turn to the independent English-language Dutch-owned *Moscow Times*, with its foreign editor and a staff of some foreign but mainly Russian journalists. It was read by many Muscovites who knew English and were interested in the country's politics. The lack of solidarity between journalists had never been quite as bad as in this period of free speech, peaking in the Chubais scandal. Accusations trailed behind almost every successful media personality. A columnist for the newspaper, Andrei Piontkovsky, had become increasingly irate at the behaviour of journalists, blurting out in disgust:

> Fifty years ago, the predecessors of this elite – the best journalists, writers and scholars of the Soviet Union – signed petitions to 'Shoot them like mad dogs!' Morals have not improved in Russia during the past half century. On the contrary. Stalin paid for dishonour far more than Berezovsky does. Stalin didn't pay some kind of measly tens of thousands of dollars per year, He allowed the elite to live or, at least, gave it the hope of survival.[125]

Journalists working for a tycoon usually pretended they were not under pressure: 'it would be pointless for them to pressure me' was the usual retort. Occasionally, editorial censorship was exposed. In one incident, *Ogonyok*'s staff was reported to have been threatened with the suspension of its wages after the magazine printed an article alleging that Chernomyrdin had shot a female bear and its cubs on a hunting trip, at a time when Berezovsky was an ally of the prime minister.[126] Berezovsky's most famous and shameless front man, Sergei Dorenko, a presenter with high popularity ratings, was brought back to ORT to batter the tycoon's enemies. Dorenko's vitriolic outbursts became legendary and earned him the name of 'killer-journalist'. He became more important to Berezovsky after he was sacked by Yeltsin from the national security council in November 1997 for failing to distance his business interests from government policy – a move, it was hoped wistfully, would put an end to oligarchic capitalism. To minimise Berezovsky's control of ORT a supervisory board was set up to support state interests. For those fans who saw Dorenko as 'a Robin Hood, cleaning out the dirt, a knight without fear or favour, let me remind you', TV critic Irina Petrovskaya wrote 'that there was a time when he used to attack his present boss, Berezovsky, with the same willing zeal he attacks Chubais today'.[127] Dorenko's 'killer' instincts were especially effective in decimating Putin's rivals in the 1999 election.

Rebuilding the state media

The information wars became shrill in advance of the elections, still two years away. This time there would be no unified support for Yeltsin, if he chose to breach constitutional rules and stand for a third time (hypothetically, by arguing that as he had been elected president under the Soviet Union the first time, it did not count). Berezovsky called him 'unelectable'. Gusinsky announced that NTV would not promote him. The main reason was that Yeltsin and the young reformers were no longer pandering to the interests of the oligarchs, whose goal was to hang onto their privileges and avoid paying taxes. Yeltsin had to fill the gaping hole in the federal budget against a background of pending catastrophe and industrial unrest. With most of the electronic media in the hands of the oligarchs, Yeltsin set out to establish a stronger media base. He needed media backing to push for a person of his choice as successor and protect himself from the Duma, which was getting ready to impeach him again. He could rely on RTR but not on ORT, when Berezovsky was paying bonuses to the management and staff that the state could not match.

On 8 May 1998 Yeltsin passed a decree to expand the fully state-controlled All-Russia State Television and Radio Company (VGTRK) into one huge holding, which would manage all its property: TV stations RTR and Kultura, Radio Russia, and the state's regional network of 89 stations. This scared not only the oligarchs, but came as a blow to local state-owned stations which had virtually won their freedom from Moscow after the breakup of the Soviet television monolith. Lacking finance, however, they had fallen under the control of regional governments which had their own agenda. VGTRK would be given tax privileges, and its debts of more than $200 million would be written off. This was despite a recent audit which showed corruption and gross misuse of funds. The most important change for private channels was that VGTRK would be in control of national transmission facilities, which had previously been under the Communications Ministry. It made all non-state companies dependent on VGTRK, which could dictate terms for signal transmission and increase rates to finance its expansion.

The oligarchs accused the Kremlin of blackmail and began a new information war, spreading inflammatory remarks in the press which the presidential spokesman complained were 'beyond reasonable limits'. The sensitive issue of the day were the striking miners in the Far East who had blocked the Trans-Siberian and other major railroads across Russia to demand the government pay their wages. Incensed at the way the oligarchic media were covering the strikes and the scorn they had poured on his new Prime Minister Kiriyenko, because he had refused to negotiate with the oligarchs, Yeltsin criticised the media tycoons publicly for the first time at an international press congress in Moscow on 26 May 1998:

> Owners of the media sometimes act as the worst censors. They openly interfere in editorial policy, decide what can and cannot be written or said. As a result, the right of citizens to receive objective and truthful information is threatened ... Unfortunately, far from all journalists have learned to make use of their acquired freedom in a rational way. I mean those cases where the norms of professional ethics have been abused; there are many such cases.[128]

NTV's position was typical of the cynicism of the day. It might have seemed that NTV journalists were supporting the miners in portraying their dire situation, and they may have been doing that as well, but they were also defending their funder Gazprom against Kiriyenko, who was forcing Gazprom to pay billions of dollars in back taxes, and had already sent bailiffs to seize assets, precisely so as to pay the wages and pensions of which NTV was accusing the government with such emotion of failing to do. They wanted Kiriyenko out, and their favourite Chernomyrdin brought back. NTV's assertion that the government was indebted to Gazprom for an amount larger than Gazprom's tax debt was repeated so frequently, and had lodged so firmly in most people's minds and in the press, that when Kiriyenko was able soundly to contradict the claim, people did not listen.

Yeltsin scaled down the aggression by calling the heads of the three major television companies to a meeting, where he said he was 'requesting', not 'demanding' that they report events honestly. They accepted his assurances that although VGTRK was being reorganised, nothing would be done to the private channels behind their backs. 'When the question goes down to the bureaucrats' level, the president's words are of crucial importance', said NTV's Oleg Dobrodeyev. In a radio broadcast, Yeltsin stressed his position:

> I will help both state-owned and non-state-owned newspapers, radio and television companies to develop. We must and will work with them only on the basis of dialogue ... Of course, journalists are not to blame for our social and economic difficulties. Nevertheless, it's very important that they feel responsible for covering these problems precisely and urgently. After all, people know of what is happening in the country largely from newspapers and tele-radio programmes .... the principle of a free press does not mean anything goes and open cynicism.[129]

The relationship between Yeltsin and the media had depended on his personality and not on the fragile democratic infrastructure, which journalists had not spent time building. It was therefore to him that the media turned to resolve problems. When the oligarchs wanted the price of their transmission services lowered that year they appealed to him as 'the steadfast defender of freedom of speech in our country'. But Yeltsin was no longer the main decision-maker. He was ill with various health problems and spent a great deal of time at his dacha. His own decisions were sometimes erratic – such as the five prime ministers that he appointed in the space of a year and a half. Increasingly, duties were taken over by the 'family'.

The fate of his own family must have also played a part in Yeltsin's decisions. Everyone knew that Yeltsin himself did not pursue luxury, but his daughters and their partners were said to be involved in business deals with the oligarchs which the press was examining as suspicious. Yeltsin had reason to fear what would happen when he stepped down. Some of the dangers he faced could be seen from the charges the Duma raised to impeach him: breaking up the Soviet Union, using force against the Duma in 1993, ruining the army, bringing about the genocide of the Russian people through policies that impoverished the country. The only rational charge, supported by Yabloko, was the launching of the war in Chechnya, especially as it was done without the consultation of any of the proper institutions. This charge might have held, but in fact impeachment failed on all counts. Nevertheless, it showed Yeltsin that it was expedient to seek a successor who would ensure the protection of his and his family's life and property, a spectre that also haunts Putin were he to retire in the near future.

In choosing between state and private media, most journalists considered state channels to be more dangerous to free speech, whatever their criticism of media tycoons. Private media were now seen not so much as the 'real' as the 'potential' independent sector. Broadcasters knew that as long as the trans-mission services were under the control of the state, it was the state that held the on/off button. It was the same with the press, where the printing presses and distribution services were mainly state-owned. Media columnist Leonid Bershidsky made this comparison: 'The Western view of Russian media tends to demonise the tycoons who own most news outlets here, but in my view the state is a far worse media owner than any robber baron. Apart from distort-ing and censoring information, it also encourages thievery and bureaucracy in the media. These factors combined turn a media company into an unmiti-gated disaster'.[130] TV critic Irina Petrovskaya's argument rested on journalists themselves. Once a state centre had been established, she said, it would not be difficult to pump out a 'party' line as ethical values in journalism were so low. A generation of journalists had grown up, she argued, who would be willing to fulfil any task if there was enough money in it. She compared this generation to those in the past who 'did at least think of their reputation, while today's don't even know what the word means, let alone the phrase "television in the public interest"'.[131]

Fear of the state was borne out in the rapidity with which the state took over in the final Yeltsin years, which Putin was able to exploit relatively easily when he came to office. With the 'family' largely in charge, television began to be reorganised without the libertarian principles Yeltsin had adhered to, intent mainly on protecting its political and financial interests after Yeltsin had gone. TV management very quickly began to take on Soviet character-istics. As well as VGTRK, the press ministry which had been disbanded, was re-established in July 1999 to form a vast Ministry of Press, Tele-Radio and Mass Communications. The previously appointed deputy head of VGTRK, Mikhail Lesin, moved over to become the minister. As the candidate put forward by Dyachenko and Yumashev, Lesin made himself useful to the 'family' in the last two years of the Yeltsin era, responsible with them for a rapid decline in media pluralism. The Union of Journalists dubbed Lesin enemy no. 1 of free speech in 2000, a prescient title as he later reaped greater benefit and influence from his success as Putin's main troubleshooter and media functionary.

Lesin formulated the statist position that later characterised Putin's media policy. The state, Lesin said, needed to be protected from the media. 'The defence of the state from the free media is a crucial problem at present. I don't agree with the view that the state is more dangerous to the media than the media is to the state. I believe the opposite'.[132] A *Moscow Times* editorial asked sarcastically: 'How can the agitprop minister defend the poor state from the media wolves?'.[133] Although much of the media found Lesin's position risible, never underestimating state power, there was truth to the fact that the state had become weak. Just as privatisation had denuded the government of a budget, it had left the Kremlin with limited media outlets, while privatised media had not brought into play a liberal and trustworthy private sector committed to building a shared and equitable society. But democratic considerations did not play a part in Lesin's rebuilding of state media. As the media had become a political tool, his goal was to strengthen state control for political and economically advantageous reasons.

Once again media matters were to be represented by a ministry, replacing two previously autonomous organisations, the state committee for the press and the federal service for TV and radio. There were two reasons for independent-minded journalists to be alarmed. First, the ministry was given the right to decide who would receive broadcast licences among privately owned media. The second reason was Lesin himself. There was an obvious conflict of interest in appointing Lesin minister when he was also the owner of Video International, the monolithic advertising agency and PR production company he had started in 1990, which had contributed to Yeltsin's 1996 election campaign and was closely embedded with television executives. Although Lesin gave up his position as shareholder in the company, no one took that seriously, as it was precisely these ties that made him valuable.

Novaya gazeta was scathing about the press minister. 'He is absolutely controllable, only the lazy have no *kompromat* on Lesin', it wrote. 'Through [him] the "family" can have not only complete influence on VGTRK ... but on all mass media, because the Lesin ministry issues licences, and getting them is a long drawn-out procedure'.[134] The newspaper spelled out the mutually beneficial relationship between Lesin and the Yeltsin 'family'. Initially, when Poptsov and Anatoly Lysenko had been in charge of RTR, Video International paid VGTRK $50 million in advance in order to place advertising on the channel, and also maintained supervisory powers. Under the 'family', Video International was allowed gradually to become the dominant partner, payment in advance was dropped, and the firm which supervised its activities was closed. After that, VGTRK was seen as virtually an offshoot of Video International and Lesin's business interests.

The August default

The financial crisis of 17 August 1998 saw the rouble devalued and a default on domestic and foreign debt payments. Ordinary people's savings and purchasing power went up in smoke once again. It brought the banks and the oligarchs to their knees. NTV was hit, ORT headed for bankruptcy; there was a 70 per cent drop in advertising on television; salaries were cut and journalists were laid off. In this atmosphere the 1995 law on state support for the media was prolonged, and newspapers cautiously accepted the lifeline. The oligarchs, however, even while their businesses collapsed hung onto their media outlets, knowing their value in restoring wealth and political influence.

In fact, economic recovery returned within the year, but the initial brutal impact of the crisis introduced a number of changes. It brought in the first left-wing government in the person of Yevgeny Primakov. To deal with the financial crisis Yeltsin's nomination of Chernomyrdin as prime minister, who would have bailed out the oligarchs, was rejected by the Duma twice. It had been Yavlinksy's clever suggestion to appoint Primakov, who espoused social democratic views. The respected Primakov offered stability and order, but journalists fell out with him almost immediately. An experienced politician, and one of the few figures who had been loyal to both Gorbachev and Yeltsin, Primakov's old communist habits betrayed him as far as his attitude to the media went. In his first week in office he had put out a gagging order on officials not to talk to the press. Access became harder and more documents were rated as classified. As one-time head of counter-intelligence, Primakov tried to install the smooth-talking PR head of the spy agency, Yury Kobaladze, as deputy head of VGTRK. To have former spies as top TV executives would have been a good campaign tool for Primakov's own presidential ambitions. The move failed (Kobaladze went to ITAR-TASS instead), but there was reason for journalists to fear the tightening of control over free speech.

With Primakov in office, the oligarchs no longer felt safe. Primakov's attempt to curb the media was linked to his attempt to demolish the power of the oligarchs and their out-of-control information wars. He threatened to 'optimise' the use of jails by filling them with 'economic criminals'. The oligarchs suddenly found themselves the target of long-simmering allegations of corruption and money laundering. With Primakov behind him, the Prosecutor General Yury Skuratov began examining the reasons behind the financial default. He launched investigations into almost 800 officials (including Chubais), who may have been speculating on the treasury bill market with insider information. Skuratov also launched a raft of investigations into the oligarchs and high officials, using documents he had received from his Swiss counterpart, Carla Del Ponte. Berezovsky and Smolensky were issued with arrest warrants (albeit while abroad and later annulled). Old scandals, like the Aeroflot case that *Moskovsky komsomolets* had exposed in 1997, resurfaced, with Berezovsky accused of diverting funds from the national airline to an offshore company in Switzerland. The case was sensitive because Yeltsin's son-in-law (Yelena's husband) had been made Aeroflot director-general under Berezovsky's watch. Other cases came up, such as allegations of impropriety by the Central Bank in using a little-known offshore firm, FIMACO, to stash the nation's foreign currency reserves. A separate investigation claimed that billions of dollars had been illegally siphoned out of Russia and laundered in a New York bank. But the Mabetex case was the most sensational because it touched on Yeltsin's family and inner circle.

A man resembling the Prosecutor General

Skuratov had begun to dig into Kremlin corruption. He claimed he had evidence that the Swiss construction company Mabetex had received highly profitable contracts to renovate the Kremlin and government buildings by paying bribes to high officials. According to Skuratov, $15 million had been put into bank or credit-card accounts for numerous officials, including Yeltsin's daughters. Yeltsin's response to this and other investigations attempting to implicate his family and Kremlin staff was to dismiss Skuratov, but the Federation Council, the upper house in whose jurisdiction these appointments were made, defiantly reinstated him. It showed how low Yeltsin's authority had fallen: he had just emerged from hospital and was unprepared for the multiple new forces jockeying for power.

On the evening of the day the Federation Council had defied Yeltsin, *kompromat* appeared against Skuratov on RTR. A one-minute fragment of a videotape was broadcast of a naked man 'resembling' Skuratov, engaged in sexual activities in bed with two prostitutes. Dorenko introduced the video, facetiously warning under-age viewers not to watch the Prosecutor General, if they wanted to retain their sense of patriotism. The videotape provoked a storm of outrage from politicians and journalists alike, who saw it as issuing from Yeltsin's desire to put a stop to the investigations. It was sleazy and tasteless and showed RTR's sycophancy to the Kremlin. RTR director Mikhail Shvidkoi fired back, saying he was 'shocked to the core' that the upper house could on one and the same day ignore the Prosecutor General's sexual misdemeanour and adopt a bill on morality, which would be used as political censorship against the media.

The press had a field day with Skuratov, fooling around with the word 'resembling', as the video was said to be too damaged to say for sure whether it was him. *Komsomolskaya pravda* printed a collage of Skuratov in uniform in bed with two women with the heading: 'The organs of the Public Prosecution have shown their might', with the sub-heading: 'the man resembling the Prosecutor General, Yury Skuratov, did not blemish the honour of his suit, resembling a uniform, because he took it off in time' (19.3.1999). Although there was little doubt that the aim of the video was to tarnish Skuratov's reputation and stop the various investigations into corruption, the media did not see Skuratov as a martyr fighting for truth and justice. During his years in office he had not upheld the judicial system in the wars between feuding Kremlin factions. He had not brought criminals to justice in the murders of Listyev, Kholodov and the more recent murder of the especially loved politician Galina Starovoytova. He irritated journalists by tantalising them with material he claimed to have on officials, then failing to produce the evidence. The Mabatex case had been put together incompetently and without sufficient proof.

The press suggested the video should be sent to the West to receive an impartial assessment of its authenticity, but the new FSB director, Vladimir Putin, was satisfied. He accepted the FSB's expert analysis that the man on the tape was Skuratov and that the orgy had been paid for by people being investigated for criminal offences by Skuratov's office. It is thought that Skuratov had been overheard on a bugged phone preparing indictments against Yeltsin's circle, including his daughter Tatyana. It appears now that the *kompromat* was arranged by Putin, but there are different versions: either Putin's operatives had managed to catch Skuratov on film with the two female prostitutes or the video was a fake. Putin used the video to try to deter Skuratov from pursuing the indictments.[135] Skuratov himself has provided conflicting accounts. In his book closest to the event, published in 2000, he writes that Putin rang and advised him that the sooner he resign, the better. 'Putin of course was in the loop on all those blackmailing efforts and games the "family" was playing', he writes.[136] More recently, Skuratov has said it was not Putin, but Security Council secretary Nikolai Bordyuzha with whom he spoke. Nevertheless, certain things became clear. When Skuratov reneged on the deal to resign, the video was handed to RTR.[137] Lesin had it broadcast as a service to the Dyachenko–Yumashev partnership. Skuratov suffered a heart attack soon after. Putin had proved his loyalty to the 'family'.

Berezovsky versus Gusinsky

Five months before the parliamentary elections, a new propaganda war started between Berezovsky and Gusinsky, now again at loggerheads, which became so vitriolic that Yeltsin tried to intercede. Chernomyrdin blurted out that it was no more than a pointless feud 'between two Jews'. The stakes were high, because the party that emerged victorious in the Duma in 1999 would determine the presidential outcome in 2000. Berezovsky was fighting on behalf of Yeltsin's successor, Putin. Gusinsky sided with his old partner, Moscow mayor Luzhkov, who was a strong candidate. He had proved his efficient management of the city and, deeply hostile to Chubais, had shown that social democratic policies for Moscow were often more successful than Chubais's free market economics for the nation.

The presidential entourage was unhappy with what they saw as oligarchic disloyalty. NTV covered Yeltsin rarely and coldly, while it featured Luzhkov frequently and warmly. NTV reported with unconcealed delight all of Skuratov's anti-Kremlin revelations. ORT's first shot across the bow was to diminish NTV by claiming it was deep in debt and that the FSB was investigating the bank accounts of Luzhkov's wife, a businesswoman whose enormous success was seen as dependent on city contracts provided by her husband's office. Luzhkov would cause 'bloodshed' as president, ranted Berezovsky. Berezovsky was Satan incarnate, Luzhkov replied. Yevgeny Kiselyov accused Berezovsky of crony capitalism that threatened to turn Russia into a 'banana republic', providing Luzhkov with a pulpit on NTV to denounce the

FSB's probe against his wife. Lofty about their own aims, virulent against the opposition, these slanders had nothing to do with real news. The conflict grew when the tax police came after Media-MOST's press, *Segodnya* and *Itogi*, and Kiselyov accused presidential administration chief Aleksandr Voloshin of preventing the company from receiving a loan that had previously been agreed.

Many years later, in 2011, the two sides in the person of Yevgeny Kiselyov and Yeltsin's daughter, Dyachenko, angrily lashed out at each other, allowing the public to get a bit closer to the truth. Kiselyov blamed the 'family' for being behind the moves that ended Gusinsky's control of NTV. Dyachenko blamed NTV for slandering Yeltsin, inundating TV viewers every day with stories about the 'insatiable family controlling a president, who was not of sound mind, and signing decrees to further their wealth'. Dyachenko was not wrong in saying this was the general impression people were left with at the time from NTV's coverage. Kiselyov hit back saying no one was accusing Yeltsin of enriching himself, but where did Dyachenko get the money to live in such style in London and abroad? Dyachenko revealed that 'wise' Chubais had warned Yeltsin not to give Gusinsky the whole of the fourth channel after the 1996 elections, telling her 'You have no idea how they will blackmail him and disinform television viewers' to push for their own presidential candidate.[138]

Nevertheless, Media MOST's only recourse in the last year of the Yeltsin era was to appeal to him as guarantor of freedom and democracy. At a press conference, editors and executives of Gusinsky's media empire – NTV, radio Ekho Moskvy, Segodnya and Itogi (represented by Dobrodeyev and Kiselyov, Venediktov, Berger and Parkhomenko respectively) accused the presidential staff of misleading Yeltsin and keeping him in the dark about the pressures being applied on 'independent' media. They suspected Voloshin had not shown their open letter of 26 July sent to Yeltsin. Part of the letter read: 'For the first time in the history of the new Russia, we are becoming witnesses to a deep and open attack on one of the main triumphs of Russian democracy: freedom of speech'.[139] The private media were being harassed and black-mailed because they were too independent, said NTV. Voloshin mocked NTV's double standards, saying it was running an 'information racket' to get more financing out of the government, although it had already received large amounts and was supposed to be a private company. Moreover, Yeltsin was still supporting NTV, giving it the same privileges as ORT and RTR to send its signal on government transmission facilities.

Free speech fair or foul?

To what extent did the 'information wars' prevent the positive results of what the exercise of free speech is supposed to provide: an understanding of the true nature of what is happening? There is no doubt that free speech was being exercised throughout the Yeltsin era; there was no monopoly of the news, there were different versions and points of view – and journalists were too aggressive, undisciplined and contradictory to be kept on a leash all the time. When they complied to promote their bosses, they did so for income or greed, but not out of political fear. That entailed they could change their approach and allegiances. It meant they felt in control of their fate, not slaves to a system. Media outlets were vigorous, robust, rowdy and dirty; pluralism and diversity existed, leaks competed with lies, providing more information on the workings of power than Russia had ever witnessed before. They exposed political dirt, corruption, greed, cruelty; and there was a great deal of it around, which the public no longer sees under Putin. The more dirt that politicians and oligarchs flung at each other, the more the public learned of political machinations and corrupt practices, confirming in many minds that conspiracy theories in Russia were not always that far from the truth.

On the other hand, there was a whole world out there which did not involve political–financial–industrial scandals. Media concentration in the hands of feuding oligarchs limited the nature of political and social discourse. The interests of a relatively small club of wealthy men did not relate to the interests of society at large. Although there was a pluralism of views, the news was selective. Instead of national debates on how to negotiate a society in transition, the headlines screamed intrigue and drama in the corridors of power. The political and personal agendas tarnished the media as a serious institution to be trusted. By distorting information, they hoodwinked and disempowered the public from understanding the world around them. Media outlets became the playthings of oligarchs, politicians and journalists – three professions which in a democracy should be characterised by a separation of powers. Their incestuous relationship and guilty secrets produced a refracted truth rather than blinding clarity.

Free speech existed, but it was being mauled and manipulated in ways that damaged its future and made it all the easier for Putin to deceive confused TV viewers. The devotee could seek the truth by reading rival media accounts, buying a variety of newspapers and watching different news bulletins, but ordinary people did not have the time, money or expertise to do this. The collaboration of a great number of journalists with their oligarch-proprietors showed that Soviet journalistic habits die hard, insulating them from the shame of being seen as flunkeys. Moreover, in the eyes of the public and due to their own PR, well-paid sophisticated journalists fell more into the class of celebrity than flunkey. The distance from serving the state in Soviet times to serving an oligarch in the new times was not that great, especially when it came with the temptation of going from rags to riches in conditions of the wild gold rush that some Russians were experiencing. The award-winning journalist Igor Svinarenko, known for his coverage of the privatisation deals, wrote about the way journalists justified their positions:

> At *Kommersant*, some of the economics writers practically had fistfights in the corridors, accusing each other of prejudice, of being on some

oligarch's payroll. It was like 'My oligarch is higher and more honest than yours, and I am more fearless and altruistic than you!'[140]

Duma elections 1999

The Yeltsin era ended with the 19 December 1999 Duma elections and a display of the dirtiest tactics in post-Soviet elections yet. Supported by an enlarged state media machine, Berezovsky and the 'family' pulled out all the stops to discredit the opposition Fatherland-All Russia bloc (Otechestvo-Vsya Rossiya) and its representatives, Primakov and Luzhkov, as future leaders of a new post-Yeltsin government. A correspondingly persistent propaganda campaign was run to promote the Putin-backed Unity (Yedinstvo) bloc, opening the way for Putin to win the presidential election. With the assistance of the media, Unity, a movement that had not existed two months earlier and lacked a party platform, managed to achieve resounding success.

Unity could gloat over the 23 per cent of votes it won, only 1 per cent lower than the communists had gained, by comparison with Fatherland-All Russia's 13 per cent. Primakov, who had been the most popular politician of the year and a promising future president, was trounced by the barrage of negative coverage from the Kremlin media. After that, he did not bother to enter the presidential race. Forecast as the next prime minister, Moscow mayor Luzhkov, having had his reputation besmirched, found it more expedient to support Putin in the presidential elections. It is believed Primakov and Luzhkov came to an understanding with the Kremlin to bow out after the parliamentary elections, ensuring that Putin would win as president in the first round.

After the 'information wars', dirty media politics in elections should not have come as a surprise, but what was happening signalled more than the usual unethical bar-room brawl of vested interests. The power exercised by the state media and press ministry indicated that the balance of forces had shifted from the private to the state sector. The OSCE's observer mission failed to detect the signs, reporting that the Duma elections 'marked significant progress in consolidating representative democracy' because voters had a broad political spectrum from which to choose and commonly recognised democratic principles were followed.[141] One needed to look at the brazen character assassination of opponents to understand just how much Kremlin media policy had changed. Working behind the scenes was a new prime minister, Putin, virtually unknown to most Russians. Yeltsin had publicly named him as his successor on 9 August, only four months before the elections. Some of the methods that were used to win showed Putin's hallmark – the same firm and ruthless decisiveness that he had already shown in dealing with Chechnya.

Whereas in 1996 there had been a frenetic contest on many levels, 1999 saw a wholly TV-dominated event, with negative coverage transmitted to potentially over 90 per cent of the population on ORT and RTR. The main offender was Berezovsky-managed ORT, which produced an unremitting stream of scurrilous and undocumented information against Luzhkov and Primakov through its 'killer-journalists' Sergey Dorenko and Mikhail Leontyev. Luzhkov, in particular, came in for ridicule every Sunday on Dorenko's programme. He was called 'the hypocrite', mocked for being short and fat, his face distorted by computer graphics to look like Mussolini or Monica Lewinsky. Reports made claims of his excessive wealth, his gigantic security service, his support for evil Scientologists, and his part in the murder of a US businessman. Sometimes Dorenko caught him out in a lie: yes, Luzhkov admitted, Moscow did not pay for the restoration of Budyonnovsk's hospital after the Chechen hostage-taking. Mostly, however, hard evidence was not produced and the information remained on an anecdotal and emotive level. Such was an interview with notorious racist Dmitry Vasilyev of Pamyat', who claimed he and Luzhkov held similar views, that Luzhkov would make a 'good Fuhrer' and that he agreed with his policy of ridding Moscow of people with 'non-Slavic origins'. That hit a sore spot, as Luzhkov had been criticised for not allowing Chechens to get residence permits in Moscow. These blows affected not only Luzhkov, but the sensibilities of viewers who were bludgeoned on a weekly basis and could only escape this personal vendetta by switching off the channel. But that was hard to do because Dorenko's shows were a sensation. The joke two weeks before the elections was that it was still two Dorenko programmes away.

The smear campaign against Primakov was not as unremitting, but it was extravagant, as in the accusation that he was incriminated in an attempted assassination of Georgian President Eduard Shevardnadze. Dorenko's attempt to show that Primakov was too old and feeble, at 70, to run as president after hip surgery, was bizarre. One such operation was shown in long and bloody detail on Dorenko's programme, doctors drilling into a bone with the same sensitivity of road workers drilling through asphalt, blood oozing, to show that no one could emerge from such a hip operation with the stamina to become president. Primakov was given the right of reply; Luzhkov chose to take Dorenko to court and won, but under the law the fine was so negligible it hardly worked as a deterrent. Dorenko was fined the equivalent of $2,000, not much for a man reputed to be earning a million dollars to do Berezovsky's bidding.

According to the EIM, ORT devoted more than one-quarter of its election news coverage to Unity (28 per cent), while Fatherland-All Russia received half that coverage (14 per cent).[142] But the impact of a one-hour Dorenko programme of negative propaganda was much more lethal than could be evaluated quantitatively. Dorenko's ratings throughout the electoral campaign far exceeded those of NTV's. According to a Romir survey, 33.9 per cent thought the most objective information came from Dorenko.

While all the television channels showed bias, not all participated in the smear campaign. As monitored by EIM, the Moscow channel TV Centre clearly promoted Luzhkov and Fatherland-All Russia and showed some bias against Unity, but its impact was not comparable with ORT as it reached only 40 per cent of the population. NTV with a reach of 73 per cent showed bias towards Fatherland-All Russia (31 per cent) compared with Unity (4 per cent), but argued it was only readjusting the balance in a skewered campaign. It ran the most successful election debates, but Unity candidates shunned them, preferring the safety of ORT. By comparison with its position in 1996, NTV was subdued, fearing the state's political and economic levers.

In this dirtiest of campaigns, the press ministry issued only three selectively chosen legal warnings. One against ORT's flagrant abuse of regulations; and two against Luzhkov's TV Centre. The second warning against TV Centre was risible: that the channel had not notified the ministry of a change of address; but as the law stated if a channel received more than one warning its licence could be revoked, the threat was serious. The Kremlin's mission to warn off rival contestants had achieved its goal. State media through the machinations of Berezovsky and Lesin had cleared the field of rivals to enable Putin to become president.

Notes

1   *Zapiski prezidenta*, Izdatel'stvo 'Ogonek', Moskva, 1994, p. 67.
2   BBC Monitoring Service, 24 April 2007. http://news.bbc.co.uk/1/hi/world/europe/6586695.stm (accessed 21 November 2015).
3   'Yeltsin's complicated legacy in the Caucasus', 19 February 2011. www.opendemocracy.net/od-russia/sergei-markedonov/yeltsin%E2%80%99s-complicated-legacy-in-caucasus (accessed 21 November 2015).
4   'Yeltsin – father of democracy?', *The Nation*, 27 April 2007. www.thenation.com/article/yeltsin-father-democracy/ (accessed 8 December 2015).
5   'On Yeltsin', 26 April 2007, JRL 103, 2007, no. 28.
6   Proshchal'naya rech' Borisa Yeltsina, *Echo Moskvy.* http://echo.msk.ru/blog/echomsk/1465886-echo/ (accessed 8 December 2015).
7   'Zerkalo', RTR, 4 February 2001.
8   *Epokha Yeltsina: Ocherki politicheskoi istorii*, ed. Yu.M. Baturin et al (a group of Yeltsin's top liberal advisers), Moskva Vagrius 2001, pp. 494–5.
9   This had been a controversial issue in international development circles since UNTAC (the UN Transitional Authority in Cambodia, which provided technical assistance in support of Cambodia's transition to democracy) recommended media liability in cases of defamation and hate speech in 1992. In 1999 the UN Special Rapporteur for Freedom of Expression reflected a growing rejection of this approach by issuing a guideline to exempt the media from liability so as to protect the public right to receive information. See Media and Elections: Legal Framework for Media and Elections, ACE, the Electoral Knowledge Network. http://aceproject.org/ace-en/topics/me/mea (accessed 25 August 2016).
10   Mikhail Poltoranina, *Vlast' v trotilovom ekvivalente: nasledie tsarya Borisa*, Moskva: Eksmo Algoritm, 2012, p. 351.
11   Baturin *et al., Epokha Yeltsina*, p. 494.
12   'Menya mozhno ubit' , glavnoe, chtob gazetu ne ubili ...' , 8 April 2014. http://www.sovsekretno.ru/articles/id/4067/ (accessed 21 November 2015).
13   RTR, 11 June 1992.
14   *Midnight Diaries*, London: Phoenix, 2000, p. 200.
15   Daniel Tilles, 'Commercially successful', *International Herald Tribune*, July 1994.

16   *Izvestiya*, 17 March 1992.
17   *Literaturnaya gazeta*, 15 July 1992.
18   Andrei G. Richter, 'The Russian press after *perestroika*', *Canadian Journal of Communication*, 20(1), 1995, pp. 7–23.
19   Ibid.
20   Ibid.
21   *Literaturnaya gazeta*, 25 November 1992, p. 10.
22   Andrei Zolotov Jr, 'Meddling publishers draw journalists' fire', *Moscow Times*, 4 March 1998.
23   The Brezhnev Constitution officially gave power to the Soviets (councils), but in reality power resided in the Central Committee of the Communist Party and not the Soviets. Since Brezhnev's death, the Constitution had been amended over 300 times.
24   *Nezavisimaya gazeta*, 4 July 1992.
25   Oleg Poptsov, *Trevozhnye sny tsarya Borisa*, Moskva: Algoritm, 2011, p. 38.
26   Ibid., p. 147.
27   *Post-Soviet Media Law and Policy Newsletter*, 1(1), 20 October 1993, p. 2.
28   Valery Vyzhutovich, 'Pod konvoem tsenzury', *Izvestiya*, 30 March 1993, p. 2.
29   *Post-Soviet Media Law and Policy Newsletter*.
30   Valery Vyzhutovich, 'R. Khasbulatov vozlagaet na pressu vinu za itogi referendum', *Izvestiya*, 28 April 1993. Yeltsin did not garner the necessary number of votes to claim a legal mandate for early parliamentary elections.
31   Vera Tolz and Julia Wishnevsky, 'The Russian Media and the Political Crisis in Moscow', *RFE/RL Research Report*, 2(40), 8 October 1993, p. 15.
32   *Moskovskie novosti*, 9 May 1993, p. 13.
33   The well-known *Rossiiskaya gazeta* was instituted in 1990 as the official paper of the USSR Supreme Soviet. After October 1993 it became the government's official paper and remains as such today.
34   *Zapiski prezidenta*, p. 361.
35   See A. Balashov, 'V Rossii poyavilis' zapretnye temy', *Kommersant*, 29 September 1993; Tolz and Wishnevsky, 'Russian Media and the Political Crisis in Moscow', p. 14.
36   Among the foreign journalists who died outside Ostankino was British freelance cameraman Rory Peck. He was posthumously awarded the Order for Personal Courage by Yeltsin. Peck's widow and friends set up the Rory Peck Trust in 1995, which today is the only organisation supporting freelance news gathers around the world. https://rorypecktrust.org/about (accessed 25 August 2016).
37   Leningrad station continued to broadcast, but it reaches only European Russia.
38   Zapiski prezidenta, p. 380.
39   Oleg Poptsov, *Khronika Vremen 'Tsarya Borisa', Rossiya. Kreml': 1991–1995*, Sovershenno Sekretno, 1995, p. 389.
40   Ibid., p. 394.
41   John Lloyd, *Rebirth of a Nation: An Anatomy of Russia*, London: Michel Joseph, 1998, p. 48.
42   30 October 1993.
43   'Po obe storony vitriny', *Literaturnaya gazeta*, 4 March 1992.
44   *Interfax*, 14 October 1993. The newspapers were *Den'*, *Narodnaya pravda*, *Russkoe delo*, *Russkoe voskresen'e*, *Russkie vedomosti*, *Russkii pul's*, *Russkii poryadok*, *Za Rus*, *Nash Marsh*, *Natsionalist, Russkoe slovo*, *Moskovskii traktir*, *Russii soyuz*, *K toporu*, *Gazeta dukhovnoi oppozitsii*. Some suspended papers, such as *Glasnost*, did not reregister.
45   Interfax, 20 October 1993.
46   *Izvestiya*, 2 December 1994.
47   *Nezavisimaya gazeta*, 16 October 1993.

48   Yeltsin chose a western-style bicameral parliamentary system with a lower house, the State Duma ('dumas' were councils used by tsars from the eighteenth century; and the name of the first four limited parliaments permitted by Tsar Nicholas II from 1906–17). The Duma of 450 seats was equally divided by majority district candidates and members of party lists. This system was changed before the 2007 election and was reintroduced for the 2016 election. An upper house called the Federation Council consisted of regional senators. Its make-up was changed by Putin in 2000.

49   For a fuller version of the 1993 elections, see Daphne Skillen, 'Media Coverage in the Elections', in Peter Lentini (ed.), *Elections and Political Order in Russia*, London and New York: Central European University Press, 1995.

50   European Institute for the Media, *The Russian Parliamentary Election: Monitoring of the Election Coverage in the Russian Mass Media: Final Report*, 1 February 1994, p. 32. Also in www.media-politics.com/EIM%20reports/12% 20Russia%2093.pdf (accessed 21 November 2015).

51   *Izvestiya*, 1 December 1993.

52   ITAR-TASS, 6 November 1993 as quoted in *Post-Soviet Media Law and Policy Newsletter*, 1(2), 17 November 1993, p. 5.

53   VTsIOM, *Monitoring*, no. 2, 1994 (March–April), p. 31; A. Olson and E. Petrenko, Parlamenskie vybory 12 dekabrya 1993 goda: sotsiologiya elektoral'nogo povedeniya, Moscow: Fond Obshchestvennoe mnenie, 1994.

54   *Izvestiya*, 2 December 1993.

55   *Obshchaya gazeta*, 22–28 April 1994.

56   '"Ostankino" vse na prodazhu', *Izvestiya*, 14 January 1994.

57   *Moscow Times*, 21 February 1995.

58   *Moscow Times*, 3 March 1995.

59   Paul Klebnikov's article 'Godfather of the Kremlin' in *Forbes*, 30 December 1996 analyses Berezovsky's part in the Listyev case and was the subject of a libel suit brought by Berezovsky in the UK. The English court ruled that the article's description of the Listyev case was tantamount to stating that Berezovsky was guilty of murder and that he was a gangland leader running a mafia-style operation. Forbes apologised and Berezovsky withdrew his suit. See also Klebnikov's book *Godfather of the Kremlin: Boris Berezovsky and the looting of Russia*, Harcourt, Inc. 2000. There are other versions of Listyev' murder and has said a number of times that those who killed Listyev head Ostankino today: 'Kollega Listyeva: Ubiits nuzhno iskat' v teletsentre', *Argumenty i fakty*, 26 October 2010, http:// www.spb.aif.ru/society/news/65901 (accessed 16 November 2015).

60   Yevgeny Yu. Dodolev, *Vlad Listyev: Pristrastnyi rekviem* , Zelenaya lampa, Moskva, 2012, pp. 44, 219; '"Ubivat" Vlada nikto ne khotel. No on meshal Badri Patarkatsishvili provodit' reform na "pervoi knopke"', 7 April 2012. http:// www.business-gazeta.ru/article/57436/ (accessed 21 November 2015).

61   Yevgeny Lekovich,'V interv'yu so mnoi Ernst nazval Lisovskogo ubiitsei Listyeva', *Slon*, 4 April 2013. http://slon.ru/fast/russia/evgeniy-levkovich-v-intervyu-so-m noy-ernst-nazval-lisovskogo-ubiytsey-listeva-927492.xhtml (accessed 21 November 2015).

62   Aleksandr Kondrashov, 'Deti kolbasy', *Literaturnaya gazeta*. www.lgz.ru/article/ 19237/ (accessed 21 November 2015).

63   Dodolev, *Vlad Listyev*, p. 106.

64   Yevgeny Dodelev interviews Vladimir Mukusev, '15-letie so dnya ubiistva Listyeva: "Vlad, vy rano ili pozdno perestrelyaete drug druga"', 1 March 2010, http://svpressa.ru/society/article/21833/ (accessed 21 November 2015).

65   Ibid.

66   'Trudnyi kharakter Vladimira Mukuseva', *Novaya gazeta*, 22 May 2006. http:// novayagazeta.spb.ru/articles/2699/ (accessed 21 November 2015).

67 Viktor Nogin and Gennady Kurinnogo, who were shot during the course of their journalistic duties during the Croatian war in September 1991.

68 MMM was headed by Sergei Mavrodi, who was Russia's fifth richest man at the time.

69 Frances Foster, 'The MMM Case: Implications for the Russian Media', *Post-Soviet Media Law and Policy Newsletter*, no. 10, 10 September 1994, p. 2.

70 Executive Igor Malashenko, editor Oleg Dobrodeev, newsreader Tatyana Mitkova, scriptwriter for *Puppets*, Viktor Shenderovich and many others.

71 Yeltsin set up the highbrow Kultura channel on 1 November 1997 after growing complaints that, unlike Soviet television which had subsidised educational and cultural programmes, Russian television was too commercial. Yeltsin halted plans to privatise Petersburg's fifth channel, which covered European Russia, to create Kultura as part of the state company VGTRK, which would be free of advertising. This commitment did not last long because of the government's lack of funds. The channel's idea of culture is traditional, mainly showing televised versions of opera and ballet, documentaries, interviews with artists, etc., and tends not to make innovative cultural programmes for a wide audience.

72 Klebnikov, *Godfather of the Kremlin*, appendix I, p. 328. This was a videotaped appeal by Berezovsky and Lesnevskaya to Yeltsin, who was away at the time of the murder of Listyev, to absolve Berezovsky of the crime and for Lesnevskaya to allege that the man behind the murder was Gusinsky. Klebnikov argues that it was unlikely to be Gusinsky.

73 *Izvestiya*, 17 March 1992.

74 Peter Klebnikov, A. G. Richter (ed), *Zhurnalistika i Voina: Osveshchenie rossiiskimi SMI voennykh deistvii v Chechne*, Moskva, 1995, p. 15.

75 Ibid., p. 9.

76 *Izvestiya*, 17 February 1995.

77 'Samaya televizionnaya familiya', *Ogonek*, no. 19, May 1996. Poptsov was removed by Yeltsin in February 1996 despite protests from RTR staff. He later headed the Moscow channel TVTs from 2000–2005.

78 European Institute for the Media, *Russia 1996 (Presidential)*, p. 75. www.media-politics.com/EIM%20reports/Russia%201996.pdf (accessed 21 November 2015).

79 *Midnight Diaries*, p. 20. The seven bankers were Boris Berezovsky, Vladimir Gusinsky, Aleksandr Smolensky, Vladimir Potanin, Mikhail Khodorkovsky, Mikhail Fridman and Vladimir Vinogradov.

80 Irina Petrovskaya, 'Predvybornaya lovushka dlya TV', *Izvestiya*, 19 April 1996.

81 *Izvestiya*, 5 July 1996.

82 *Izvestiya*, 3 April 1996.

83 *Komsomolskaya pravda*, 15 May 1996.

84 European Institute for the Media, *Russia 1996*, p. 35.

85 *Geroi dnya*, NTV, 11 June 1996. Nikolai Savidze was RTR's main political presenter.

86 *Itogi*, NTV, 9 June 1996.

87 'O chem Prezident sovetuetsya s "vnesistemshchikami"', 21 February 2012 RADIO FINAM FM 99. https://www.youtube.com/watch?v=9aLCsg-aobc (accessed 21 November 2015).

88 Baturin et al., *Epokha Yeltsina*, p. 572.

89 15 November 1996. The transcript of the tape, leaked to Aleksandr Khinshtein presumably by the FSB with whom he was known to have close ties, shows the casual and cynical way Chubais and his team went about manipulating the public. Khinshtein also reveals that the FSB had gathered a fairly large amount of *kompromat* against former St Petersburg mayor Sobchak, which Korzhakov had been trying to get into the press without success, as it had been blocked by

Chubais and the election team, knowing that a blow against Sobchak, seen as a popular democrat, would tarnish Yeltsin as well.

90 'The big lie: alive and well', *Moscow Times*, 13 November 1999.
91 Klebnikov, *Godfather of the Kremlin*, p. 220. His information comes from interviews he took with Colonel Streletsky, head of the anti-corruption department of Korzhakov's Presidential Security Service, who put the amount at £1 billion; and the Washington-based Center for Strategic and International Studies that put it at $2 billion.
92 Marshall Goldman, *Oilopoly: Putin, Power and the Rise of the New Russia*, London: Oneworld, 2008, p. 64.
93 *Financial Times*, 1 November 1996, quoted in Andrei Piontkovsky, 'Modern-day Rasputin', *Moscow Times*, 12 November 1997.
94 'Reyting iz karmana nalogoplatel'shchika', *Pravda* 5, 14–21 June 1996.
95 *Midnight Diaries*, pp. 36–8.
96 European Institute for the Media, *Russia 1996*, p. 31.
97 Ibid., p. 74.
98 Ibid., p. 75.
99 'Glas Naroda', NTV, 1 February 2000.
100 Natalya Rostova, 'Ne schitayu, chto zhurnalistika nepremenno dolzhna byt' obektivnoi', *Slon.ru* 13 November 2009. http://www.74rif.ru/Kiselev.html (accessed 22 November 2015).
101 *Moscow Times*, 29 May 1998.
102 Dozhd' TV, 19 August 2015, also at: https://slon.ru/posts/55302 (accessed 22 November 2015).
103 *BBC Russkaya sluzhba*, 28 February 2012. www.bbc.co.uk/russian/russia/2012/02/120227_berezovsky_facebook_letter.shtml?print=1 (accessed 22 November 2015).
104 *Ekho Moskvy*, 2 April 2013. www.echo.msk.ru/blog/shenderovich/1044108-echo (accessed 22 November 2015).
105 *Ekho Moskvy*, 1 April 2013. www.echo.msk.ru/blog/pozner/1043926-echo (accessed 22 November 2015).
106 Anna Kachkaeva, 'ORT nachinaet ... i vyigryvaet?' *Zakonodatel'stvo i Praktika Sredst Massovoi Informatsii*, issue 5 (9), May 1995, p. 2.
107 Andrei Zolotov, 'Newspaper stake sale approved', *Moscow Tines*, 23 March 1997.
108 *Moscow Times*, 19 October 1996.
109 The other authors were privatisation chiefs Alfred Kokh, Pyotr Mostovoi, Maksim Boiko and Aleksandr Kazakov.
110 Dozhd' TV, 19 August 2015; also see Slon.ru https://slon.ru/posts/55302 (accessed 22 November 2015).
111 Sobchak i Sokolova s Alfredom Kokhom: 'Vlast' – neeffektivnaya trata zhizni' #03 (56) March 2013. http://www.snob.ru/magazine/entry/58102 (accessed 22 November 2015).
112 Jonas Bernstein, 'Bank scandal gets murkier', *Moscow Times*, 18 July 1997
113 Research conducted by Floriana Fossato and Anna Kachkaeva in RFE/RL, Rossiiskie Informatsionnye Imperii. http://archive.svoboda.org/archive/dossier/rumedia6/(accessed 22 November 2015).
114 *Russian Journal*, 31 March–6 April 2001.
115 3 and 9 April; 26 April; 28 February; 24 April 1996, respectively.
116 Sergei Agafonov, 'Skhema upravdoma, ili o tom, kak v Rossii vozrahdaetsya politicheskaya tsenzura', *Izvestiya*, 15 April 1999; 'Biznes I pressa', 17 April 1997.
117 Anna Golembiovskaya, *Nashe 'krugosvetnoe puteshestvie' s Igorem*, Khudozhstvennaya literatura, Moskva, 2011, p. 171.
118 Ibid., p. 179.
119 *Vremya*, ORT, 26 April 1996, 21.00.

120 Adam Jones, *Izvestia: A Case Study.* http://adamjones.freeservers.com/russia2. htm#N_126_ (accessed 22 November 2015).
121 20 February 2003.
122 '"Russkii kur'er" soshel distantsii', *Kommersant*, 1 April 2005.
123 Vladimir Pribylovsky 'Novye Izvestiya dead. who's next?' *The Moscow Times*, 28 February 2003.
124 Andrei Zolotov Jr, 'Critics say muckraker has dirty hands', *Moscow Times*, 18 November 1997.
125 'Year's longest assassination', *Moscow Times*, 6 January 1998.
126 Andrei Zolotov Jr. 'Meddling publishers draw journalists' fire', *Moscow Times*, 4 March 1998.
127 *Izvestiya*, 22 November 1997.
128 I am quoting from the full Russian text which was handed out, some of which was reported in Andrei Zolotov Jr, 'Yeltsin lashes out at media tycoons', *Moscow Times*, 26 May 1998.
129 Irina Petrovskaya, 'Ne strelyaite v perevodchika', *Izvestiya*, 30 May 1998.
130 'State merits low TV rating', *Moscow Times*, 19 June 1998.
131 'Govorit i pokazyvaet Tsentral'noe televidenie', *Izvestiya*, 23 May 1998.
132 Svetlana Smetannaya, 'Ved' ni odno SMI u nas eshche ne zagubleno', *Kommersant*, 22 July 1999.
133 23 July 1999.
134 Bulat Stolyarov, 'Kremlevskii retranslyator: Lesin syadet na svobodu slova', 12–18 July 1999.
135 Allen C. Lynch, *Vladimir Putin and Russian Statecraft*, Washington, DC: Potomac Books, 2011, p. 49.
136 Yu. I. Skuratov, *Variant drakona*, Moskva: Detektiv-Press, 2000, p. 147.
137 Yu. I. Skuratov interviewed on *Hard Day's Night*, TV Dozhd, 31 July 2013.
138 'Moya istoriya s NTV', Ekho Moksvy, 14 April 2011. www.echo.msk.ru/blog/ umasheva/766188-echo; 'Yevgeny Kiselyov rasskazal to, o chem umolchala Yumasheva v istorii o gazpromizatsii NTV', Forum Moskvy, 15 April 2011. http://forum-msk.org/material/news/6056927.html (accessed 22 November 2015).
139 *Moscow Times*, 24 July 1999, p. 3.
140 Alfred Kokh and Igor Svinarenko, *A Crate of Vodka*, New York: Enigma Books, 2009, p. 397.
141 OSCE (ODIHR), 'Elections to the State Duma 19 December 1999. Final Report', p. 1. www.osce.org/odihr/elections/russia/16293 (accessed 22 November 2015).
142 European Institute for the Media, *Monitoring of Media Coverage during the Parliamentary Elections in the Russian Federation in December 1999, Final Report*, p. 2. http://www.media-politics.com/EIM%20reports/Rus%2099%20Fina l.pdf (accessed 22 November 2015).

8 The Putin regime: patrimonial media

Journalistic freedom has turned into a tasty morsel for politicians ...
(Putin, 8 July 2000)

I The Putin Project

The success of the Putin Project was predicated on controlling the media. The question of 'Who is Mr Putin?' was genuinely perplexing, since he was brought into the limelight only when Yeltsin announced him as his successor, which was no more than seven months before he became president. The public knew less about Putin's pre-history than about any other leader, including Chernenko. The project went with the potentially dangerous reversal of policy from Yeltsin's free and open society, supposed to be in transition to a western liberal democracy, to an unclear system that was packaged as authoritarian democracy. In time, this hybrid became steadily more regressive as it moved from soft to harder authoritarianism and its sham democracy changed titles from 'managed' to 'sovereign' to 'majority' democracy. Initially, however, Putin was no more than a transitional figure. The point of the 'project' was to turn him into an unbeatable presidential candidate.

The rebuilt Kremlin media machine was put into motion to secure a smooth succession and retain the entrenched privileges of oligarchic capitalism. The top-down action, as the state sought once again to impose its project on an unwitting society, flouted the Yeltsin ethos where obstructive state power had been restrained. The Kremlin project would still use the ballot box but, whereas in 1996 Yeltsin felt it his duty to energetically campaign for office and dance for his supper, despite his heart condition, the young judo-master Putin would be given a dignified passage to power through the newly refined arts of image-making. The project required delicate handling and the professional expertise of the so-called 'political technologists'.

The concept of 'political technology' has a drama to it absent in the West. We talk of public relations and media consultancy without any sense of the magical frisson Russians attribute to the art of persuasion, which they tend to apply according to Machiavelli's *tractatus* on power. Nor do they seem to see anything unethical in his realpolitik. One of the first PR companies in Russia proudly called itself 'Niccolo M'. According to Putin's initial spin doctor, Gleb Pavlovsky, Putin would be promoted by virtue of the politics of 'non-political power' – 'power without representation or the consideration of the interests of those being governed'.[1] The idea was to distance the leader from those to whom power is delegated on the tsar–boyar model, where peasants rebelled against the boyars while the tsar remained sacrosanct (*tsar' khochet, boyare ne dayut*). For the leader to maintain this aura, Pavlovsky applied his 'no alternative' strategy. He had been one of the bright young things Mala-shenko had brought into the team during Yeltsin's 1996 re-election campaign, and it was there that he learned the value of stirring up 'mythological fears' about the communists – fear of hunger, civil war, instability – so that people could be manipulated into thinking there was no alternative to Yeltsin.

Pavlovsky's strategy for the Putin regime was not to trample openly on freedoms, but to find more sophisticated ways of subjugating society to the state. In this way the myth of democracy could be retained, while changing the thrust of Yeltsin's liberal policies. In his 1996 'scenarios and technologies', Pavlovsky began to develop his art of persuasion influenced by the obscure language of French philosophy and postmodernism, hugely fashionable with the educated urban elite. Propaganda methods which 'fetishise' television no longer work, he said. The idea of 'information dramaturgy' was a more effective way of influencing the consciousness of the masses by transforming events into 'interesting and accessible plots (anecdote, scenario, myth – all these being aspects of socio-political dramaturgy)':

> The aim of propaganda and counter-propaganda is to create a window of inculcation on the level of the Real Socialising of the Mass Person, on the level of mass communications. The struggle to win is not determined by the administrative control of the media, but by dominating the grass roots level of mass communications – if you like, on the level of 'family chatter' and 'folk gossip'.[2]

Although in the 1996 elections Pavlovsky's ideas were one among many in the pot, the playacting and simulated reality of dramaturgy was central to the Putin project. One strand was to dissociate Putin from the dirt of politics. If we look at the regime's policy statements, most of them have been articulated not by Putin but by those representing him: managed and majority democracy by Sergei Markov, sovereign democracy by Vladislav Surkov. This distancing continues to this day where Putin removes himself from decisions and from blame. It was not his plan to free Khodorkovsky as a PR gesture before the Sochi Olympics, but the amnesty committee's; it was not he who enforced the annexation of Crimea but the will of the people expressed in their referendum. When the NTV group went to see Putin to ask him to intervene in saving the channel, his reply that he could not interfere in the work of an independent body such as the Prosecutor-General made satirist Viktor

Shenderovich snort: 'Ah – and I didn't know!'. There was a contradiction, of course, in the script between distancing Putin from political actions and ascribing to him the role of sole leader, without an alternative. It was the latter script that proved more successful, most of the domestic and foreign press assuming that nothing happened in the country without Putin's blessing.

In his role of figurehead, as part of the cult of personality his PR office had orchestrated, Putin has appeared in many carefully crafted personae. In one of the earliest, just after he had been elected president, he stands in braided navy cap and greatcoat looking out steely-eyed into the Barents Sea from the bridge of the nuclear submarine Karelia – master at the helm. In varying forms of dress and undress, he has featured as a superhero and a sex symbol: in judo poses, bare-chested riding a horse, fishing and swimming in Siberia, stroking (semi-drugged) Amur tigers and in a strange bird-like contraption taking the lead to head migrating cranes in the right direction. After a while the scripts flagged and when it turned out that the two fragments of ancient Greek pottery he was supposed to have found in the Black Sea had been a stunt, it didn't really matter. His spokesman, Dmitry Peskov, complained: 'Of course, they were left there or placed there. It's completely normal. There's no reason to gloat about it'.[3] Machismo and youth were important to the Putin image, so when he approached 60, there was nothing much his PR men could do when YouTube went viral with stories of probable cosmetic surgery and Botox treatment to explain the disconcerting puffiness around his eyes and cheeks. The weariness with the Putin image after a decade was revived only by the Crimean 'victory'.

Pavlovsky's 'no-alternative' strategy went to work as soon as Putin was named Yeltsin's heir. The war in Chechnya provided the first opportunity to show that there was no alternative to Putin as the strongman who had the situation in hand. He was tough (*krutoy*) and his liberal use of criminal slang (*blatnoy yazyk*) confirmed it. The unprecedentedly dirty campaign in the 1999 parliamentary elections ensured there would be no political alternative to Putin and the Unity party. Pavlovsky explains: 'To convince the voters of something that seems to contradict their natural, most personal interests, you have to present it as an expression of power to which there is no alternative'. The real forces, he said, should not be transparent, because 'technological power does everything that needs to be done but doesn't tell you what it's doing'.[4]

Pavlovsky is unfazed about revealing Machiavellian intentions; cynicism is so ingrained in the political system that the idea of fair play hardly enters into the picture. An ambitious journalist and intellectual, Pavlovsky has had a chequered career: as a dissident exiled to the Komi Republic, after he had informed on colleagues to escape being sentenced to a labour camp; as an editor of numerous journals, initiator of intellectual discussion clubs, founder of the news agency Postfactum; and in the 2000s founder of some of the first news websites in the country through his think tank, the Foundation for Effective Policy. He has had no qualms in discussing the deceptive underpinning of political technology and the way it has permeated the regime's scripted reality. In this model, the façade of democracy is retained, but the props are hollow. Attempts are made to reconcile what is irreconcilable in concepts such as 'managed democracy' and 'dictatorship of the law'. Elections are held without undue rigging by rejigging electoral procedure beforehand, loyal opposition parties joust in fake contests, and parliament has returned to a rubber-stamp body, resembling the Supreme Soviet. A manipulated world where words and institutions are drained of their real meaning required a large public relations staff settled in the presidential administration and a chief ideologue to hold the framework together.

This was the role of Vladislav Surkov, the Kremlin's grey cardinal and an ideologue as important to Putin as Mikhail Suslov was to Brezhnev. Surkov has helped to design the spirit of the times: cynical, wealthy, manipulative. A half-Chechen who concealed his roots, he is described as hip, a conceptual artist who writes lyrics for rock bands and at the same time initiates huge pro-Putin rallies of the youth league Nashi with their skinhead mentality and the burning of books. Surkov has apparently written a novel about a corrupt PR consultant prepared to sell his soul for money, but he denies it, although it is written in his wife's name, and the whole of Moscow's elite gathered to see its stage adaptation.[5] Playing games was part of the political technologists' world, a self-referential hall of mirrors where truth gets distorted. Richard Sakwa writes: 'Surkov's philosophy from the first was that there is no real freedom in the world, and that all democracies are managed democracies, so the key to success is to influence people, to give them the illusion that they are free whereas in fact they are managed'.[6] Surkov stated: 'freedom is when you have (a car) to ride and things to buy'.[7]

The oxymoronic 'managed' democracy

What was 'managed' democracy? Sergei Markov, one of Putin's early propagandists, argued that post-communist Russia would be best served by 'interweaving' its well-established authoritarian traditions with democratic institutions, providing the conditions for 'Putin's regime of personal power'.[8] This power, he said, would be modelled more on de Gaulle than on Russia's own Byzantine emperors or the Latin American dictators (the Pinochet model was particularly popular). Its economics would be dirigism; its ideology – nationalism; its patriotic rhetoric a reminder that Russia would not bow down to the West. Managed democracy would ensure a stable pro-government majority in both houses of parliament, and put an end to the direct elections of unruly governors. In effect, democracy would lose its main advantage, the possibility of kicking out those in power, because it would be prevented from doing so by those managing it. 'Managed democracy' was therefore a nonsense, an oxymoron that fitted in the postmodernist arsenal of wordplay. It was not a new term – 'guided' or 'managed' democracy had been instituted by Sukarno in Indonesia in 1957, with the same goal of emasculating representative government. The policies announced by Markov were all implemented in due course, which has restricted democracy's ability to free itself from its managers in the future.

What part did 'managed' democracy allot to freedom? Markov and the officials and journalists who lined up behind Putin repeated in chorus that freedom had never existed under Yeltsin; that it was all anarchy and disorder. The aim, therefore, was to protect the weak against unlimited freedom by applying Putin's slogan of 'dictatorship of the law', another unhelpful oxymoron. By fudging liberty with licence, Markov was able to play to the Russian public's widely-held belief of freedom as the carrier of violent, profligate behaviour. Nor was Markov coy about how the media would be subdued: 'there will be firm control over the mainstream media through financial–political control of its owners and through administrative–economic control of media owners over their journalists'. Markov does not flinch from calling this type of democracy 'manipulative' democracy and sees nothing unfair in using manipulation as a tool to hoodwink society because, as he argues, it keeps politics within the electoral system and does not resort to police methods.

The plan then was to enforce regime change under Putin, base it on imperialist principles of statism and nationalism, remove the political freedoms society was beginning to enjoy, and implement this radical change without coercion or bloodshed. Political technologists were vital to this scenario by becoming the army that replaced a bloody Pinochet style takeover. Instead of violence, there would be hard-core manipulation.

Initially Putin was not in control of the project to make him a leader, nor did he have his own team. According to Pavlovsky, his team looked more like 'raisins in a biscuit' embedded in Yeltsin's 'family'. If Yeltsin had thought Putin would preserve his legacy, he made a fateful mistake. The 1998 August default had caught Yeltsin off guard and he looked to a strong man to hold the country together; moreover, he had always put greater trust in military men. Yeltsin's liberal aide Georgy Satarov says he stopped considering civilians such as Nemtsov and Kiriyenko. 'Putin was a chronological accident, the last in the chain', he told me. The choice of candidates was also obviously limited by the 'family', even if Yeltsin made the final decision. When Yeltsin resigned, it was the first time a Russian leader had given up power voluntarily, but there was nothing democratic about his 'tsarist gesture' in naming an heir, or what another newspaper mocked as 'hereditary democracy'.

For a person who had not harboured presidential ambitions, Putin was a lucky man. Everything fell into his lap. Yeltsin had transferred power to him, he had the 'family's' Kremlin administration at his disposal, political technologists were working out his ideological messages, state television was pushing him forward in the public eye, and numerous state journalists were complicit in the scheme. His early policies largely followed those set out by Yeltsin, but he managed to push them through more successfully because the nationalist majority in parliament was eager to support him. What is seen as

Putin's trademark of bringing order and stability to society originated in Yeltsin's state of the nation address of 6 March 1997 on 'Order in power, Order in the country'. Aware of the uses to which a law and order policy could be put, Yeltsin's message spelled out that 'dictatorship and suppression do not lie at the basis of establishing order, but rather a communality of aims, reason and accord, the energy of reconciliation and construction'.[9] Putin's hardline version settled for a 'dictatorship of the law'. 'In a weak state a person is helpless and unfree', he writes. 'The stronger the state, the stronger is personal freedom'.[10]

The fact that Putin came to power as the price of oil took off was remarkably fortunate for him as well. Such an economic advantage would have transformed opportunities for Gorbachev and Yeltsin in building their freer visions of society. In April 1986 when the Chernobyl nuclear reactor exploded and Gorbachev was dealing with the consequences of an almost bankrupt state, the price of oil was $10 per barrel. Throughout the 1990s it hovered between $14 and $19 per barrel while Yeltsin was struggling to pay wages and pensions and repay the Soviet Union's foreign debt. A month before Yeltsin retired, in November 1999, the price of oil took off to $25 per barrel. On Putin's watch it rose steadily to an average of $33 in 2003, $63 in 2006, skyrocketing to an all-time high of $143 in July 2008. Since then, the global financial crisis of 2008–9 has seen oil prices falling, which has serious repercussions for a regime that did not use the oil boom years enough to build the country's infrastructure or substantially raise the wages of lower-income groups living in neglected towns and villages.

While oil prices soared, it was not difficult to raise people's living standards, increase salaries and pensions and restore confidence in a society that had suffered economic turmoil. From 2000 to 2008 annual economic growth in real terms averaged 7 per cent, annual real wages rose by almost 15 per cent and the federal budget was continually in surplus. Thanks to media propaganda, people believed their prosperity was due to Putin's leadership. He had put things in order, showed the oligarchs their place, and presided over a booming economy. With television on his side, there was no one to say that he had established order at the expense of freedom, that he had kicked out troublesome oligarchs but installed his own cronies and those who did not meddle in politics, who continued to plunder society. In 2014, according to Credit Suisse, 110 billionaires owned nearly one-third of Russia's wealth. Putin himself is rumoured to be worth $40 billion, while the annual cost of bribery, as estimated by Transparency International is $300 billion, equivalent to the size of Denmark's gross domestic product.[11]

As Machiavelli said, *fortuna* is not enough to make a leader. Putin quickly showed he would not be an obedient tool of the 'family'. He had a strong personality, he was a clever tactician and he held firm views developed during his KGB days. He was quick to position his own people in government, mainly those from St Petersburg and the *siloviki* groups (those connected with security, the police and the military). By 2007, according to sociologist Olga

Kryshtanovskaya, one-quarter of the country's senior bureaucrats were *silo-viki*; the proportion rising to three-quarters if people affiliated to the security services were included.[12] The system of government that developed was a network of shifting alliances operating behind the scenes with Putin as the main arbiter. Vladimir Pribylovsky has described the system succinctly: 'In Russia, official political parties (i.e. those registered with the Ministry of Justice) play a subordinate role to these administrative/economic groupings. It is the clans and patron–client networks, which lack any official or judicial status, that are the real players in the country's political life'.[13] This network of informal associations is kept together not by laws but by the old system of 'rules of the game', now expressed in mafia language as 'having an understanding' (*po ponyatiyam*). To stay in power, Putin needs to negotiate a delicate balance between these groups.

The 'illusions of the masses', said top independent pollster Lev Gudkov of the Levada Centre, were maintained by the belief that Putin's regime would preserve high standards of living and by the fact that no alternative rivals were permitted on the stage.[14] Putin's consistently high ratings of 70–80 per cent were more a response to him personally than to individual policies. When figures were broken down, such as with regard to his policy in Chechnya, his popularity tended to fall to between 30 to 35 per cent. An obedient mainstream media covered up the ugly picture of greed, conflict and corruption, focusing on the pleasures of a prospering, enriched society as seen not only in its mainstream television news but through the plethora of tabloids, celebrity gossip magazines and 'glossies' covering beauty, fashion and lifestyle, all of which grew rapidly with the economic upswing, encapsulated in the adopted word, *glamur*.

An indication of Putin's beliefs came in his Millennium Message while he was still prime minister. In it he revived the old chestnut of the 'Russian national idea',[15] the ultra-conservative values that were the mainstay of autocratic tsarist Russia. They were, he said, statism, patriotism and Russian greatness (*derzhavnost'*).[16] There had been no widespread urge for these values during the democratic transition and when several intellectual groups approached Yeltsin to suggest a reworking of the 'national idea' he was surprised, but asked his advisers to cobble something together. He was against the tsarist term 'national idea' and suggested calling the project 'An Idea for Russia'. His liberal advisers could not see its relevance to democracy and modernity either; moreover, the acceptance of any one state ideology, as the Communist Party had, was now prohibited by the Constitution. Nevertheless, his advisers set to work organising public discussions and distributing a series of public service announcements on television about honesty and cooperation, and that was the end of it. In a document handed to Yeltsin, one young adviser suggested two ideas for Russia: don't piss in the street and paint your fence.[17] Good advice, which meant make your life pleasant and comfortable and don't prevent others from doing the same. The Yeltsin ethos had no belief in 'exceptionalism' or messianic 'missions' that have been reanimated under Putin.

If democracy was too multifaceted to contain a national idea, Putin's narrow vision, borrowed from Russian autocracy, was popular. Not only the masses, but the professional classes, journalists and people in public life, who could have been taken for democrats of sorts or at least people with not entirely definable but not jingoistic views, seemed to be genuinely enthralled by the Putin rhetoric of greatness and statehood. At the best of times Russia is a hyperactive, nervous society, but there was more than the usual hysteria in the air when Putin took up the presidency, a thrill at the idea of enthronement. Because so little was known about Putin, people could fantasise and imagine him to be whatever they wanted. And what they wanted was the opposite of Yeltsin. People saw democracy as having failed, not that it had only just begun.

Still, enough was known about Putin to wonder about the uncritical response to this middle-ranking KGB operative espousing authoritarian views smattered with democratic phrases. Was it an indication of the level of conservatism in Russian society and its elite to embrace him so wholeheartedly, and what did western leaders and analysts have in mind when they greeted him so readily as a partner and ally? Tony Blair was the first foreign leader to rush to St Petersburg before the elections and give Putin's candidacy a boost. In due course, George W. Bush looked into his eyes and 'saw his soul'. He called him 'PootyPoo'. The belief in Putin as an ally in the war on terror and an advocate of free market economics was undoubtedly more important to western leaders than any adherence to democratic principles, the West having profited considerably (no questions asked) from Russia's oil and mineral assets and the capital flight into western financial structures. The Russian public came to see moral preaching about democracy as no more than 'double standards'.

It is not with surprise that we should look at Putin's extreme authoritarianism today; there was enough evidence in 1999. Almost the first piece of public information about him was when he returned the Andropov plaque to the walls of the Lubyanka, where it had been ripped off during the freedom celebrations after the 1991 coup. In 1999 he was probably the first person in five decades to propose a toast to Stalin in the Kremlin at a military graduation ceremony on Victory Day. Both acts were as audacious as his sayings of killing Chechens in outside toilets or calling them 'animals' and oppositionists 'traitors'. There were hardly any signs that he espoused liberal values. Many people thought he was charming; his critics said he had been trained to be charming as a KGB recruitment officer. In personal attitudes he was old-fashioned, macho and sexist, but traditional values are widely accepted in Russian society. He showed little imagination about the global modern world, dredging up values from the past that would later make up Russia's 'national idea'.

Allegations of corruption when he was mayor Sobchak's deputy in Petersburg were never properly investigated, although he was in charge of the lucrative domain of privatisation of property. One accusation against him of rigging contracts in an import–export kickback scheme for food supplies worth $92 million was exposed by prominent democrat Marina Salye, a member of the City Soviet. Sobchak declined to sack Putin and said the accusations were groundless. Petersburg newspapers had reported the investigation at the time, but Salye felt that voters should be reminded before the elections, especially as she was horrified that most of her liberal colleagues were intent on voting for Putin. She was only able to get her article 'Putin Is "President" of a Corrupt Oligarchy' published online.[18] The *Moscow Times* also reported the previous allegations, but no Russian-language national outlet touched the story.[19] Some months later Salye was 'warned', and she vanished from political life into a remote village in the Pskov region, coming out only before she died to repeat her tale.[20]

In April 2000 academic Michael McFaul, later to become US Ambassador to Moscow (2012–14), during the heat of anti-Americanism, argued that despite ominous signs it would be wrong to conclude that Putin was an anti-democrat: 'The Russian president is simply too modern and too Western-oriented to believe in dictatorship. Rather, Putin is indifferent to democratic principles and practices, believing perhaps that Russia might have to sacrifice democracy in the short run to achieve "more important" economic and state-building goals'.[21] By 2003 McFaul and a co-author conceded: 'the evidence of an erosion of democracy … under Putin is now overwhelming'.[22] Obviously, the political technologists' spin was persuasive with the West as well, at least for a while. Yelena Bonner brushed aside the dithering, bluntly announcing in 2000 the birth of a new Stalinism. Diplomat-hero of the 1991 coup, Boris Pankin, sussed Putin out fairly accurately: 'He has known what he wants right from the start – Soviet power without communists'.[23]

Presidential elections, 26 March 2000

A word blurted out indiscreetly by Putin's campaign officials summed up the presidential elections – 'asymmetric'. Angered by allegations from the opposition media, especially Gusinsky's newspaper *Segodnya*, that they had violated procedure, the Putin team sent a letter to the media on 4 March 2000 saying they reserved 'the right to use all means in our arsenal to implement an asymmetric response to acts of provocation'. The sentence was quickly withdrawn, but there it was – 'an asymmetric response' – an open threat to the media. In fact, the Kremlin had already been using asymmetric methods to destroy the level playing field and crush alternative choices.

The mudslinging of the earlier 1999 parliamentary election had cleared the field of opponents. Putin declined to make use of his free broadcasting time and showed his ignorance of the democratic process by saying he would not sell himself 'like Tampax or Snickers'. (Why Tampax? remonstrated Yelena Tregubova later: 'for every post-Soviet woman, that is the main (if not the only) democratic achievement that's been experienced'.)[24] When a reporter asked Putin to outline his policies, he replied: 'I won't tell you'. Although Putin did not say much, he was rarely off the screen in his capacity as acting president, travelling extensively around the country and behaving as if he had already won the race. The EU Tacis monitoring report called it a 'virtual' election, an early hint of what came to be known as Putin's 'virtual' or 'imitation' democracy.[25]

When Putin's image was seen to be too tough, ORT called in killer-journalist Mikhail Leontyev to interview him at home in the presence of his fluffy white poodle. The only serious television interview he gave was not to his own people but to David Frost for the BBC on relations with Nato, although the Russian press complained it could not make out which way he was leaning. He offered no electoral manifesto, but his views could be gleaned from his Millennium Message, an open letter to the press and an interview he gave to three Moscow journalists, published first in *Kommersant* on 10 March under the title Iron Putin, and a week later in book form as *First Person: Conversations with Vladimir Putin.*

By comparison with the money spent on Yeltsin's 1996 re-election, campaign financing was low: Putin's at $10 million and Yavlinsky's at about $15 million. However, the journalist Yuliya Latynina showed how the picture changed if 'administrative resources' that were used to promote Putin were taken into account. She calculated: 'out of the $170 billion gross domestic product, six to seven percent has been spent on elections in various ways – with state companies changing directors; with private companies changing owners; with loans given to the "right" governors; and with taxes forgiven to the "right" corporations'.[26]

According to the European Institute of the Media (EIM), Putin received almost one-third of all coverage in the national media. On TV news, he received close to 50 per cent of the total time. He even received the greater amount of coverage in the communists' *Pravda* (1 per cent more than their own candidate, Zyuganov), confirming that pro-Putin forces had made a deal with the Communist Party. The main democratic candidate, Yavlinsky, received the most negative coverage (41 minutes), but Putin received his share (29 minutes).

Given that the election had been clinched before it started, media coverage was not particularly hostile, except in the case of ORT. With Berezovsky zealously promoting Putin from behind the scenes, ORT not only gave far more hours to Putin (30 per cent, as compared to the next candidate, Yavlinsky, at 12 per cent), but conducted a vicious campaign against Yavlinsky.[27] ORT claimed that Yavlinsky had accepted huge donations from foreign sources, such as George Soros; accused him of exceeding the legal limits on campaign spending; alleged he had undergone cosmetic surgery to improve his appearance and, in a staged event, showed a group of gays announcing their support for him at a press conference – hardly positive publicity in a homophobic society. By constantly linking Yavlinsky to Gusinsky's media, ORT gave the false impression that NTV was biased in Yavlinsky's favour. In fact, NTV gave more coverage to Putin (29 per cent) than to Yavlinsky (14 per cent), and its coverage was more positive than negative. For Yavlinsky, however, the little positive coverage he received came from NTV.

NTV was playing safe, though giving opposition candidates a voice. It was in an unenviable position. NTV had earlier asserted its right to promote whatever candidate it wanted, mainly with Yavlinsky in mind, but it was uncertain how far it could step out of line. It had backed the wrong horse in the parliamentary elections and was taking a critical stance on the second Chechen war. It now faced the wrath of the Kremlin, which was putting pressure on it financially. Press Minister Lesin also held a Damocles' sword over ORT and Moscow's TV Centre, announcing a month before the elections that their licences would be up for tender. TV Centre, under its new general director Oleg Poptsov, was fairly even-handed in its coverage, but Luzhkov had already succumbed to the Putin camp. More surprising was the threat to ORT. As Berezovsky was using his influence and money to orchestrate Putin's rise to power, this could only be a warning that he would no longer be top dog on the channel. When ORT received its licence the following year, Berezovsky was no longer in charge.

There had been a great deal of reshuffling of top posts and poaching of journalists from commercial channels before the elections. Most sensational was state RTR's new boss, Oleg Dobrodeyev, whom many considered a TV guru. He had shocked the industry by resigning from NTV, where he and Yevgeny Kiselyov had been the creative duo. Some accused Dobrodeyev of abandoning a sinking ship, but he had been at loggerheads with his colleagues for a long time over the channel's criticism of the Chechen war. Earlier, during the Kosovo conflict, like most Russian nationalists, he had firmly supported their brother Slavs in Serbia and chaffed at Gusinsky's neutrality in the conflict. As soon as Dobrodeyev resigned from NTV to go 'nowhere', as he said, he was snapped up by Putin. Dobrodeyev became the head of RTR and the whole VGTRK state complex. He has remained in the post ever since, for 16 years so far. ORT's Konstantin Ernst, who was appointed head of ORT before the elections, has remained in post for the same period of time. It used to be a joke in Soviet times that one man had headed Gosteleradio for as long as 14 years, until finally removed by Gorbachev. The pro-Putin broadcasters, who showed their worth in promoting the new authoritarian politics in this first Putin election, have outdone even what was considered the 'stagnation' of the Brezhnev period.

Putin won 52.9 per cent of the vote. A serious piece of investigative journalism published six months later in the English-language *Moscow Times* turned up evidence to show that 2.2 million stolen or falsified votes in regions with questionable electoral reputations, such as Dagestan and Tatarstan, had been decisive in preventing a second round.[28] It is unlikely that Putin would have lost the elections, but it would have made a huge dent to his 'no-alternative' image. Interestingly, the eight-page report received no immediate response from the Electoral Commission and nothing substantial in the Russian press, except for a furious attack by *Izvestiya* against foreigners meddling in Russian affairs.

The second Chechen war

After more than a decade, open censorship returned to Russia with the military campaign in Chechnya. As we saw in Chapter 2, the war that started in September 1999 was so interwoven with Putin's rise to power that the suspicion has never receded that it was specially instigated for that purpose. Chechnya was Putin's winning card in the elections as well. It was a popular war not only with the public but with journalists. Apart from long-standing anti-Chechen animosity among Russians, the situation had turned ugly with greedy Chechen warlords, massive hostage-taking for big money, stories of torture and slave labour. Some journalists had also been kidnapped and Berezovsky is said to have paid millions to free them. It was all qualitatively different from the first Chechen war of 1994–6 when Russian journalists had defied Yeltsin's reasons for going to war and had helped bring hostilities to an end. At that time, they had reported from conflict areas within Chechnya and interviewed Chechens on the ground. Now the situation had changed. Journalists were embedded with the armed forces, the war was filmed on television from permitted military positions, and information came from the Ministry of Defence.

The Rosinform centre had been set up as the exclusive source of information on the war, placing a virtual ban on Russian and international correspondents getting into Chechnya. Journalists wishing to visit Chechnya were required to obtain additional accreditation from the Mozdok military headquarters in North Ossetia, which was almost always thwarted. Journalists working in neighbouring Ingushetia were required to hire armed security guards, who made sure they did not slip into Chechnya secretly. If they managed to cross the border, usually by bribing officials, they were often arrested, detained, interrogated for hours, and in the case of international journalists, threatened with expulsion. At the same time PR tours were organised for journalists to promote the Kremlin's picture of the war. It was left to reporters such as Anna Politkovskaya and the human rights activist and writer Natalya Estemirova, assassinated in the course of their work, to show Chechnya in later years from the point of view of a suffering population and a human tragedy

Although support for the war initially stood at 71 per cent, the Kremlin knew how quickly public opinion could change if accurate information got out on television. Only the independent press published stories about atrocities committed by Russian troops, the killing and plundering of civilians, and the indiscriminate razing of the previously elegant capital of Grozny. Just how threatening the Putin regime could be to independent-minded journalists was seen in the Babitsky affair.

The Babitsky scandal

Andrei Babitsky was a long-standing reporter on Radio Liberty, a US Congress-funded radio station which was popular in Russia, employing mainly Russian reporters and transmitting their take on events. Hostility to Babitsky lay not in the venue (in this case), but in his reporting, which officials perceived as favouring Chechen rebels, and which many independent journalists also found not to their taste. There was a mixed response to his report on the beheading of Russian servicemen by Chechen militants and his attempt to defend the rebels:

> Chechens cut the throats of soldiers not because they are sadists with an inclination to treat soldiers with particular cruelty, they are trying to show war in a clearer, more visible, distinct way, to reach out to public opinion and explain that war is really happening, a frightening cruel war.[29]

After his last phone call to the office on 15 January 2000, Babitsky disappeared. Information leaked to a colleague suggested he had been detained by Russian forces while attempting to leave Grozny and was held in the notorious Chernokozovo 'filtration' prison camp. Military officials at first denied that they knew anything about his whereabouts, but later admitted he was in their custody. Only after growing protests from journalists and the personal intervention of US Secretary of State Madeleine Albright, who happened to be visiting Moscow, did the authorities agree on 2 February to bring Babitsky back to Moscow and release him. But on 4 February Putin's press office announced that the federal authorities were no longer responsible for Babitsky's fate, as he had volunteered to be exchanged for a group of soldiers captured by Chechen rebels. An FSB video clip of the exchange shown on television seemed to prove the opposite: a grim-looking Babitsky appeared unwilling to be handed over to masked men under a convoy of arms. Branches of the security services denied any knowledge of a swap, although the defence minister told ORT he wouldn't be sorry if ten Babitskys were exchanged for one Russian soldier. Chechen rebel leaders had no knowledge of a swap taking place either.

Many of Babitsky's colleagues feared he had been killed in a botched FSB job. Undaunted by official threats, sections of the media kept the case in the public gaze. *Obshchaya gazeta*'s editor, Yegor Yakovlev, gathered willing newspapers to bring out a joint special emergency issue of his paper, which came out in times considered to be of great danger to free speech. The inconclusive video, contradictory accounts by officials and the issuing of national and Interpol arrest warrants for Babitsky all fed suspicions that Babitsky had been set up.

Finally, on 25 February, officials announced that Babitsky had been detained in a prison in Dagestan with a false Azerbaijani passport. Prosecutors said he would be charged with holding a fake passport and for alleged links to Chechen rebels. Babitsky announced he would go on hunger strike. That seemed to do the trick. On the same day Putin intervened, upbraiding the interior ministry's handling of the case and suggesting Babitsky should be released, although the charges were not dropped for some time. Official vindictiveness did not end there. Babitsky's wife had rushed to Dagestan to see him, but when Babitsky was flown back to Moscow in an empty plane she was not informed, and had to make her own way back.

On NTV and at press conferences, an exhausted Babitsky related his account of the story. His captors had taken away his documents and given him the fake passport. He had been transported across Chechnya into Dagestan in the trunk of a car. He had not agreed to be traded for prisoners of war, as the FSB had claimed. He knew that the masked men, who had taken him away after the swap, belonged to a pro-Kremlin Chechen group; but he did not know who his captors were in the last few weeks. He could not be certain they were FSB, but one of his guards used secret services slang. During his incarceration in the Chernokozovo detention camp he had been beaten, but nothing in comparison to others, he said – inside, it was like the Stalinist and Nazi concentration camps.

When Putin was asked about Babitsky in his conversation with journalists during the electoral campaign, he called him a 'traitor':

PUTIN: He worked directly for the enemy. He wasn't a neutral source of information. He sided with bandits ... that's what happens to people who fight on the side of the enemy ...
INTERVIEWER: Journalists don't fight.
PUTIN: What Babitsky did was more dangerous than firing a gun.
INTERVIEWER: And how about freedom of speech?
PUTIN: We understand freedom of speech differently. If you mean direct participation in a crime, I will never agree with you. Shall we repeat his opinion on decapitation?[30]

In the book version of the newspaper article, Putin's remarks about Babitsky were deleted. It was still unacceptable to speak in such rough terms. In this interview he also calls Oleg Kalugin a traitor – perhaps more understandably, given Kalugin was formerly head of the Leningrad KGB and vocal in denouncing the secret services during *glasnost*. At that time Kalugin was seen as a hero. Officially, not any more.

Puppets – the cherry on the cake

A test of the limits on free speech was NTV's witty political satire *Puppets*, which Yeltsin had put up with for years. These mini masterpieces were the cherry on the cake of free speech in the 1990s. All prominent politicians came under fire routinely in these sharp skits, but the new political climate proved to be less tolerant. The first blow came from St Petersburg University's rector and other dignitaries, who were part of a group that had nominated Putin for president. They signed a petition, claiming the show had committed a criminal offence and that Putin had been defamed 'with a special rage and frenzy'. This kind of talk sent alarm bells to journalists such as

Leonid Radzikhovsky, writing in the daily *Segodnya*, that obeisance and fawning were conditioned reflexes not only with the gullible masses but among the intelligentsia:

> We are now seeing the beginning of a stormy romance between a section of the intelligentsia and Putin. So far the romance is one sided – Putin doesn't even smile back. But small things don't stop those who are rushing to 'swoon at his feet with love'. They know who they are and who *he* is. In fact, the oddest thing is that not all by far love Putin for the same reasons that Dorenko loves Berezovsky and Berezovsky loves Dyachenko. Many playing up to the authorities are disinterested – they just aren't able to live any other way.[31]

This attitude of deference was revived on a big scale under Putin. Famous film director Nikita Mikhalkov's documentary about Putin was described by critics as cringingly subservient. When Kremlin policies needed support, most notoriously on the day of the Crimea referendum in March 2014 to decide its union with Russia, there was no problem in finding hooray intellectuals. More than 500 signatures appeared on the Ministry of Culture's website in one day – celebrity figures who could not remain 'cold-hearted observers' of the fate of Crimea; while the Union of Writers expressed in language not noticeably literary that 'fascist thugs' and the 'West's destructive forces' had carried out a coup in Kyiv which would soon, like the Third Reich, begin to burn books. In contrast to Soviet times, many intellectual opponents signed a robust counter-assault on *Novaya gazeta*'s site. The event was called a 'war of signatures'.

Those who had wished to ban *Puppets* would have been outraged by the scriptwriter Viktor Shenderovich's lampoon that came out for International Women's Day during the 2000 presidential campaign, showing the Duma as a brothel and politicians as prostitutes, most of them eager to oblige Putin for a price. Attired in outlandish women's clothes and make-up, the communist Zyuganov-puppet appeared as a sadomasochist in black leather, democrat Yavlinsky was virginal, and parliamentary speaker Seleznyov and Moscow Mayor Luzhkov were madams from rival brothels:

SELEZNYOV: Well, how do you like them?
PUTIN: What is this?
SELEZNYOV: They're all ready to love you.
YAVLINSKY: That's not true.
SELEZNYOV: He's just a tease … What's your orientation?
PUTIN: The traditional kind. But, of course, there will be some innovations.
SELEZNYOV: Wonderful! We have something for every taste … Some sado-
    masochism – you want to give it a try?
ZYUGANOV: Hit me!
PUTIN: What for?

ZYUGANOV: And then I'll hit you! And then you'll hit me again! … In front of everyone, publicly!

PUTIN: No …

SELEZNYOV: You don't understand anything. You're just very young still. Later, closer to election time, he'll quietly give in to you. But in front of everybody – he has to seem terrible![32]

When the political campaign against Gusinsky began, NTV received a written ultimatum from the Kremlin's chief of staff Voloshin which set out three points: to stop reporting on corruption, the Chechen war, and to remove the puppet depicting 'the first person' (written in large letters). Shenderovich obliged, removing the puppet from the next skit which was set in the Old Testament desert; bringing him in instead as a burning bush, issuing his version of the ten commandments through Moses (Voloshin), who chants Thou shalt not kill – 'except in outhouses and people of Caucasian nationality', and so on through the commandments.[33] But the fun soon came to an end. It was not the sharp skits that made Putin incandescent, but one where he is depicted as Tiny Zaches from an E. T. A Hoffmann story about an evil dwarf who is perceived by villagers to be beautiful because of a magic spell. Shenderovich was surprised to find out that it was not his 'powerful literary metaphors' that had offended Putin, but the size of tiny Zaches.[34]

Puppets ran on NTV between 1994 and 2002. There were 362 episodes.

II Putin and free speech

Throughout his time in office Putin has paid lip service to free speech while overseeing its precipitous decline. In the beginning, if he disliked the message, he complained that the media outlet was not 'genuinely' independent; if free speech was exercised by his opponents, he claimed they were abusing their freedom. His support of free speech is proclaimed in speeches over the past 16 years. In his first open letter in 2000 he claimed that 'now, already, our press is free for ever'.[35] In his first state-of-the-nation address he announced that 'free speech is and will remain an unshakeable value of Russian democracy'.[36] In 2014 he said, 'Free media, the right of citizens to receive and spread information, is a fundamental principle of any democratic power … and must be strictly observed'.[37]

As 'imitation democracy' started to work immediately, it follows that free speech, its centrepiece, would not be authentic either. In the first state-of-the-nation address, Putin took a paternalistic approach. The media are immature, they need time to develop and he will not interfere in this, but 'we are obliged to guarantee journalists real freedom and not freedom for show'. His first step was to shift the media's dependence from the private to the state sector, so that they would not interfere with the regime's interests:

> We have not yet managed to draft precise democratic rules that would guarantee the fourth estate's genuine independence. I would like to stress 'genuine'. Journalistic freedom has turned into a tasty morsel for politicians and major financial groups and a convenient instrument of infighting between clans.

The giveaway phrase is that free speech is too 'tasty' to share. Although Putin accurately describes the infighting between clans, he omits to say that he represents one of these clans, or that pressure is an aspect of the state as much as the private sector:

> The economic inefficiency of a significant proportion of media outlets makes them dependent on the commercial and political interests of the bosses and sponsors of these media outlets. This makes it possible to use the media for settling scores with competitors and, sometimes, even to turn them into mass disinformation outlets and into a means of struggle against the state.

In a democracy, there is nothing illegal about 'struggling against the state' if there is no call for violent overthrow, no incitement to riot, no exposure of classified information. In fact, it is part of democracy to call the state or government to account. NTV and other opposition journalists humorously noted that Putin aligned himself with Louis XIV's *l'état, c'est moi*. In Putin's mind, to attack the barbarism taking place in Chechnya or the FSB's persecution of Babitsky was to be anti-state, even treasonable, rather than simply critical of government conduct.

Putin: the state as a coy damsel

It is interesting to examine Putin's off-the-cuff remarks about the media. In public Putin is usually affable and polite, but every now and then, especially when he relaxes or gets angry, he blurts things out that arguably illuminate what he really thinks. On these occasions, Putin invariably shows contempt for the media as a free institution. His exasperated outburst after Anna Politkovskaya's murder showed how little respect he held for her or even for her bravery.

On a few occasions Putin has used macho imagery about the media that he seems to find amusing. At a 2004 press conference in the Kremlin, Putin's jokey reply to journalists who accused him of muzzling the media was: 'a real man should always try and a real lady should always resist', he said. He elaborated: 'the authorities have always tried to avoid criticism, while the media have always tried to unearth everything they can to draw the authorities' attention to their errors'.[38] The analogy annoyed media professional Yelena Rykovtseva, one of the few women journalists who took exception to this remark: 'Those in power don't just "try", but "violate" primitively, and the press "surrenders" without showing much in the way of "resistance".[39] It was not the first time Putin had baited the media for 'unmanly' responses to state pressure. He seemed to be saying: either fight or stop complaining. In 2006 another jocular female metaphor slipped out, this time to Western journalists in Shanghai inquiring about the state of media freedom. 'If you have nine pregnant women, it doesn't mean one of them will give birth in a month. You need time to mature'.[40] Putin obviously felt these were light-hearted remarks, but (as Freud might agree) they are all sexual and derisory. In 2010 the only comment he could make about the internet was that half of it was 'pornographic'.

Putin: journalism and spying

In an interview on CBS's *Sixty Minutes* with Mike Wallace in 2005 Putin declared that journalism was like spying. 'You know, journalism, as it relates to collecting information, differs little if at all from intelligence work', he said.[41] He said much the same a few years earlier to Larry King: 'Intelligence people are very close [in] their duties to the stuff in mass media. The same purpose to gather information, to synthesize it and to present it for the consumption of the decision makers'.[42]

How far does Putin take this analogy? As a case officer stationed in East Germany recruiting a network of foreign nationals to work as spies for the KGB, he would have had contact with Soviet and German journalists. The relationship between foreign correspondents and intelligence operatives working abroad is always tense. Both are seeking information and snoop to get it. Accredited journalists hold the advantage by having access to places that are off limits to others: they have contacts, knowledge and clout and can be valuable informants to their intelligence agencies, be it the KGB, CIA or MI6. Carl Bernstein, of Watergate fame, after studying the relationship between the CIA and the press in his country, wrote in 1977 that 400 US journalists had secretly carried out assignments for the CIA in the past 25 years, but that this consensus had been shredded during the Vietnam War.[43] Today, without the same deference in the West to spy agencies, the relationship is more varied: some journalists may pass on small bits of information, others may be involved in complex schemes.

Despite this, there is a principled difference between journalists and spies in their function and method of operation, between openness and deceit, between serving the public interest and serving the state. Ideally, the exposé-conscious journalist is the mirror opposite of the secret service operative. The professions are as mutually exclusive as the sacred is to the profane. Of course the hack may well prostitute his profession – journalism has long been called the world's second oldest profession, a saying much quoted in Russia – but a journalist who violates his responsibility to protect the public (including a foreign public) and his sources from the state is profaning the profession.

The journalist-spy comes together in ways that are generally considered acceptable only when the cause is widely lauded, such as the 'fight against fascism' in the Second World War. The wars in, say, Vietnam and Iraq have not had that consensus. The same legendary aura surrounded the *Pravda* correspondent Mikhail Koltsov reporting from the Spanish Civil War, when the Soviet Union supported the fight against fascism while the western allies remained aloof. Koltsov was honoured by Ernest Hemingway in his novel *For Whom the Bell Tolls* in the character of Karkov: 'He had more brains and more inner dignity and outer insolence and humour than any man that he had ever known'.[44] But for all Koltsov's brilliant reporting and cooperation with the NKVD, on his return home he was tortured in the Stalinist camps and executed either in 1940 or 1942 on the false charge of spying for the enemy. The Russian journalist-spy is an altogether different phenomenon from glamorous western spy-journalists such as Ian Fleming and Graham Greene.

During the Soviet period journalists posted abroad would be expected to snoop for the KGB and GRU: that was something they had to live with, whether they liked it or not. The opposite was also true: spies masqueraded as journalists. When Putin thinks of journalist-spies he must have this picture in his mind. It follows there was nothing new in turning journalists into servants of the state. With a cynical KGB eye, all he had to do was to observe the journalist community in the 1990s, when so many were prepared to use the media as an instrument for enrichment, to know how manipulable they were. It may well explain the feeling of contempt he seems to have for them. It may also have made him feel he could clamp down on the media early in his term of office without resistance. Maybe, because of this, he feels journalists cannot be trusted. He has demonstrated this many times. On one occasion, responding to criticism in front of relatives of sailors trapped in the *Kursk* submarine, he shouted angrily: 'Who's saying that? Television? Then it's lies, lies, lies'.[45] Perhaps Putin's distrust of journalists is connected with his doubt that anything approximating the truth exists. In the interview with Mike Wallace he said: 'I worked in intelligence and know how information and information bulletins are made. After all, this is determined to a considerable extent by the political attitudes and bias of those who do it'. The assumption is that there is no truth-telling, only propaganda – the dominant view of his political technologists and the ruling elite. It follows that journalists need to be managed to gather 'trustworthy' information that reflects appropriate interests, which is what the Doctrine of Information Security, his main media policy document, sets out to do.

Some journalists have remarked on Putin's inability to understand what free speech is. Radio Ekho Moskvy editor, Aleksei Venediktov, said he was amazed by Putin's profoundly Soviet view of the media: 'Your job is to support the state', he told Venediktov. When Venediktov explained that the media weren't meant to be instruments of the state, Putin did not understand: 'for him there was the state press and the anti-state press'.[46] Mikhail Berger is also quoted as saying to a German journalist that Putin refused on principle to talk to journalists from Gusinsky's press: 'I only speak to people who share my opinion', he said.

The first three journalists Putin invited to visit him on becoming president is telling. One of them, ORT's Sergei Dorenko, was not surprising, as his propaganda had helped to bring Putin to power. But the other two were the most ultra-radical conservative editors in the country: Valentin Chikin, editor of the old hardline communist newspaper, *Sovetskaya Rossiya*, and Aleksandr Prokhanov, editor of the nationalist–imperialist-racist newspaper *Zavtra*. Both men played important roles in opposing Gorbachev's party reforms and used their newspapers as mouthpieces of the 'red-brown' parliamentary forces to attack Yeltsin's democratic changes. They supported the anti-democratic 1991 coup. They were out-on-a-limb right-wingers considered by many as the 'loony' fringe.

If Putin's preference lies with the ultra-conservative media, does he receive rounded information? From what Putin's press secretary has said, news gathering has remained extremely important for Putin – 'sometimes we're wondering what is the limit for a human being for absorbing this huge amount of information', Dmitry Peskov has stated.[47] According to him, staff work around the clock to prepare TV digests and recordings for him from traditional media and internet; and he follows TV news in English and German. But according to Pavlovsky, Putin's information is not diverse. 'Russian authorities do not have reliable information. It depends ... on more or less trusted officials and such information is always changed and corrected, because it is in the interest of any trusted official to remain a trusted official'.[48] There are the public opinion polls that cannot be fully trusted (with the exception of the independent Levada Centre), nor are respondents necessarily reliable. The consequence of suppressing free speech usually has a boomerang effect and this was most visibly demonstrated when the administration was caught unawares by the anger aroused at the Putin–Medvedev presidential swap in 2011.

Putin's fear of not having the situation under control determines all arrangements with journalists. As a wide-eyed 24-year-old reporter working in the Kremlin pool, Yelena Tregubova describes the pressure put on journalists in her book, which caused a sensation when it was published in 2003. It may have been the reason for a bomb exploding outside her apartment door four months later, or perhaps it was because she had embarrassed Putin by revealing a flirtatious lunch he had invited her to when he was FSB chief. It was certainly the reason for her being sacked by *Kommersant* a few weeks later. Restrictions demanded by the Kremlin press service began immediately Yeltsin announced his retirement, she says, before Putin had become president. Under the press service's new head, Aleksei Gromov, questions to Putin were forbidden unless they had been approved by him beforehand, and the same rule applied to questions to delegates who accompanied Putin on official visits. What amazed Tregubova was that most of her colleagues did not remonstrate (she says they acted like 'mutants'), but simply competed to establish good relations with Gromov on his terms: in fact, there was even the thrill that they might become 'the new elite of journalism!'.[49]

The same scenario was repeated in the White House, the seat of the administration, when Putin changed places with Medvedev in 2008 to become prime minister. Accredited journalists had been in the habit of roaming the corridors and dropping in on officials (only the fifth floor around the prime minister's office was exempt), but the rules changed in advance of Putin moving in. Reporters were confined to the press room; they could meet senior sources and aides if they had received their consent, as well as permission from the press secretary, and a press officer had to escort them there and back. The White House pool could only look back with nostalgia to the days when reporters had been allowed to sit in on cabinet meetings during the Chernomyrdin period between 1992 and 1998.[50]

Putin never experienced or witnessed the euphoria of *perestroika*. A few months after Gorbachev came to power he was posted to Dresden in East Germany. He remained abroad from August 1985 until early 1990. Mary Elise Sarotte points out that from the viewpoint of a Soviet loyalist, what Putin might have seen in Dresden before the Berlin Wall came down probably filled him with horror, especially when tens of thousands of East Germans clashed violently with police, army and Stasi forces at the Dresden railway station trying to leave the country after Honecker had closed the borders.[51] From what Putin has himself revealed, his experience was not pleasant. As the senior person on duty in the Soviet Cultural Centre when the building was besieged by angry crowds threatening to break in, he says his main concern was to conceal top secret dossiers on German agents who had worked for the KGB. Taking a few bodyguards with him, Putin went outside to calm the protesters, fooling them into thinking he was only a translator and that there were no officials in the building.[52] The experience left him angry and resentful at Moscow's disloyalty in offering no support to KGB officers on the ground; and one of Putin's traits, on which most agree, has been his staunch loyalty to his old bosses and the institutions he has worked for.

Not only Putin, but many Russians, see scenes of people's liberation from the point of view of bloody revolution. Jubilant protesters are seen as rioting, anarchic mobs. Moreover, in this case, Putin was the hated enemy that had propped up a repressive regime. Putin probably took back hostile images from East Germany's liberation, just as Andropov did when he served as Soviet ambassador in Hungary after the Soviet Union put down the uprising in 1956. This experience influenced Andropov's repressive anti-dissident policy of 'containment' when he became the KGB's powerful chief. Instead of Stalin's all-embracing terror, Andropov's method of instilling fear in the population was to target selected high-profile dissidents (Solzhenitsyn, Sakharov, Bukovsky), incarcerating or exiling them at home or expelling them from the country. Andropov's policies have undoubtedly had an impact on Putin, who has found ways of containing or 'managing' important sections of the media and the 'tastiest' of them all – television.

Putin's first nine months in power

Among the independent media there was a growing apprehension of the state taking control, each day bringing fresh evidence of journalists being harassed, making it more difficult to get a story or talk to officials. Yet freedoms were so much taken for granted that it did not seem likely they could simply vanish in a puff of smoke. One journalist expressed her irritation at what she saw as wishful thinking on the part of the democrats: 'Nothing in Putin's image seems to have perturbed the Russian "democratic" and "reformist" political elite. The democrats seem to have simply closed their eyes to the dangers posed by this creeping sabotage of democratic institutions'.[53] In a survey carried out in 2000, only one-third of the public thought free speech was endangered.[54]

VGTRK executive Oleg Dobrodeyev saw the state as the natural guarantor of freedom and stability: 'Big state-owned television companies are better protected and less subject to political whims, and they have no political games of their own to play, which is very important when applied to our political land-scape'.[55] Such political naivety about a state without interests was common; not so with Yevgeniya Albats, who responded that the state was the 'largest oli-garch of them all'.[56] When a Petersburg journalist wanted to know what lib-eral-minded Nikolai Svanidze, state RTR's top presenter, had to say about safeguarding free speech in a situation where KGB officers were dominating the regime, he snapped: 'What exactly do you have against the KGB? Would it be preferable to put Berezovsky in their place?'. This became the dominant narrative, repeated endlessly in the state media. RIA Novosti was among them:

> Opinion polls indicate that media freedoms of the nineties have been rejected ... Society was exasperated by free-and-easy illiterate journalists, their indiscriminate use of all sources of information and methods of getting it ... It was an open secret that television during that period turned into one of the most corrupt areas of the 'grey' Russian economy. The private media empires ... were exploited ultimately not to serve society, but to promote the commercial and political interests of businessmen.

It was hard to defend the oligarchs and their leading journalists who had abused their exercise of free speech, and even comic to see them posturing as martyrs, but in 2000 they were fighting not only for their survival but for the survival of free speech. But they had lost the high moral ground to mount a campaign against what had become the massive media propaganda machine they had allowed to develop.

To show that Putin and the regime were intent on grabbing control of the media from the start, it is worth looking at Putin's first nine months in power, from March to the end of 2000. The move against the media oligarchs was swift. Gusinsky's Media MOST empire was the first on the hit list.

Masked commandos burst into its offices in May 2000, two months after Putin became president, and in a series of raids tried to nail Gusinsky on various criminal charges, all of which failed. Another ploy followed. NTV's investor, Gazprom Media, had always been accommodating, but it suddenly called in payment of a \$211.6 million loan. At the same time a reshuffle took place in Gazprom Media with Press Minister Lesin putting Alfred Kokh in charge – a 'hired killer', responded NTV satirist Shenderovich,[57] referring to Kokh's bitterness after the NTV book scandal. All this was nothing compared to the shock when Gusinsky was thrown into Butyrskaya prison for embezzling state property. Had the Kremlin gone too far, asked sociologist Boris Kagarlitsky? 'Before, the oligarchs were untouchable. Not even political rivals could be thrown in jail for corruption, since it was obvious that all members of the elite could, and should, be jailed on these grounds, including those who were jailing others'.[58] Whatever reservations one might have had about Gusinsky's role in the political life of the country, the purpose of his arrest was clear. 'Those who dare criticise the Kremlin should watch out', Yevgeniya Albats concluded.[59]

Gusinsky was released a few days later and the charges were dropped. He fled to Spain. From there he broke the news that he had been blackmailed into signing an agreement on 10 July by Kokh and Lesin to hand over his media holding to Gazprom in exchange for a cash payment, debt forgiveness and a pledge to end the criminal prosecution against him. He produced the pledge with the signatures for the media to see – so-called appendix 6. When Gusinsky's story hit the press, the Kremlin responded immediately. Putin said he was outraged and Prime Minister Mikhail Kasyanov reprimanded Lesin publicly, but no further action was taken against him. Instead, showing what it meant to break an 'understanding' with the Kremlin, the Prosecutor-General's office attempted to have Gusinsky extradited first from Spain, later from Greece, and to obstruct every attempt he made to save his empire and pay his debts. By early 2001 NTV had already been raided 27 times.

The campaign against Gusinsky took a pause during the *Kursk* nuclear submarine accident, which Putin handled so badly it could have been his undoing. The *Kursk* sank in the Barents Sea killing all 118 sailors on board during ten days in August. If Putin had not taken five days to return from holiday in Sochi, if the authorities had felt they could make decisions on their own and accepted foreign aid from ships close to hand, evidence shows the sailors might have been saved. It was a disaster for Putin's image at a time when the press was still uncowed and able to expose him and his officials.

The authorities withheld information, misinformed reporters and distraught relatives, and allowed only state television RTR access to the scene. In disgust, NTV, ORT and independent newspapers undertook their own investigations. *Komsomolskaya pravda* printed a list of the names of the sailors on board, which it bought from a naval officer for \$600, because naval command declared it to be a military secret. One of the most infamous scenes was NTV's footage of a meeting between officials and relatives of the dead crew.

When the distraught mother of one sailor began to shout at officials, a medic approached her from behind, injected her with a sedative, and she was carried from the room. The whole of Russia watched as a grieving woman who had dared to criticise the government was silenced. When NTV was accused of being unethical in its coverage, the company replied: 'Would you have preferred that we operate like the government network? Our correspondents reported that the reality was ten times more dreadful'.[60]

The *Kursk* tragedy showed how a catastrophe could be made worse when officials covered up information, but the lesson Putin took from the incident was to ensure he would never again be exposed. *Glasnost* had begun with the exposure of major disasters, but now cover-ups and lies on a scale which reporters had thought would be impossible were happening again. State pressure on the media became more intense. It hit Berezovsky a few months later, as he revealed in an open letter he wrote to Putin. He had received an ultimatum from a highly placed official to sell his 49 per cent share in ORT to the government in the next two weeks or go the way of Gusinsky. He wrote a prescient letter in defence of private media:

> It will be easier for you to govern, the people will live more peacefully, and there will be far fewer people to raise unpleasant questions; after all, they won't have the powerful defence that TV *glasnost* gives them. You won't have to curtail your vacation and immediately look for money to help families of the dead. And one fine day, people will wake up and discover that they have unanimously approved the sending of the Russian army to some far-off country to supply fraternal assistance.[61]

Not long in retirement, Yeltsin could not restrain himself from criticising Putin's handling of the crisis. Of course he should have returned immediately from Sochi, Yeltsin said. It was incumbent on the head of state to show 'human compassion'.[62] Putin was particularly ridiculed when CNN's Larry King interviewed him several weeks later and asked: 'What happened to the *Kursk*?' Putin replied with a slight smirk: 'It sank'. Apologists jumped to his defence – what else could he have said to such a stupid question. An anecdote in multiple variations was born. Question: 'What happened to truth in our country?' Answer: 'It sank'.

Berezovsky's favourite anchor, Sergei Dorenko, unstinting in his critical coverage of the handling of the *Kursk* accident and the Chechen war, whose muckraking journalism had earlier helped Putin win the elections, was taken off the air. Dorenko believed the order came from Putin. He revealed at a press conference that he had been invited to see Putin several times and Putin had asked him to join his team. Dorenko had politely refused, but he was less flattering now, telling Bloomberg television: 'He wants me to be a laser beam that creates him, because without television he doesn't exist'. *Moskovsky komsomolets* was pleased to see the back of Dorenko, who had blackened their patron Luzhkov's name: 'Farewell, snitch!' ran its headline, mocking the new union that had been forged in the face of persecution between sworn enemies Dorenko and Kiselyov.[63]

In many ways Dorenko, the killer-journalist, exemplified the late 1990s oligarch-backed style of journalism. Telegenic, charismatic and unethical, his buccaneering forays into television exuded the spirit of *volya*: freedom to do what he wanted, to enrich himself, to sneer at opponents, to accuse them without proper evidence. At the same time, he was not easily intimidated: he openly defended private media and commented wryly on Putin. 'Not I, nor my colleagues on NTV, fully associate the interests of our native land, our Russia, with the state machine, which the president heads. The State and Russia are not one and the same thing'.[64] The audience loved him, because he was dramatic and outspoken. He may have been Berezovsky's attack dog, but he was not going to be anything as dull as the state machine's loyal mouthpiece. In due course, however, he became part of the obsequious Putin landscape.

Nor did the new politics suit Berezovsky, who found himself at loggerheads with the president he had pushed to power. Rather late in the day, he tried to transfer his ORT shares to a trust, managed by his favourite journalists, and keep the channel from turning into a Kremlin propaganda outlet. He began to oppose Putin in public, to finance political parties and started a philanthropic foundation. But when prosecutors reopened the Aeroflot case and summoned him for questioning into the embezzlement of nearly $1 billion, Berezovsky fled to Britain before the year had ended, where he was given political asylum. He became Russia's bogyman, the Kremlin's most hated person, heaped with all manner of vile deeds. In reply, Berezovsky pursued and financed events from abroad to denounce Putin, to expose his alleged involvement in the apartment bombings and the death of Litvinenko in London from polonium 210.

A good deal of what happened to Berezovsky's shares in ORT was revealed in the sensational case of *Berezovsky* v. *Abramovich* in the High Court in London in 2011. Putin's determination to wrest the shares from Berezovsky were negotiated through Roman Abramovich and hammered out at meetings in different parts of the world. According to Berezovsky, the threat delivered to him from Putin was to surrender all his business interests or they would be seized, and a colleague was thrown into prison as a 'hostage' to force him to submit. The ORT shares were sold to Abramovich for £150 million as part of the general package Berezovsky received.

In the space of this short period of Putin's first nine months, a number of media institutions also came under the hammer. The Judicial Chamber for Information Disputes, the media regulator that was highly respected during its seven years' work, was abolished. The Freedom of Information Act, which Yeltsin had been trying to push through since 1997 against the unwavering opposition of the bureaucracy, was dropped. A new one was passed in 2010 already in conditions that made it unlikely to be implemented properly. The guide to curbing the media, the Doctrine of Information Security was drafted.

So-called press enemy no. 1 Lesin was involved in most of the repressive measures, but the media were still sufficiently bold to give Putin third place in infamy. The year ended with Putin's request to reinstate the music of the Soviet national anthem, which liberals considered an insult to the victims of repression.

A year into Yeltsin's retirement, he gave his only interview to *Komsomolskaya pravda*. He had been particularly upset about the return of the Soviet anthem, which he associated with party bureaucracy. He was diplomatic about Putin's 'tact and sensible firmness' in relation to Berezovsky. Was there a threat to free speech, the journalist asked. 'You could look at it like that but you don't need to', Yeltsin replied. 'There's no threat to free speech. I'm more concerned that some people take this freedom to mean that everything is permissible; they lose a sense of proportion'.[65] Yeltsin might have been thinking more of the kind of problems he had faced. Later, privately, in conversation with Boris Nemtsov, who used to visit him in retirement, his views were harsher. Nemtsov says: 'He was extremely annoyed that free speech began to erode under Putin and that the institution of elections was being destroyed. He didn't speak publicly about it, but he spoke to me about it repeatedly'.[66] Nemtsov confirms that Yeltsin's public silence was probably connected with the deal he had made with Putin for his and his family's immunity from prosecution. 'Otherwise', Nemtsov adds, 'knowing Yeltsin's character, it is impossible to understand why he has kept quiet all this time'.

III Doctrine of Information Security

As we saw in Chapter 2, the September 2000 Doctrine of Information Security established an ideological framework for controlling the media. It was an entirely KGB/FSB document, approved by Putin, drafted by the Security Council, the powerful Kremlin advisory body then headed by Sergei Ivanov, Putin's long-time associate and fellow KGB veteran, and stacked with former KGB generals. In attendance were the seven new presidential plenipotentiaries, five of whom were generals in the military, police or security services. They represented the new division of the country into seven federal districts, bringing the regions more closely under the control of the Kremlin. They would ensure regional media did not go out on their own trajectory. It was nothing if not an FSB document.

What, one might ask, in a supposed democracy, in peacetime, were the media doing in a document concerned with intelligence and national threats to the Russian Federation? As suspicion and paranoia are integral to the military and security services, it comes as no surprise that they would be on the outlook for national threats, but if all domestic media that were private and independent were considered threats, it meant that the authors of the Information Doctrine were already identifying them as 'the enemy within' long before they began to be called 'fifth columns' 12 years later. If, as well, foreign media were seen as hostile and a challenge to Russia's superpower status, then it indicated how early in the regime Russia returned to cold war suspicions.

Several months before the publication of the doctrine, a secret document from the Kremlin's presidential administration was leaked to *Kommersant*, recommending conspiratorial methods of controlling society. The media section of the document, which was leaked in April (the comprehensive document was leaked a month later and has been reposted online by Karen Dawisha),[67] has been dubbed Version Number 6, after Chekhov's story *Ward Number 6* about a lunatic asylum, so sinister are the implications behind the text. Because society is not 'morally' prepared to accept the 'suppression of opposition' and the 'takeover of the media and information communications', Version Number 6 suggests a dual agenda should be followed: one to be open (official), the other to be hidden. The aim of the hidden agenda is:

> to take control of different media outlets, designate the use of specially gathered information, including that of an incriminating nature. Drive the opposition media and media sympathetic to the opposition to financial crisis, remove their licences and certifications, create the conditions by which the actions of every concrete opposition media outlet can be controlled or disabled.[68]

This subversive document, backing FSB entitlement to meddle behind the scenes, shows the kind of thinking that went on in the president's team while the façade of democracy was being created. Overall, the document confirms the repressive intentions behind the Doctrine of Information Security, as well as the different attempts since 2000 to blackmail and disable media standing in the way of the Kremlin.

More than a few political analysts ignored the dangers of the Information Security Doctrine at the time because it was not legally binding. The doctrine, together with other keynote statements, such as Sergei Markov's on 'managed' democracy and Putin's Millennium Message, have clearly acted as blueprints with long-term perspectives that have been implemented with almost military precision. Their extraordinary longevity has been noted by Dawisha and co-authors Hill and Gaddy, who commented that 'to a remarkable degree, the goals he outlined in the Millennium Message remain the priority today, more than twelve years later'.[69] Today, 16 years later, the doctrine's goals on the media remain the same: to prevent ungovernable sections of the media from interfering with 'trustworthy' messages that the Kremlin wishes to communicate to the Russian people and the world. There has been no cut-off point to these goals; instead, these trustworthy messages turned into propaganda, hate speech and lies in Putin's third term.

The two major threats, privately owned media and foreign media, were considered dangerous because they had their own interests at heart or they had an interest in the truth. Left to their own devices, private media would disseminate a pluralism of views that would interfere with the regime's attempt to build a semi-monopoly on opinion at home. Foreign media failed to convey the country's domestic and foreign objectives properly, and disseminated western values which competed with the regime's attempts to celebrate Russia's traditional norms. Inevitably, the tenor of the document was punitive. 'In the text you often find words that define an information war and an information weapon, but you don't have any words about democracy', noted media rights advocate Oleg Panfilov.[70]

Private media ownership and foreign media have received special and separate attention over the years. The assault on the private sector and on media oligarchs has been ongoing. Although the most sensational clampdown occurred when Gusinsky and Berezovsky were hounded out of Russia, the screws tightened after every major crisis. The Information Security Doctrine itself was rushed forward for publication after the *Kursk* crisis as a warning to the media to stop its criticism over Putin's handling of the accident. The screws tightened further after the terrorist hostage-taking of *Nord-Ost* and Beslan, after the Yukos trial, after the colour revolutions and the wars with Georgia and Ukraine. Because the process of curbing the media went in fits and starts, the political technologists' tactics of mystification as to whether or not Putin supported free speech and democracy seemed to work in allaying the worst fears.

The regime concealed its intentions so well that each blow against private media was seen usually as the last, as there would be no need for further Kremlin clampdowns in a supposed democracy. In 2003, when television channels were under state control, political analysts assumed the press would be left alone. The print runs of newspapers were low: *Kommersant*, with a circulation of about 115,000 copies at the time was hardly a menace in the enormity of Russia, yet because it was the main business newspaper it was suspect and pressure was put on Berezovsky in exile to sell. By 2005–6, after Kremlin-friendly owners had bought most of the press, people assumed the small alternative sector that remained would be safe, if for no other reason than to let officials boast that free speech was not dead. But with disaffection in 2012 and Putin's act of defiance over Crimea, censorship spread to all domains of free expression and the internet and it became more a matter of counting on two hands what national independent outlets remained.

In the case of foreign media, the strength of anti-western feeling depended on major events taking place outside Russia. Fear of the colour revolutions led to the setting up of the international satellite broadcaster RT, and its huge and rapid expansion after the Ukraine crisis of 2014. New laws were adopted to prevent the spread of foreign-funded organisations with 'foreign' ideas of human rights.

The overkill and fear shown by the regime to any form of protest are hard to explain except in terms of the FSB preponderance in the administration. Observing a protest demonstration in 2006 of no more than 2,000 protesters, dwarfed by police and OMON anti-riot squads, former presidential candidate Irina Khakamada was stunned: 'It's just laughable. So many dogs, so many policemen, all the streets closed off, helicopters flying around. For me, it's paranoia'.[71] The flow of petro dollars together with political apathy, at least up to 2009, gave no cause for such fierce reprisals, especially as these liberal protests were not usually accompanied by violent Molotov-throwing rioters, burning of cars and window-breaking. But the fears of a kleptocracy at its ill-gotten gains, and the lack of legitimacy in its farce of democracy, engendered uncertainty and the possibility of what Gleb Pavlovsky calls Russians' tendency to nihilism when 'everything can change at any moment'.[72] The FSB mentality and Putin's own instincts appear not to be satisfied with anything less than what the doctrine called 'informational and psychological influences on the mass consciousness of society'. Fingers itching to engineer the soul have been held back only by the need to retain some democratic credentials.

In the next two sections we will see how the Doctrine of Information Security's goals were implemented in (i) the assault on privately owned media and (ii) the control of foreign media and western influence.

(i) The assault on private media

In dismantling media freedoms, Putin destroyed what had been Yeltsin's greatest achievement. It is hard to build and easy to destroy. It took one year, 2001, for the Kremlin to destroy the private media empires and begin hacking away at fragile democratic institutions that had only begun to take root. That year there were still three main competing television stations: state-owned (RTR), hybrid (ORT), private (NTV). By the end of the year all three were virtually under state control.

The takeover of NTV was the most dramatic blow to free speech. Its talent and professionalism had been an inspiration to quality journalism. However gross the interference of Gusinsky's business interests in its journalism, he had given something back to society in creating the first viable media complex in Russia. He had ensured that his media outlets had highly trained journalists and state of the art equipment. At least this was more than Berezovsky had done, throwing money into the media mainly for short-term self-serving gains. There was of course hubris to the fall of the tycoons, so much extravagance and such lavish projects, such as Gusinsky's satellite network NTV Plus, all done by cosying up to power and borrowing as much money as they wanted without a flicker of concern about paying taxpayers back.

Gusinsky's financial borrowings made him vulnerable. As the earlier anti-crime raids had not ensnared him, prosecutors took advantage of the massive debts Media Most had run up with Gazprom and other banks (up to $1.5 billion). In November 2000, Gazprom Media had written off Media Most's debts in exchange for an increased stake in NTV from 30 per cent to 46 per cent. Gusinsky and his top managers held 49.5 per cent of NTV's shares and, of that, 19 per cent was collateral on a Credit Suisse First Boston loan guaranteed by Gazprom. When Gazprom Media got the backing of a minority US shareholder, Capital Research Management, holding a 4.5 per cent share, it called in the loan. Gusinsky hoped he could save NTV by negotiating a deal with CNN's media mogul Ted Turner, in a consortium with George Soros. But before negotiations went too far, Gazprom Media swooped on an NTV shareholders' meeting on 3 April 2001 and threw Gusinsky and his associates off the board. NTV refused to accept the decision because of contradictory court rulings and submitted two lawsuits to challenge the shareholders' meeting. Boris Jordan, a US banker of Russian descent, replaced Gusinsky as director general of NTV. Alfred Kokh, director general of Gazprom-Media, became NTV board chairman.

On 14 April 2001 without bothering to wait for court appeals to be resolved, Gazprom-Media sent private armed guards to break into the NTV studios at 4 a.m. on Easter Sunday, conveniently when Putin and Lesin had flown to Chechnya, so the break-in would have to compete for news headlines. Things moved quickly. The following week the new management closed *Segodnya* and *Itogi*, the latter a joint venture with *US Newsweek*. *Newsweek* pulled out and the joint news and current affairs ventures that had been so plentiful in the 1990s declined.

About 70 demonstrations were held in support of NTV, one brought out 15,000 people, the largest for a decade in Moscow. But the enmities that had accrued within the journalist community meant that mobilising massive support was unlikely. The Union of Journalists held meetings, petitions were signed and when the joint *Obshchaya gazeta* special emergency edition came out it was endorsed by 62 publications from different parts of the country. Small demonstrations were held, one in Pushkin Square on 17 May 2000 with about 2,000 people, which I went to. The old free-and-easy atmosphere that had been taken for granted over the last decade had vanished, especially the sense of a 'right' to be there, without having to look suspiciously at the police. TV presenter Vladimir Pozner explained why so few colleagues came out to support each other:

> One is cowardice, the desire to gain the good will of the authorities. Another is greed, the desire perhaps to grab a piece of this very sweet pie. Another is envy, because NTV has remained Russia's most professional channel and this brings out malice. There are many factors, but I'd say that of course the main reason is stupidity. People don't understand, looking on silently or washing their hands of the way their colleagues are being treated, that this is a sample of what will inevitably happen to them precisely because they are silent.[73]

Those who maintained that there was no political motivation behind the takeover (such as Chubais) would have closed their eyes to the details of the case. Media Most's crime was to have taken out a multimillion-dollar loan without having the funds to pay it back, but ORT and RTR were in the same position. ORT had not repaid a huge loan issued in 1998 and VGTRK (which ran RTR) had even more sins to its name. Yelena Rykovtseva, basing her investigations on the Audit Chamber's report of February 2001, showed that Media Most's viability as a successful company was far greater than that of VGTRK. NTV's advertising revenue of $60 million was twice as high as VGTRK's, which was a loss-making company that had taken out loans higher than it needed to buy expensive foreign cars and securities. Its advertising income was lower because it was paying for its middleman, Video International, the company founded by Lesin. Rykovtseva concluded that if the two companies were measured by the same yardstick, 'VGTRK would have long since been declared bankrupt, its chairman Oleg Dobrodeyev would be under investigation and media minister Mikhail Lesin, who worked with VGTRK since its creation in 1991 and was largely responsible for its financial matters, would be sitting in prison'.[74]

There was a personal dimension to Putin's attack on Gusinsky. Vladimir Pozner talked of a 'vendetta' between them and their falling out on two occasions,[75] and it was said at the time that Gusinsky had threatened him with words to the effect that 'without us, you're nothing'. Putin more or less confirmed many years later that 'some' oligarchs had come to him when he was acting prime minister and told him 'you should understand, you'll never be president'.[76] There is little doubt that the oligarchs felt their money and influence entitled them to behave badly. One story from Gusinsky's PR office tells of him barking orders to Prime Minister Chernomyrdin, as if he were a junior partner. Former *Kommersant* editor Andrei Vasilyev passed on to me what Berezovsky had told him: that Gusinsky had tried to blackmail Putin, and Putin had asked Berezovsky's advice about what to do. Berezovsky had replied: 'you're the president, go for him'.[77] At the time Berezovsky was supremely confident the same thing would never happen to him. Perhaps he had forgotten his boast after the 2000 elections that he could 'have a monkey elected president using one TV channel'. He ended up losing both his channels.

The Kremlin's war with the media empires produced bitter resentment in the journalist community. It pitted journalist against journalist, raised moral issues that had been neglected, and pushed employees into being heroes or scabs. Instead of coming out in solidarity with NTV, the other two channels, RTR and ORT, gave more time on air to the Prosecutor-General's accusations than to Media Most's lawyers. Political and personal dramas went public as colleagues accused each other of treachery and deceit.

In an open letter, VGTRK chief Dobrodeyev called Yevgeny Kiselyov a hypocrite, saying he should stop pretending NTV had ever been independent, as it had always been a Kremlin channel. He accused Kiselyov and Gusinsky of covering the war in Chechnya negatively as a bargaining point, and they would change their tone if the Kremlin prolonged their credit. In the process, Kiselyov was risking his colleagues' jobs, while he himself 'will be whisked away on his boss's jet, his boss's yacht'.[78] When Dobrodeyev learned how Gazprom-Media had been kicked out of its premises, however, he began to behave erratically. Announcing his resignation as head of VGTRK, feeling 'profound guilt' towards Putin for 'acting spontaneously and impulsively', he rushed over to NTV. Perhaps he was appalled by what he called the 'burial of television news journalism', as the high quality of NTV's news service had largely been his creation. Some, including a former friend and protégé, Vladimir Kara-Murza, were sceptical of Dobrodeyev's motives. Kara-Murza stopped him in the hall at NTV and asked him what he was doing there. Dobrodeyev said: 'Volodya, freedom of speech is not just you. And you should have a greater degree of freedom to understand this'. As far as Kara-Murza was concerned, Dobrodeyev had come to sow discord and divide the loyalties of colleagues, many of whom still kept in touch with their former mentor. 'Dobrodeyev left for one night … just to pull us apart. Putin didn't sign his resignation, so it turns out he stayed at RTR and scattered us'.[79]

Some of NTV's best journalists were among the 40 who resigned, led by Kiselyov.[80] Two top presenters stayed on: Tatyana Mitkova, who eventually replaced Kiselyov; and leading presenter of infotainment, Leonid Parfyonov, who was infuriated with Kiselyov's politics. Parfyonov wrote an open letter, accusing Kiselyov of treating people like 'cannon fodder' and making a nonsense of both freedom and speech: 'I can no longer stand listening to your preaching in the reporters' room – those ten minutes of hatred'.[81] Kiselyov hit back at Parfyonov's 'arrogant individualism', slagging him off for being a 'poseur and coward'. In this round of insults, the new NTV boss, Alfred Kokh, praised Parfyonov's taste and style, to which satirist Shenderovich responded on the NTV website: 'We have bad taste, Mr. Kokh, but we are not morons. And we know what will happen if ("when") you come to power at NTV'.[82]

The editorial team that resigned from NTV was invited by Berezovsky to work on his private channel, TV6. He had made peace with Gusinsky and together they hoped to prevent the state from encroaching upon their space. Both owners were working as émigrés from abroad. TV6 had been a minor family channel, but it was the second private channel and the fourth network in terms of national reach. The original staff protested at the rude influx from NTV, but Berezovsky had given guarantees that people would not be left without a job. However, the 'persecuted', as media professor Anna Kachkaeva said, pushed out their neighbours. The channel's recent head, Aleksandr Ponomaryov, felt ashamed at having persuaded his team to think they were lucky to work with such glittering colleagues. Instead, he said, 'they came as if no one had been here before them'.[83]

The Kremlin's determination to crush the NTV rebels had not abated and it turned its attention to TV6, embroiling it in legal wrangles. The fact that the channel's reporting had become less oppositional was not enough to save it. Although Berezovsky held a 75 per cent share in the channel, a 15 per cent stake was held by Lukoil-Garant, a pension fund owned by Russian oil giant Lukoil. Berezovsky offered to buy their shares, but the fund refused. Lukoil, like other vast corporations, had their reasons for staying on good terms with the Kremlin, if they wanted to gain licences, export quotas and favourable tax treatment. The Kremlin's fist was obvious when Lukoil-Garant acted against its own financial interests to bring a bankruptcy suit against TV 6, demanding that the station be liquidated at a time when it was actually beginning to make money. It invoked a rarely used clause of the Russian law on joint-stock companies, which stated that a company can be liquidated if its debts excee-ded its assets for two years running. TV6 had been unprofitable, but its ratings had doubled since the arrival of NTV's journalists and its advertising had increased. The channel's managers were about to break even and believed they would make a profit the following year, but the court refused to consider the company's financial position as of January. Significantly, this clause had already been repealed as inappropriate by the Duma a few months earlier, but it did not take effect until 1 January 2002. TV6's screen blanked out at mid-night on 21 January 2002 for insolvency by order of Press Minister Lesin. Sports came on the screen the next day. To add to the dirty dealings, a video of Yevgeny Kiselyov engaging in sexual activities with two women appeared on the website kompromat.ru. It was presumed to have been filmed secretly by the FSB.

A last chance for independent television remained with a tender set for March 2002 for the vacated TV6's licence – now called TVS. The Federal Tender Commission, responsible for awarding broadcasting licences, still retained liberal members from Yeltsin's years, some of whom discussed the stress they were under to do the right thing. A number of professional groups were bidding, but Kiselyov's team won in the end. Its consortium, Media Socium, was selected because it was backed by a large group of oligarchs (such as Chubais, now chief of the energy grid, and aluminium magnate Oleg Deripaska), which gave it the financial advantage. It also meant that no single investor would be able to influence the editorial line. The deal compromised Kiselyov in the eyes of former supporters because of his efforts to stay on top at all costs, even if it meant working with a Kremlin-backed consortium. Yeltsin had made a suggestion that he head the consortium as a guarantor, but the offer was vetoed by Putin. Instead, it was headed by Yevgeny Prima-kov, a rival turned ally of Putin. The deal was seen as a cynical marriage of convenience to appease everyone.

It didn't. TVS was plagued not only by financial troubles and infighting among the oligarchs but also by management and legal disputes and conflict among the journalists. The oligarchs claimed the journalists wanted too much money, the journalists said the oligarchs were not putting enough money into the station, and they had not been paid for months. TVS broadcast precisely for a year, from June 2002–3. It was taken off the air by Lesin because of its financial problems (illegally, since the media law stipulates that a channel can be taken off the air only by a court order, and there was none) and replaced by a state-run sports channel (without a public tender). The government had become less concerned about covering its tracks now that it had a monopoly on television. It was rumoured that Chubais and Deripaska separately had tried to buy the channel, but to no avail. Obviously, Putin was not prepared to take any chances with the elections imminent in 2003 and 2004.

TVS was the last major 'independent' private nationwide territorial channel in Russia. Its demise left the Kremlin in de facto control of all the major television news stations and networks. It had taken the television industry back to the Soviet era, where no private media had been allowed to exist. Censorship had returned, not in word but deed. The situation differed from that of the Soviet Union only in that some pluralism still existed in smaller television channels and other media outlets. But from now on the vast majority of television viewers would be spoon-fed.

Information Security Doctrine: (ii) the foreign threat

As the Information Security Doctrine shows, the West was perceived as a threat early in Putin's presidency, although it was not until later that action was taken. Loss of superpower status was felt deeply in Russia's nationalist circles; an overblown sense of humiliation at the loss of parity with the USA and a constant anxiety for its own sovereignty and national interests. These fears manifested themselves during the colour revolutions that took place in countries of the former Soviet Union: Georgia's Rose Revolution (2003), Ukraine's Orange Revolution (2004) and Kyrgyzstan's Tulip Revolution (2005). To Putin and his entourage these popular rebellions were not expressions of local discontent with corruption and crony capitalism, but attempts by the West to weaken and divide Russia. When Putin experienced Russia's own protest movement in 2012, he snapped that it was time to 'break the Anglo-Saxon monopoly on the global information streams'.[84]

Plans to challenge US media hegemony came early in the Putin regime – in 2001 when Press Minister Lesin returned from a trip to the USA, smarting from a US State Department report that criticised his ministry's record on free speech. He called a press conference at home, putting forward projects to improve Russia's image abroad. 'I've long ago stopped being ashamed of the word "propaganda"', he said. 'We need to propagandise Russia in the international market, its positive side, or we'll look like bears in their eyes, wandering the streets growling'.[85] Lesin mentioned various projects he had in mind: to fund US free speech NGOs, to publish a document that would expose 'free speech and free activity of the media in the USA', and to organise a big campaign promoting Russia on US media. Nothing came of these ideas, but RT, when it emerged, was Lesin's brainchild.

Originally called Russia Today (news from Russia was not good publicity and the name was abbreviated), RT was Russia's English-language 24-hour satellite TV news channel, also coming out in Spanish and Arabic, to vie with the likes of BBC World, CNN, Al-Jazeera and other international broadcasters. With a start-up capital from the state of $30 million in 2005, it was receiving between $300 and $500 million by 2015, with Russian and foreign staff resident in Moscow and Washington. As the Kremlin's mouthpiece, RT justifies Russia's rollback of democracy and downplays most popular political movements aspiring to democracy, whether in Ukraine or Syria, as manifestations of anarchy, chaos and western interference. RT claims to have reached a billion viewers on YouTube, but in the UK its daily audience in 2015 was 90,000, less than such obscure channels as Zing and Viva.[86]

Unlike Russia's home channels, RT is not prohibited from displaying a pluralism of views on non-crisis events and sometimes invites interesting guests that do not get to be regulars on western television, such as Noam Chomsky, Slavoj Žižek, Julian Assange. It claims to provide an alternative perspective on major global events. Seeing things differently would have been a valuable television strategy and one located in Russia's own literary tradition of 'estrangement', but just as the Formalists were rejected by Soviet ideologues, Russia's creative past was not a source of inspiration for Putin's executives. They claimed to be different, but remained trapped in a narrow, authoritarian tradition. More often the pluralism of RT resided in broadcasting marginal views, conspiracy theories and crackpot ideas; anything to break the Anglo-American mould and annoy its advocates. To counter British politics, it has given a good deal of time to the controversial views of George Galloway and Nigel Farage; to aggravate Americans it gives a platform to 'truthers', who believe 9/11 was the work of the US government and not Islamist militants. There is nothing RT likes better than US race riots, which take Russian memories back to the endless propaganda of the 1920s and 1930s of Ku Klux Klan lynchings. RT engages in Russian diplomacy's favourite game of tit for tat and 'whataboutism'. When RT's editor Margarita Simonyan was asked why the station gave airtime to 'truthers', she replied that it was morally comparable to western media coverage of the 1999 apartment bombings. She herself did not believe in 'truthers' but – 'what about western media reports saying that Vladimir Putin was behind the bombings?'[87]

On closer inspection, the political technologists have created yet another postmodernist phenomenon in RT. This could be witnessed in the sensational 2011 poster campaign, which won international advertising awards and was displayed on countless billboards and full-page newspaper advertisements around the world. The poster depicted the face of US President Barack Obama and Iranian President Mahmoud Ahmadinejad superimposed over each other with the question: 'Who poses the greater nuclear threat?', followed by RT's logo – 'question more'. It was glib but thought-provoking, although the latent message was actually saying something about the nature of truth. If you cannot distinguish between two such opposed figures as Obama and Ahmadinejad, what does it tell us about truth, except that there is no truth. This is RT's standard message: stop criticising us and our versions of democracy, because our truth is as good as yours. 'I don't believe in unbiased news', says Simonyan,[88] repeating Putin's views conceived in his spy days that news only reflects vested interests.

RT's first broadcast in December 2005 was coordinated with two policy moves designed to decrease the West's influence on Russia. One was Surkov's announcement on 6 February 2006 of the doctrine of 'sovereign democracy', a new label to attach to the regime's democracy that reflected the fear, ever since Kosovo, that its sovereignty was threatened by western aggression. Sovereign democracy confirmed the right of countries to determine their own domestic and foreign policy without interference from outside. It did not practise what it preached, as we see later in the interventions in Georgia and Ukraine, accusing the West's democracy-promotion NGOs of fomenting the colour revolutions. Russia's policy may also have been fear of the UN's new policy of 'responsibility to protect', that had come into effect a few months earlier, in September 2005, and gave the international community the responsibility to intervene in a country if citizens' human rights were grossly and systematically violated, a consequence of the tragedies in the Balkans and Rwanda.

The other policy move to counter democracy promotion came with the January 2006 amendment to the Law on Non-Governmental Organisations, an attempt to close down NGOs which received any level of funding from western international development agencies or private philanthropic foundations. The amendment introduced further bureaucratic reporting requirements and draconian rules on financial accounting. The NGOs that were targeted were mainly those supporting human rights and environmental issues, media and election training. The demands became even more severe, as we will see, in Putin's third term in office, when NGOs were labelled 'foreign agents'.

Editor of *Profil'* ('Profile'), Georgy Bovt, explained the attempt to tighten control over foreign NGOs as a Soviet-era phenomenon: 'These people have enormous difficulty understanding the difference between civic and political activity, especially since in their day and age "political" was almost always synonymous with "subversive". Your average KGB colonel in the late-Soviet era would have found it hard to believe that a foreign organization could do anything in Russia without a hidden agenda'.[89] It was the reverse side of the time when the Communist Party, with an agenda in mind, had funded communist parties all over the world. Some western critics share the Kremlin view that foreign-funded NGOs are 'stooges' of a more malign western agenda. While it is true that US or foreign capitalist values are promoted in certain NGOs concerned with marketisation, for the most part there has been no agenda to democracy-promotion NGOs other than to provide training and awareness in fostering liberal values, which is why donors were originally invited into the country in the Yeltsin era and why they are now vilified under the Putin regime. If these NGOs instil ideas of regime change in their struggle against authoritarianism, corruption and censorship, it is because of the regime's violations of democratic values. Because Putin refuses to acknowledge that Russia is not a democracy, he needs to find other reasons, such as 'foreignness' to prevent the dangers they represent.

To compete with foreign-funded NGOs, an umbrella institution called the Public Chamber (Obshchestvennaya palata) was set up to provide grants for NGOs on a smaller scale. This was one of the regime's 'virtual institutions', officially independent, as required of institutions designed to oversee the state, yet imposed from above and connected with the state. In other words, they tended to fund GONGOs – a term for NGOs that represent an arm of repressive governments. In 2007 Putin attacked the civil society community as 'jackals' scavenging at foreign embassies: 'who count on the support of foreign funds and governments and not the support of their own people'.[90] Human rights NGOs could not count on the support of the Public Chamber when state officials were harassing some of the best and most worthy of them, such as the Committee of Soldiers' Mothers, whose heroic members exposed military abuses and travelled to the most dangerous parts of Chechnya in search of their lost sons. In the absence of free media, civil society was taking the brunt of public oversight.

Without foreign-funded NGOs, the population would learn less about human rights violations in their country. It was in 2006 that the Soldiers' Mothers exposed one of the worst cases of 'hazing' in the army, a form of ritualistic indoctrination which is widespread. It concerned a 19-year-old conscript, Andrei Sychev, of the Chelyabinsk Tank Academy, who had been beaten and tortured and refused medical treatment, as a result of which he had to have both legs and his genitals amputated. A whistle-blower, one of the army doctors, leaked the information to the Soldiers' Mothers, who took the story to the media. The Defence Minister, Sergei Ivanov, heard of the case from journalists at a press conference three weeks later and replied confidently that nothing serious had happened or he would have been informed. The furore could not be stopped. Putin personally intervened to order the ministry to conduct the investigation quickly and provide Private Sychev with financial compensation and housing. Earlier, Sychev's mother had complained to the press that she had been repeatedly offered money by unknown officials to drop the case.[91]

How many of the multifarious abuses in the country have seen the light of day? If we take cases of hazing for one year, 2005, by the military's own count there were 2,798 cases of abuse, 16 soldiers killed, and an additional 276 men who committed suicide. Since Sychev's case, despite continuing figures of killings, beatings and suicides, the Defence Ministry has done little to eradicate brutality in the armed forces. At least through human rights NGOs cases occasionally come out into the public domain. Although suspicious of the West, the Kremlin has not been queasy about hiring vastly expensive foreign PR companies to improve its image on the global stage. Ekho Moskvy reported that due to the US PR firm Ketchum's vigorous lobbying, Putin was named *Time* magazine's 2007 Person of the Year.

As part of the onslaught against the media, a case was instigated against the most successful media NGO, the Educated Media Foundation (formerly Internews), which was funded by a variety of foreign grants. Its remit was the training and development of regional television stations. As one of the first NGOs of 1992, Internews trained about 15,000 journalists, producers, media managers, media lawyers and web designers throughout the regions over its 15 years of work. Its popular director, Manana Aslamazyan, had nurtured some of the most sophisticated and prosperous of the 500 independent regional stations that flourished in the 1990s, especially stations in Moscow, Yekaterinburg, Tomsk, Novosibirsk and Krasnoyarsk. The last of these TV stations, Tomsk-2, was forced to close down in 2015, despite strong local protest.

As usual, a pretext was found to destroy the former Internews. In January 2007 Aslamazyan was detained at Moscow airport for not declaring a trivial amount of excess cash. She had forgotten to mention that she had the equivalent of $2,567 more in cash than the allowed limit of $10,000. Instead of a fine, she was charged with smuggling, which could mean up to five years in prison, and the foundation was accused of money laundering. It was raided by the economic crime unit, which confiscated all its documents, computers and servers, effectively terminating the foundation's activities. A petition in Aslamazyan's defence, signed by over 2000 people from all over the world, was sent to Putin. The charges against her were eventually dropped, but the foundation had been destroyed completely. The former Internews was the first of the media NGOs to be targeted.

Terrorism in Nord-Ost *and Beslan*

With the Kremlin in control of the main national television networks, who was to say whether government mismanagement, corruption and deceit were being covered up? Journalists on the third channel, NTV, had not been entirely tamed after a decade of free broadcasting, and there were newspapers and smaller electronic media still working robustly, although their impact was uncertain when over 90 per cent of the population received most if not all of their knowledge of the world from the large state TV stations. Two of the bloodiest tragedies connected with Chechen terrorism, which took place during this period, showed that even the huge lies exposed by the remaining media could not affect Putin's general popularity.

It is worth remembering how the first major hostage drama, which took place in June 1995 in Budyonnovsk, was resolved by comparison with the Putin regime's methods. A band of about 130 Chechen fighters led by the notorious rebel leader Shamil Basayev had indiscriminately dragged civilians off the streets of this southern Russian border town, herding over 1,000 people into a hospital, with the result that 147 civilians were killed. There were no government attempts at cover-ups; in fact, Prime Minister Chernomyrdin's negotiations took place in a phone conversation on television – the famous scene of Chernomyrdin's call: 'Shamil Basayev, can you hear me?' To save civilian lives, journalists were permitted to go to a press conference demanded by the rebels, and rebels were allowed to leave the hospital with a group of volunteer hostages, including 20 journalists, who were released after they had crossed the border into Chechnya. The takeover did not pass without some botched-up Russian commando raids and unnecessary killings, but the crisis ended in peace talks, negligent security ministers were sacked, and the media reporting was open and thorough. One of the reasons so many were killed in hostage-taking in the 2000s was the lack of open and trustworthy information available.

The major terrorist attacks in the 2000s took place at the Dubrovka Theatre in Moscow during the performance of a musical, *Nord Ost*, on 23 October 2002 (the siege is referred to as *Nord-Ost*); and in a school in Beslan in North Ossetia on 1 September 2004. In both instances the authorities obstructed journalists and blocked information. As the *Kursk* accident had shown, the instinctive reaction of the authorities was to lie and cover their tracks. Again, by withholding information, a great number of lives were lost. The tensions at Beslan were so great that the OSCE Representative on Freedom of the Media defined the situation as a triple credibility gap: between the government and the media, the media and citizens and government and citizens.

In the *Nord-Ost* siege, Chechen terrorists held 916 hostages for three days until special forces ended the standoff by pumping an unknown gas into the closed hall, disabling hostages as well as terrorists. The horrifying detail was that out of the official figure of 130 dead, only five were actually killed by the terrorists; the rest were poisoned by the gas. There were so many questions: why were all 41 terrorists killed while they were unconscious when they could have been questioned? Why were unconscious people crammed into buses and left to die when they needed artificial respiration immediately? Why did the authorities refuse to reveal the name of the gas that was used, leaving doctors unable to treat patients with proper antidotes to save their lives? If the gas was a military secret, as the authorities maintained, where was the debate about the ensuing cost in lives? On 31 October the Ministry of Health announced the drug to be a powerful opiate fentanyl, but its precise composition has remained a mystery.

Having learned his lesson from the *Kursk* tragedy, Putin was on the spot. He asked forgiveness in his television speech for not being able to prevent so many deaths, but immediately hailed the assault a success: 'We have achieved the virtually impossible'. Western newspapers were shocked at the callous indifference to human life, but the Russian dynamic from the public was different. Putin was praised for his quick and firm actions that had prevented a bloodbath. According to VTsIOM, 85 per cent of respondents backed Putin's handling of the siege. The independent media expressed horror. *Kommersant* ran the headline 'Overkill', quoting a witness: 'they poisoned us like cockroaches'. The *Moskovsky komsomolets* headline 'Saved or killed?' asked, 'why are we being offered only one version – everyone could have died, but only some did'. Aleksandr Minkin retorted: 'We now know what Putin meant by "wiping them out in the outhouses"'.

Scenes that were splashed across the media of a dead Chechen leader after the storming of the theatre showed him with a bottle of cognac by his side, although hostages confirmed they had not seen him smoke or drink. The Chechen 'black widows' among the suicide bombers (those whose husbands had been killed in the war) were portrayed as drug addicts with needle marks on their arms, who died with syringes at their feet.[92] Whether or not these shots were doctored was taken up ten years later by Kseniya Sobchak in one of those rare moments in Russia when journalists publicly accost their colleagues to try to get to the bottom of things. Sobchak read out a statement that REN TV's Olga Romanova had written on the internet: 'People working on TV at the time knew very well where that bottle had come from; correspondent Arkasha Mamontov went to the buffet to get it, opened it and put it by the corpse'.[93] Sobchak was interviewing Mamontov on TV, with Romanova on the phone. Mamontov denied her allegations and said he wasn't even in the building at the time. Did she see it herself? She had not, and would not name who had, but she said there were a lot of witnesses and dared him to take her to court.

To clamp down on criticism, the Press Ministry was busy handing out 'warnings' that threatened the licences of undaunted media outlets. The government's own *Rossiyskaya gazeta* received a reprimand for publishing a front-page photo that showed doctors in white coats dragging a dead body from the theatre. NTV was singled out for interviewing hostages' relatives and allegedly live reporting on the movements of special forces around the theatre building, which they denied; and soon after Boris Jordan, who had replaced Yevgeny Kiselyov at the channel, was also removed. Radio Ekho Moskvy was in trouble for taking a cell-phone call from the theatre and airing interviews with hostages, as well as a half-hour interview with a terrorist. Later, editor Aleksei Venediktov said it was the right decision to give the hostages and their relatives the right to speak; 'but I met with the press minister and I agreed with him that terrorists shouldn't go on the air anymore'.[94] The ministry had warned that statements from terrorists could contain coded messages.

By comparison with *Nord-Ost*, the handling of the Beslan school siege was even worse. The use of censorship and false information is thought to have contributed to the ensuing slaughter in which at least 334 people died, of whom 186 were children. In this horrendous crisis, when teachers and schoolchildren were packed into a hall in extremely hot weather with little food and water for two-and-a-half days, surrounded by explosives, officials made unprecedented efforts to muzzle and harass journalists, and are even suspected of drugging two of them. It showed the Kremlin's obsession with the media and with controlling its image. Officials of PR departments of all the security structures involved in the hostage rescue operation (Interior Ministry, FSB, the Prosecutor-General's Office) arrived in Beslan on the first day ostensibly to keep the public informed, in fact to obstruct journalists.

The official lies were outrageous, and newspapers said so: 'a chronicle of lies' (*Moskovsky komsomolets*); 'lies provoked terrorists' aggression' (*Novaya gazeta*); '54 hours of lies ended with children dying' (*Russky kuryer*). 'One cannot defeat terror with lies ... but the official accounts were filled with lies', said Ekho Moskvy's editor Aleksei Venediktov; 'those who were taken hostage in Beslan paid a very high price for these lies', said Professor Yasen Zasursky, dean of Moscow State University's journalism faculty.

Defying information received on the ground in Beslan, state broadcasters announced the number of hostages as three times lower than in fact there were, claiming the rebels held 350 people when the actual number was 1,200. Survivors later told journalists that suppressing information and minimising the importance of what had happened enraged the terrorists and might have increased their aggressive behaviour towards the hostages. The terrorists were listening to the news on radios and taunted hostages: 'Maybe we should kill enough of you to get down to that number'. Many of the casualties occurred as Russian forces stormed the school after explosions went off in the gym and a fire started. Later evidence indicated that rocket flamethrowers thrown by the military from outside started the fire which killed the hostages.[95]

When CNN, the BBC and radio Ekho Moskvy were sending out live reports of the storming of the school, and correspondents from the smaller REN TV were doing their best to keep information flowing by phoning through the latest news, as they were too far from the scene to get footage (Russian journalists were pushed further from the scene than their foreign colleagues), and NTV, after a pause, remembered its previous professionalism and began to broadcast without breaks for several hours, even managing to show video filmed by hostage-takers inside the hall – while all this was taking place on the ground, state television's First Channel and Rossiya broadcast their normal afternoon schedules. An hour into the battle, First Channel interrupted its programmes with news from Beslan for ten minutes and then began to show a soap called *Women in Love*. Rossiya stayed with Beslan for an hour and then resumed its normal entertainment schedule.[96]

No official representatives gave interviews. Putin was once again in Sochi when the crisis started and although he returned to Moscow he was kept at a distance, so as not to appear embroiled in the crisis. He said a few words on television on the third day and paid a brief visit to Beslan, arriving and leaving in the middle of the night. It was said he was being protected from the wrath of mothers who had lost their children. The worst indictment of Putin came from the Beslan Mothers' Committee, who asked him not to attend the memorial ceremony for their children. The worst indictment of state television came when grieving parents and relatives physically attacked state television crews for reporting lies about the number of hostages and hushing up the scale of the tragedy.

Without official information, independent journalists did what they could, speaking to anguished relatives, which was prohibited to state channels, and piecing together the tragedy from survivors' accounts. Doctors had been warned not to talk to the press. The 4 September issue of *Izvestiya* was devoted to photos of the assault with a full-page front cover of a man carrying the limp half-naked body of a schoolgirl. A few days later, *Izvestiya*'s respected editor, Raf Shakirov, was sacked for being 'too emotional'. It was said the paper's owner, Vladimir Potanin, who had brought an end to *Izvestiya*'s halcyon days, had asked Shakirov to resign after receiving a reprimand from the Kremlin.

There was still the issue of Anna Politkovskaya's mysterious 'poisoning'. Many public figures had tried to act as mediators, but the authorities were particularly concerned to keep Politkovskaya away from the scene and prevent her from making use of her contacts with Aslan Maskhadov, the moderate Chechen leader, to persuade him to help end the siege. This was not regarded positively by the authorities. Writing for the UK's *The Guardian*, Politkovskaya explained that an FSB man at the military airport in Moscow had offered her a seat on a flight to Rostov. On that flight she had drunk a cup of tea and woke up in a hospital bed in Rostov. 'The nurse tells me that when they brought me in I was "almost hopeless". Then she whispers: "My dear, they tried to poison you". All the tests taken at the airport have been destroyed – on orders "from on high", say the doctors'.[97]

The other incident of poisoning took place in Vladikavkaz, the capital of North Ossetia. Georgian journalist Nana Lezhava, of Rustavi-2 TV, was given a cup of coffee during an FSB interrogation and came to her senses the next day in an isolation ward. Tests taken in Georgia later showed she had been drugged. Other journalists were harassed and detained, including a familiar name, Andrei Babitsky, who was prevented from flying to Beslan by being sentenced to five days in prison in Moscow for alleged hooliganism.

Many journalists were shocked at the extent of state television's subservience. NTV revealed a semi-official memo that had been circulated during the siege to state journalists, demanding censorship on almost everything, from troops deployed to names and nationalities of witnesses, relatives and hostages. Forbidden, too, were: political analyses of the crisis and options for tackling it; close-ups of crying relatives and, after the siege, of corpses; words such as 'special operation' and, of course, the phrase (for a whole year already) 'war in Chechnya', especially as, according to officials, what had happened was not connected with Chechnya but with international terrorism, and reports alleged that Arabs had been seen at the school. Deputy news editor at the Rossiya channel, Yevgeny Revenko, sought to fend off criticism for transmitting false information by saying journalists were merely reporting the authorities' statements and – 'it must rest on their conscience'.[98]

Veteran broadcaster, mentor of *perestroika*'s golden youth, Eduard Sagalayev, would have none of it:

> During Beslan, I'm talking to [my former colleagues] and I'm saying, 'I understand you couldn't say anything about the true number of hostages, but why couldn't you show the parent holding the sign "There Are More Than 800"? You could have told the Kremlin that the cameraman was to

blame – "It was beyond our control". You could have fired the cameraman. But show it!

And they answered, 'Eduard, you don't know who we have to deal with'. But I know perfectly well who they're dealing with. And what I'm worried about now is the state of my own colleagues.[99]

If journalists working on state television had an opportunity en masse to protest and reject the subservience Putin and his officials had imposed on them, this was the time to do it. The crisis made a mockery of the stability and order Putin had touted. The Chechen fiasco had triggered not only *Nord-Ost* and Beslan but a whole spate of suicide bombings. The mismanagement, lies and callousness peaked in Beslan and could have stirred feelings of moral outrage, reviving the spectacular spirit journalists had shown during *perestroika* and the early Yeltsin years, but that did not happen. 'It is tempting to blame Vladimir Putin', wrote journalist Arkady Ostrovsky, 'but the truth is more complicated ... Russian TV has been complicit in the shrinking of its independence ... they are not helpless pawns'.[100] When Sagalayev and Irina Petrovskaya sponsored a protest letter over Beslan, Sagalayev said a flood of hatred poured down on him. 'They said I was looking for cheap popularity'.

Beslan was a point of no return for Putin and those journalists who crossed the Rubicon with him. It meant acceptance of Putin's increasingly authoritarian regime in exchange for rewards. The oil economy was booming, Moscow-based TV journalists were well paid and people were enjoying a higher standard of living than ever before. Those who did not become Putin followers gradually moved into alternative and social media.

After Beslan, Putin consolidated his political dominance. He insisted that sweeping political changes had to be made to combat terrorism although, as commentators have noted, the changes made after crises never had anything to do with the original problem. In this case changes were made to the electoral system: an end was put to the direct election of regional governors, who had been a major independent force under Yeltsin; and an end to the election of independent members of parliament, who had made up half the Duma and provided a way that popular independent figures, often liberals, could get into parliament. This brought an end to meaningful elections and the genuine rotation of government. The earlier Duma and presidential elections of 2003–4 had already seen the liberal parties Yabloko and Union of Right forces wiped out, and the communists losing half their votes to nationalist and statist parties. In effect, in so short a period of time, Putin held all the levers of power in his hands.

Andrei Illarionov, Putin's chief economic adviser who had steered the booming oil economy, resigned at the end of 2005 after regular outbursts of anger at the erosion of democracy, especially after Khodorkovsky's imprisonment and the redistribution of Yukos to pro-Putin factions. He saw the fault not only in Putin but in the public's indifference:

To begin with, Chechnya's freedom was violated and many people died in that war, but many citizens of Russia decided that this did not concern them. Next media freedom was violated, but many citizens of Russia decided that this did not concern them either. Then private business freedom was violated, but Russians decided that this did not concern them either. Next the freedom of political parties and the freedom to elect governors and local authorities were violated; then the freedom of operation of non-governmental organisations, freedom of religious convictions and freedom of expression on the internet were violated, but citizens of Russia thought all the time that this did not concern them and that they did not need to defend this. As a result, no freedom remains in Russia now.[101]

The 'patrimonial' media

Having taken control of the major television networks, the Kremlin turned to media outlets which it considered second rank in importance. These were the privately owned national newspapers and second-league electronic outlets. The Kremlin's almost obsessional drive to add to the list of media it already had under its control has led today to what can be called a 'patrimonial media', because of the uniquely Russian relationship that has developed between private media tycoons and the Kremlin.

In this relationship the state has invited or allowed Kremlin-friendly oligarchs to acquire media outlets as long as they keep their journalists in check on the state's behalf. Deals are done behind closed doors. The first step usually requires pressure to get owners to sell, as we saw in the case of Gusinsky and Berezovsky, but preferably done without the drama, which it is possible to do with less powerful individuals. The second step is to negotiate with a friendly oligarch, often a long-time Putin associate, who would understand his duty to the state or be bound by clan loyalties. Media property acquired in this way belongs to the owner only in the relationship of servitor to master. If the owner does not abide by the rules of the game, the property can be retrieved. One can call this extortion, if we look at it in terms of Russia's political mafia mentality; or we can look at it in terms of the pull of history and Russia's autocratic legacy.

Putin has borrowed extensively from Russia's past to prop up his own statist system, and the submissive relationship that has developed between media and the state is not dissimilar to feudal relations that existed in Russia for centuries, basically from the twelfth to the nineteenth centuries. Historian Richard Pipes uses the term 'patrimony' to define Russia's type of feudalism where 'conflicts between sovereignty and property do not and cannot arise because, as in the case of a primitive family run by a paterfamilias, they are one and the same thing. A despot violates his subjects' property rights; a patrimonial ruler does not even acknowledge their existence'.[102] It was possible to push people into this old pattern once the principles of democracy and the Yeltsin era had been devalued and destroyed.

Compared with Russia, feudalism of the Western European type was a very different system, based on contracts and rights that had developed between vassal and lord. In Russia the law played no role, as private and state property were almost indistinguishable. The Russian landlord held land on condition of state service in a non-reciprocal relationship: what the sovereign (*gosudar'*) gave, he could take away. Interestingly, Pipes shows that this autocratic system was largely accepted by landowners and there were only three significant attempts to change it.[103] An acceptance of the tied and binding relationship we see today between private media owners and the state has roots in this patrimonial mentality where oligarchs, at least publicly, appear to maintain a harmonious relationship with the state. To take the comparison one step further: formally, the landlord did not own his serfs either (*krepostnoe pravo*), so that both landowner and serf were committed to serve the tsar. A journalist's relationship in this recreated feudal set-up would incline naturally to furthering the interests of the state over and above that of his media boss. In this patrimonial system of ranking both the media owner, however wealthy he may be, as well as the journalist, lack independence and are bound to serve Putin, as the figure of the personalised state.

There are probably few countries in the world where the media industry, with thousands of outlets and networks criss-crossing Russia's vast spaces, submits to the will of a leader in a capitalist system; even, say, in such a despotic capitalist state as Pinochet's Chile. In repressive capitalist societies private media owners of major television stations and newspapers do not have such enforced ties: they either willingly support and promote a regime through their outlets or their media are banned or they are in perpetual struggle against the regime. It is not customary for a wealthy private tycoon to submit so abjectly to the state. By contrast, in a communist country, such as China, the media have not been allowed to partake in China's rampant capitalist enterprise and have largely remained in the position of the Soviet media under Brezhnev in the 1970s. Some commentators point to a similarity with Russia in Turkey's media, based on an extreme form of patrimonialism called 'sultanism'.

Strictly speaking, those who talk of the 'Sovietisation' of the media today are inaccurate, except in so far as the Soviet system also replicated the patrimonial one. Of course we understand the comparison but it misses the point, because for the media to be 'Soviet' would be to nationalise them, whereas what we see is a tortuous attempt to create a capitalist version of bonding with the state. The patrimonial system offers other virtues to the regime, because to have a tied owner is preferable to one you have to entice or lobby to support you. The set up plays to the same political technologists' script where owners and their media outlets appear to be private and independent, but are chained down by a variety of external factors. Formally, the regime can and does insist that private independent media exist in robust form.

Those who dismiss the patrimonial relationship as a façade and hence no more harmful than a matter of playing games, do not take into account the trauma of normalised lying. In the first place it encourages the schizoid approach to reality that characterised the Soviet system. It produces wary, cautious, alienated relationships within the journalist community and society, making any journalistic endeavour to try to create a fourth estate less likely. It changes the relationship to work. It demands a patriarchal response and dampens critical thinking. It dramatically changes the impact of censorship when it is turned into self-censorship.

Self-censorship places the blame on the individual. If obstructions to free speech are so intrusive that a person gives up the struggle, it is still the case that no one has forced the person to give up. Self-censorship turns the journalist into a victim, much in the same way as a rape victim, if he or she has failed to stand up and denounce the rapist, whatever his or her reason. It may be because the collective culture would revile the individual or because the state would crush him or her. This makes Putin-style censorship more perverse than Soviet censorship, where journalists were under the heel of the editor and the editor was under the heel of *Glavlit*. It was not their fault, then, if the final stamp came from a faceless bureaucracy. Of course, if you wanted, you were free to complain, for which you might lose your job or go to prison, but in most cases it would not affect the fate of the article. That was the whole point of using Aesopian language so as to wriggle through *Glavlit*. But in self-censorship it is possible to publish if you have the guts. When President Medvedev told journalists on a number of occasions in 2010 to ask him anything they wanted, no one came forth with serious questions. It was as if the necessary reflexes no longer worked.

The jet-setting billionaire oligarchs may not personally be happy about owning media assets; certainly there is criticism from investors that these enormous oil and metal empires are straying from their core business. When the foreign press talks of media being 'awarded' to loyal cronies, it may not be seen as a reward at all but more like a duty. If you cannot use your media outlet for personal ends (like Gusinsky and Berezovsky did), and if it is not a profit-making endeavour (if it is news and not celebrity tabloids), it becomes more of a burden than an asset.

Russia's private media owners have been co-opted into working within this patrimonial system, where property is private in law but feudal in fact. Most private outlets are parts of large media holdings owned by oligarchs, who also possess and run massive industrial and financial corporations. Some media tycoons go back to the Yeltsin era, such as Vladimir Potanin. Most of the newcomers are part of Putin's clique. Ekho Moskvy's editor, Venediktov, who has had opportunities to talk to Putin, confirms the feudal mentality: 'Putin thinks that journalists are instruments of the owners of the media. He told me so. And if the owner is good, the instrument will be safe; but if the instrument is bad, the owner has to be changed'.[104]

Patrimonial media ownership

After the crisis year 2005 following the Beslan siege, the turnover in news-paper acquisitions and smaller TV channels became fierce. Pressure was put on owners to sell to pro-Putin oligarchs, sometimes using intimidation and *kompromat*. In 2001 Gusinsky had sold all that remained of his media outlets in Russia. Berezovsky hung on for longer, financing his newspapers from abroad, but from 2005 he also began to sell. Many outlets since then have been sold and re-sold several times over the last decade. The new ownership networks tend to be complex, but they all show increasing concentration in the hands of oligarchs and corporations that form a tight web of business and media interests linked with the Kremlin political elite.

The last independent national private channel, REN TV, with a small (4 per cent) share of viewing but with a prestigious name, went under the hammer in 2005. Owner Irena Lisnevsaya said in 2014 that she had been under pressure to sell for two years. REN TV depended on support from Anatoly Chubais by virtue of his position as director of the electricity monopoly Unified Energy Systems, which held 70 per cent of shares in the television company. Chubais had been pressured into selling the block of shares to Yury Kovalchuk, a close Petersburg friend of Putin. Lesnevskaya had tried to see Putin, with whom she was acquainted, without luck; but she managed to persuade former German chancellor Gerhard Schroeder, now an executive in the gas industry in Russia, to speak on her behalf and suggest that he buy some of the shares. Lesnevskaya hoped the German input would protect her channel. Schroeder asked Putin if he would permit him to buy a block of shares out of Chubais's portfolio. Putin replied: 'No. Chubais's block will go to the state; you can buy shares from Lesnevskaya's portfolio'. It caused the journalist Pavel Lobkov, who was taking an interview with Les-nevskaya on Dozhd' TV online to gasp: 'What a deep understanding the head of state has of share ownership in TV companies!'.

TIKHON DZYADKO: Do you think that now ten years later Vladimir Vladi-mirovich Putin is just as knowledgeable about the mechanism of media joint-stock companies?

LESNEVSKAYA: Of course, much better than you or I because the details aren't made transparent to us ...

DZYADKO: It turns out that these people decide the ideological work of the media.

LESNEVSKAYA: No, I think they only implement Vladimir Vladimirovich's requests and grab everything they can. It's unlikely they sit and direct and watch.

LOBKOV: I'm dashed if I can see Yury Valentinovich Kovalchuk inspecting all his 148 media outlets.

LESNEVSKAYA: I don't think he knows what's going on there. Why should he? There are specially trained people receiving special salaries for that, managers who are responsible for ideology.[105]

REN TV was Kovalchuk's first media acquisition. Since then his National Media Group has become the largest and most influential media holding in the country. Among its acquisitions (either which it owns or has a majority stake in) are St Petersburg's Fifth Channel, *Izvestiya*, radio Russian News Service, the entertainment channel holding STS-Media and the advertising monopoly Video International. The First Channel, 25 per cent of which had been in Roman Abramovich's hands since Berezovsky had been forced to sell his shares, was now bought by Kovalchuk for a rumoured $150 million.[106] That gave him three national TV channels. Yury Kovalchuk (and his brother Mikhail) are among Putin's most trusted friends. His St Petersburg-based bank Rossiya is known as the main bank that serves the Putin entourage. For that reason, it was targeted for sanctions by the US after the Crimea standoff. The National Media Group had been put together by Mikhail Lesin in an apparently mysterious and 'unethical' manner. This happened during President Medvedev's term in office, and enraged him to such a degree that Lesin was sacked in the harshest tones for 'systematic violations of discipline', including not observing 'the rules of state service and the ethical behaviour of a state servant'.[107] The attack may point to murky business negotiations or to political rivalry, for Lesin has always been Putin's man and until his death the most powerful player in media politics under his regime.

During the 2012 protest movement, Lesin was brought back to deal with the new dangers to the regime. Appointed as head of Gazprom Media, he was there to make patrimonial rearrangements. Yuliya Latynina, a journalist who has managed to decipher the hugely tangled network of media ownership relations, analysed the process. As soon as Lesin was installed, Gazprom Media bought out billionaire oligarch Vladimir Potanin's media company Profmedia, which added considerably to Gazprom Media's stable of TV and radio stations, newspapers, cinemas, film production and online portals. Previously Gazprom Media had been attached to the parent company, Gazprom, but under Lesin it was bought by Gazprombank, controlled by the Kovalchuk brothers. That meant, says Latynina, that 'practically all television channels, radio stations and other major assets not already owned by the state have now come under the control of the Kovalchuk brothers'.[108]

Putin's fear of 'monopolisation' by private media, as expressed in the Information Security Doctrine, must have been assuaged by his friend Kovalchuk holding the vast share of the private sector in his hands. Kovalchuk has, in effect, also acquired a monopoly of the advertising market. As owner of Video International (originally founded by Lesin), Kovalchuk owns 70 per cent of the advertising market. The other 30 per cent belongs to Alcasar, which sells advertising for NTV. Through Gazprom Media, however, which has controlled NTV ever since Gusinsky was kicked out, Kovalchuk's group has influence over NTV as well. With the advertising industry in his hands, Latynina believes Kovalchuk rivals the 'Soviet media behemoth Gosteleradio'.[109] This is the ownership pattern that exists in 2016, but the incestuous interweaving of different serving oligarchs shifts frequently, securing the political needs of the regime.

The ownership of major newspapers and journals also changed to more loyal hands in 2005: *Nezavisimaya gazeta, Moskovskiye novosti, Trud, Versiya* ('Version'), *Ogonyok*. The most important acquisition was the broadsheet daily *Kommersant* with its publishing house, previously owned by Berezovsky and his business colleague Badri Patarkatsishvili, and sold to metals tycoon Alisher Usmanov in 2006. Although Usmanov bought the newspaper through his own iron ore company, Metalloinvest, he was also director-general of Gazprominvest Holding, fully owned by Gazprom. The boomerang always returns to the Kremlin.

In this way Russia's wealthiest men, high up on Forbes's list of the richest people on the globe, who have made money in energy and finance and may have no interest in the press, hold on to even relatively modest media outlets and have started investing in the internet. Alisher Usmanov, in 2013 the richest man in Russia (and the UK, where he is a resident and owns one-third of Arsenal Football Club), with a £13 billion fortune, controls the biggest internet provider in the Russian-speaking world (Mail.ru) and later bought stakes in social networking site Vkontakte and the schoolfriends' site Odnoklassniki. Another billionaire media tycoon, Aleksandr Mamut, owner of Britain's largest book chain Waterstones, entered the media business in 2006, mainly buying into internet and social media. Together with Potanin, he holds the rights to the Cyrillic segment of LiveJournal and, through their media company Afisha-Rambler-SUP, they own the web portal Rambler and news sites (such as lenta.ru).

Despite their Midas-like wealth, the patrimonial relationship means media owners jump when called upon. In 2011, when a scandal occurred in Usmanov's journal *Kommersant-Vlast'*, which published a photograph of a spoiled ballot paper with insulting graffiti about Putin, it ended with the sacking of the general director and a number of journalists. During the heated atmosphere of the Crimean crisis, Mamut sacked the editor and a journalist at lenta.ru, when they received a warning from the media regulator, Roskomnadzor. Critics noted scornfully that some owners were sacking journalists now even before the Kremlin asked them to. Every tycoon fears competitors and rivals more powerful than him, who may jostle him out of the way. 'When a publisher is told that he may lose his business if he does not fire an independent-minded editor or close a publication, his decision to comply is certainly economic. And just as certainly, it is political', writes Masha Gessen.[110] It raises Russian eyebrows, however, when foreigners do the same. Condé Nast was mocked when it removed a highly critical article on Putin from the Russian edition of the magazine *GQ* but not from the US one.

Alternative information sources: (i) traditional media

A few traditional outlets have shown a proven record of independent and uncompromised journalism, against all attempts to deny their editorial autonomy. One of the longest lasting beacons of freedom has been radio Ekho Moskvy, which started broadcasting in 1990. Most truth seekers follow its news, programmes and blogs. To be 'alternative' in the media world courts danger and its editor, Aleksei Venediktov, a familiar figure with his halo of wiry hair, has had numerous physical threats. Since an axe on a chopping block was left outside his apartment in 2009, he is accompanied by a body-guard. Venediktov calls Ekho the 'mausoleum', because it has become the Kremlin's showcase to give the impression that free speech exists. Venediktov likes to point out that the radio's main shareholder is state-controlled Gazprom Media, which owns 66 per cent of the station, with the journalist collective owning the rest. Theoretically, Ekho hangs by a thread and could be closed at any moment. On occasion Putin has ranted against its coverage, and during the protest movement in 2012 accused it of pouring verbal 'diarrhoea' on him. At other times Venediktov has been invited to Putin's meetings with trusted media executives. Venediktov's recipe for success has been to invite a wide spectrum of political opinion on the website's blogs, embracing most of the liberal great and good, as well as mavericks and a handful of pro-Putinists. Among the latter have been Prokhanov, Dorenko and Margarita Simonyan. Venediktov insists that Ekho's aim is professionalism: to provide alternative, not oppositionist, information.

Its wide range of opinions is both what keeps it afloat and causes internal conflicts. 'I create a model of society with my radio programmes. If we had a free press in the country, I wouldn't have to', he says.[111] Venediktov is tough, sometimes rude with his audience and intransigent with the authorities. In 2014, warned by Press Minister Lesin to sack a journalist or be sacked, he refused to take orders. The incident involved an old scandal over former Defence Minister Sergei Ivanov's son, who had all charges dropped against him after running over a pensioner on a pedestrian crossing. When Ivanov's son drowned in an accident, Ekho's Aleksandr Plyushchev tweeted that there was a 'higher justice' after all (he later apologised). Venediktov's defiance was based on the radio station's charter and on the media law, that it was up to the editor to make decisions on the staff and up to the journalist collective to decide whether to fire the editor. Venediktov won this round, and he has won many others, but the authorities have become more vindictive since the Ukraine crisis. Political problems also come with advertising losses, as companies fear the impact that politics will have on their businesses. Ekho currently has four million listeners, who tune into the radio station daily, and more than three million a month who read the site. One of the reasons the radio is still on the air, says Venediktov, is that the Kremlin also needs a pluralism of information.

The newspaper *Novaya gazeta*, the heroic crusader against the Chechen war and corruption, sees itself in opposition to the Kremlin. It has paid a high price for its independence, with six of its journalists murdered. 'We don't serve the powers that be, we're in conflict with them', says deputy editor Vitaly Yaroshevsky. Against all the odds, it has retained its purity. As a rule, it will not report the well-known rants of Zhirinovsky or Prokhanov, which get well covered elsewhere. Nor does it use leaks suspected to be from the FSB ('people have come offering money'), because it could be an attempt to incriminate them. 'The authorities never ring to demand anything from us, they know we're not under their control', says Yaroshevsky. 'They wouldn't want to ring us, we might do something about it'. As a result, the staff gets half the salary of those at *Izvestiya*, says Yaroshevsky, while he doesn't get a bonus or a special car or medical insurance. 'But you're not ashamed to work here', he says.[112]

Novaya, as it is known, started in 1993 and comes out three days a week. Its print run in 2014 of 242,650 shows it is doing well (by comparison with *Kommersant*'s at 81,390 and the pro-Putin 'yellow' newspaper *Komsomolskaya pravda* at 183,215). The paper is known for its frank investigations, among which have been articles about business firms directly connected to Putin, ministers using shady means to build luxurious villas on the Black Sea, money disappearing from Sochi Olympic Games constructions, and Putin's so-called palace (it was referred to as 'a palace built for Putin'), which was hurriedly resold.

There have been many attempts to close or bankrupt *Novaya*. In 2003 judges slapped $1.5 million damages against it in two defamation cases: one for alleging that Krasnodar region's top judge was living well beyond his means; the other alleging a bank's money-laundering activities. This was an astonishing fine given that the previous 54 libel cases came to a total of only $50,000. In the end, after *Novaya* offered an apology, the defendants agreed to an amount that would allow the paper to continue publication. In the internet age, it is regularly the target of cyberattacks. On one occasion, in April 2011, the attack was so strong that its website, which typically received 70,000 to 120,000 visitors every day, was getting 70,000 visit requests every 14 seconds.[113]

The paper is 51 per cent owned by the journalist collective. Gorbachev is a supporter, his 10 per cent shares managed by oligarch Aleksandr Lebedev (with 39 per cent), who is also owner of London's *Evening Standard* and other media outlets in the UK. Lebedev's commercial ventures have suffered heavily as a result of his connection with the paper; and whether Gorbachev's name will help is a moot point, since it made no difference when he was on NTV's board in 2001.

Another staunch outlet, the liberal weekly, *Novoye Vremya* (also using its English title, the *New Times*), survives with a small print run of loyal supporters. Bought by Irena Lesnevskaya after she was forced to sell REN TV, she gave the paper as a gift in 2013 to its editor, Yevgeniya Albats, an outspoken journalist, also from the *perestroika* era. As well, the public can turn to an old standby, the Russian-language foreign broadcasters, such as Radio Liberty and the BBC Russian Service: both have cut their radio services but continue their websites.

Other sources in the press can be called 'fellow-travellers': they allow a certain amount of political freedom and do what they can. A powerful editor such as Pavel Gusev, who owns the profitable tabloid *Moskovsky komsomolets*, will play a fine balancing act and see what he can get away with. A number of papers are in this category (*Novyye Izvestiya, Argumenty i fakty*). Business media, such as *Kommersant*, are given a freer rein, perhaps because of a felt need for accurate information in the financial domain, but even this changed in Putin's third term. Foreign-owned business newspapers, *Vedomosti* ('Gazette') and *Forbes* were sold to Russians, and Russia's own RBK, a large media holding consisting of publishing ventures, a wire agency, website and TV channel that was not scared of investigating suspicious financial ventures, owned by oligarch Mikhail Prokhorov, was pressured into sacking editors and senior journalists in 2016. The last straw it seemed was RBK's coverage of the Panama Papers and in particular the personal life and business affairs of Putin's younger daughter, who had been operating under an assumed name. Prokhorov, the last remaining billionaire supporting opposition media, fell into line in the patrimonial system once gun-toting police stormed his premises and threatened his 10 billion-dollar financial empire.

(ii) Internet and social media

Russians used to say, 'it's not news if it's not on television'. That saying remains true today for the majority of the population, but the spread of internet and social media has fractured the regime's hold on information and television's monopoly. From 2001 there have been attempts to restrict the internet, but it was not until 2007, coming up to the elections, when regular internet users had reached over 29 million, 20.8 per cent of the population, that serious methods of control began to be considered.[114] As Russia has tried to avoid falling into the category of non-democratic states, such as China, Belarus and Turkmenistan who have built firewalls, the FSB hired hackers and young 'patriotic' bloggers instead to crash systems, spam opposition websites and flood chatrooms at required moments. Denial of service hacker attacks were particularly common when protest demonstrations were being organised.

Online users have continued to increase rapidly. By 2010 there were almost 60 million in the country – the highest number in Europe.[115] Russians have been enthusiastic users of social networking sites, with President Medvedev leading the way with his website and Twitter account. In 2011 the number of bloggers in the Russian LiveJournal segment exceeded two million, making Russia the second 'LiveJournal addict' country after the United States, with its five million bloggers.[116] In 2016 there were over 102 million internet users,[117] but as we have seen users and social networkers are not necessarily avid news followers. Nevertheless, the increase of social media from 2011 gave a huge boost of confidence to the educated urban class and to the protest movement. Newspapers set up their own websites, and many independent online news sites and blogs became required reading for anyone seeking reliable information. In January 2011, when a suicide bomber blew himself up at Moscow's Domodedovo Airport, the news was first broken on Twitter at 16.44, after which international news sites picked up the story, and only two hours later did Russia's state-run TV channels announce the attack.

Cooperation between traditional and citizen journalists on the internet has encouraged civic activism and self-help. Because of the Putin regime's terrible record of responding to emergencies, people turned to the internet to solve their problems. During the 2010 wildfires that raged through central Russia after the worst heatwave for more than a century, with Moscow choking in hazardous smog from peat bogs surrounding the city, not only did officials play down the impact of the disaster and its death toll, they were incapable of offering standard health and safety guidance. The blogosphere became the survival call centre. People on social media set up a round-the-clock system to monitor and exchange information, organise units of firefighters, set up early warning systems and find volunteers to provide medical help:

> Yesterday we went to Kulebaki to bring them everything they needed – firefighting equipment, food, protective devices that were purchased with bloggers' money. Our mission to the 'hot spot' was organized by i_cherski, who, as you know, is filling in voluntarily for our temporarily incompetent leadership at the Ministry of Emergency Situations.[118]

By filling the gap in the information space, the internet reawakened political activism. It brought people together to fight the battle to preserve Khimki's oak forest from highway construction; car owners in Moscow connected online in the 'blue bucket' campaign against VIP cars using their flashing blue lights to travel at high speeds, causing accidents; meetings were organised online against the unpopular governor of Kaliningrad, which led to his resignation. In Putin's dysfunctional system, the internet was taking on the job of being 'more than an internet', which had been the role of the media before most outlets had been taken over by state alliances. The internet was now journalist, social worker and local councillor.

Out of this tumultuous traffic emerged a new breed of informal political leaders. The most famous and audacious was Aleksei Navalny, an anti-corruption campaigner and blogger, who was brave enough to say what everyone knew: that Putin's United Russia party was a party of 'swindlers and thieves'. The slogan went viral and became part of a large web campaign against corruption and electoral fraud. Navalny's charisma lay in his irreverent humour, shrewd tactics and serious research. A former member of Yabloko, with two degrees in law and finance and a stint at Yale University,

Navalny initiated some of the most imaginative anti-corruption projects on the internet. He took on state corporations, defending the interest of minority shareholders, suing companies to force disclosure of accounting documents. He posted the results of his investigations on his blog (navalny.livejournal.com), until he was put under house arrest in 2014 and forbidden by the court to use the internet. He first made his name after revealing leaked documents of a \$4 billion scam at the state-owned pipeline company Transneft. The website he created (rospil.info) holds information on corrupt government procurement deals; and he continues to be a constant thorn in the side of the government, providing documentation of alleged corruption. Whistle-blowers and crowdsourcing have turned his lonely crusade into a national campaign.

Such personal popularity, when most public figures stand in Putin's shadow, has thrust Navalny up against Putin and raised the hypothetical question of what he would be like as president. Although a symbol of the liberal opposition, he is a nationalist, which gives him a wider appeal than democrats could attain but makes him suspect with some of the opposition, especially as in the past he has been involved in Russian marches, where nationalists are prone to making Nazi salutes and talk of 'Russia for Russians'. He has toned down his nationalist rhetoric since becoming the focus of public interest, but still asks controversial questions. In the 'Stop feeding the Caucasus' campaign, which to some has racist connotations, Navalny speaks of the size of the federal subsidies to Chechnya and the implications that has for keeping the ruthless tyrant Kadyrov in power. He is one of the driving forces behind the attempt by candidates of small democratic parties to stand for elections, he himself having won a stunning 27 per cent of votes in the Moscow mayoral elections in 2013.

The internet has broadened the protest movement to the literary and artistic world, linking it to conceptual art, rock music, theatre and street performance, such as Pussy Riot's punk acts. Dissident writers and artists have participated in public debates and blogs to counter the pro-Putin *glitterati*. Satire returned in the wildly funny *Grazhdanin Poet* series ('Citizen Poet'), produced by former *Kommersant* editor Vasilyev, recited by the lovable actor Mikhail Yefremov and written by the literary virtuoso Dmitry Bykov in rhymed verse, imitating famous poets and laced with political innuendos. One of their sharpest skits was '20 years and bugger all to show for it' (*Dvadtsat' let – ni khrena net*). The series was first tried on Dozhd' TV for a pittance ('for two Mojitos', interjects Yefremov), and became hugely popular with the urban elite, playing to full houses on tour to major cities ('they didn't want to miss out before we got thrown into prison', interjects Yefremov). The spirit of rebellion came to a peak with the rigging of elections in 2011–12.

IV Putin's third presidential term: truth and alternative realities

The tandem politics of Medvedev–Putin had destroyed the no-alternative-to-Putin strategy. Feeble though Medvedev's presidential term had been, it opened up new vistas and choices, and brought excitement to the upcoming 2011–12 elections. When Medvedev nominated Putin for president on 24 September 2011, saying the decision had been planned long ago 'in the period when our comradely alliance was being formed',[119] anger and frustration broke the 12-year political silence. The presidential swap may not have been planned in this way, because Medvedev had implied earlier his wish to seek a second term, but the lack of a contest did not go down well.

Putin's attempt to grab another six or perhaps 12 years of power led to the largest wave of protests since the fall of the Soviet Union. As president, Medvedev had amended the Constitution to extend the presidential term from four to six years – fortunately not seven, which was what Putin considered the best length of time. It meant Putin could be in power until 2024. He had already spent eight years as president and another four as prime minister. Theoretically, he could be in power for a total of 24 years. Even Brezhnev had only managed 18 years in the country's totalitarian past. His record could be equal to Stalin's 24 years in power.

The call for 'Russia without Putin' became a serious challenge to his legitimacy and terrified a regime striving to hold on to power by any means. It seemed to catch Putin unawares when he was first booed by a disgruntled crowd at a martial arts fight. Putin had succumbed to the 'habit of adoration', Gleb Pavlovsky said, himself having been dropped from the presidential team for criticising Putin's return.

Two events in particular struck fear at the heart of the regime, both expressing people's power: (1) the opposition protest movement in Moscow from December 2011; and (2) Kyiv's Euromaidan that toppled the corrupt reign of President Yanukovich in November 2013 and rejected closer integration with Russia in favour of Europe. From the regime's point of view, the two were connected, although the loss to its sphere of influence in the region was not as threatening to the existence of a plundering elite as a liberated pro-western, pro-democracy, anti-corruption Ukraine and the encouragement that would give to the home-grown protest movement that had developed. The Doctrine of Information Security's anticipation of threats from internal and external enemies had, in the eyes of its FSB advocates, come to pass in these two events.

The reactionary forces Putin unleashed in his third term plunged Russia into its darkest period, resembling some of the unedifying moments of Soviet and tsarist history in its embrace of intolerance, jingoism and violence. Contempt for free expression poured into every aspect of life. Not only politics but morality too were in the dock. The regime hit out at non-traditional lifestyles, non-conformist beliefs, religious and sexual orientations. Those who opposed the regime's Ukraine policy were pilloried as disloyal, unpatriotic and treasonable. De facto censorship was imposed on grounds of obscenity, blasphemy and sedition – words with imprecise meanings that could ensnare anyone in their trap.

Although state-controlled media were in a position to blast their version of events over any large-scale dissent, the situation was considered so dangerous that the offensive went to new levels. Accusing the West of stoking rebellion in Moscow and Kyiv, the regime broke its tenuous ties with the western camp and in the process dropped the pretence of being a democracy western style – although still clinging to the word. Instead, it turned to the Orthodox Church and its anti-western, anti-modern views to articulate a new 'democratic' identity based on Russia's 'traditional' values and what were seen as the virtues of the 'Russian world'. These features were largely defined in negation of liberal cosmopolitanism, which was 'un-Russian' (*nerussky*).

As we saw in Chapter 1, the unreformed Orthodox Church, with its mixture of capitalism and medievalism, chimed with Putin's assertive revisionism in a church–state alliance that was aptly described as 'Orthodox Church FSBism' (*pravoslavnyy FSBism*). It was no surprise that, aside from political repression, free speech's other enemies were resurrected – religious dogma and conformism – the threats to free speech that concerned J. S. Mill as much as political repression. The church–state alliance justified ultra-nationalists dredging up old chauvinist and xenophobic views that tsarist vigilante groups such as the Black Hundreds had represented. The most symbolic image of this regression was a Cossack in uniform lashing members of the Pussy Riot group with his knout as the young women tried to protest at the Sochi Winter Olympics: tsarist brutality in the modern age. Given the right to arbitrate on fundamental questions of morality and decide what was to be considered 'depraved and corrupt', the Orthodox Church decreed that being gay or swearing or blaspheming were not Russian values.

What is un-Russian?

Presumably, Pussy Riot is un-Russian, the LGBT (lesbian, gay, bisexual, transgender) community is too, as well as all political opponents, free thinkers and critical inquirers. Words were bandied around indiscriminately by state-affiliated media to vilify liberals and non-conformists as 'fifth columnists', 'traitors', 'Russophobes', 'foreign agents' and 'undesirables'. It was as close as Russia had come to Stalinist enemy mania, which could not but ring alarm bells when 'enemies of the people' had been thrown into labour camps and shot.

The most un-Russian of values were human rights, a part of the western liberal package of freedoms which, as we saw in Chapter 1, was feared and rejected by the Soviet Union and the Orthodox Church long before the Putin regime regurgitated it. Human rights NGOs were to be labelled 'foreign agents' if they received any financing from western donors. An amendment passed in November 2012 required NGOs that carried out 'political activities' to register with the Ministry of Justice as 'foreign agents', stamp 'foreign agent' on all their publications and websites and to submit to frequent bureaucratic surveillance. Most of the NGOs refused on principle to register. As far as they were concerned, the term was libellous, with Stalinist and cold war implications of treacherous intent. When the ministry hesitated to implement the law, Putin pushed it forward in a speech addressed to the FSB at the height of the protest movement, saying that 'no one had a monopoly on the right to speak in the name of Russian society, especially not structures managed and financed from abroad and thus inevitably serving other interests'.[120] Prosecutors launched a nationwide campaign to inspect and search hundreds of NGOs, raiding offices, seizing documents and records, fining and suspending those that had not registered. Many have since closed down, unable to receive Russian donations and afraid to apply for western grants for fear of stigmatising the organisation and those involved with it.

The net was cast to miss social service charities but catch human rights organisations, women's and LGBT rights groups, environmental activists and the Moscow offices of international organisations such as New York's Human Rights Watch and Amnesty International. Golos, the Russian independent election monitor, which had inspired volunteers in their masses to go out and observe the notorious 2011 parliamentary elections, was constantly harassed even though it claimed not to have received foreign funding since 2012, raising contributions from online sponsors. Nevertheless, it was cynically labelled a 'foreign agent' a month and a half before the September 2016 parliamentary elections, disqualifying it and its observers from admission into polling stations. Earlier, one of the few remaining media training NGOs, the Regional Press Institute in Petersburg, headed for 21 years by Anna Sharogradskaya, was labelled a 'foreign agent' and made to pay a large fine (the equivalent of $6,800), when she boycotted the law. The label is 'disgusting', she told me. 'It implies not only that you are a traitor, but that you are being paid to betray your country'. Another media rights organisation, the *Glasnost* Defence Foundation with its well-known director Aleksei Simonov, and the only outfit left that monitors the death and persecution of journalists, investigated by the indomitable Boris Timoshenko, has been slapped with the 'foreign agent' label. The word *glasnost* in the foundation's name points to it as one of the first NGOs in the country, and its logo – '*glasnost* is a tortoise crawling towards free speech' – poignantly ironic.

By June 2016 there were 102 groups on the Justice Ministry's list of active 'foreign agents'. But death by strangulation was not enough, and on 23 May 2015 Putin signed another bill giving prosecutors the power to declare foreign and international organisations 'undesirable' (*nezhelatel'nyy*) and ban their activities if they present a threat to the constitutional order, its defences or its security. This was a pretext to threaten or oust major international human rights watchdogs, some of whom have already left the country because of the difficulties they face. Heads of defiant NGOs face criminal prosecution and fines of between $6,000 and $10,000 or up to six years behind bars.

The laws on 'un-Russian' behaviour were adopted one by one with great speed at the height of the Moscow protest movement, passed almost unanimously by parliament and signed immediately into force by Putin. On 30 June 2013 the law that bans propaganda for homosexual and non-traditional sexual relations to minors was adopted by 430–0 votes and one abstention.[121] This law prohibits holding gay pride events, speaking in defence of gay rights or equating gay and heterosexual relations, which can result in fines of up to $31,000. In the same year laws were passed that made offending religious feelings a criminal offence punishable by up to three years in prison – seen as a response to the *Pussy Riot* case – and passed 308–2; a bill outlawing advertisements on abortion, often the main form of birth control; and the ban on swearwords, basically targeting four 'obscene' words and their thousands of derivatives, collectively called *mat*, used with relish by anyone from thugs to poets of genius like Pushkin. Such laws have left a fog of confusion. Was Tchaikovsky un-Russian because he was a closet gay, and should *Swan Lake* be banned for minors?

According to the Orthodox Church, faith, nationalism, belief in the Fatherland are Russian values. According to Putin, Russian morality involves patriotism, self-sacrifice, family and spiritual values. In the West, Putin explained on television, people are more pragmatic and consider personal success as the greatest good. 'People in the Russian world' have a sense of 'higher moral destiny', because a person thinks 'less of himself and more of the outside world', said Putin - even those people who have made billions, he added.[122] This meant that human obligations were more important than human rights, and that individualism should give way to serving the state. Putin has admitted that as a divorced man he cannot claim to be a role model, but he failed to mention living with a female partner and children in a normal non-traditional relationship although as Putin's private life is taboo and only gossiped about, this remains in the realm of conjecture. Putin has always endorsed traditional conservative values, but not until now did they begin to take on the status of a national ideology, with Putin reaching out for reinforcement to nationalist and xenophobic parties in the West; Viktor Orban in Hungary, Marine Le Pen in France, providing a loan to her far-right party. The shock of the Brexit referendum and the demented vitriol of Donald Trump as a Republican nominee for the 2016 presidential race gave a huge boost to the Putin regime's widespread use of demagogy and abusive public discourse. Trump, said Putin, is 'brilliant and talented, an absolute leader in the presidential race'.[123] Sections of western society channelling their frustration against governments seen as mealy-mouthed liberals 'soft' on migration played well to Putin's tactics of scapegoating and enemy mania.

The term 'un-Russian' raises the same hackles among Russia's liberals as the term 'un-American' did under McCarthyism in the early 1950s, when thousands of alleged communist sympathisers were accused of being disloyal and subversive. The American 'psychosis' at the peak of the 'red scare' equated political criticism with hatred of one's country. There is the same edge to the current debate in the West as to whether computer wizards who have leaked classified information to the mainstream media are heroes or traitors. When the UK's *Guardian* editor Alan Rusbridger was asked whether he loved his country, after having published surveillance tapes leaked by Edward Snowden, he said he was surprised by the question because of the illegitimacy of equating criticism with betrayal. He replied, 'Yes, we are patriots and one of the things we are patriotic about is the nature of democracy, the nature of a free press and the fact that one can, in this country, discuss and report these things'.[124]

Rusbridger's response adheres to a system of universal values, that being a patriot does not depend on loving your country, right or wrong, but abiding by democratic principles valid for everyone. By ghettoising 'un-Russians', Putin returns to the divisiveness of Lenin's formula of those with and against us or, in terms of religious sectarianism, the pious against the heretic. Putin's academic mouthpiece, Sergei Markov, having already defined 'managed' democracy, now cobbled together a new idea that would allow Russia to call itself a democracy – this time, a 'majority' democracy:

> Russia defines its political system not as a liberal democracy with an emphasis on the rights of minorities but as a democracy that respects the rights and wishes of its majority ... [and aims] to protect it as much as possible from an aggressive minority ... LGBT lifestyles are immoral and sinful, and while individuals have the right to live as they please, they have no right to promote such behaviour among others who find it alien and offensive ... Russia is effectively pioneering a new concept: the 'zoning of public space'. LGBT minorities are free to pursue their chosen lifestyles and values, but only within private zones.[125]

For a country that in its history has endorsed the Pale, pogroms, spy mania and the deportation of ethnic minorities, to talk of 'zoning' people with impunity shows the extent of Russia's unwillingness to be responsible for its actions, the depth of its amnesia and the capacity to dissemble without a blink. It was only in 1989 that Yury Afanasyev had caused a sensation by mocking the 'esteemed aggressively obedient majority' of time-servers that had for 70 years propped up a repressive and dysfunctional Communist Party, and already the same issues, in the same terms, were cropping up again: Russian history spinning in its isolation, playing mirror image games with itself. The 'aggressive minority' is accused of causing Russia's social and economic ills, and the scapegoating device is working successfully once again. The lack of a free press means there is no one to force the issue, to remind the public of what it so easily forgets, and to sort out the political complexity.

The main criticism of a majority democracy is its potential for mob rule, expressed long ago by de Tocqueville as the 'tyranny of the majority'. Today the term 'majority rule' more often refers to an electoral system, which in the modern age tends to be limited by the separation of powers, the rule of law, the free press and other pillars of democracy, none of which has an independent existence in Russia. As Putin enjoys enormous popularity with the majority, it is convenient to stigmatise the minority and claim that its 'aggressive' non-traditional ideas have been boosted by western propaganda. One of the state media's main arguments is to point to the West's spineless permissiveness which is so 'excessive', Putin says, that people are seriously talking about registering parties 'whose aim is to promote paedophilia'.[126] It appears then that the minority is depraved, sodomite-and-paedophilia-loving as well. This is bizarre, but the lack of free media enables such nonsense to be voiced.

The mutation of free speech

By manipulating the concept of free speech, Putin ideologues have tried to ridicule democracy's 'sacred cow' – in the words of one-time editor Vitaly Tretyakov. The intention to make free speech politically expedient and capable of dividing society from its opposition has created attitudes Yeltsin always feared because he knew it would lead to separating the 'clean' from the 'unclean'. It was autocratic Russia's standard way of flushing out opponents. Today, among the elite that stands behind Putin's regime, the level of cynicism is so high that the threat of free speech has mutated into a denial that it exists. Thus, while Putin continues to proclaim free speech has not been subverted, his gurus juggle with its meaning. Propped up by Marxist-Leninist antecedents devaluing free speech as bourgeois liberal ideology and by more recent postmodernist views that truth is relative, it is easy for Putin's PR gurus to mould notions of free speech in ways that will assist the Putin regime's control of the media. But because the regime fears losing credentials within the Western community, it is necessary to devalue the pre-eminence that democracies give to free speech.

Tretyakov set himself this task early in the regime: 'In democratic societies freedom of speech exists not because it is the highest value, but because this society's survivability and expansion cannot be secured without it. Freely expressed thought is easier for government to control than thought unexpressed'.[127] Censorship, says Tretyakov, is imposed indirectly 'so that the "sacred cow" of freedom of speech remains inviolable'. Because he, like many of his colleagues, is unable to envisage how free processes in society can work, any more than did the critics J. S. Mill argued with in the nineteenth century, he claims it is impossible for any society to allow free and diverse ideas to exist because that would inevitably interfere with unity and, if necessary, the conduct of war:

> Freedom of the press, pluralism of opinions can thus lead to the disintegration of the society or the state, which, by the way, we clearly saw in the history of the USSR disintegration in 1987 to 1991. The Russian leadership has learned this lesson very well.

Basically, the concept of opposition is not acceptable to Russian authoritarian thinking unless it is 'loyal', hence controllable. The argument, often repeated today, is that what may seem to be free speech is not, actually. What might have been thought to be free speech under Yeltsin was not; it was anarchy and chaos because if freedom is not 'managed' people will suffer. The fundamental assumption of Western thought and practice that free speech goes with regulation, checks and balances, the rule of law and other practising democratic institutions that are real even if not perfect, is dismissed as pulling the wool over citizens' eyes. The double standard of western democracies, Tretyakov believes, is that they claim to be free but are actually controlled by 'politically correct or behind-the-scenes or psychological methods or at least never directly on behalf of the government'. But who is pulling these strings? Typically, it is assumed the state does the controlling, because there is no belief in the view that representative government and civic institutions can work responsibly.

Political correctness arouses particular contempt from Putin ideologues. As the notion involves a desire not to offend or discriminate against diversity, it asserts the integral part minority views play in liberal democracies; views that are especially important, said Mill, because they do not conform. This flies in the face of Sergei Markov and his colleagues' aim to justify eliminating minority views as delinquent and alien to society. Of course, Russia's frequent taunts about the West's political correctness play to a darker script, attempting to stir up divisions in the West over traditional Enlightenment-era freedoms and the views of cultural and religious minorities, such as Islam, especially set against the background of international terrorism, war and migration. There is no doubt that these conflicts raise difficult questions and heated disagreements, but the debate in the West is taking place openly while Russian television does not tolerate an alternative agenda.

Without the witch-hunt rhetoric against opponents and minorities that gained momentum during the Moscow anti-Putin protests, the majority of Russians might not have been as prepared to accept the unprecedented hate propaganda that followed two years later against Ukrainians.

(i) 'Bolotnaya' – the protest movement

The word 'Bolotnaya' came to denote the protest movement in Moscow and some of the larger cities. Literally, it referred to the city square, Bolotnaya Ploshchad, in central Moscow, where some of the main protests had been held. The word had resonance, meaning 'bog' or 'swamp' – Yeltsin had once said that only free discussion would ever pull Russia out of the bog – and it was here that many Russians tried to regain their freedom and self-respect by making their voices heard. 'We exist', Aleksei Navalny proclaimed.

The protests were about values, not economics. The protesters were educated, professional and internet savvy, sometimes the children of the super-rich. They had come, writes professor Yuly Nisnevich, to meet others like themselves 'who were equally unwilling to be subjected to humiliation and lies'.[128] The protests were undoubtedly influenced by the first flush of the Arab Spring, which had helped to oust long-term tyrants. The Arab Spring's slogans of freedom and human dignity, the demand that people would no longer be humiliated and marginalised as they had been for decades, highlighted the Russian condition when once again, in words so often used before, people were being pushed around like a 'herd of cattle'.

The protest movement began the day after the parliamentary elections on 4 December 2011 in outrage at widespread vote rigging. For the first time the internet had been used to spread evidence of electoral violations. Amateur videos and online testimonies of ballot stuffing and repeat voting were posted on YouTube and other sites by thousands of volunteers, who had gone out to monitor the ballot. Whether or not Navalny's campaign to persuade voters to vote for any party except Putin's United Russia was effective, the mood was not with Putin. Even officially United Russia limped in with less than 50 per cent of the vote, losing its two-thirds majority and the ability to rewrite the Constitution at will. As Putin's legitimacy was based on his popularity, the protests and his own poor showing in the presidential elections three months later, on 4 March 2012, had serious implications. The OSCE reported that almost one-third of polling stations registered irregularities during the count.[129] Officially Putin won almost 64 per cent of the vote, but in Moscow he managed only 47 per cent. Given electoral fraud and voter coercion, analysts calculated that he might have actually scored no more than 30–35 per cent in Moscow. Having lost the most important city in Russia, the question was whether he could maintain credibility.

The protests exuded a liberating, almost carnival atmosphere. As well as the rallies, there were debates, happenings and performance art – the most famous being Pussy Riot's punk prayer. Creative protests were devised, such as the circle of unity formed by people holding hands along the Garden Ring road (*Sadovoye kol'tso*), a 10-mile loop around the Kremlin; and a similar circle of protesters driving cars and hooting round the Ring, flying white balloons and ribbons symbolic of the movement. For Putin, the reference of the white ribbons to the 'orange' ribbons of the 2004 Ukraine revolution was like a red rag to a bull: his response was to call them 'condoms'. As for the protest movement, he derided it as a conspiracy by the US State Department through its funding of Russian democracy-training NGOs.

Although the protests set out to be peaceful, the overreaction by the riot police, with 300 to 700 people being detained at some rallies, only helped the movement gather momentum. Massive rallies on 10 and 24 December on Bolotnaya Square and Sakharov Prospekt with 100,000 people were held to protest the results of the Duma elections. On the eve of Putin's inauguration on 6 May 2012, a 20,000-strong protest on Bolotnaya saw the most brutal clashes with riot police, which activists claimed were deliberately provoked. A Gazeta.ru correspondent observed police dragging women by their hair, spraying gas and beating people indiscriminately. Navalny's pain as the police almost break his arm frogmarching him to a police van can be witnessed on YouTube.[130] The demand for honest elections turned into general calls for an end to the corruption, inequality and lawlessness associated with Putin's rule.

Although the majority of protesters were young (between 20 and 45 years), the ethos was inclusive. It involved the Solidarity movement activist Ilya Yashin, who had first raised the cry against rigged election results; anti-corruption blogger Navalny; socialist Sergei Udaltsov; the flamboyant socialite journalist Kseniya Sobchak; the Khimki forest environmentalist Yevgeniya Chirikova; Putin's former finance minister Aleksei Kudrin and billionaire oligarch Mikhail Prokhorov. Together with them were some of the 'young' democrats, now from an older generation, who had kept the flame burning in such opposition groups as the Other Russia (Drugaya Rossiya) and the Dissenters' Marches of 2008–11 (Boris Nemtsov, Gary Kasparov, Vladimir Ryzhkov), as well as the National Bolsheviks (Eduard Limonov), who had held protest meetings every 31st of the month for several years in defence of the right to free assembly enshrined in article 31 of the Constitution.

There was a 'new kind of community and communication', wrote sociologist Aleksei Levinson excitedly about the movement; 'its very existence or rather, the amazing and inspiring fact of its emergence, was intoxicating'.[131] When people asked who the organisers were, the answer was Facebook and Twitter. Either because of the new digital technology or because of lessons learned from past history, that the 'means' of protest were as important as 'ends', the spontaneous and leaderless rallies had an organic flow. Repeated demonstrations in support of those detained in prison displayed solidarity. It was significant that police had instructions to grab anarchist posters depicting Kropotkin and Makhno; these classic anarchist forms of communalism and mutual aid went entirely against the regime's understanding of anarchy, drummed into every TV viewers' head, as dire chaos and disorder. The lack of leadership was one reason why the Leninist Limonov quit the movement and soon found his niche in the Kremlin camp. It can be argued that it was not so much the type of organisation, as the movement's isolation from the majority of society that made it unsustainable in the face of the tough police backlash.

Catching the mood of the moment, a new internet TV station appeared giving full coverage to the protest movement. Called Dozhd' TV, it had emerged out of the radio station Serebreny Dozhd' ('Silver Rain') and later moved to cable until the regime began to harass it. Dozhd' called itself the optimistic channel and spoke to the internet generation. Owned by Natalya Sindeyeva and her businessman husband Aleksandr Vinokurov, this was Moscow's sophisticated rich elite. They moved their studio into a famous converted chocolate factory Krasny Oktyabr ('Red October') in the city's fashionable art district and were vital as part of the liberating mood that flourished for a few years. It was behind a number of websites and magazines of which Slon.ru still remains. Dozhd' employed young, hard-hitting journalists, and brought back some of the excitement of television in the 1990s. It showed its hand from the start by inviting liberal public figures to read the articles of the Constitution on air. The station ran a white ribbon as its logo during the protests, justifying its policy of being 'more than' journalists by hoping to become 'mediators' between protesters and the state.

Alternative realities: internet versus TV

Analyst Stanislav Belkovsky called the protesters ROGs – the Russian educated city dweller in English (*russkyy obrazovannyy gorozhanin*), who did not want to be oppressed by the rest of society's low political consciousness, encouraged by state TV.[132] Levada Centre's Boris Dubin put it this way: 'Internet Russia came out on the square, while TV Russia stayed at home'.[133] Society had become polarised by the news bulletins people followed. Liberals and truth seekers went to the internet and hardly ever switched on television, while the majority followed the main terrestrial news channels as people had always done. Those who followed news of the protests on internet said they felt they were living in a parallel universe from those whose information came from TV. Mainstream TV journalists themselves insisted they would no longer pretend the protests were not happening after their channels initially responded with silence. But the arsenal of lying that began to emerge from pro-state channels was far more disturbing than the original silence.

The concept of 'Soviet reality' (*sovetskaya deystvitel'nost'*), as we saw in Chapter 4, was a way of encouraging people to be part of something that was fictive. It had to be called 'Soviet' precisely because it was not real, otherwise it would have been obvious. There is no need to talk of real reality. As we have seen, 'realities' have been invented at different periods of Russia's history as ways of deliberately limiting the real world and forcing it into a framework that subscribed to an official ideology. It meant that an alternative ideology and the rest of the multifarious world outside could be blocked out. In Putin's third term TV became the reality conveyor by which most Russian citizens lived.

Previously the internet had escaped overt censorship partially because Putin did not understand information technology. In his reductive way of thinking, he had earlier dismissed the internet, and had largely ignored Medvedev's enthusiasm for social media, his 2.5 million Twitter followers, and his project for building a Silicon Valley in Skolkovo, near Moscow. Putin rarely uses the internet himself. He has always been happier in marathon live television discussions, where he is able to charm the invited subservient audience without ever confronting hard questions, speaking for four hours or more in the tradition of communist leaders.

The protest movement and the Ukraine crisis changed Putin's approach to the internet. In his eyes, the regime was being subverted by the combined forces of the IT crowd and foreign funders, inciting NGOs and protesters to rebel. He lashed out at the internet as 'a special CIA project'. That was how it had been conceived, Putin said in April 2014, and it is 'still developing in this way'.[134] The protest movements, he said, had been a conspiracy organised by the US State Department. It was in this period that the first serious attempt to clamp down on the internet was made.

The regime had used its propaganda machine in the past to channel bias, 'asymmetry', exaggeration and lies, although its main success had been in eliminating pluralism and alternative views from the mainstream. Before the Ukraine campaign, television had already begun to take uglier forms. NTV's two-part documentary *Anatomy of Protest* in 2012 alleged that footage of people standing in a queue receiving 'money and biscuits' were protesters being paid by the US State Department. As information spread online from those who had witnessed the episode being faked with a rent-a-crowd, the internet hit back. Bloggers responded on social networking sites, hackers got into the NTV website and covered its logo with the words 'violence, stupidity, lies', words which start with the same letters as NTV. For a while cries of 'Shame' followed NTV crews, and a rally of 400 people demonstrated 'Against Brazen Lies on NTV' outside the Ostankino building, where one-quarter of them were detained. Some of NTV's staff felt ashamed and apologised for their channel. But not NTV's executive, Vladimir Kulistikov: 'My people, who are making ratings for NTV, they are quite all right. All the others can go, I don't care about them. But nobody left this company, by the way! Why? Maybe I pay them too much money!'.[135]

Worse was to come when apparently faked information was used as evidence to pin criminal charges on Left Front activist, Sergei Udaltsov. Grainy footage from a hidden camera showed him supposedly plotting with foreign backers, including a Georgian leader from the Rose revolution. He was also accused of planning to secure financing from a fraudulent bank and hiring Chechen rebels to carry out provocations in Moscow. As a result of the documentary's allegations, the powerful Investigative Committee opened a case against Udaltsov, who was sentenced to four-and-a-half years for plotting mass riots at the 6 May Bolotnaya demonstration. So was Leonid Razvozz-hayev, who had fled to Ukraine and alleges he was tortured into signing a false confession, abducted and brought back to Russia. They were among 30 people arrested that day who have endured different fates as a result of the notorious trials and the court's insistence that mass riots had taken place.

(ii) Putin: Crimea returns to its 'home port'

It was as if the FSB's Information Security Doctrine written in 2000 had been drafted especially to bring Crimea back into the bosom of Russia. A national threat had been found, in a self-fulfilling prophesy, and rewarded with imperialist aggrandisement. The Security Doctrine's justification for gaining control of the media to protect the country's national interests received its most cynical expression in the annexation of Crimea and destabilisation of Eastern Ukraine. The finely honed state-controlled media machine pumped out nationalist passions to the point of mass psychosis, winding up hatred against Ukraine and the West. Here we see the doctrine's 'trustworthy' messages in action. Putin's Ukrainian adventure could not have succeeded without 14 years of media pummelling, concealed censorship and financial inducements. It showed how dangerous the inane media squabbles of the 1990s had been to allow things to come to such a pass.

Just as the Kremlin's 'virtual' democracy was a fiction, so was its fake version of events in Ukraine, claiming that a fascist, neo-Nazi junta had seized power in Kyiv, compelling Russia to intervene and 'protect' Crimea's Russian majority. The fact that no one had been hurt was beside the point. Moreover, according to a Ukrainian survey conducted in 2011, 71 per cent of Crimeans were content living in Ukraine.[136] By comparison, more than 100 people had died in Kyiv from police brutality unleashed by Ukraine's pro-Russian President, Viktor Yanukovich. If, from the West's point of view, Kyiv's revolutionary movement was a protest against corruption and a desire for closer ties with Europe, for Putin it was a personal humiliation which ruined his plans for incorporating Ukraine into a Eurasian customs union. The bonds between Ukraine and Russia were close, but there were also tensions. Russians stereotype Ukrainians as their country cousins (in the derogatory term *Khokhol*), while Ukrainians cannot forget the Holodomor, the man-made famine under Stalin that took over three million lives. Russia's sense of superiority made Ukraine's rejection all the more humiliating, but Putin's aggression has had the opposite effect on Ukraine. As indicated in polls conducted by Andrii Bychenko, head of Kyiv's respected Razumkov Centre, it has helped to consolidate Ukraine's sense of nationhood and brush away the remnants of Soviet mentality (this poll did not include the separatist areas). The centre's data show that if in 2011 only 17.8 per cent said they would vote to join Nato if there was a referendum, in 2015 43.3 per cent were in favour.[137]

A decade previously, in 2004, Russia had been ignominiously rejected by Ukraine's Orange revolution, and the Russian experts it had sent over to rig elections in favour of Yanukovich had almost literally been thrown out of the country. Some of the usual suspects were back, notably the Kremlin's ideologue, Surkov, orchestrating operations in Crimea. He was one of the first to be placed on the US's blacklist of sanctions after Crimea's annexation. Surkov's postmodernist scenarios could be detected in the fabrications and theatricality the Russian media passed off as reality. Levada Centre's Lev Gudkov monitored the impact of TV's daily disinformation on the population:

> An atmosphere of complete unprecedented hysteria has been created in Russia, arousing passions and uncertainty, and imposing the idea that Russians in Ukraine are under threat – 67 per cent of respondents think that radical Ukrainian nationalist organisations of some sort are to blame; and 54 per cent think that in such a situation Russia can quite legally deploy troops into the country and impose order. This is the result of the intense false aggressive propaganda of the past weeks … [the belief] that a coup has taken place and that it is not just nationalists who have

come to power but bandits, Nazis, fascists and followers of Bandera, although few have any idea who Stepan Bandera was.[138]

Nothing could be worse for Russians than the name of Bandera. With Ukraine's unhappy history wedged between Stalin and Hitler in the Second World War, Bandera was a Ukrainian patriot who had at first been imprisoned but was later supported by Nazi Germany in his fight for independence from Soviet rule. Meanwhile, the Ukrainians themselves had made a serious mistake in the first days of Euromaidan when a motion was passed in parliament to remove the status of Russian as a possible second official language where a region wished to make it such – a constant fear of Russia's diaspora in the near-abroad. Although the bill was repealed five days later by the acting president, the damage had been done. It was full sail ahead after that for Russian TV to stoke extravagant fears of Ukrainian nationalism, especially of the small militant Right Sector party which had played a leading role in the early street battles. How exaggerated that was could be seen in the Ukrainian elections a few months later when the party received 1.80 per cent of the vote.

It was also true that anti-Semitism had blighted Ukraine's history, especially the pogroms of the late nineteenth century under the Russian Empire, as well as the collaboration of some groups with the Nazis, but anti-Semitism was entrenched in Russia as well, and its current policy of hatred of Ukrainians and overt discrimination against minorities showed Russia had not progressed very far in its tolerance threshold. Mikhail Khodorkovsky's response speaking in Kyiv was that the number of fascists in Kyiv was no greater than on the streets of Moscow and Petersburg. To which Mikhail Leontyev replied on his programme *Odnako,* (14.03.2014), that Khodorkovsky had a 'pathological hatred of his own country'. The over-heated political climate allowed no room for discussion.

The spin that Russia's TV gurus devised for the hate-Ukraine campaign was to put Euromaidan into a Second World War script. The repeated use of the words fascists, Nazis and anti-Semites to brand Ukrainians forced Russian minds back to the horrors of the Great Patriotic War. The word 'punisher' (*karatel'*) had been used only to refer to the Nazi SS troops, but it was now being used against Ukrainian fighters. In Putin's triumphalist annexation speech in Moscow, he called Ukrainians opposed to Russia 'nationalists, neo-Nazis, Russophobes and anti-Semites' who had resorted to 'terror, murder and pogroms'.[139] In the same speech he referred to opponents of the war at home as 'national traitors' (*natsional-predateli*), a term from Hitler's *Mein Kampf*, that had journalists scurrying to find out which other politicians had used such an abhorrent term. A good script also pays attention to music and voice, all of which were carefully orchestrated for news broadcasts to provide an atmosphere of menace. Dmitry Kiselyov, having already achieved infamy in his gay bashing, performed theatrically every Sunday, swaying slightly and gesticulating with his hands in balletic poses, talents he had not displayed earlier in his career.

Aggressive and outlandish lies were disorientating, but viewers and bloggers began unravelling reports shown in Russian broadcasts. Only those browsing the net, however, would know of the volume of them. There were lies of different kinds, some overstepping all ethical boundaries. There was the First Channel's footage of panicked Ukrainians in cars fleeing to Russia from right-wing fascists, except that a Ukrainian blogger proved that it had taken place at the Polish border; or a photo of a child claimed to have been killed in Donetsk, who had died in Aleppo, Syria, a year earlier.[140] The use of images of children was a favourite, sometimes taken from movies, as well as the fake story of the crucified child discussed in Chapter 4. One Russian blogger simply got angry when a state newspaper reported that the upper house of parliament had 'unanimously' approved the use of military force in Ukraine, and published screen shots that showed only 90 of the body's 166 members had voted.[141] Another news story reported that the Ukrainian government was building a 'concentration camp' for pro-Russian supporters, only it was an EU-funded project to build a holding centre for illegal migrants.[142] There were lies big and small, but never ending. The First Channel allotted almost 32 per cent of its time to the conflict in Ukraine, ignoring domestic issues.[143]

From Ukraine's point of view it has been tricky to find the right balance between protecting free speech and dealing with Russia's hate messages channelled through cable and satellite operators to its Russian-speaking Ukrainian audience. After Crimea's annexation, Ukraine's broadcasting council called for an end to the transmission of Russia's leading channels based on information 'threatening Ukraine's national security, sovereignty and territorial integrity, promoting war, violence, cruelty, spreading interethnic and racial hostility'.[144] At least 15 channels have been suspended by a series of court orders and some of Russia's journalists and top TV executives have been barred from entering the country until the end of 2017. On the other side, the separatists have closed down Ukrainian channels in Eastern Ukraine and the Russians have closed them in Crimea.[145] Initially, conscious of its Euromaidan principles, Ukraine attempted to deal with Russia's propaganda war in legitimate ways, but as the fighting and killings have continued anti-Russian sentiment has taken harsher forms. The decommunisation law passed by the Ukrainian parliament in April 2015 is particularly damning in its 'history' clause, making it illegal to express 'contempt' for nationalist figures and organisations of Ukrainian independence in the last century. Censorship in this area, so fraught with controversy and lies between Russia and its neighbours, cries out for examination and closure. In the meantime, the EU has countered Russian disinformation with its own strategic communications plans publishing since September 2015 online newsletters *Disinformation Review* and *Disinformation Digest*, which analyse examples of pro-Kremlin propaganda and convey the EU and Nato positions. In a nine-month period the newsletters identified 1,649 'disinfo-stories' in 18 languages but mainly in Russian (173 in English).[146]

Let it 'rain'

To prop up the mountain of lies, the regime pulled out all the stops on a number of fronts: assaults on the internet, further closures of traditional media, and a new spate of draconian laws. A few weeks after the Kyiv protests began, Putin announced that the huge state news agency RIA Novosti, which had started its life with the beginning of the Second World War in 1941, was to be liquidated. The director general since 2004, Svetlana Mironyuk, first heard of it from the media. Although a major state institution, Mironyuk had turned RIA into a reasonably trustworthy news outfit and had initiated other highly considered PR projects, such as the Valdai forum, where Putin meets with foreign guests. The old RIA team ended its reign with an impartial report on its own demise as 'the latest in a series of shifts in Russia's news landscape, which appear to point toward a tightening of state control in the already heavily regulated media sector'.

RIA has been replaced by a larger body called Rossiya Segodnya that incorporates RT and other outlets broadcasting to the outside world. Dmitry Kiselyov replaced the professional Mironyuk, but then talent was not the issue. RT's budget increased by 30 per cent for 2015 to $330 million, with plans to add French and German services to the already existing ones. Rossiya Segodnya's budget was almost tripled to $152 million, which would include the new Sputnik News (replacing Voice of Russia). Commentators have assumed that this expansion would be used not only for information wars with the West but as cover to increase espionage networks – a return to the large-scale use of the journalist-spy.

Hot on the heels of RIA's demise came the crackdown on Dozhd' TV. Because of Dozhd' TV's great success as a digital news channel, it began broadcasting on major cable and satellite networks and gained an audience of 12 million. Its troubles began when it conducted a survey on the anniversary of the Leningrad blockade in January 2014, asking viewers whether it would have been possible to save hundreds of thousands of lives if the city had surrendered to the Nazis. Such much-needed debate has always been attacked as desecrating the memory of those who died. On this occasion, it acted as a pretext for Duma deputies to ask prosecutors to examine whether an 'extremist' act had been committed. Although Roskomnadzor found no evidence of wrongdoing, most of the cable and satellite providers unanimously removed the channel from their packages, effectively ending its operations. Such coordinated action would not have happened without instructions from above, said the Dozhd' staff, who had been told privately that their even-handed coverage of the Kyiv protests had annoyed the Kremlin.

Dozhd' lost 80 per cent of its audience, it was unlawfully kicked out of its elegant office space in central Moscow and was forced to move several times, at one point broadcasting from a flat. It was almost 25 years ago that *Vzglyad* had resorted to producing video tapes of their programmes out of a flat after being closed down during Gorbachev's turn to the right – and now it was happening again. Dozhd' limped on from month to month; its future looking particularly bleak after a law was adopted that would ban advertising on pay channels from January 2015, although this has since been softened. 'Let it rain', wrote journalist Aleksandr Minkin, among the channel's many staunch fans who organised a 'marathon' fundraising that has kept the channel afloat. Dozhd' is no longer broadcast on major networks, but it is surviving online through subscriptions. It is watched by about 4 million in Russia, and as neighbouring countries listen less to Russian television its audience has expanded to 20 million, taking into account Smart TV, cable to the Baltics and Eastern Europe, and the net.

Internet websites that had remained largely free from censorship were now targeted. This was hastened by a law adopted in March at the height of the Ukraine crisis, which allowed sites to be blocked by prosecutors without a court order. Alternative news sites – grani.ru, Kasparov.ru, EJ.ru and Aleksei Navalny's sites – were blocked for 'participation in unsanctioned mass action'. Another law, the so-called anti-bloggers law that came into effect on 1 August 2014, forced websites publishing posts or articles that receive more than 3,000 readers a day to register as a media outlet. This subjects them to the same stringent regulations and fines as it does the media if, say, they used foul language or unwittingly spread false information. By September 2014 Roskomnadzor had blocked access to more than 600 websites deemed by prosecutors to be 'extremist'.

In the same month of March 2014, the editor of one of the most flourishing news sites – lenta.ru – was sacked for allowing an interview with Ukrainian Right Sector's Dmytro Yarosh, who said: 'Sooner or later we are destined to fight against the Moscow empire'.[147] Sixty-nine of lenta.ru's journalists resigned saying: 'The problem is not that we have nowhere to work, but that it seems you have nothing to read'.[148] The highly respected editor, Galina Timchenko, connected her sacking with the growing popularity of the site during the Ukrainian events. 'When we passed three million users daily and 20 million hits ... I realised that such a large audience was bound to attract the attention of the authorities or the oligarchs: it could not avoid being a matter of concern'.[149] Timchenko and her team have relocated to Latvia and started a new site (meduza.io).

Also hounded out of his company was the founder of the social networking site VKontakte, Russia's equivalent of Facebook, but at the time more popular than it with over 100 million users. Its young entrepreneur, Pavel Durov, named the most promising Northern European leader under the age of 30, saw himself as an anarcho-capitalist. In a manifesto of how Russia could become a twenty-first century leader, he said of free expression: 'Abolish taxes and limitations on everything connected with the information sphere. Russia must become the first major information offshore, which will attract all progressive people of the world'.[150] Inevitably, he was often in trouble, but the tipping point came with Ukraine. In March 2014 he revealed that the FSB had tried to pressure him to disclose data about Ukrainian protest leaders and to shut down Aleksei Navalny's anti-corruption pages.[151] After riot police had descended on his office in Petersburg and the internet Mail.ru Group, owned by Putin acolyte Alisher Usmanov, secretly bought majority shares in VKontakte, Durov began to sell his own 12 per cent shares in the company. He resigned and left Russia. 'I'm out of here', he said, taking his latest ideas about mobile messaging apps with him to the Caribbean islands, where he has been granted citizenship.

The spate of new legislation that had started with the protest movement and continued at a rapid pace after the Ukraine crisis had media lawyers reeling. Galina Arapova of the Centre in Defence of Media Rights, based in Voronezh, said there had been nothing like it in the 18 years she has been in the field. 'I have the feeling that the state Duma is concerned with no other problem than regulating what the media write, for whom they write, and in what form', she said. Not only the media, but the whole system of distribution of information was under attack. She pointed out that to call for the return of Crimea you could get five years, to swear in the media is safe only if it's in a foreign language, if you distribute inaccurate or libellous information you could be ordered to withdraw the material from the site or to destroy the whole issue of a newspaper without any compensation, to deny or distort the essence of patriotism your site can be blocked.[152]

One of the most significant laws that came into force in January 2016 limited foreign ownership of media to 20 per cent. This law has targeted the country's glamour and lifestyle media industry. Since the 1990s western capital had been vital in developing this vast sector of non-political magazines and niche journals. Although an extra year's grace has been allowed, large publishing houses, such as the Swiss Edipress and the German media giant Axel Springer have already pulled out, declaring it is no longer profitable working in Russia in hostile conditions and a falling rouble. Axel Springer has also sold its Russian edition of the magazine *Forbes*, popular for its investigations of the elite and super-wealthy, one of the two business outlets with foreign owners that survived from the 1990s. The new owner is the glossy magazine publisher ArtComMedia run by Aleksandr Fedotov, whose first words were that the magazine would be 'depoliticised'. The other business venue, the daily *Vedomosti* was owned by the *Financial Times*, the *Wall Street Journal* and the Finnish magazine publisher Sanoma, each of which have now sold their shares to Demyan Kudryavtsev, a one-time Berezovsky ally and former head of the Kommersant publishing house. Sanoma has also sold him its English-language newspaper the *Moscow Times*, an independent paper for 22 years which has produced four Pulitzer Prize winners and could always be relied on to discuss news blocked by the Russian media. Although it has now been demoted into a weekly, it has hired liberal journalist Mikhail Fishman to be editor. Kudryavtsev says he intends to respect the editorial independence of these papers, but no one can tell at this stage how these new ownership patterns will evolve. Previously, in 2012, foreign companies were prevented only from owning majority stakes. Now foreign owners, including Russian businessmen who hold dual citizenship, will have to decide which Russian legal entity they wish to sell to (and which will be approved by the authorities), or whether to exit the country.

By corralling the whole glossy glamour sector with its readers' unquenchable thirst for western fashion, luxury goods and lifestyles, Putin may be asking for trouble. This is what made money worthwhile in the Putin glamour years, and it is unclear whether people will be happy to give up *Cosmopolitan* and *Vogue* (or *Men's Health* and *National Geographic*) for the new church–state mantra of traditional Russian morality. While the Duma has gloated over the imminent return of its 'information sovereignty', the law may have serious repercussions on the country's already affected economy. In 2013 the fashion market was worth \$53 billion.[153] In the balance between politics and economics in Putin's third term, it is the former that wins, although it was the latter that had initially made him popular. With the country's push towards isolationism, the Kremlin may feel it necessary to start taking steps in weaning its population off *haute couture* and tourist travel abroad. After all, what is the point of Crimea? And celebrity magazines like *Tatler* had become a nuisance, exposing the private lives and foibles of the powerful.

The franchised Russian-language versions of the glossy magazines have provided an escape route for women journalists wanting to practise their profession, but unwilling to make the political compromises necessary to work on news and current affairs. At present 80 per cent of students at Moscow State University's faculty of journalism are women, and many have this in mind. If the Kremlin's goal is to demonise western glamour as immoral and decadent, this will be another route cut off for them.

Truth or television reality?

Since Dozhd' TV's short incursion on cable ended, there has been no relief from the wall-to-wall television coverage of Ukraine, later Syria and Turkey, reflecting Kremlin-dominated reality. As Navalny puts it, the TV-viewing public has become 'zombified'. Normally, television reflects society, but if the blanket of lies on television is so overwhelming that it produces a seeming psychosis in its audience, reality begins to reflect television. Television becomes the big lie (*lozh'*), and through daily repetition the normal state of affairs. As we saw in Chapter 4, normalising lies was the Soviet state's standard method of resolving problems and suppressing discontent. By playing up Russia's humiliation at the hands of the West, the return of Crimea became a euphoric moment; what journalist Konstantin Von Eggert called a 'collective therapy session for the nation as a whole, which seemed to relish the chance to spit in the face of "ungrateful" Ukrainians, NATO "aggressors", "American imperialists" and even history itself'.[154]

As we have seen, Russia is quick to assume the position of victimhood, which Putin has encouraged by denying its 'humiliation' has anything to do with its own governance. The sense of victimhood may begin to explain the unbelievable, that Russians of all sorts accepted the crudest of lies about people they have regarded as quasi-brothers and sisters. Television has done nothing like this in Russia before. The lies of the Stalinist era, much of which Putin propagandists have utilised, came before the advent of television, conveyed by radio, film and the press. In Putin's third term television was used to demonise opponents, sentence Bolotnaya protestors, break up friendships over Ukraine, and damage relations with the West. It has caused havoc with minds and, as Russians say, 'powdered the brains', pushing people to behave in untypical ways. Reactions from well-known journalists has also caught people by surprise. Andrei Babitsky, called a 'traitor' by Putin in 2000, agreed 'absolutely' with his right to take the population of Crimea 'under protection'.[155] He was soon fired by Radio Liberty and departed to help the separatist 'republic' of Donetsk set up its own television station. Meanwhile, Aleksandr Nevzorov, with his predilection for 'hooray patriots', was outraged by Crimea's annexation, expostulating that 'you don't steal boots from a wounded man when he is lying unconscious'.[156]

Dehumanising the enemy is a well-researched psychological process of stirring intense hatred in people towards opponents, pushing them to behave in ways that in normal conditions they would not countenance. It is a well-known ploy for manipulating support for a war that would otherwise be regarded as unacceptable and murderous. It can lead to increased violence and human rights violations, and has led to genocide in the Holocaust, the former Yugoslavia and Rwanda. By presenting Ukrainians as Nazis and fascists, Russian television made them less than human, evil and criminal, capable of such gross acts as burning people in Odessa or crucifying children. According to the philosopher Igor Chubais, three great post-Soviet myths have been punctured by the TV campaign against Ukraine. The belief that the tragedy of the Great Patriotic War was so devastating that war is impermissible. The myth of familial relations with Ukraine – that although Russians are capable of fighting anyone, including Chechens and Georgians, only, in Chubais's words, 'anti-Russian nonhumans' could fight Ukrainians. Third, the myth that people of Orthodox faith would never kill each other, or even renounce each other, as seen previously in the unshakeable support for Serbia, notwithstanding revelations of atrocities. These have been such fundamental principles of the Russian order of things that their destruction must inevitably have severe repercussions.

Hate speech in journalism is reprehensible, even criminal, but it was rewarded by Putin with prizes to 300 media personnel for their 'high professionalism and objectivity in covering events in the Republic of Crimea'. Leaked by the newspaper *Vedomosti*, the ceremony had been kept secret and the president's decree no. 269 did not appear in public records. Was it embarrassment? No, say critics, more likely fear of names being revealed to

Ukraine and the rest of the world. The leak, said an Ekho Moskvy blog, made it feel 'as if a mole had turned over a carefully set up network of agents to the enemy'.[157] The usual suspects, such as TV presenters Vladimir Solovyov and Arkady Mamontov were on the list. The biggest prize went to Vladimir Kulistikov, then director general of NTV (known now as 'Information Gestapo') 'For Services to the Fatherland, Grade Two'– a man regarded as the most 'crass cynic of them all'.[158] Such an exceptionally large number of awards must have been considered necessary to prevent any flagging of the propaganda machine. By comparison, President Medvedev had granted only 11 awards for coverage of the Russia–Georgia–South Ossetia war in 2008. The awards carry financial benefits and privileges, which Gleb Pavlovsky has said are necessary on all occasions: if you were doing the work out of principle it would be considered suspicious.

Television professionals responsible for disinformation cannot pretend to distance themselves from collaborating in a war that has resulted in more than 9,000 deaths in Ukraine and many deaths in Russia. Increasingly, liberal journalists have taken the position that propagandists whose coverage is responsible for deaths, prison sentences based on faked TV information and persecution should not be allowed to use the term 'journalist'. Nor should they get away with it in the USA because of the First Amendment. In April 2015 former Prime Minister Mikhail Kasyanov and journalist Vladimir Kara-Murza lobbied Congress to expand the Magnitsky Law, that bans travel to the USA and freezes assets, to include television personalities whose smear campaigns, they said, led to Boris Nemtsov's brazen assassination in full view of the Kremlin walls. They provided a document with examples from journalists (all Putin prizewinners) who 'month after month, vilified and denounced (Nemtsov) in government-controlled media outlets as a "traitor", the "fifth column" and an "enemy of Russia"', said Kara-Murza. 'This was not journalism or the exercise of freedom of speech. This was state-sponsored incitement to murder'.[159] Kara-Murza suffered a near-fatal collapse some months later from the effects of an unknown toxin, yet another political activist who has refused to be intimidated among the list of those who have died or been lucky enough to survive mysterious acts of poisoning allegedly committed by the FSB.

The collapse of ethical and professional standards can be witnessed in other spheres of information. The growing army of internet trolls, who can be found in their thousands all over Russia, is another sector of paid liars willing to reinvent reality. Their jobs are secret and their work anonymous. Like trolls everywhere, Russian trolls sow discord, post inflammatory and abusive messages, obstruct discussion and deface sites, but not for their private antisocial and delinquent purposes, although they may do that as well, but to sabotage Putin's critics. *Novaya gazeta* first exposed a troll factory in St Petersburg disguised as the Internet Research Centre, operating around the clock, with trolls working 12-hour shifts, two days on, two days off. Trolling has become a lucrative industry which now involves not only troll factories but, according to Dozhd' TV's Ilya Klishin, numerous advertising agencies working for the Kremlin on secret contracts. 'It seems like a joke', he says:

> but thousands of hired bloggers 'go to work' every day, writing online about Vladimir Putin's greatness and the decay of the West. They're on Facebook, Twitter, news sites, and anywhere else where the Kremlin feels threatened and outnumbered. Fresh instructions arrive every day in emails, specifying what to say and where to post it, all with the aim of bolstering Putin's presidency amidst war and economic crisis. Sadly, it's working. People have trouble believing the scope of the Kremlin's Internet invasion, thinking it incredible that the government could be capable of such sophisticated, targeted manipulation. And yet that is exactly what Putin's social media team has achieved.[160]

With most of the alternative media suppressed, online news sites reduced and bloggers under threat, trolls are having a field day. An ex-troll, Lyudmila Savchuk, confirmed that the main messages were all much the same – 'Putin is great', 'Ukrainians are Fascists', 'Europe is decadent'. She juggled with three virtual identities as a housewife, student and athlete, leaving 100 comments on an average day.[161] The average pay is good, between $700 and $1,000 a month. In one factory employees worked in teams of three, one playing the role of Putin critic, the other two defending his honour.[162] Russian trolling has been exported abroad, especially during the height of the Crimea crisis. The UK's *Guardian* revealed what it believed to be an orchestrated pro-Kremlin campaign in its newspaper and elsewhere, denigrating in abusive terms any comment criticising Russia or Putin, despite the best efforts of its moderators at prevention.[163]

Russian/Soviet history is such fertile soil for lies, that the shutdown of critical faculties by the public to bursts of propaganda may be as much a symptom of fear as, in the case of Crimea, celebration. It is a knee-jerk response to the Kremlin's demands. Journalists and trolls who are complicit in creating the 'reality' of lies have helped to restore the Soviet mentality of parallel worlds, where people live between official lies and private lives. They have encouraged the detritus of Soviet oppression with the rise of public abuse, the vigilante mentality, informants, snitching, 'anonimki', and the disintegration of values. They have assisted in purveying imperialist fantasies, such as Putin's 'lost' territory of *Novorossiya* (New Russia), which does not exist – but then Soviet maps were never reliable and eliminated or included landmarks as politics dictated. The voice of television, stentorian, triumphalist or sneering has created its own reality to keep the incumbent elite in power.

A coherent picture of Putin's third term in office emerges when the Moscow and Kyiv protests are seen together. That is the way state media played it, linking traitors in the Moscow protests with Kyiv's treacherous behaviour, wrapping a victimised Russia in a blanket of enemy mania. Tellingly, Putin displayed an almost childish rage at being thwarted by Kyiv; more generally, at failing to sell the Russian vision to many of his 'near abroad' neighbours, yet still clinging to denial politics of the brutal imperial legacy Russia and the Soviet Union bequeathed to their neighbours, and insisting on inflicting a corrupt 'authoritarian democracy' on them now. The combination of imperial aggression and historical amnesia makes the Putin regime delusional and dangerous, as it normalises a defensive system of lies that breeds its own logic. Hanging on to power by distracting the nation with more drama, the regime moves the theatre of war from Ukraine to Syria to Turkey, inventing new lies. It is not difficult after the Ukraine crisis to support another tyrant in Bashar al-Assad, even while he is accused of atrocities against his own people.

So far, Putin's cynical world has been propped up by mainstream media and a population enjoying higher living standards and enthralled by imperialist rhetoric. It is a moot point how long the Grand Inquisitor's trade-off of freedom for material prosperity can last when the nation has been boxed socially and economically into a corner. The rouble has fallen, the heavily dependent oil economy has seen prices plunging, trade agreements with Europe and Turkey have been disrupted. About 200 of Putin's top cronies are affected by US and EU sanctions and if they are anxious not to display disloyalty at present, the balance of forces behind the scenes will inevitably change. Not only is Russia burdened with the huge costs of military intervention, it must maintain its conquest of Crimea and the separatist zones of Eastern Ukraine. The question by the opposition has been posed as the TV set versus the fridge. Russians have endured hard times many times, and nationalist fervour may reanimate the intrepid spirit of wartime heroism, but this is not what created Putin's extraordinary popularity.

Russia can pretend to be victimised and distort its history only while it suppresses free speech. Without debate and catharsis, it can continue to indulge in wishful thinking and self-deception. As the regime works to ban all effective venues that allow free speech, the situation will become more tyrannical and oppressive. On the other hand, the regime could use the 2018 elections to ameliorate the problems of its own making, and Putin could choose to step aside and anoint a successor. Much will depend on how the population responds to the thrill of superpower adventures against increasing austerity and Russia's growing pariah status in the West.

Notes

1 Ivan Krastev and Tatiana Zhurzhenko, 'The politics of no alternatives or how power works in Russia: an interview with Gleb Pavlovsky', *Transit*, 6 September 2011. www.eurozine.com/articles/2011-06-09-pavlovsky-en.html (accessed 20 November 2011).
2 'The President in 1996: Scenarios and Technologies of Victory', a Report from Pavlovsky's Foundation of Effective Politics, quoted in Ivan Zasursky, *Rekonstruktsiya Rossii: mass-media i politika v 90-e*, Izdatel'stvo MGU, 2001, pp. 66–7.

3   *Mail Online*, 6 October 2011. www.dailymail.co.uk/news/article-2045848/Vladim
    ir-Putins-Black-Sea-scuba-diving-treasure-stunt.html (accessed 20 November 2011).
4   Krastev and Zhurzhenko, 'Politics of no alternatives'.
5   Peter Pomerantsev, 'Putin's Rasputin', *London Review of Books*, 33(20), 20 Octo-
    ber 2011. www.lrb.co.uk/v33/n20/peter-pomerantsev/putins-rasputin (accessed 20
    November 2015).
6   'Surkov: 'Dark prince of the Kremlin', *Open Democracy*, 7 April 2011. www.op
    endemocracy.net/od-russia/richard-sakwa/surkov-dark-prince-of-kremlin (accessed
    20 November 2015).
7   Oleg Shchedrov 'Reporter's death fuels fear for Russia media freedom', *Reuters*,
    8 October 2006.
8   'Manipulyativnaya demokratiya', *Nezavisimaya gazeta*, 2 March 2000.
9   Intellektual'naya Rossiya. www.intelros.org/lib/elzin/1997.htm.
10 *Kommersant*, 25 February 2000.
11 Karen Dawisha, 'The Putin Principle: How it came to rule Russia', May–June
    2015. www.worldaffairsjournal.org/article/putin-principle-how-it-came-rule-russia
    (accessed 20 November 2015).
12 *The Economist*, 24–31 August 2007.
13 'Clans are marching', *Open Democracy*, 30 May 2013. www.opendemocracy.net/
    od-russia/vladimir-pribylovsky/clans-are-marching (accessed 20 November 2015).
14 'Priroda "Putinizma"', Levada Centre, 16 December 2009. www.levada.ru/2009/
    12/15/lev-gudkov-priroda-putinizma (accessed 20 November 2015).
15 Putin here uses the term *rossiiskaya* referring to all Russia's citizens and not
    russkaya referring to ethnic Russians only. However, the tsarist-era phrase 'the
    Russian world', currently in popular use, is *russkii mir.*
16 'Rossiya na rubezhe tysyacheletiya', delivered on 30 December 1999. www.ng.
    ru/politics/1999-12-30/4_millenium.html (accessed 20 November 2015).
17 Author's interview, 16 June 2014.
18 *Antikompromat*, 18 March 2000. http://anticompromat.org/putin/salie.html (accessed
    20 November 2015).
19 *Moscow Times* (weekend), 4 March 2000.
20 It took Masha Gessen two years to persuade Salye to talk to her (*The Man
    without a Face: The Unlikely Rise of Vladimir Putin*, London, Granta, 2012, Ch. 5).
21 'Democracy in Danger', *Moscow Times*, 9 March 2000.
22 McFaul and James M. Goldgeier, '"New Russia" ailing: stand up, Mr Bush', *Los
    Angeles Times*, 21 September 2003.
23 '10 years of what?', *Moscow Times*, 17 August 2001.
24 *Baiki kremlevskogo diggera*, Ad Marginem, 2003, p. 271.
25 *Tacis: The European Union's project for Capacity Development in Election
    Monitoring*, Briefing Document no. 6, 13 March 2000, pp. 1–2.
26 'How much the elections actually cost', *Moscow Times*, 29 March 2000.
27 European Institute for the Media, *Monitoring the Media Coverage of the March
    2000 Presidential Elections in Russia. Final Report. August 2000*. www.media-pol
    itics.com/EIM%20reports/Rus%202000%20final%20.pdf (accessed 20 November
    2015).
28 The investigation was headed by Yevgeniya Borisova; and this special issue of
    the English-language newspaper came out in both English and Russian, 9
    September 2000.
29 'Boy vozle ploshchadi Minutka v Groznom- lish' odin epizod iz mnogikh, 'Lib-
    erty Live' Radio Svoboda, 24 December 1999. http://web.archive.org/web/
    20000304001929/www.svoboda.org/archive/crisis/caucasus/1299/ll.122499-1.shtml
    (accessed 20 November 2015).
30 'Zheleznyi Putin', *Kommersant*, 10 March 2000.
31 'Kuklobortsy', No. 29, February 2000.

32 Yulia Solovyova, 'The world's oldest professions', *Moscow Times*, 18 March 2000.
33 'Usilenie vertikali', 28 March 2000. www.youtube.com/watch?v=ZasYm9Rs8UA&
    list=PLJQXkdGK444vCyYu-fSdvIlec2CHP67Kg&index=219 (accessed 29 Novem-
    ber 2015).
34 Bul'var Gordona archives, 25 September 2007. http://bulvar.com.ua/gazeta/a
    rchive/s39_32539/3838.html (accessed 29 November 2015).
35 *Kommersan*t, 25 February 2000.
36 8 July 2000, Grani.ru. http://grani.ru/Politics/Russia/President/m.32401.html
    (accessed 20 November 2015).
37 MKRU 1 October 2014. www.mk.ru/politics/2014/10/01/putin-rossiya-ne-nam
    erena-stavit-internet-pod-totalnyy-kontrol.html (accessed 20 November 2015).
38 'Putin: Russian media as free as any other', *RIA Novosti*, 23 December 2004,
    JRL 8514, no. 2.
39 'Why bother to try if no one resists?', *Russia Profile*, 15 March 2005.
40 'Putin shows his lighter side in Shanghai', Henry Meyer, Associated Press, 16 June
    2006. www.washingtonpost.com/wp-dyn/content/article/2006/06/16/AR20060616
    00923_pf.html (accessed 20 November 2015).
41 Interview on CBS *Sixty Minutes* with Mike Wallace, 8 May, 2005. Ministry of For-
    eign Affairs of the Russian Federation. www.mid.ru/brp_4.nsf/e78a48070f128a
    7b43256999005bcbb3/a8ebb19dd698fdf2c3256ffe0031388f?OpenDocument (accessed
    20 November 2015).
42 *Larry King Live*, 'Russian President Vladimir Putin discusses domestic and for-
    eign affairs', *CNN*, 8 September 2000. http://edition.cnn.com/TRANSCRIPTS/
    0009/08/lkl.00.html (accessed 20 November 2015).
43 'The CIA and the media'. *Carl Bernstein site*. www.carlbernstein.com/magazine_
    cia_and_media.php (accessed 20 November 2015).
44 London, Jonathan Cape, 1946, p. 221.
45 Leaked stenograph, 'Vstrecha s rodnymi', 22 August 2000. www.kommersant.ru/
    k-vlast/get_evlast.asp?id_article=12
46 Anne Applebaum, 'Soviet-style terror has the media at bay', *Sunday Telegraph*, 4
    March 2001.
47 Jill Dougherty, 'How the media became one of Putin's most powerful weapons',
    The Atlantic, 21 April 2015.
48 *Osoboe mnenie with Tatyana Fel'gengauer*, 17 February 2014. http://echo.msk.
    ru/programs/personalno/1260026-echo/#element-text (accessed 20 November
    2015).
49 *Baiki kremlevskogo diggera*, Ad Marginem, 2003, pp. 249, 276. Tregubova was
    given political asylum in the UK.
50 Anatoly Medetsky, 'Stricter rules for press in Putin's White House', *Moscow
    Times*, 6 May 2008.
51 *Guardian*, 1 October 2014.
52 Oleg Blotsky, *Vladimir Putin: Doroga k vlasti*, Moscow: Osmos Press, 2000, pp.
    259–266.
53 Vera Kuznetsov, *Norasco-Russia Journal*, 7 February 2000.
54 Agency of Regional Political Surveys, Interfax, 20 July 2000.
55 Raisa Zubova, 'State media play stabilising role in today's Russia', RIA Novosti,
    21 April, 2004.
56 *Moscow Times*, 15 June 2000.
57 Forum.msk.ru, 15 April 2011. http://forum-msk.org/material/news/6056927.html
    (accessed 20 November 2015).
58 *Moscow Times*, 23 June 2000.
59 *Moscow Times*, 15 June 2000.
60 Sylvie Braibant and Carole Sigman, 'Television's big picture', *Le Monde diplomatique*,
    February 2001, JRL, 5099.

61   *Moscow Times*, 6 December, 2000.
62   'Ya ne o chem ne zhaleyu', *Komsomolskaya pravda*, 8 December 2000.
63   6 February 2001. Dorenko was dismissed from ORT a few months after he was taken off the air.
64   Deadline.ru/ SMI, 11 July 2000.
65   'Ya ne o chem ne zhaleyu'.
66   'Yeltsin byl by na Bolotnoi', 1 February 2012. www.svoboda.org/content/article/ 24469668.html. Nemtsov said much the same on Ekho Moskvy, 27 April 2007 (accessed 20 November 2015).
67   *Reform of the Administration of the President of the Russian Federation.* http://m iamioh.edu/cas/academics/centers/havighurst/cultural-academic-resources/putins-russia/reform-presidential-admin-landing/index.html. (accessed 20 November 2015). See also Karen Dawisha, *Putin's Kleptocracy: Who Owns Russia?*, New York, Simon & Shuster, 2014, p. 252ff.
68   www.masterandmargarita.eu/estore/pdf/erru01_versionsix.pdf, III.3:1.
69   Fiona Hill and Clifford G. Gaddy, *Mr Putin: Operative in the Kremlin*, Washington, DC, Brookings Institution Press, 2013, p. 211.
70   Francesca Mereu, 'More media headaches forecast after "bad year"', *Russian Journal*, 13–19 January 2001.
71   T. Miles, 'Russian riot police dominate at opposition rally', Reuters, 16 December 2006.
72   Krastev and Zhurzhenko, 'Politics of no alternatives'.
73   Radio Liberty, 29 January 2001.
74   'Double standards in television row', *Russian Journal*, 17–23 February 2001.
75   'Two titans meet', Pozner interviewed by Walter Cronkite, 2001, Russia Project. http://russiaproject.org/transcript/titans.html (accessed 20 November 2015).
76   Documentary film 'Prezident', presented by Vladimir Solovyov, *Rossiya 1*, 26 April 2015.
77   Author's interview, 30 November 2013.
78   *Izvestiya*, 10 April 2001.
79   Andrei Zolotov Jr., 'VGTRK chief rushed to NTV', *Moscow Times*, 16 April 2001.
80   Among them were leading presenters Svetlana Sorokina, Marianna Maksimovskaya, Mikhail Osokin, Vladimir Kara-Murza, Viktor Shenderovich.
81   *Kommersant*, 7 April 2001.
82   Torrey Clark, 'Resignations, bitter reproaches at NTV', *Moscow Times*, 10 April 2001.
83   Lev Kadyk, 'Mne dazhe nelovko za vse svoi propovedi', *Kommersant*, 23 April 2001.
84   'Putin talks NSA, Syria, Iran, drones in RT interview', 12 June 2013. http://rt. com/news/putin-rt-interview-full-577/ (accessed 20 November 2015).
85   *Vremya novostei*, 28 February 2001.
86   Dominic Lawson, 'This is Russia Today, bringing you no news at all about, er, Russia', *Sunday Times*, 2 November 2014.
87   Nikolaus von Twickel, 'Russia Today courts viewers with controversy', *Moscow Times*, 17 March 2010. www.themoscowtimes.com/news/article/russia-today-courts-viewers-with-controversy/401888.html (accessed 20 November 2015).
88   *Guardian*, 19 December 2009.
89   'A dual dilemma for NGOs', *Moscow Times*, 15 December 2005.
90   *BBC News*, 21 November 2007. http://news.bbc.co.uk/1/hi/world/europe/7105467. stm (accessed 20 November 2015).
91   *News.ru.com*, 30 January 2006. www.newsru.com/russia/30jan2006/sichev.html (accessed 20 November 2015).

92 Mark Mackinnon, 'Kremlin dusts off propaganda machine', *Globe and Mail* (Canada), 30 October 2002, JRL, 6522.
93 Dozhd' TV, 14 November 2012. http://tvrain.ru/articles/ksenija_sobchak_i_arka dij_mamontov_o_rassledovanii_korruptsii-332902/ (accessed 20 November 2015).
94 Sophia Kishkovsky, 'Voice of calm', *New York Times Magazine*, 10 November 2002, JRL 6544.
95 Andrei Smirnov, 'New remains discovered in Beslan: incompetence or crime?', *Eurasia Daily Monitor*, 4 March 2005. http://web.archive.org/web/20080223150119/ www.jamestown.org/edm/article.php?article_id=2369369 (accessed 20 November 2015).
96 Irina Petrovskaya, *Izvestiya*, 4 September 2004.
97 'Poisoned by Putin', 9 September 2004.
98 'State-controlled TV newsman defends station against criticism of hostage crisis coverage', AP, 13 September, 2004.
99 Kim Murphy, 'Critics blame Kremlin for cautious media', *Los Angeles Times*, 17 October 2004. http://articles.latimes.com/2004/oct/17/world/fg-press17/2 (accessed 20 November 2015).
100 'Lessons of Beslan', *Variety*, 31 January, 2005.
101 *Kommersant*, 5 May 2006.
102 Richard Pipes, *Russia under the Old Regime*, London: Penguin, 1995, p. 23.
103 Ibid., p. 184.
104 *El Mundo* (Spain), 27 February 2008.
105 *Hard Day's Night*, Dozhd' TV, 5 February 2014.
106 'Yury Kovalchuk+1', Kommersant.ru 9 February 2011. http://kommersant.ru/ doc/1581792 (accessed 20 November 2015).
107 'Mikhail Lesin uvolen za nesoblyudenie etiki', *Kommersant*. 19 November 2009, www.advertology.ru/article75626.htm (accessed 20 November 2015).
108 'The new state media behemoth', *Moscow Times*, 18 December 2013.
109 Ibid.
110 'All politics is economic'. *New York Times*, 15 April 2013. http://latitude.blogs.nytim es.com/2013/04/15/how-politics-controls-russias-media-business/?_r=0 (accessed 20 November 2015).
111 Natalya Rostova, 'Aleksei Venediktov – nash aktsioner – Kreml', *Novaya gazeta*, 10 April 2008. www.novayagazeta.ru/data/2008/25/29.html (accessed 20 November 2015).
112 Author's interview, 2 June 2011.
113 11 April 2011. www.themoscowtimes.com/sitemap/free/2011/4/article/cyber-atta ck-paralyzes-novaya-gazeta-site/434777.html (accessed 20 November 2015).
114 Internet World Stats. www.internetworldstats.com/euro/ru.htm (accessed 20 November 2015).
115 Ibid.
116 Sputnik International, 5 March 2011. http://en.rian.ru/analysis/20110305/ 162878541.html (accessed 20 November 2015).
117 www.internetlivestats.com/internet-users/russia (accessed 20 July 2016).
118 'Online cooperation as an alternative for government?', *Global Voices*, 30 August 2010. http://globalvoicesonline.org/2010/08/30/russia-online-cooperation-as-an-a lternative-for-government/ (accessed 20 November 2015).
119 *Newstube*, www.newstube.ru/media/medvedev-vydvinul-putina-v-prezidenty (acces sed 20 November 2015).
120 *Kremlin.ru*, 14 February 2013. http://kremlin.ru/events/president/news/17516 (accessed 20 November 2015).
121 The one abstention was Ilya Ponamaryov.
122 NPK TV Rossii (Narodno-Patrioticheskii kanal Rossii) , 18 April 2014. www. youtube.com/watch?v=dGBYoJgH4D0 (accessed 20 November 2015).

123   YouTube, 17 December 2015. https://yandex.ru/video/search?filmId=w4LCX9SY UXI&text=%D0%BF%D1%83%D1%82%D0%B8%D0%BD%20%D0%B8%20 %D1%82%D1%80%D0%B0%D0%BC%D0%BF (accessed 4 August 2016).
124   *Guardian*, 3 December 2013.
125   'Russia should create private zone for LGBT', *Moscow Times*, 5 February 2013.
126   Meeting at Valdai, Kremlin.ru, 19 September 2013. http://en.kremlin.ru/events/p resident/news/19243 (accessed 20 November 2015).
127   'Svobodny li SMI Rossii?' Rossiiskaya gazeta, 19 November 2003. www.rg.ru/ 2003/11/19/smi.html (accessed 11 November 2015).
128   'Passionarii i pragmatiki', 6 December 2012. www.gazeta.ru/comments/2012/12/ 05_a_4880689.shtml (accessed 20 November 2015).
129   *Guardian*, 6 March 2012.
130   www.youtube.com/watch?v=ayjfU8Zv5nI (accessed 19 November 2015).
131   'The free city of Moscow: reflections on Russia's protest movement', *Open Democracy*, 5 April 2012. www.opendemocracy.net/print/65217 (accessed 19 November 2015).
132   'Narod ROGonosets', *Moskovsky Komsomolets*, 7 December 2012.
133   'Na ulitsy vyshla Rossiya interneta. Rossiya televizionnaya ostalas' doma, *Executive.ru*,   27   January   2012.   www.e-xecutive.ru/management/practices/ 1577992-boris-dubin-na-ulitsy-vyshla-rossiya-interneta-rossiya-televizionnaya-osta las-doma (accessed 19 November 2015).
134   Media Forum of Independent, Regional and Local Media, *Kremlin.ru*, 24 April 2014. http://kremlin.ru/news/20858 (accessed 19 November 2015).
135   Ellen Barry and Michael Schwirtz, 'Russian TV broadcast besmirching protesters draws a furious reaction', *New York Times*, 24 March 2012. www.nytimes. com/2012/03/25/world/europe/russian-show-besmirching-protesters-stirs-outrage. html?pagewanted=all&_r=0 (accessed 19 November 2015).
136   Razumkov Centre and Fridrikh Naumann Foundation, 8 April 2011. http://p odrobnosti.ua/763117-bolshinstvo-krymchan-schitajut-ukrainu-rodinoj-opros.html (accessed 19 November 2015).
137   Talk at King's Russia Institute, London, 18 May 2015.
138   Radio Svoboda, 18 March 2014. www.svoboda.org/content/article/25301303.htm l (accessed 20 November 2015).
139   Obrashchenie prezidenta rossiiskoi federatsii, *Kremlin.ru*, 18 March 2014. http:// kremlin.ru/news/20603 (accessed 20 November 2015).
140   A panel analyses Russian propaganda, Broadcasting Board of Governors, June 2014. www.bbg.gov/blog/2014/06/04/panel-analyzes-russian-propaganda (accessed 20 November 2015).
141   Ellen Barry and Ravi Somaiya, *New York Times*, 5 March 2014. www.nytimes. com/2014/03/06/world/europe/for-russian-tv-channels-influence-and-criticism.htm l?_r=0 (accessed 20 November 2015).
142   Stephen Pifer, 'The Russian propaganda machine – is it winning?', 2 paragraphs, 4 May 2014. http://2paragraphs.com/2014/05/the-russian-propaganda-machine-a t-work (accessed 20 November 2015).
143   *Monitoring of Russian TV Channels 2015 Final Report*, joint report by a number of NGOs and funded by the EU, pp. 33–4. www.memo98.sk/data/_media/Mon itoring%20report_final-FF.pdf (accessed 20 November 2015).
144   'Censorship in Ukraine: providers stop broadcasting Russian TV channels', Sputnik News Agency, 25 March 2014. http://sputniknews.com/voiceofrussia/news/2014_ 03_25/Ukrainian-providers-stop-broadcasting-Russian-TV-channels-4793/ (accessed 20 November 2015).
145   As the violence has spread, the Russian Union of Journalists and two Ukrainian journalists' unions have been cooperating to protect colleagues.

146 *Disinformation Review*, 26 July 2016. http://us11.campaign-archive2.com/?u=
cd23226ada1699a77000eb60b&id=a413e08635&e=d96d846e11 (accessed 2 August
2016).

147 'Eto pozor i ...', *Lenta.ru*.13 March 2014. http://lenta.ru/articles/2014/03/13/lenta
(accessed 20 November 2015).

148 Dorogim chitatelyam ot dorogoi redaktsii, *Lenta.ru*, 12 March 2014. http://lenta.
ru/info/posts/statement (accessed 20 November 2015).

149 Nataliya Rostova, 'Mozhet, u kogo-to eto trafik, a u menya- auditoriya', 18 March
2014. http://slon.ru/world/galya_galya-1072609.xhtml (accessed 20 November
2015).

150 Grazhdanskie manifesty, Afisha live, 18 May 2012. www.afisha.ru/article/pavel-
durov-vkontakte/ (accessed 20 November 2015).

151 '"VKontakte" otpravilo Pavla Durova v otstavku', Interfax, 21 April 2014.
http://m.interfax.ru/372931 (accessed 20 November 2015).

152 *36ON.ru*, 10 December 2014. http://36on.ru/news/interview/51104-galina-arapova
-uzhestochenie-zakonodatelstva-v-sfere-smi-eto-katastrofa (accessed 20 November
2015).

153 Kate Abnett, 'East of Eden: how Russia's isolationism is impacting fashion,
part two – retail', *Business Fashion*, 20 November 2014. www.businessoffa
shion.com/articles/global-currents/east-eden-russias-isolationism-impacting-fashi
on-part-two-retail (accessed 20 November 2015).

154 'All politics are local: Crimea explained', *World Affairs*, September/October
2014.   www.worldaffairsjournal.org/article/all-politics-are-local-crimea-explained?
utm_source=World+Affairs+Newsletter&utm_campaign=bdcd4b86d1-September_
23_2014_WNN&utm_medium=email&utm_term=0_f83b38c5c7-bdcd4b86d-29463
2861 (accessed 20 November 2015).

155 *Novaya gazeta*, 17 April 2014. www.novayagazeta.ru/news/1680987.html (accessed
20 November 2015).

156 'Bezumets net v Kremle – oni pragmatiki', Snob, 24 March 2014.www.snob.ru/p
rofile/20736/blog/74068 (accessed 20 November 2015).

157 Isaak Rozovsky, 'Nagrada nashla "geroev"', *Ekho Moskvy* 5 May 2014. http://
echo.msk.ru/programs/persontv/1641612-echo (accessed 18 November 2015).

158 Kulistikov and his retirement for health reasons discussed by K. Larina and I.
Petrovskaya, 'Chelovek iz Televizora', *Ekho Moskvy*, 17 October 2015. http://
echo.msk.ru/programs/persontv/1641612-echo/ (accessed 18 November 2015).

159 Carl Schreck, 'Nemtsov allies press US to punish Russian "propagandists"',
RFE/RL, 23 April 2015. www.rferl.org/content/russia-us-politics-opposition/
26973575.html (accessed 18 November 2015).

160 'How Putin secretly conquered Russia's social media over the past 3 years',
Global Voices, 30 January 2015. http://globalvoicesonline.org/2015/01/30/how-p
utin-secretly-conquered-russias-social-media-over-the-past-3-years (accessed 18
November 2015).

161 'Trolling for Putin: Russia's information war explained', Digital, 7 April 2015.
http://digital.asiaone.com/digital/news/trolling-putin-russias-information-war-exp
lained (accessed 18 November 2015).

162 Andrei Malgin, 'Fabrika trollei. Novye podrobnosti', *Livejournal*, 21 March 201.
http://avmalgin.livejournal.com/5323826.html (accessed 20 November 2015).

163 Chris Elliott, 'The readers' editor on ... pro-Russia trolling below the line on
Ukraine stories', *Guardian*, 4 May 2014. www.theguardian.com/commentisfree/
2014/may/04/pro-russia-trolls-ukraine-guardian-online See also Adrian Chen,
'The agency', *New York Times Magazine*, 2 June 2015. www.nytimes.com/2015/
06/07/magazine/the-agency.html?_r=0 (accessed 20 November 2015).

Conclusion

'Posterity will avenge me', exclaimed Radishchev, Russia's pioneer freethinker, a few months before he committed suicide in 1802. It seems Radishchev must wait longer before the nation acclaims him for his struggles in the name of free speech.

Following the route of Radishchev's *Journey from St Petersburg to Moscow*, the clever young journalist Andrei Loshak stopped at the small town of Torzhok, near Moscow, where Radishchev's fellow traveller had expounded his noble thesis on free speech and censorship. The traveller was heading the other way, to Petersburg, to request permission from Catherine the Great's officials to set up a free printing press in the town. Loshak filmed the town, now a neglected corner of the country where citizens worry about the lack of ambulances, doctors and jobs. He dropped in at the local paper to ask the editor how things were going, and was she able to criticise local officials? We are absolutely free, she replied, we don't have censorship. Our paper is 70 per cent good news because we have good officials. And you know how it is with our journalism, the political situation, we have to show 70 per cent because we don't want to scare people and focus on bad things.[1] This was in 2014 during the Ukraine crisis. It confirms the sinking feeling that things in Russia never change.

As we saw in Chapter 2, Russia's history has not moved in a straight progressive line, but more in the manner of Lenin's shuffle of one step forward, two steps back. TV's two top critics were overwhelmed by the ugly turn of events on television. Shocked at the hate-Ukraine campaign, Arina Borodina said: 'Our news over the past two weeks ... will go down as the blackest ever in the history of Russian television'.[2] Almost a year later, in February 2015 Irina Petrovskaya found watching television traumatic. She wrote on Facebook: 'I've been doing this since 1992. The last six months have been worse than all the others. I'm not joking when I say I'm at my wits' end'. That meant that 31 years after the start of *glasnost* television was again a propaganda tool, journalists were collaborating in the destruction of free thought, and the public was happy with what they saw on their screens – evidence of Russia's intractability, and the difficulty of modernising and democratising the country.

The progress made in the Gorbachev and Yeltsin eras to open up society and allow free speech to flourish have been pushed back by the Putin regime and, as we have seen, without fierce resistance from the media or the public. Russia's two-headed Janus, that resonant symbol of Russia's divided identity, now resolutely looks back, revelling in nostalgia and imperialist dreams. The red-brown groups, with their communist–nationalist–imperialist views and shared hatred of liberalism, who had tried to depose Yeltsin in the 1990s and were considered by many at the time to be on the loony fringe, are the dominant players in Putin's geopolitical tactics. After Nina Andreyeva's letter in 1988 when party stalwarts had tried to suppress the media, reformers were stunned by the lack of any opposition among themselves. How much has been learned if the silence is almost as deafening today?

The lack of hope has whittled down the resolve of many in the media who had struggled to safeguard media independence. As we have seen, the prospects for free speech had already been grossly limited before the annexation of Crimea; since then, free speech has been hammered on all sides by laws, public denunciations, media closures, sackings, beatings and arson attacks on web dissidents, more than a million websites blocked and finally the assassination of such a significant internationally recognised political opponent as Boris Nemtsov. Because over the last 16 years Putin has been allowed to seize almost all the levers of power, there seems no end to Russia's fortress mentality. The result has led to a wave of emigration, to add to the other waves since the nineteenth century that have drained Russia of its talent and enriched the outside world. Many in the new wave are well-known media professionals. Leonid Bershidsky, once founder and editor of the business journal *Vedomosti* ('they killed off my life's work') has left for Germany and is working for Bloomberg ('I have no desire to ... pay a single kopek for Crimea'). Masha Gessen has returned to the USA because of anti-gay propaganda and the fear that authorities could remove her children from her and her gay partner.[3] Many émigrés continue to write for and about Russia. Will their voices ring as loud as Herzen's did from London? Today the strongest voices come not from elite property-boom London, although Putin's émigré nemesis Mikhail Khodorkovsky has chosen it for his Open Russia foundation, which finances anti-Putin opposition abroad and at home and aims to keep the vision of a future liberal Russia alive. The main émigré bolt-holes are in Ukraine and Latvia. Yevgeny Kiselyov was one of the earliest to move to Ukraine after Putin's takeover of television channels. Many more have followed since, including the independent Crimean Tatar television channel ATR, which Roskomnadzor had refused to register after the annexation of Crimea.

In Russia only a few of the respected independent outlets remain, and even they may be working on borrowed time: the main ones are Ekho Moskvy, *Novaya gazeta* and Dozhd – a radio, a newspaper and a TV website. Because they are marginal to society, the regime still allows them to remain as showcases of freedom. Television is what matters and all the nationwide channels and most of the regional ones are in Putin's orbit. There is no doubt that liberal democracy and pluralism have been devastated. But Russia has enjoyed a more sustained period of freedom than ever in its history, some 15 years taking the Gorbachev and Yeltsin years together, and they have left their footprints. Moreover, Russia is too vast and varied to ever say categorically that there is no free speech; and given its quasi-free economy and some of the West's freedoms, a total blanket of information would be impossible to implement without the terror of the 1930s and the regional network Stalin had built. Even in its darkest years, Russia has always had writers, journalists, artists and scientists brave enough to tell the truth. The Magun and Rudnev statistic of a 19 per cent 'value minority' continues to function: pockets of free thought crop up, a variety of media outlets keep working on the sidelines, the human rights tradition is experienced in the ways of repression, and the ineffable spirit of protest and struggle in Russia has an effervescent quality. Bucking the system is as much a national characteristic as political passivity.

But those in Russia who hoped and worked for a free society, despite periods of brilliance and courage, have not been able in the past 31 years to lay down permanent foundations for the existence of free speech. What is distinctive, is that they did have a chance to grasp what Dostoyevsky called this 'terrible gift' and failed to do so as a community. In this book I have tried to show that much of the problem has been in a lack of understanding of the dynamics of freedom and democracy, and a preference for social and material values to civil and political ones, although the western experience shows that for a humane and prosperous society to exist the one does not go without the other. Have lessons been learned about how to advance free speech when the next occasion arises, or will everything be done on the hoof, without reflection, as it was done this time?

Notes

1 'Puteshestvie iz Peterburga v Moskvu osobyi put', seriya 4: Vyshnii Volochok-Torzhok, 20 December 2014, Dozhd'. https://www.youtube.com/watch?v=tJav4fLp 674 (accessed 18 December 2015).
2 'Chelovek iz televizora', 8 March 2014, Ekho Moskvy. http://echo.msk.ru/program s/persontv/1273410-echo/#element-text (accessed 18 December 2015).
3 Robert Coalson, 'Some who left: a new wave of Russian emigration', 21 April 2015. www.rferl.org/content/russia-emigration-emigrants/26970465.html (accessed 18 December 2015).

Index

eBooks
from Taylor & Francis

Helping you to choose the right eBooks for your Library

Add to your library's digital collection today with Taylor & Francis eBooks. We have over 50,000 eBooks in the Humanities, Social Sciences, Behavioural Sciences, Built Environment and Law, from leading imprints, including Routledge, Focal Press and Psychology Press.

Free Trials Available

We offer free trials to qualifying academic, corporate and government customers.

Choose from a range of subject packages or create your own!

Benefits for you
- Free MARC records
- COUNTER-compliant usage statistics
- Flexible purchase and pricing options
- 70% approx of our eBooks are now DRM-free.

Benefits for your user
- Off-site, anytime access via Athens or referring URL
- Print or copy pages or chapters
- Full content search
- Bookmark, highlight and annotate text
- Access to thousands of pages of quality research at the click of a button.

eCollections

Choose from 20 different subject eCollections, including:

- Asian Studies
- Economics
- Health Studies
- Law
- Middle East Studies

eFocus

We have 16 cutting-edge interdisciplinary collections, including:

- Development Studies
- The Environment
- Islam
- Korea
- Urban Studies

For more information, pricing enquiries or to order a free trial, please contact your local sales team:

UK/Rest of World: **online.sales@tandf.co.uk**
USA/Canada/Latin America: **e-reference@taylorandfrancis.com**
East/Southeast Asia: **martin.jack@tandf.com.sg**
India: **journalsales@tandfindia.com**

www.tandfebooks.com